IBM DB2 9.7 ~~Advanc~~ed
Administration
Cookbook

D0732254

Over 100 recipes focused on advanced administration
tasks to build and configure powerful databases with
IBM DB2

Adrian Neagu

Robert Pelletier

BIRMINGHAM - MUMBAI

IBM DB2 9.7 Advanced Administration Cookbook

First published: March 2012

Production Reference: 1200212

Published by Packt Publishing Ltd.
Livery Place
35 Livery Street
Birmingham B3 2PB, UK.

ISBN 978-1-84968-332-6

www.packtpub.com

Cover Image by Sandeep Babu (sandyjb@gmail.com)

Credits

Authors

Adrian Neagu

Robert Pelletier

Reviewers

Nadir Doctor

Marius Ileana

Nivasreddy Inaganti

Nitin G. Maker

Drazen Martinovic

Eldho Mathew

Acquisition Editor

Rukshana Khambatta

Lead Technical Editor

Hithesh Uchil

Technical Editor

Arun Nadar

Project Coordinator

Leena Purkait

Copy Editor

Brandt D'Mello

Proofreader

Aaron Nash

Indexer

Monica Ajmera Mehta

Production Coordinator

Shantanu Zagade

Cover Work

Shantanu Zagade

About the Authors

Adrian Neagu has over 10 years of experience as a database administrator, mainly with DB2 and Oracle databases. He has been working with IBM DB2 since 2002.

He is an IBM DB2 Certified Administrator (versions 8.1.2 and 9), Oracle Database Administrator Certified Master 10g, Oracle Certified Professional (9i and 10g), and Sun Certified System Administrator Solaris 10. He is an expert in many areas of database administration, such as performance tuning, high availability, replication, and backup and recovery.

In his spare time, he enjoys cooking, taking photos, and catching big pikes with huge jerkbaits and bulldawgs.

I would like to give many thanks to my family, to my daughter Maia-Maria, and my wife Dana, who helped and supported me unconditionally, and also to my colleagues, my friends, to Rukshana Khambatta, my acquisition editor, for her patience, and finally to Robert Pelletier and Marius Ileana, who have provided invaluable advice, helping me to climb up the cliffs of authoring.

Robert Pelletier is a Senior DBA Certified Oracle 8i, 9i, 10g, and DB2. He has 12 years of experience as DBA, in production/development support, database installation and configuration, and tuning and troubleshooting. He has more than 30 years of IT experience in application development in mainframe central environments, client-server, and UNIX. More recently, he has added expertise in Oracle RAC 11gR2, 10gR2, 9i, DB2 UDB DBA, ORACLE 9iAS, Financials, PeopleSoft, and also SAP R/2 & R/3. He is renowned for his expertise among many major organizations worldwide and has a solid consulting background in well-known firms.

I would like to thank my wife, Julie, and son, Marc-André, for their positive and unconditional support, and also to Adrian Neagu, who helped me a lot for coauthoring this book, and all the Packt publishing team for making this possible. I would also like to thank my clients and colleagues who have provided invaluable opportunities for me to expand my knowledge and shape my career.

About the Reviewers

Marius Ileana is an OpenGroup Certified IT specialist currently working in banking industry.

Working for six years in IBM Romania as a part of middleware team and also being a two-year support specialist, he has been involved in various IBM-related technologies and enterprise grade deployments.

He holds many IBM certifications including IBM Certified DBA for DB2 9 on LUW. Since Java development is one of his hobbies, he is also a Sun Certified Programmer for Java™ v1.4. His areas of expertise include AIX, HACMP, WebSphere Application Server, DB2 UDB, and design and development of J2EE™ applications.

His current focus areas include the architecture and development of a general-purpose monitoring solution, Portal solutions, and data visualization.

Nitin G. Maker is an IBM Certified DB2 UDB DBA with around 11 years of IT experience, primarily in IBM DB2 Universal Database Technologies. He has demonstrated excellent capabilities in various roles as Data Architect/Database Administrator/DataWarehouse Architect, Applications Administrator, Upgrade Specialist, and Technical Team Leader.

Nitin has worked with many leading software houses in India and also completed assignments in the USA, UK, and Sri Lanka. He is currently based in Pune, with his family, and enjoys making new friends, listening to music, and following sports.

Drazen Martinovic graduated at the Faculty of Electronics, Machinery and Shipbuilding, Split, Croatia, in 1996. He worked in DHL international d.o.o. as a Unix administrator—IT support administrator—for 11 years. He then started to work as a database administrator for DB2 for LUW. He has been an IBM Certified Database Administrator (DB2 9 for Linux, UNIX, and Windows), since last year.

He works in the Raiffeisenbank Austria d.d. Zagreb bank as a Database Administrator for DB2. It has over 2000 employees.

Eldho Mathew is a DB2 LUW, Linux and AIX certified administrator with 8 years of proven expertise in various aspects of building, administrating, and supporting highly complex 24x7 operational and warehouse database servers. He has handled highly complex and critical systems for many top branded customers in UK.

www.PacktPub.com

Support files, eBooks, discount offers and more

You might want to visit www.PacktPub.com for support files and downloads related to your book.

Did you know that Packt offers eBook versions of every book published, with PDF and ePub files available? You can upgrade to the eBook version at www.PacktPub.com and as a print book customer, you are entitled to a discount on the eBook copy. Get in touch with us at service@packtpub.com for more details.

At www.PacktPub.com, you can also read a collection of free technical articles, sign up for a range of free newsletters and receive exclusive discounts and offers on Packt books and eBooks.

http://PacktLib.PacktPub.com

Do you need instant solutions to your IT questions? PacktLib is Packt's online digital book library. Here, you can access, read and search across Packt's entire library of books.

Why Subscribe?

- ▶ Fully searchable across every book published by Packt
- ▶ Copy and paste, print and bookmark content
- ▶ On demand and accessible via web browser

Free Access for Packt account holders

If you have an account with Packt at www.PacktPub.com, you can use this to access PacktLib today and view nine entirely free books. Simply use your login credentials for immediate access.

Instant Updates on New Packt Books

Get notified! Find out when new books are published by following @PacktEnterprise on Twitter, or the *Packt Enterprise* Facebook page.

Table of Contents

Preface

IBM DB2 LUW is a leading relational database system developed by IBM. DB2 LUW database software offers industry leading performance, scale, and reliability on your choice of platform on various Linux distributions, leading Unix systems, such as AIX, HP-UX, and Solaris, and also MS Windows platforms. With lots of new features, DB2 9.7 delivers one the best relational database systems on the market.

IBM DB2 9.7 Advanced Administration Cookbook covers all the latest features with instance creation, setup, and administration of multi-partitioned databases.

This practical cookbook provides step-by-step instructions to build and configure powerful databases, with scalability, safety, and reliability features, using industry standard best practices.

This book will walk you through all the important aspects of administration. You will learn to set up production-capable environments with multi-partitioned databases and make the best use of hardware resources for maximum performance.

With this guide, you can master the different ways to implement strong databases with high-availability architecture.

What this book covers

Chapter 1, DB2 Instance—Administration and Configuration, covers DB2 instance creation and configuration for non-partitioned database and multipartitioned database environments.

Chapter 2, Administration and Configuration of the DB2 Non-partitioned Database, contains recipes that explain how to create a database and get operational in simple and easy steps. In this chapter, you will also learn how to configure your database for its mission and prepare it for automatic maintenance, so its operation is worry-free.

Chapter 3, DB2 Multipartitioned Databases—Administration and Configuration, contains recipes that explain how to create and configure a multipartitioned database and its related administration tasks. This chapter will also teach us how to add and remove new partitions, how to perform add, remove, and redistribute operations on database partition groups, and much more.

Chapter 4, Storage—Using DB2 Table Spaces, covers physical aspects of storage, the foundation of a database. In this chapter, we will cover configuring SMS and DMS table spaces, altering table spaces, and dropping table spaces.

Chapter 5, DB2 Buffer Pools, covers caching. Here, you will learn how data is read from the disk, to buffer pools. And as reading from memory is faster than reading from disk, the buffer pools play an important part in database performance.

Chapter 6, Database Objects, covers Multidimensional Clustering (MDC), Materialized Query Tables (MQT), and Partitioning as the key techniques used for efficient data warehousing. Combined with database partitioning, these deliver a scalable and effective solution, reduce performance problems and logging, and provide easier table maintenance.

Chapter 7, DB2 Backup and Recovery, covers the major aspects of backup and recovery, as is practiced industry-wide, the preferred solutions, and how we can implement some of these methods.

Chapter 8, DB2 High Availability, mainly covers High Availability Disaster Recovery as a HA solution and DB2 Fault Monitor, which is used for monitoring and ensuring the availability of instances that might be closed by unexpected events, such as bugs or other type of malfunctions. The reader will learn how to implement HADR using command line and Control Center, about synchronization modes, how to initiate takeover and takeover by force, how to configure and open a standby database in read-only mode, and more.

Chapter 9, Problem Determination, Event Sources, and Files, has recipes for various tools used for diagnostics, inspection, and performance problem detection, such as `db2mtrk`, for gathering memory-related information, `db2pd`, a very powerful tool used for problem determination, `db2dart`, also a very powerful tool with wide applicability, that can be used for virtually any problem that may arise, `db2ckbkp`, for backup image checking, and `db2support`, used mainly for automating diagnostic data collection.

Chapter 10, DB2 Security, speaks about the main security options used to harden and secure DB2 servers. It is about instance-level and database authorities, data encryption, roles, and securing and hiding data using Label Based Access Control.

Chapter 11, Connectivity and Networking, covers many network-related configurations that apply to DB2 servers and clients, such as node cataloging, setting up connections to DRDA serves, and how to tune and monitor the Fast Communication Manager.

Chapter 12, Monitoring, covers an important part of a DBA's work, ensuring the database is available and that nothing hinders its functionality.

Chapter 13, DB2 Tuning and Optimization, provides general guidelines, as well as insightful details, on how to dispense the regular attention and tuning that databases need, using a design-centered approach. Our tips, based on best practices in the industry, will help you in building powerful and efficient databases.

Chapter 14, IBM pureScale Technology and DB2, represents mainly an introduction to pureScale technology. We will cover the principal administration tasks related to members, instances, and caching facilities. The reader will also learn about monitoring, backup and recovery methods, and special features that exist only in pureScale configurations.

What you need for this book

Unless you have access to a facility that has DB2 installed, you can install a trial version of DB2 on your own PC for learning purposes. Make sure you have the required hardware and operating system.

We must stress the importance of using a sandbox environment in order to duplicate the recipes in this book. Some recipes are intended for demonstration purposes and should not be done in a production environment.

Who this book is for

If you are a DB2 Database Administrator who wants to understand and get hands-on with the underlying aspects of database administration, then this book is for you.

This book assumes that you have a basic understanding of DB2 database concepts, and sufficient proficiency in the Unix/Linux operating system.

Conventions

In this book, you will find a number of styles of text that distinguish between different kinds of information. Here are some examples of these styles, and an explanation of their meaning.

Code words in text are shown as follows: "Partitioned indexes facilitate data maintenance by making `rollin` and `rollout` operations easier."

A block of code is set as follows:

```
SELECT DISTINCT
   STORE,  INTEGER(SALESDATE)/100
FROM POS.SALES
```

When we wish to draw your attention to a particular part of a code block, the relevant lines or items are set in bold:

```
db2 "CREATE TABLE POSP.MQT_REFTBLS AS ( … )
 . . .
 MAINTAINED BY SYSTEM
 DISTRIBUTE BY REPLICATION"
```

Any command-line input or output is written as follows:

```
CREATE GLOBAL TEMPORARY TABLE TMP_INVCDET

LIKE POSP.INVCDET

ON COMMIT DELETE ROWS

NOT LOGGED

IN POSTEMP8K;
```

New terms and **important words** are shown in bold. Words that you see on the screen, in menus or dialog boxes for example, appear in the text like this: "Navigate to **Database partition groups**, right-click, and choose **Create....**"

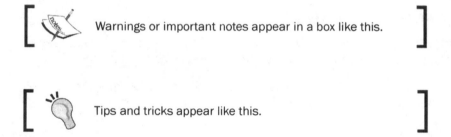

Warnings or important notes appear in a box like this.

Tips and tricks appear like this.

Reader feedback

Feedback from our readers is always welcome. Let us know what you think about this book—what you liked or may have disliked. Reader feedback is important for us to develop titles that you really get the most out of.

To send us general feedback, simply send an e-mail to feedback@packtpub.com, and mention the book title through the subject of your message.

If there is a topic that you have expertise in and you are interested in either writing or contributing to a book, see our author guide on www.packtpub.com/authors.

Customer support

Now that you are the proud owner of a Packt book, we have a number of things to help you to get the most from your purchase.

Downloading the example code

You can download the example code files for all Packt books you have purchased from your account at http://www.packtpub.com. If you purchased this book elsewhere, you can visit http://www.packtpub.com/support and register to have the files e-mailed directly to you.

Errata

Although we have taken every care to ensure the accuracy of our content, mistakes do happen. If you find a mistake in one of our books—maybe a mistake in the text or the code—we would be grateful if you would report this to us. By doing so, you can save other readers from frustration and help us improve subsequent versions of this book. If you find any errata, please report them by visiting http://www.packtpub.com/support, selecting your book, clicking on the **errata submission form** link, and entering the details of your errata. Once your errata are verified, your submission will be accepted and the errata will be uploaded to our website, or added to any list of existing errata, under the Errata section of that title.

Piracy

Piracy of copyright material on the Internet is an ongoing problem across all media. At Packt, we take the protection of our copyright and licenses very seriously. If you come across any illegal copies of our works, in any form, on the Internet, please provide us with the location address or website name immediately so that we can pursue a remedy.

Please contact us at copyright@packtpub.com with a link to the suspected pirated material.

We appreciate your help in protecting our authors, and our ability to bring you valuable content.

Questions

You can contact us at questions@packtpub.com if you are having a problem with any aspect of the book, and we will do our best to address it.

1

DB2 Instance— Administration and Configuration

In this chapter, we will cover:

- ▶ Creating and configuring instances for non-partitioned environments
- ▶ Creating and configuring a client instance
- ▶ Creating and configuring instances for multipartitioned environments
- ▶ Starting and stopping instances
- ▶ Configuring SSL for client-server instance communication
- ▶ Listing instances
- ▶ Attaching to instances
- ▶ Dropping instances

Introduction

The main focus of this chapter is DB2 instance creation and configuration, for non-partitioned database and for multipartitioned database environments.

Creating and configuring instances for non-partitioned environments

A DB2 instance can be defined as a logical container or as a logical context for databases. It can also be described as a layer between DB2 software binaries, a database, and its objects. Also it provides a level of isolation between databases; for example, it is possible to have two or more databases on the same environment, with the same name, but under different instances. It also provides and ensures the communication layer between clients and databases.

Getting ready

For this recipe (and almost all recipes in this book), we will use two servers running Red Hat Enterprise Linux Server x64 release 5.5 (Tikanga), named nodedb21 and nodedb22. The hostnames are optional, but our recommendation is to set up an identical environment to avoid confusion during reading and applying the recipes.

As install location for the IBM DB2 9.7 Enterprise Server Enterprise software product, we will use the directory /opt/ibm/db2/V9.7 on nodedb21. On nodedb22, we will install DB2 Client software to location /opt/ibm/db2/V9.7_clnt. The instance owner will be db2inst1 on nodedb21 and db2clnt1 as client instance owner on nodedb22. Also, on nodedb21, we will create a second instance owner user named db2inst2, to demonstrate how to create an instance manually.

How to do it...

The default method to create an instance is during the IBM DB2 9.7 Enterprise Server Edition software installation. The other possible option is to use the db2icrt command.

In Linux and Unix, every instance is created under a dedicated user, called the instance owner. To create an instance in Linux and UNIX you have to be the root user; on these platforms, we are limited to one instance per user. On Microsoft Windows platforms, you may have more than one instance created under the same user.

Usually, if you set up the software in graphical mode you do not have to create the users manually—you can do this using the wizard. In our recipes, we want to reuse the same groups (db2iadm1 and db2fadm1) for the non-partitioned and the multipartitioned instance and database setup. For the multipartitioned setup we will have the same groups defined on both servers; because we have to deal with security regarding permissions, here, we should create the groups with the same group ID (GID):

1. Create primary groups with the same GID on both servers:

```
[root@nodedb21 ~]# groupadd -g 1103 db2iadm1
[root@nodedb21 ~]# groupadd -g 1102 db2fadm1
[root@nodedb21 ~]#
```

```
[root@nodedb22 ~]# groupadd -g 1103 db2iadm1
[root@nodedb22 ~]# groupadd -g 1102 db2fadm1
[root@nodedb22 ~]#
```

Downloading the example code

You can download the example code files for all Packt books you have purchased from your account at http://www.packtpub.com. If you purchased this book elsewhere, you can visit http://www.packtpub. com/support and register to have the files e-mailed directly to you.

2. Run db2setup from the IBM DB2 9.7 Enterprise Server Edition software installation kit.

> Instance owner user db2inst and fenced user db2fenc will be created during installation. The groups db2iadm1 and db2fadm1 will automatically fill in on the screen.

3. To create a new instance during the installation with db2setup in graphical mode, navigate through configuration steps 1 to 6 and, at step 7 you will find **Create a DB2 instance** option checked; this is the default option.and let as it is.Click **Next**.

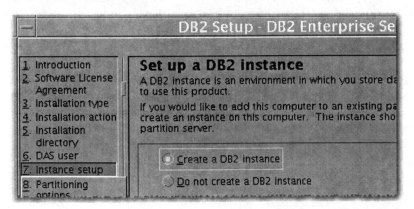

4. At step 8—**Partitioning options**—you will find **Single partition instance** option checked ; this is the default option and let as it is. Click **Next** and finalize installation. If installation was successful, we have a new instance named db2inst1 created.

Another way to create an instance is to use the db2icrt command. This method is suitable in the case that you install the DB2 software with db2_install (manual installation), or that you do not check the **Create a DB2 instance** option during installation with db2setup. Other scenarios would be if you drop an instance and want to create a new one, or if you want to create an additional instance.

5. As mentioned previously, in Linux and Unix, every instance has to be created under an instance owner user. As a `root` user, we will create the user `db2inst2` as instance owner and `db2fenc2` as fenced user; set passwords identical to the individual usernames:

```
[root@nodedb21 ~]# useradd -g db2iadm1 db2inst2
[root@nodedb21 ~]# useradd -g db2fadm1 db2fenc2
[root@nodedb21 ~]# passwd db2inst2
Changing password for user db2inst2.
New UNIX password:
Retype new UNIX password:
passwd: all authentication tokens updated successfully.
[root@nodedb21 ~]# passwd db2fenc2
Changing password for user db2fenc2.
New UNIX password:
Retype new UNIX password:
passwd: all authentication tokens updated successfully.
[root@nodedb21 ~]#
```

6. At this step, set the communication protocol to TCP/IP. The instance communication protocol is set up using the `DB2COMM` variable. We can set this variable no protocol managers will be started and will lead to communication errors at the client side.

```
[db2inst2@nodedb21 ~]$ db2set DB2COMM=TCPIP
[db2inst2@nodedb21 ~]$
```

7. Next, as user `root`, edit `/etc/services` and add `db2c_db2inst2 50002/tcp` entry (highlighted in bold in the listing bellow). Port `50002` will be assigned to `db2inst2` instance. Port `50001` corresponds to the `db2c_db2inst1` service name and was added at `db2inst1` instance creation. Port names prefixed with DB2 are reserved for inter-partition communication, a subject that we're going to discuss later on.

```
db2c_db2inst1     50001/tcp
DB2_db2inst1      60000/tcp
DB2_db2inst1_1    60001/tcp
DB2_db2inst1_2    60002/tcp
DB2_db2inst1_END        60003/tcp
db2c_db2inst2 50002/tcp
```

 If you choose to use only port numbers for SVCENAME database manager parameter you do not need to edit this file.

8. As `root` user, create instance `db2inst2`, using the previously created users as instance owner and fenced user:

    [root@nodedb21.~]# /opt/ibm/db2/V9.7/instance/db2icrt -a SERVER ENCRYPT -p db2c_db2inst2 -u db2fenc2 db2inst2

    DBI1070I Program db2icrt completed successfully.

    [root@nodedb21 ~]#

    We need to explain a little bit about the options used for creating instance `db2inst2`:

    - The `-a` option indicates the authentication type; the default is `SERVER`. Using the `-a` option, the following authentication modes are available: `SERVER`, `CLIENT`, and `SERVER ENCRYPT`. We may change it later by modifying the `AUTHENTICATION` or the SRVCONN_AUTH instance parameter.
    - The `-u` switch is used to set the fenced user.
    - The `-p` option is used to specify the port or its corresponding service name used for client communication, as defined in `/etc/services`. The port or service name may be changed later by modifying the `SVCENAME` database manager parameter
    - For MS Windows platforms, we don't have the `-a` option to specify the authentication mode. The `-p` option in Windows has a different meaning; it is used to specify the instance profile. The `-u` option is for specifying the account name and password used that will be included in the Windows service definition associated with the instance.

To use the **Control Center** for managing an instance locally or remotely, you need to have DB2 Administration Server (DAS) up and running, on the server.

To check the status of DAS, execute the following command, as DAS owner user, which is in our case dasusr1:

[dasusr1@nodedb21 ~]$ db2dascfg get dasstatus

ACTIVE

[dasusr1@nodedb21 ~]$

Usually, it is installed and created during IBM DB2 software installation. If there is no DAS created, you should create it using the dascrt command. The steps are similar to those for creating an instance—create a group and a user. It has to be created by specifying the owner.

For example, /opt/ibm/db2/V9.7/instance/dascrt –u dasusr1.

How it works...

In Linux or Unix, when an instance is created, the db2icrt command *builds up* under the instance owner home directory, the sqllib directory, as a collection of symbolic links pointing to the IBM DB2 software installation home directory. If you want to see what is executing db2icrt in the background, you need to include the -d option to enable debug mode. This explains what happens behind the scenes for the steps mentioned earlier. Usually, this switch is used for detailed diagnostics, and should be activated at the request of IBM support.

Almost all files and directories from sqllib directory are symbolic links to the corresponding installation path (DB2HOME). A short listing inside sqllib directory looks like this:

```
[db2inst1@nodedb21]/home/db2inst1/sqllib>symlinks -v .
other_fs: /home/db2inst1/sqllib/map -> /opt/ibm/db2/V9.7/map
other_fs: /home/db2inst1/sqllib/bin -> /opt/ibm/db2/V9.7/bin
other_fs: /home/db2inst1/sqllib/ruby64 -> /opt/ibm/db2/V9.7/dsdriver/
ruby64
```

On MS Windows platforms, the db2icrt command creates a service. The binaries are actually copied and a service associated with the instance is created.

On a generic Windows machine we'll create an instance named db2win. Initially, the associated service has the status set to stopped and the startup type set to manually. If you want the service to start automatically at system boot, you have to change its startup type to automatic.

To create instance db2win, execute the following command under a privileged user:

```
C:\Windows\system32>db2icrt db2win
DB20000I  The DB2ICRT command completed successfully.
```

To find the associated Windows service with db2win instance, execute the following command:

```
C:\Windows\system32>sc query state= all  | findstr "DB2WIN"
SERVICE_NAME: DB2WIN
DISPLAY_NAME: DB2 - DB2COPY1 - DB2WIN
C:\Windows\system32>
```

There's more...

The db2isetup graphical tool might be used also for creating instances; this tool is available only on the Linux and Unix platforms.

On Linux and Unix you have the possibility to create a non-root type instance using the installer. You are limited to only one non-root instance per server.

Updating instances using the db2iuptd command

Usually this command is used to update an instance after an upgrade to a higher version, or migrate an instance from a lower product level such as Workgroup Edition to Enterprise Edition. Also it might be used for instance debug using the -d option. Like db2icrt, this command has its own particularities on MS Windows operating systems. To find the available options and related descriptions of this command issue db2iuptd -h. For non-root type instances exists a variant of this command named db2nruptd.

Creating and configuring a client instance

Usually, this special type of instance is used for cataloging nodes and databases to which you want to connect using this client. Compared to server instances there are some limitations, as it cannot be started or stopped, and you cannot create databases under it. Mainly, it is used by the DB2 Client and DB2 Connect products.

Getting ready...

On nodedb22 we will create the instance owner db2clnt1 and fenced user named db2fenc1. For creating a client instance, we'll use the -s option of the db2icrt command.

How to do it...

1. Install DB2 Client in the /opt/ibm/db2/V9.7_clnt location on nodedb22, without creating an instance; to do this during installation, check at step 6—**Instance setup**—*Defer this task until after installation is complete*.

2. Next, create users on nodedb22—db2clnt1 as the client instance owner and db2fenc1 as fenced user—and set passwords identical to the usernames:

```
[root@nodedb22 ~]# useradd -g db2iadm1 db2clnt1
[root@nodedb22 ~]# useradd -g db2fadm1 db2fenc1
[root@nodedb22 ~]# passwd db2clnt1
Changing password for user db2clnt1.
New UNIX password:
Retype new UNIX password:
passwd: all authentication tokens updated successfully.
[root@nodedb22 ~]# passwd db2fenc1
Changing password for user db2fenc1.
New UNIX password:
Retype new UNIX password:
passwd: all authentication tokens updated successfully.
[root@nodedb22 ~]#
```

3. As user `root`, create the client instance `db2clnt1`:

```
[root@nodedb22 ~]# /opt/ibm/db2/V9.7/instance/db2icrt -s client -u
db2fenc1 db2iclnt1
DBI1070I  Program db2icrt completed successfully.
[root@nodedb22 ~]#
```

How it works...

Mainly you need to setup a client instance when you have plans to administer DB2 servers remotely with tools that are using non-Java based connections such as **Control Center** or Toad for DB2. The same scenario is applicable when you are using CLI for remote administration or command execution and also in this category are non-java based application clients.

There's more...

In the previous section we used the term non-java clients. However, this not totally exact for older type JDBC or JDBC-ODBC bridge connections using type 1 and 2 drivers. Type 3 and 4 JDBC drivers have implemented internally the entire network communication stack; this is the main reason for their independence from client instances and external network libraries. A good example for a tool that is relying only on JDBC type connections is the new Optim Database Administrator recommended by IBM to be used in future for database administration.

See also

The *Communication with DRDA servers (z/OS and i/OS)* recipe in *Chapter 11, Connectivity and Networking*

Creating and configuring an instance for multipartitioned environments

The IBM DB2 database multipartitioned feature offers the ability to distribute a large database onto different physical servers or the same SMP server, balancing the workload onto multiple databases that are working as one, offering a very scalable way of data processing. We may have all the database partitions reside on the same server, this method of database partitioning is called logical partitioning. There is another scenario when the database partitions are spanned on different physical servers; this partitioning method is called physical partitioning.

An instance in a multipartitioned configuration is not very different by a non-partitioned instance, if it is running on a logical partitioning scheme. To use only physical partitioning, or physical partitioning combined with logical partitioning, an instance must be configured as shared across all the database partitions. In this recipe, we will use the last scenario.

The instance is created once on one node; on the other participant nodes, you have to create just the instance owner user with the same user ID (UID) and GIDs and the same home directory as on the instance owner node. In the following recipe, we will configure servers for the purpose of multipartitioning and will create a new instance named db2instp.

Notice that in this recipe we will use node and partition termsinterchangeably

Getting ready

To install a multipartitioned instance, we need to prepare a suitable environment. For this recipe, we will use the two Linux servers named nodedb21 and nodedb22, mentioned before. nodedb21 will contain the instance home and will export it through NFS to the nodedb22 system. We will also use a new disk partition, defined on nodedb21, for instance home /db2partinst, which, in our case, is a Linux LVM partition. We will create users on both servers with the same UID, and will install IBM DB2 ESE in a new location or DB2HOME—/opt/ibm/db2/V9.7_part on nodedb21 with the **create a response file** option. On nodedb22, we'll also install IBM DB2 ESE, in the location /opt/ibm/db2/V9.7_part, using the response file created during installation on nodedb21.

How to do it...

1. Because this is not a Linux book, we do not cover how to install NFS or how to create a new Linux partition. As a preliminary task, you should check if you have NFS and portmap installed and running on both servers.

2. As user root, execute the following commands on both servers:

   To check if we have NFS and portmap on nodedb21:

   ```
   [root@nodedb21 ~]# rpm -qa | grep nfs
   nfs-utils-lib-1.0.8-7.6.el5
   nfs-utils-1.0.9-44.el5
   [root@nodedb21 ~]# rpm -qa | grep portmap
   portmap-4.0-65.2.2.1
   [root@nodedb21 ~]#
   ```

   To check their current status on nodedb21:

   ```
   [root@nodedb21 ~]# service nfs status
   rpc.mountd (pid 3667) is running...
   nfsd (pid 3664 3663 3662 3661 3660 3659 3658 3657) is running...
   rpc.rquotad (pid 3635) is running...
   [root@nodedb21 ~]#
   [root@nodedb21 ~]# service portmap status
   portmap (pid 3428) is running...
   [root@nodedb21 ~]#
   ```

Set up NFS for sharing the instance home

1. To automatically export /db2partinst on system boot, add your hostnames or the corresponding IP numbers to the /etc/exports file. On nodedb21, add the following line in /etc/exports:

```
/db2partinst          10.231.56.117(rw,no_root_squash,sync)
  10.231.56.118(rw,no_root_squash,sync)
```

2. To export the partition immediately, execute the following command:

```
[root@nodedb22 ~]# exportfs -ra
[root@nodedb22 ~]#
```

3. On nodedb22, as user root, create a directory /db2partinst, used as mount point for /db2partinst, exported from nodedb21:

```
[root@nodedb22 ~]# mkdir /db2partinst
[root@nodedb22 ~]#
```

4. In /etc/fstab on nodedb22, to mount /db2partinst on system boot, add the following line:

```
nodedb21:/db2partinst /db2partinst nfs
  rw,timeo=300,retrans=5,hard,intr,bg,suid
```

5. To mount the partition immediately on nodedb22, issue the following command:

```
[root@nodedb22 ~]# mount nodedb21:/db2partinst /db2partinst
[root@nodedb22 ~]#
```

Creating the instance owner and fenced user

1. On nodedb21, create the instance owner db2instp and the fenced user db2fencp. Instance home will be located in /db2partinst/db2instp:

```
[root@nodedb22 ~]# useradd -u 1316 -g db2iadm1 -m -d /db2partinst/
db2instp db2instp
```

```
[root@nodedb22 ~]# useradd -u 1315 -g db2fadm1 -m -d /db2partinst/
db2fencp db2fencp
```

```
[root@nodedb22 ~]# passwd db2instp
```

```
Changing password for user db2instp.
```

```
New UNIX password:
```

```
Retype new UNIX password:
```

```
passwd: all authentication tokens updated successfully.
```

```
[root@nodedb21 ~]# passwd db2fencp
```

```
Changing password for user db2fencp.
```

```
New UNIX password:
```

```
Retype new UNIX password:
passwd: all authentication tokens updated successfully.
[root@nodedb21 ~]#
```

2. Repeat step 1 on `nodedb22` and ignore any warnings.

Set up SSH for client authentication

In a physical multipartitioned environment, any instance owner user has to be able to execute commands on any participant node. To ensure this, we need to establish user equivalence or host equivalence between nodes. Actually, we have two methods: one is with RSH, which is less secure and the other is using SSH, which is secure. With SSH, there are two methods: one is host-based authentication and the other is client-based authentication. Next, we will implement client-based authentication; this method fits better with a small number of partitions, as in our example.

1. As user `db2instp` on `nodedb21`, execute the following commands:

```
[db2instp@nodedb21 ~]$ cd ~
[db2instp@nodedb21 ~]$ mkdir .ssh
[db2instp@nodedb21 ~]$ chmod 700 .ssh
[db2instp@nodedb21 ~]$ cd .ssh
[db2instp@nodedb21 .ssh]$ ssh-keygen -t rsa
Generating public/private rsa key pair.
Enter file in which to save the key (/db2partinst/db2instp/.ssh/
id_rsa): Enter passphrase (empty for no passphrase):
Enter same passphrase again:
Your identification has been saved in /db2partinst/db2instp/.ssh/
id_rsa.
Your public key has been saved in /db2partinst/db2instp/.ssh/id_
rsa.pub.
The key fingerprint is:
2b:90:ee:3b:e6:28:11:b1:63:93:ba:88:d7:d5:b1:14 db2instp@nodedb21
[db2instp@nodedb21 .ssh]$ cat id_rsa.pub >> authorized_keys
[db2instp@nodedb21 .ssh]$ chmod 640 authorized_keys
```

2. As user `db2instp` on `nodedb22`, execute the following commands:

```
[db2instp@nodedb22 .ssh]$ cd ~/.ssh
[db2instp@nodedb22 .ssh]$ ssh-keygen -t rsa
Generating public/private rsa key pair.
Enter file in which to save the key (/db2partinst/db2instp/.ssh/
id_rsa):
```

```
/db2partinst/db2instp/.ssh/id_rsa already exists.
Overwrite (y/n)? y
Enter passphrase (empty for no passphrase):
Enter same passphrase again:
Your identification has been saved in /db2partinst/db2instp/.ssh/
id_rsa.
Your public key has been saved in /db2partinst/db2instp/.ssh/id_
rsa.pub.
The key fingerprint is:
87:36:b4:47:5a:5c:e5:3e:4e:e9:ce:5b:47:2c:ce:6b db2instp@nodedb22
[db2instp@nodedb22 .ssh]$ cat id_rsa.pub >> authorized_keys
[db2instp@nodedb22 .ssh]$
```

3. Go back on `nodedb21` and issue the following commands to set up a host trust relationship:

```
[db2instp@nodedb21 ~]$ cd ~/.ssh
[db2instp@nodedb21 .ssh]$ ssh-keyscan -t rsa
nodedb21,10.231.56.117 >> known_hosts
# nodedb21 SSH-2.0-OpenSSH_4.3
[db2instp@nodedb21 .ssh]$ ssh-keyscan -t rsa
nodedb22,10.231.56.118 >> known_hosts
# nodedb22 SSH-2.0-OpenSSH_4.3
[db2instp@nodedb21 .ssh]$
```

4. Verify that the client authentication is working; on `nodedb21`, issue `ssh nodedb22 date` (do it the other way around—now it should work without asking for a password):

```
[db2instp@nodedb21 .ssh]$ ssh nodedb22 date
Thu Jun  9 16:42:33 EEST 2011
[db2instp@nodedb21 .ssh]$ ssh nodedb22
[db2instp@nodedb22 ~]$ ssh nodedb21 date
Thu Jun  9 16:42:48 EEST 2011
[db2instp@nodedb22 ~]$ ssh nodedb22 date
Thu Jun  9 16:42:55 EEST 2011
[db2instp@nodedb22 ~]$ ssh nodedb21
[db2instp@nodedb21 ~]$ ssh nodedb21 date
Thu Jun  9 16:43:07 EEST 2011
[db2instp@nodedb21 ~]$
```

Install DB2 ESE software with a response file option

A response file is a text file containing installation and configuration information such as paths, installation options etc. It can be created and recorded using interactive installation and replayed by other installations to perform the same steps.

1. Launch db2setup, and, at step 4 of the installation wizard (**Install action**), check the **Install DB2 Enterprise Server Edition on this computer and save my setting in a response file** option. Provide the complete path to the response file.

2. At step 5, specify /opt/ibm/db2/V9.7_part for **Installation directory**.

3. At step 7 (**Partitioning option**), check **Multiple partition instance**.

4. Next, for DB2 instance owner, choose db2instp and, for fenced user, choose db2fencp. On the next screen, choose **Do not create tools catalog**. At the end of installation, we will find (in the directory chosen at step 4 of installation wizard) two files with .rsp extension; you need to copy just db2ese_addpart.rsp to nodedb22 and issue on nodedb22, from the installation directory:

    ```
    ./db2setup -r <your path>db2ese_addpart.rsp
    DBI1191I  db2setup is installing and configuring DB2 according to
    the response file provided. Please wait.
    ```

Configuring communication for inter-partition command execution

1. The communication method of inter-partition command execution is controlled by DB2RSCHCM registry variable. Because our choice is SSH for inter-partition command execution, you must next set the DB2RSHCMD variable to point to SSH executable DB2RSHCMD=/usr/bin/ssh. If this variable is not set, the rsh method is used by default:

    ```
    [db2instp@nodedb21 ~]$ db2set DB2RSHCMD=/usr/bin/ssh -i
    ```

2. To verify the current DB2 registry variables, issue the following command:

    ```
    [db2instp@nodedb21 ~]$ db2set -all
    [i] DB2RSHCMD=/usr/bin/ssh
    [i] DB2COMM=tcpip
    [i] DB2AUTOSTART=YES
    [g] DB2FCMCOMM=TCPIP4
    [g] DB2SYSTEM=nodedb21
    [g] DB2INSTDEF=db2instp
    ```

Configuring the nodes

In the `db2nodes.cfg` file, database partition configuration file, located in `$INSTANCEHOME/sqllib`, set the participant nodes. Define three nodes—two on `nodedb21`, partition number 0 with logical port 0 and partition number 2 with logical port 1 and one on `nodedb22`, partition 1 with logical port 0. After adding the nodes we should have the following structure:

```
0 nodedb21 0
1 nodedb22 0
2 nodedb21 1
```

How it works...

Instance `db2instp` knows about the current nodes by reading their definition from db2nodes.cfg database partition configuration file. The logical ports and number of maximum partitions per server are limited by the range defined within `/etc/services` file as follows:

DB2_db2inst1

60000/tcp DB2_db2inst1_1

60001/tcp DB2_db2inst1_2

60002/tcp DB2_db2inst1_END 60003/tcp

The structure of `db2nodes.cfg`, in some cases, can be further elaborated with optional information such as `resourcenames` or `netnames`; in our case being a simple setup used for demonstration purpose we have defined only the nodes, hostnames, and the logical ports.

Under Unix and Linux, db2nodes has the following complete format:

dbpartitionnum hostname logicalport netname resourcesetname

Under MS Windows, db2nodes has the following complete format:

dbpartitionnum hostname computername logicalport netname resourcesetname

There's more...

DB2 has two utilities to verify that communication between nodes is working: `db2_all` and rah. You can also issue practically any administrative command (backup, restore, setting parameters, and so on) across the database partitions with these utilities.

An example of using `db2_all` for verification:

```
[db2instp@nodedb21 ~]$ db2_all uptime
  11:54:02 up 17:11,        1 user,       load average: 0.07, 0.03, 0.00
nodedb21: uptime completed ok
  11:54:03 up 17:11,        0 users,      load average: 0.10, 0.03, 0.01
nodedb22: uptime completed ok
```

```
  11:54:03 up 17:11,        1 user,      load average: 0.07, 0.03, 0.00
nodedb21: uptime completed ok
```

The same using rah:

```
[db2instp@nodedb21 ~]$ rah uptime
```

```
  14:56:19 up 35 days, 18:09,      1 user,    load average: 0.08, 0.02, 0.01
nodedb21: uptime completed ok
  14:56:20 up 35 days, 18:09,      0 users,   load average: 0.00, 0.00, 0.00
nodedb22: uptime completed ok
  14:56:20 up 35 days, 18:09,      1 user,    load average: 0.08, 0.02, 0.01
nodedb21: uptime completed ok
```

Obviously, there is also a possibility of using a shared disk, formatted with a concurrent file system, such as, IBM's GPFS or Red Hat GFS, for instance home, and used for sharing across the nodes instead of using NFS exports.

On Windows, it is not recommended to edit the db2nodes.cfg file manually; use the

The following commands instead:

- ▸ db2nlist—to list database partitions
- ▸ db2ncrt—to add a database partition server to an instance
- ▸ db2ndrop—to drop a database partition server to an instance
- ▸ db2nchg—to modify a database partition server configuration

See also

The *Converting a non-partitioned database to a multipartitioned database on MS Windows* recipe in *Chapter 3, DB2 Multipartitioned Databases—Administration and Configuration*

Starting and stopping instances

There are several situations in which an instance must be stopped and started, for example, after you change some parameters that are not dynamic, or after applying a fixpack.

Getting ready

We have, at disposal, a couple of different ways to start or stop an instance. We can use, say, db2start for starting and db2stop for stopping; these commands are available for execution in the command line or from DB2 CLI. We can also start or stop an instance from the **Control Center**. In Windows, you can also start and stop an instance by starting and stopping the service associated with it.

How to do it...

1. The current instance is set by the environment variable DB2INSTANCE or the global registry variable DB2INSTDEF, in case DB2INSTANCE is not set. This is applicable mostly for Microsoft Windows platforms where there could be more than one instance per user.

   ❏ On Microsoft Windows:

   ```
   C:\Documents and Settings>db2ilist

   DB2_02

   DB2WIN

   C:\Documents and Settings>set DB2INSTANCE

   DB2INSTANCE=DB2_02
   ```

   Now, if we issue db2stop or db2start, only instance DB2_02 will be affected.

   ❏ On our Linux server nodedb21:

   ```
   [db2inst1@nodedb21 ~]$ echo $DB2INSTANCE

   db2inst1
   ```

2. As the db2inst1 instance owner, stop instance db2inst1 with the db2stop command, and start it with db2start:

   ```
   [db2inst1@nodedb21 ~]$ db2stop

   06/09/2011 17:55:21     0    0    SQL1064N  DB2STOP processing was
       successful.

   SQL1064N  DB2STOP processing was successful.

   [db2inst1@nodedb21 ~]$ db2start

   06/09/2011 17:55:29     0    0    SQL1063N  DB2START processing was
       successful.

   SQL1063N  DB2START processing was successful.
   ```

3. As the multipartitioned instance owner db2instp, stop instance db2instp with the db2stop command, and start it with db2start:

   ```
   [db2instp@nodedb21 sqllib]$ db2stop

   06/09/2011 19:03:47     1    0    SQL1064N  DB2STOP processing was
       successful.

   06/09/2011 19:03:48     0    0    SQL1064N  DB2STOP processing was
       successful.

   06/09/2011 19:03:49     2    0    SQL1064N  DB2STOP processing was
       successful.

   SQL1064N  DB2STOP processing was successful.

   [db2instp@nodedb21 sqllib]$ db2start
   ```

```
06/09/2011 19:04:02      1    0    SQL1063N  DB2START processing was
   successful.
06/09/2011 19:04:06      2    0    SQL1063N  DB2START processing was
   successful.
06/09/2011 19:04:06      0    0    SQL1063N  DB2START processing was
   successful.
SQL1063N  DB2START processing was successful.
```

4. Using the **Control Center**, right-click on db2inst1 and issue *stop* and *start*.

How it works...

In the process of starting an instance, memory structures are allocated and the instance starts listening for connections on the ports assigned by the SVCENAME database manager configuration parameter. At *stop*, existing connections are disconnected and memory is deallocated.

There's more...

Other options that can be used to start and stop an instance are the DB2 CLI commands, START DATABASE MANAGER and STOP DATABASE MANAGER. For Windows, we have as alternate option to start or stop the service associated with the instance. To set the instance for automatic start on Linux or Unix, at system boot, you can use the instance-level registry variable DB2AUTOSTART=YES or the db2iauto -on <instance name> command.

Configuring SSL for client-server instance communication

Databases can contain sensitive information; these days, the main concern is related to the security of data stored in tables as well as those sent over the network. One method of securing network communication between server and client is **SSL**, which is actually an abbreviation for **Secure Socket Layer**. We do not delve further into too much theory. Mainly, SSL addresses the following important security considerations: authentication, confidentiality, and integrity. Mainly SSL encryption and other network communication or also named data in transit encryption methods protects against unauthorized packet interception and analysis performed by an interposed person between a client and a server, also known as eavesdropping.

The DB2 instance has built-in support for SSL. DB2 relies on Global Security Kit for implementing SSL. GSKit is included in the IBM DB2 ESE software installation kit or is downloadable for free from IBM's website. Next, we'll show how to implement a secure connection between a DB2 server and a DB2 client.

Getting ready

For the next recipe, we will use nodedb21 (db2inst1 instance) as server and nodedb22 (db2clnt1 instance) as client, where we have installed DB2 Client in previous recipes. You need to ensure that you have GSKit libraries in LD_LIBRARY_PATH. In our case, the libraries that are located in /home/db2inst1/sqllib/lib64 are pointing to the /opt/ibm/db2/ V9.7/lib64 location.

How to do it...

1. The first step is to add the gsk8capicmd_64 executable in our PATH.

    Include the following in .bash_profile:

    ```
    PATH=$PATH:$HOME/bin:$HOME/sqllib/gskit/bin
    ```

    Execute source .bash_profile to reinitialize the user environment.

2. To create a key database on the server, execute the following (for more information about gsk8capicmd_64, execute gsk8capicmd_64 –help):

    ```
    [db2inst1@nodedb21 ~]$ gsk8capicmd_64 -keydb -create -db "/home/
    db2inst1/keystoredb2inst1.kdb" -pw "db2cookbook" -stash
    [db2inst1@nodedb21 ~]$
    ```

3. Create a self-signature and self-sign the key database on the server:

    ```
    [db2inst1@nodedb21 ~]$ gsk8capicmd_64 -cert -create -db "/
    home/db2inst1/keystoredb2inst1.kdb" -pw "db2cookbook" -label
    "db2cookbooksignature" -dn "CN=www.packtpub.com,O=Packt
    Publishing,OU=Packt Publishing"
    [db2inst1@nodedb21 ~]$
    ```

4. Extract the signature for signing the client key database:

    ```
    [db2inst1@nodedb21 ~]$ gsk8capicmd_64 -cert -extract -db "/home/
    db2inst1/keystoredb2inst1.kdb" -label "db2cookbooksignature"
    -target "/home/db2inst1/db2cookbook.arm" -format ascii -fips -pw
    "db2cookbook"
    [db2inst1@nodedb21 ~]$
    ```

5. Next, create the client key database:

    ```
    [db2inst1@nodedb21 ~]$ gsk8capicmd_64 -keydb -create -db "/home/
    db2inst1/keystoreclientdb2inst1.kdb" -pw "db2ckbk" –stash
    [db2inst1@nodedb21 ~]$
    ```

6. Import the self-signed certificate into the client key database:

```
[db2inst1@nodedb21 ~]$ gsk8capicmd_64 -cert -add -db "/home/
db2inst1/keystoreclientdb2inst.kdb" -pw "db2ckbk" -label
"db2cookbooksignature" -file "/home/db2inst1/db2cookbook.arm"
-format ascii -fips
[db2inst1@nodedb21 ~]$
```

7. To enable SSL as communication protocol on nodedb21, execute the following:

```
[db2inst1@nodedb21 ~]$ db2set DB2COMM=tcpip,ssl -i
[db2inst1@nodedb21 ~]$
```

8. Enable SSL as communication protocol also on the client side:

```
[db2clnt1@nodedb21 ~]$ db2set DB2COMM=tcpip,ssl -i
[db2clnt1@nodedb21 ~]$
```

9. Next, on nodedb21, set SSL-related parameters on the server instance; then, stop and start the instance:

```
[db2inst1@nodedb21 ~]$ db2 "update dbm cfg using ssl_svr_keydb /
home/db2inst/keystoredb2inst1.kdb"
DB20000I  The UPDATE DATABASE MANAGER CONFIGURATION command
completed
successfully.
[db2inst1@nodedb21 ~]$ db2 "update dbm cfg using ssl_svr_stash /
home/db2inst/keystoredb2inst1.sth"
DB20000I  The UPDATE DATABASE MANAGER CONFIGURATION command
completed
successfully.
[db2inst1@nodedb21 ~]$ db2 "update dbm cfg using ssl_svr_label
db2cookbooksignature"
DB20000I  The UPDATE DATABASE MANAGER CONFIGURATION command
completed
successfully.
[db2inst1@nodedb21 ~]$ db2 "update dbm cfg using ssl_svcename
50004"
DB20000I  The UPDATE DATABASE MANAGER CONFIGURATION command
completed
successfully.
[db2inst1@nodedb21 ~]$ db2stop
06/09/2011 19:08:39     0    0    SQL1064N  DB2STOP processing was
successful.
SQL1064N  DB2STOP processing was successful.
[db2inst1@nodedb21 ~]$ db2start
06/09/2011 19:08:45     0    0    SQL1063N  DB2START processing was
successful.
SQL1063N  DB2START processing was successful.
```

Description of SSL-related parameters used on the server side:

▸ SSL_SVR_KEYDB specifies a fully qualified filepath of the key file to be used for SSL setup at server side

▸ SSL_SVR_STASH—specifies a fully qualified filepath of the stash file to be used for SSL setup at server side

▸ SSL_SVR_LABEL—specifies a label of the personal certificate of the server in the key database

▸ SSL_SVCENAME—specifies the name of the port that a database server uses to await communications from remote client nodes using SSL protocol

▸ Be careful to set the correct paths, otherwise SSL won't work.

10. Copy /home/db2inst1/keystoreinstclient.kdb and /home/db2clnt1/ keystoreinstclient.sth to nodedb22.

11. On nodedb22, set SSL DB2 client instance-related parameters:

```
[db2clnt1@nodedb22 ~]$ db2 "update dbm cfg using SSL_CLNT_KEYDB /
home/db2clnt1/keystoreclientdb2inst.kdb"

DB20000I  The UPDATE DATABASE MANAGER CONFIGURATION command
  completed successfully.

[db2clnt1@nodedb22 ~]$  db2 "update dbm cfg using SSL_CLNT_STASH /
home/db2clnt1/keystoreclientdb2inst.sth"

DB20000I  The UPDATE DATABASE MANAGER CONFIGURATION command
  completed successfully.
```

Description of SSL-related parameters on the client side:

SSL_CLNT_KEYDB specifies the fully qualified filepath of the key file to be used for SSL connection at the client side

SSL_CLNT_STASH specifies the fully qualified filepath of the stash file to be used for SSL connections at the client side

12. Next, copy GSKit libraries to the client's DB2HOME/lib64 directory:

```
[root@nodedb22 ~]# cp /opt/ibm/db2/V9.7_part/lib64/libgsk8* /opt/
ibm/db2/V9.7/lib64/

[root@nodedb22 ~]#
```

How it works...

SSL establishes the connection between client and server using a mechanism called **handshake**. There is a lot of information on the Internet about SSL and its working. Briefly, these are the steps for SSL handshake:

1. The client requests an SSL connection, listing its SSL version and supported cipher suites.
2. The server responds with a selected cipher suite.
3. The server sends its digital certificate to the client.
4. The client verifies the validity of the server's certificate (server authentication).
5. Client and server securely negotiate a session key.
6. Client and server securely exchange information using the key selected previously.

There's more...

In this recipe, we used a self signed certificate, which is fine for testing or internal use. For production environments, you should use trusted certificates signed by a third-party certification authority.

Other methods for encrypting data in transit can be implemented by using `DATA_ENCRYPT` and `DATA_ENCRYPT_CMP` as authentication methods. Also using port forwarding with SSH tunnels is a good option.

See also

Chapter 10, DB2 Security

Listing and attaching to instances

On a server environment, you may have many instances belonging to one DB2 installation or DB2HOME; obviously, you need to know about them and their name. For this purpose, you have the ability to use some specific commands to list them.

You also need to connect to these instances from remote locations to perform administration tasks; this, in the DB2 world, is called attaching.

Getting ready

In this recipe, we'll show how to list instances and attach to local and remote instances. Again, we'll use `nodedb21` as server and `nodedb22` as client.

How to do it...

Commands related to creating an instance are performed by the root user; listing is no exception and must be performed as root.

Listing instances

1. The command to list current instances is db2ilist. It lists the instances that belong to one DB2 copy. List instances created in DBCOPY1:

   ```
   [root@nodedb21 ~]# /opt/ibm/db2/V9.7/instance/db2ilist
   db2inst1
   db2inst2
   ```

2. The same command from multipartitioned DB2HOME or DBCOPY2:

   ```
   [root@nodedb21 ~]# /opt/ibm//db2/V9.7_part/instance/db2ilist
   db2instp
   ```

Attaching to instances

1. On nodedb22, catalog db2inst1 both as TCPIP and SSL, on our client instance db2clnt1, created before. Because we set up SSL as a separate communication method for the db2inst1 instance, we have to specify it as the security method when cataloging the node (security SSL) with the SSL dedicated port. Catalog the nodes, as follows:

   ```
   [db2clnt1@nodedb22 db2dump]$ db2 "CATALOG TCPIP NODE NODE21_S
   REMOTE nodedb21 SERVER 50004 SECURITY SSL REMOTE_INSTANCE
   db2inst1 SYSTEM  nodedb21 OSTYPE  LINUXX8664"
   DB20000I  The CATALOG TCPIP NODE command completed successfully.
   DB21056W  Directory changes may not be effective until the
      directory cache is refreshed.


   [db2clnt1@nodedb22 db2dump]$ db2 "CATALOG TCPIP NODE NODE21_1
   REMOTE nodedb21 SERVER 50001 REMOTE_INSTANCE  db2inst1 SYSTEM
   nodedb21 OSTYPE  LINUXX8664"
   DB20000I  The CATALOG TCPIP NODE command completed successfully.
   DB21056W  Directory changes may not be effective until the
      directory cache is refreshed.
   ```

2. List the cataloged nodes:

   ```
   [db2clnt1@nodedb22 ~]$ db2 "list node directory"

   Node Directory

   Number of entries in the directory = 2
   ```

```
Node 1 entry:
Node name                      = NODE21_S
 Comment                       =
 Directory entry type          = LOCAL
 Protocol                      = TCPIP
 Hostname                      = nodedb21
 Service name                  = 50004
 Security type                 = SSL
 Remote instance name          = db2inst1
 System                        = nodedb21
 Operating system type         = LINUXX8664


Node 2 entry:

 Node name                     = NODE21_1
 Comment                       =
 Directory entry type          = LOCAL
 Protocol                      = TCPIP
 Hostname                      = nodedb21
 Service name                  = 50001
 Remote instance name          = db2inst1
 System                        = nodedb21
 Operating system type         = LINUXX8664
```

3. Attach to instance `db2inst1`, using first the SSL port, and next the TCP/IP port:

```
[db2clnt1@nodedb22 ~]$ db2 "attach to NODE21_S user db2inst1
using db2inst1"


    Instance Attachment Information


 Instance server      = DB2/LINUXX8664 9.7.4
 Authorization ID     = DB2INST1
 Local instance alias = NODE21_S


[db2clnt1@nodedb22 ~]$ db2 " attach to node21_1 user db2inst1
using db2inst1"


    Instance Attachment Information
```

```
Instance server       = DB2/LINUXX8664 9.7.4
Authorization ID      = DB2INST1
Local instance alias  = NODE21_1
```

4. Attaching to an instance with the **Control Center**:

    In **Control Center** navigate to instance db2inst1, right-click, and choose **Attach**.

How it works...

Instances are registered in a file named global register. This file is always updated when an instance is created or dropped.

When you attach to an instance from a client, you can see that the port on the server is changing its status from *listening* to *established*:

```
[root@nodedb21 ~]# netstat -nlpta | grep 5000*
tcp        0        0 0.0.0.0:50001             0.0.0.0:*
LISTEN       19974/db2sysc 0

tcp        0        0 0.0.0.0:50003             0.0.0.0:*
LISTEN       26082/db2sysc 0

tcp        0        0 0.0.0.0:50004             0.0.0.0:*
LISTEN       19974/db2sysc 0

tcp        0        0 10.231.56.117:50001       10.231.56.118:49321
TIME_WAIT    -

tcp        0        0 10.231.56.117:50004       10.231.56.118:48187
ESTABLISHED 19974/db2sysc 0
```

This appears on nodedb21, after attaching to instance db2inst1, using the SSL port 50004.

There's more...

There is a straightforward method to verify that one instance is listening on its assigned port from a client. For this purpose, you can try to connect with telnet on that port:

```
[db2inst1@nodedb22 ~]$ telnet nodedb21 50004
Trying 10.231.56.117...
Connected to nodedb21.
Escape character is '^]'.
```

This means that our port assigned to SSL is listening. To detach from an instance, simply issue the DETACH command.

Another indirect method to list instances on a server is to use the discovery process provided by Configuration Assistant or Control Center locally or remotely.

See also

Chapter 11, Using DB2 Discovery

Dropping instances

There could be situations when it is necessary to drop an instance. An instance might be dropped by using the db2idrop command.

Getting ready

In this recipe, we will drop the instance db2inst2, created previously.

How to do it...

1. The command for dropping an instance is db2idrop. You have to be user root to drop an instance. First, we need to ensure that the instance is not active. If the instance has active connections and it is active, the db2idrop command fails.

2. Stop the instance by force:

   ```
   [db2inst2@nodedb21 ~]$ db2stop force

   07/12/2011 16:38:27     0   0    SQL1064N  DB2STOP processing was
   successful.

   SQL1064N  DB2STOP processing was successful.

   [db2inst2@nodedb21 ~]$
   ```

    If the instance hangs for some reason, the db2_kill command might be used. It will bring down the instance abruptly. However, be careful running this, because your databases running under this instance remain in an inconsistent mode.

3. As the user root, issue the following command to drop db2inst2:

   ```
   [root@nodedb21 ~]# /opt/ibm/db2/V9.7/instance/db2idrop db2inst2
   DBI1070I  Program db2idrop completed successfully.
   ```

How it works...

On Linux and Unix, `db2idrop` actually deletes the `sqllib` directory from the instance owner home. Therefore, it is recommended to save anything you have placed in this directory such as UDFs or external programs.

On Windows, `db2idrop` removes the service associated with the instance.

There's more...

As a best practice, before the instance is dropped, it is recommended to save the information related to that instance in a server profile file. In case you plan to recreate the instance and configure it as before, you can simply import the server profile after the instance is created again.

To export the instance profile, use **Control Center** | **Tools** | **Configuration assistant** | **Export profile** | **Customize**.

In the **Export** tab, you have plenty of options to export; choose anything you consider worth being saved.

2

Administration and Configuration of the DB2 Non-partitioned Database

In this chapter, we will cover:

- ▶ Creating and configuring DB2 non-partitioned databases
- ▶ Using configuration advisor
- ▶ Creating a database from an existing backup
- ▶ Configuring automatic database maintenance
- ▶ Managing federated databases, connecting to Oracle and MSSQL
- ▶ Altering databases
- ▶ Dropping databases

Introduction

This chapter provides recipes in order to create a database and get operational in simple and easy steps. We will do so in a manner that respects best practices in the industry.

You have created an instance named db2inst1 on nodedb21, in the previous chapter. You will prepare for available disk space. You will then be able to configure your database for its mission and prepare it for automatic maintenance, so its operation is worry free.

While the nature of these recipes makes them useful right away, it is strongly recommended that they be attempted in a test environment first. We suggest you execute the commands individually, so you can learn as you go along.

Creating and configuring DB2 non-partitioned databases

We will discuss here how to create a single-partitioned database, which is sufficient for most database applications and is the most common configuration for small- to medium-sized databases.

If you plan on having a **Business Intelligence** (**BI**) database, you should be planning for a partitioned database. You can estimate one processor core for every 300 GB of data. We will cover this topic in *Chapter 3, DB2 Multi-partitioned Databases—Administration and Configuration*.

Getting ready

Gather as much technical information as you can about the hardware or virtual machine(s) you have at your disposal, for this database. Identify in which instance you will create your database, and ensure you will have enough memory and disk space for what you need.

Identify the location where you will create the table spaces (filesystems for Unix platforms, disk drives on Windows servers) and how much available space you will have. Make sure the instance owner has read and write permission in the directory that you will specify for your new database.

Best practices in the industry recommend separating data, indexes, lobs, and transaction logs on separate filesystems (or disk drives, on Windows systems). Depending on your installation, a filesystem can be defined as a single virtual disk on a NAS/SAN RAID 5 device, or a logical volume, spread on many physical disk drives. Check with your storage administrator for the best configuration—get as many disks/spindles as possible.

Decide on a data strategy—consider the database's mission and growth potential. Allow for possible partitioning, or table partitioning. MDC could also be a possible avenue. Decide on a naming convention for mount points and databases. The effort you spend on planning will save much time and money down the road.

Now perhaps you just want to get to the matter right away. We'll create a simple database; I'll explain the details as we go along.

How to do it...

1. Log in as the target instance owner.

   Start **Control Center** and make sure the instance is started. Or, start the instance from the command line:

   ```
   [db2inst1@nodedb21 ~]$ db2start
   SQL1063N  DB2START processing was successful.
   ```

2. Choose the instance.

   Expand the **All Systems** node in the left pane of the **Control Center**. Choose the node and instance.

   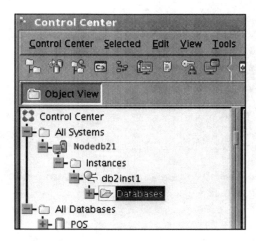

3. Create the database.

   Right-click on the **Databases** folder. A pop-up menu appears; select **Create Database** and start with the **Standard** option. We'll use default options for now.

   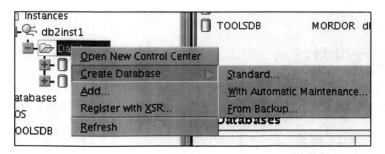

We'll create a database called **NAV**, located in **/data/db2**, with the same alias. You can add a comment if you wish; I would suggest putting in the name by which the users know this database. Since they probably don't know the database name as **NAV**, we'll put in **Aviation Geo Data**.

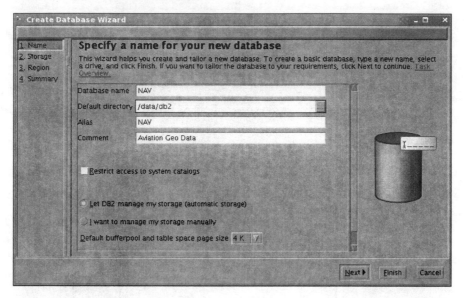

We will also select **Let DB2 manage my storage (automatic storage)**; this will enable DB2 to use automatic storage.

Avoid prefixing schema, table spaces, or database objects with db2, ibm, sys, or syscat. This may induce confusion with objects belonging to DB2. When installing the DBMS, DB2 will ask you to create an instance called db2inst1, by default. You can safely use this instance name or bypass this step and create one later with your own naming convention.

How it works...

DB2 creates and catalogs a database for us. It's basically an empty shell with a catalog, user space, and temporary space. This database will have to be customized to fit your needs.

There's more...

Here are some features to consider before creating a database; some cannot be changed easily when created, so, if you want to change settings, you may even have to export the data, recreate the database with the new settings, and then reimport the data.

Command preview

While creating the database with the **Create Database Wizard**, there will be a summary report of the operation when DB2 is about to create your database.

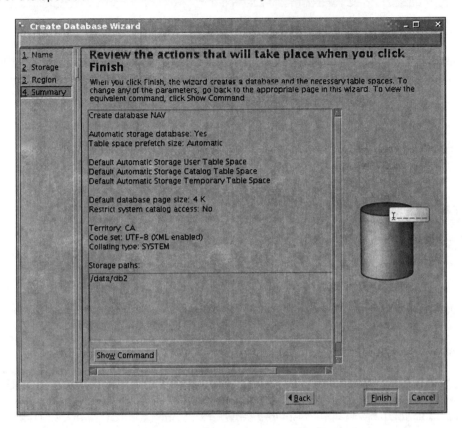

A **Show command** button lets you preview the create database command. You can click on **Finish** to execute the command now, or do it later on.

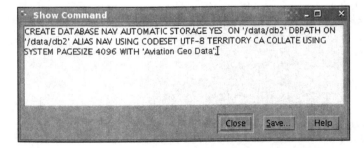

You can copy this command and paste it into a script, so you can create the database manually from the command line, if you wish.

Automatic storage

With automatic storage, DB2 simplifies database file maintenance. DB2 uses the storage path you put in the *default directory* and manages automatically all table space containers for the database. You may add storage paths; DB2 will create, extend, or add containers in these storage paths. You don't have to worry about container file naming convention or extending containers to allow for free space.

In DB2 Express C version and Enterprise Server Edition (ESE), automatic storage is the default option present in the **Control Center**'s create database dialog. Once a database is created with automatic storage, it cannot be reset after creation. Note the command used for an automatic storage database. No table space definitions are required, since DB2 will create the three main table spaces, CATALOG, USER, and SYSTEM Temporary table spaces.

```
CREATE DATABASE NAV
AUTOMATIC STORAGE YES
ON '/data/db2'
DBPATH ON '/data/db2'
ALIAS NAV
USING CODESET UTF-8
TERRITORY CA
COLLATE USING SYSTEM
PAGESIZE 4096
WITH 'Aviation Geo Data';
```

All that is needed for maintenance is to check for filesystem availability. Fortunately, there are tools in DB2 to help you do this; we'll see this later with the health monitor.

Perhaps you have your own naming convention and prefer to manage containers yourself; in that case, automatic storage should be off. With the **Control Center**, you just have to select **I want to manage my space manually**, on the first screen. You can create a database using the command center with the **AUTOMATIC STORAGE NO** option or manually from the command line, using a script. Note the three required table spaces and their container definitions:

```
CREATE DATABASE NAV
AUTOMATIC STORAGE NO
ON '/data/db2' ALIAS NAV
USING CODESET UTF-8
TERRITORY CA
COLLATE USING SYSTEM
PAGESIZE 8 K
CATALOG    TABLESPACE  MANAGED BY DATABASE USING (
   FILE '/data/db2/db2inst1/NODE0000/nav/catalog.dbf' 6400 )
   AUTORESIZE YES MAXSIZE 500 M
USER       TABLESPACE  MANAGED BY DATABASE USING (
   FILE '/data/db2/db2inst1/NODE0000/nav/user.dbf' 6400 )
   AUTORESIZE YES MAXSIZE 500 M
TEMPORARY TABLESPACE  MANAGED BY DATABASE USING (
   FILE '/data/db2/db2inst1/NODE0000/nav/temp.dbf' 6400 )
   AUTORESIZE YES MAXSIZE 500 M;
```

The file size in the `create database` command is in pages; you cannot specify M or G for megabytes or gigabytes.

Adaptive self-tuning memory

Adaptive self-tuning memory, introduced with v9.1, removes the burden on the DBA to tune memory utilization. It is enabled, by default, for single partition databases. This allows DB2 to automatically distribute memory allocation for buffer pools, lock lists, package cache, and sort memory. For example, when less memory is required from buffer pools, it can be freed from buffer pools to allow more space for sort memory.

File and directory permission on database objects

When instance and database directory permissions are created by DB2, you should not modify any of those. With automatic storage, you would normally find the database files under the following directory hierarchy:

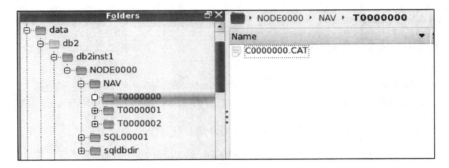

Let's explain the directory hierarchy we just saw earlier:

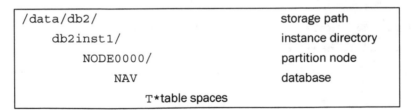

UNIX links

You can define your containers or storage path in DB2 to point to a symbolic link. The operating system will follow it through. In this example, I moved a container but left a symbolic link to point to the new container location.

Use this carefully in sandbox environments first. This can be useful to get you out of a disk-based issue with minimum impact.

For example:

```
[db2inst1@nodedb21 ~]$ db2 connect to nav


   Database Connection Information

 Database server        = DB2/LINUXX8664 9.7.4
 SQL authorization ID   = DB2INST1
 Local database alias   = NAV


[db2inst1@nodedb21 ~]$ db2 quiesce database immediate
DB20000I  The QUIESCE DATABASE command completed successfully.
```

On the Linux command line, go to another filesystem, to which the instance owner has write access (/data1, in our case):

```
[db2inst1@nodedb21 ~]$ cd /data1
```

Create a directory to move a container to:

```
[db2inst1@nodedb21 data1]$ mkdir -p db2/db2inst1/NODE0000/nav
```

Go to this directory and copy the original container there:

```
[db2inst1@nodedb21 data1]$ cd db2/db2inst1/NODE0000/nav
[db2inst1@nodedb21 nav]$ cp /data/db2/db2inst1/NODE0000/nav/nav_tbls.dbf
```

Go back to the original directory and rename the original container:

```
[db2inst1@nodedb21 data1]$ cd /data/db2/db2inst1/NODE0000/nav/
[db2inst1@nodedb21 nav]$ mv nav_tbls.dbf nav_tbls.dbf.scrap
```

Create a link:

```
[db2inst1@nodedb21 nav]$ ln -s /data1/db2/db2inst1/NODE0000/nav/nav_tbls.
dbf nav_tbls.dbf
```

Confirm link is done:

```
[db2inst1@nodedb21 nav]$ ls -al nav_tbls.dbf
lrwxrwxrwx 1 db2inst1 dba 45 2011-07-01 16:29 nav_tbls.dbf -> /data1/db2/
db2inst1/NODE0000/nav/nav_tbls.dbf
```

Bring the database back on line:

```
[db2inst1@nodedb21 ~]$ db2 unquiesce database;
DB20000I  The UNQUIESCE DATABASE command completed successfully.
```

If you query a table in that table space, the data will be there.

Make sure you use this feature wisely, as part of a well thought-out plan; otherwise, this introduces another level of complexity. You may want to use automatic storage instead.

Default codeset

The default codeset is UTF-8, except when defined otherwise. This cannot be changed after creation.

Territory

The default territory is US, except when defined otherwise. This cannot be changed after creation. The combination of the codeset and territory or locale values must be valid.

Collate using

The default setting is _SYSTEM_. Ensure this setting is compatible with codeset and territory. This cannot be changed after creation.

Control files

There are no equivalent commands to manipulate control files in DB2. In our example, you will find them in /data/db2/db2inst1/NODE0000/SQL00003/.

The following files reflect the equivalent of Oracle's control file information. These files should not be tampered with. db2rhist.asc and db2rhist.bak contain historic information about backups, restores, and other changes to the database. db2tschg.his contains a history of table space changes. For each log file, it contains information that helps to identify which table spaces are affected by the log file. This information is used for table space recovery. You can browse it with a text editor.

The log control files contain information about active logs. The files, SQLOGCTL.LFH.1 and its mirror copy, SQLOGCTL.LFH.1, are located, in our example, in /data/db2/db2inst1/NODE0000/SQL00003/SQLOGDIR, which contains the actual log files.

SQL00003 is a directory containing db2 configuration files for the NAV database. Other databases will be mapped to SQL0000x, according to the respective order of database creation. These log control files will be used by db2 when processing recovery, to determine the starting point in the logs to begin the recovery.

See also

▶ *Creating database from existing backup* recipe in this chapter

▶ *Chapter 3*, DB2 multipartitioned databases—Administration and Configuration

Using Configuration Advisor

The configuration advisor will help you configure the best settings for the database mission, using this server's hardware configuration. You can then accept or cancel the proposed settings.

Getting ready

Obtain as much information as possible on the database size, future growth, number of concurrent users, and so on.

How to do it...

1. Select database **Configuration Advisor...**.

   Go to the left pane of Control Center, and expand the databases node. Right-click on the **NAV** database, and select **Configuration Advisor...**.

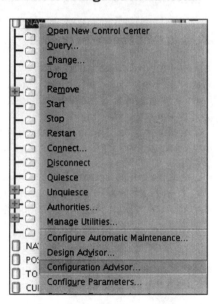

   A first screen will ask you to confirm whether this is the database you want to configure; then, click **Next**.

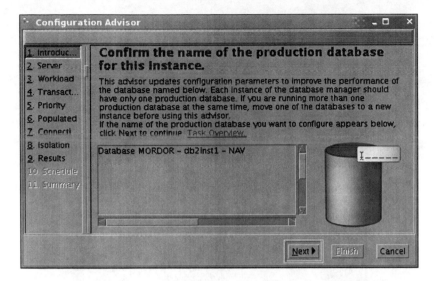

2. Choose how much memory you want to allocate to this database.

   You will see a slider bar and the amount of physical memory available on the server. Allow around 300-500 MB for the operating system, or ask your system administrator how much space is needed. Then, you will have to divide the remaining space for each of the active databases. Click **Next**.

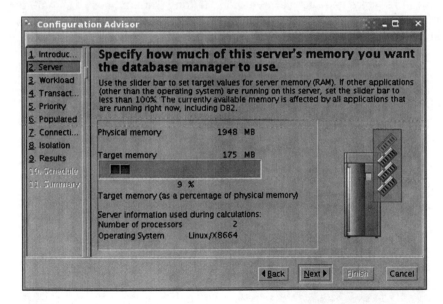

In our example, I have two gigabytes available for system memory, so I leave 500 MB for the operating system; that leaves me with 1,500 MB available. The NAV database is quite small, so even 175 MB would be enough. Now, click **Next**.

3. Select type of work load.

    For an OLTP database, select **Transactions (order entry)**, and click **Next**.

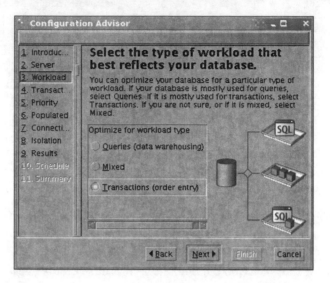

Choose your typical transaction's characteristics.On this screen, we estimate the load on the database. We never really know how many queries we may encounter per unit of work, so it's safe to select **More than 10 (long transactions)**. Estimate or obtain the number of transactions per minute on the database; 3000 transactions a minute should be fairly representative of a production OLTP database. Click **Next**.

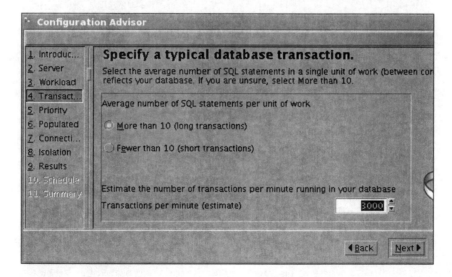

4. Choose the database's priority between performance and recovery:

For OLTP, we would recommend choosing *performance*. We will leave the setting on *both*, for this scenario. This will choose the best values to balance between transaction performance and recovery time.

5. Tell the advisor if the database contains data:

    If you have loaded data since the database has been created, select *yes* and click **Next**.

6. Estimate the number of applications connected to the database:

    Enter the number of local and remote applications and click **Next**.

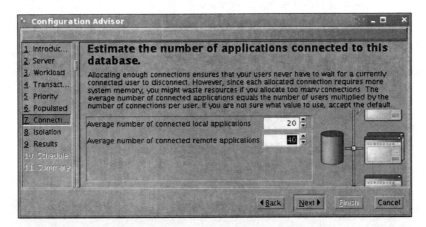

7. Select the appropriate isolation level for your database:

    Click **Next**. I chose the default value, **Cursor stability**, to minimize lock duration.

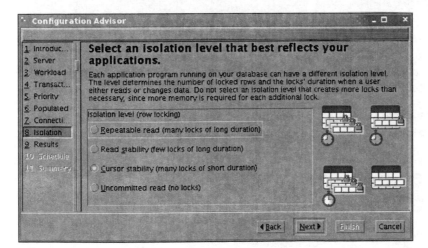

8. Review the proposed configuration recommendations.

    You can take some time to review the proposed configuration recommendations; when you are ready to continue, click **Next**.

9. Schedule this as a task or do it right now.

    You can choose to create a task with the proposed configuration recommendations, and schedule this task for another time frame.

    Or, select **Run now...** and click **Next**.

    Review the actions that will apply the new settings and click **Finish**. You will see the progress indicator and the results of the action.

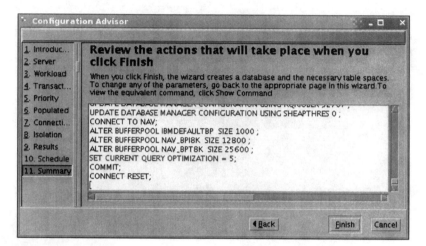

How it works...

The configuration advisor takes the current setting for the database configuration and optimizes those parameters to suit the database for OLTP processing. Commands used are: get database or get database manager (db/dbm) configuration (cfg) and update database or update database manager (db/dbm) configuration (cfg).

We suggest you copy the results into a script and run it manually through the command line, for historic and documentation purposes. You might want to track performance improvements with parameter change history.

There's more...

The configuration advisor is not only used for a newly created database; you might just as well run this utility on an existing database. For an existing database, you want to make sure table and index statistics are fairly recent. See the Collecting object statistics and the RUNSTAT utility recipe in *Chapter 13, DB2 Tuning and Optimization*.

Main configuration characteristics of OLTP databases

Since an OLTP database requires many users to frequently read small amounts of data, it is best to allow more memory for buffer pools and less for sorts.

Log archiving is used in order to enable online and/or table space backups without quiescing the database. It is also required if you wish to set up HADR, so that archived logs can be sent over to the DR site.

Recommendations:

- ▶ Smaller extents
- ▶ Less prefetch
- ▶ Small page size
- ▶ Separate indexes and data
- ▶ Multiple buffer pools

Main configuration characteristics of DSS databases

Since a DSS database requires a few users to read a large amount of data, it is best to allow more memory for sorts and less for buffer pools. Data is usually extracted from production OLTP databases, so your backup strategy may be different.

Recommendations:

- ▶ Large extent size
- ▶ Prefetch across all devices
- ▶ Large page size (32 KB)
- ▶ Spread tables and indexes across all devices
- ▶ Single buffer pool
- ▶ Allow 50 percent of useable memory to buffer pools and 50 percent to SHEAPTHRES

Main configuration characteristics of mixed processing databases

We have both the advantages and the inconvenience of both configurations. Perhaps the best approach here would be to optimize the database for transaction processing during the day and DSS processing, or analytic processing, outside daytime hours.

This may require down time between settings.

Another solution would be to somehow throttle the resources to ensure optimal response for OLTP while permitting let's say 25 percent of CPU time and disk I/O activity for OLAP.

We recommend having separate resources for different missions, when possible. Have one or several machines for use in a partitioned database for DSS processing and one separate machine for OLTP processing. Avoid having one machine for multiple missions as this may result in a single point of failure.

See also

▸ *Chapter 4, Storage—Using DB2 Table Spaces*

▸ *Chapter 5, DB2 Buffer Pools*

▸ *Chapter 13, DB2 Tuning and Optimization*

Creating a database from an existing backup

Let's suppose you want to copy a production database into a QA server. You can prepare a script using the GUI. It will walk you through the process, and will allow you to save the script. With the GUI, you can also schedule this script as a regular task so you can refresh your QA environment on a weekly basis or at any frequency you wish.

Getting ready

Identify the backup you want to recover, and do a verification to make sure it's valid. In our example, we'll start here from a cold (offline) backup stored on disk, so there is no tape command or `rollforward` to do.

How to do it...

1. Make sure the backup is valid.

   Log in as instance owner. Go to the backup location and, from the operating system command line (Linux in this example), type `db2ckbkp`:

   ```
   [db2inst1@nodedb21 ~]$ cd /maint/backups
   [db2inst1@nodedb21 backups]$ db2ckbkp   NAV.0.db2inst1.NODE0000.
   CATN0000.20101114190028.001


   [1] Buffers processed:  #######


   Image Verification Complete - successful.
   ```

2. Restore the database:

   Within the Control Center's GUI, right-click on the Databases folder and select **Create database**, and on the next sub menu, **From Backup**.

3. Define location information for the new database:

   Let's say you want to create a development database from a production database. Both databases have the same name. Copy your production backup file on your development server.

   Enter the source database NAV, and the target database, NAV, located in directory /data/db2; logs, if any, will be stored in /data/db2/logs. Click **Next**.

4. Select the backup image to use:

   On the next screen, leave **Media Type** to **File System**, and click **Add** to specify the filesystem directory where the backup is located. In our example, this is in /maint/backups. Locate the backup you want—NAV.0.db2inst1.NODE0000. CATN0000.20101114190028.001.

   ```
   [db2inst1@nodedb21 ~]$ cd /maint/backups/

   [db2inst1@nodedb21 backups]$ ls -al *001

   -rw------- 1 db2inst1 dba 25186304 2010-11-14 19:00
   NAV.0.db2inst1.NODE0000.CATN0000.20101114190028.001

   -rw------- 1 db2inst1 dba 20992000 2010-11-15 18:15
   POS.0.db2inst1.NODE0000.CATN0000.20101115181505.001


   [db2inst1@nodedb21 backups]$
   ```

   You see from part of the filename, 20101114190028, that the date is November 14, 2010 and the time is 19:00:28. You can now click **Finish**; the new NAV database will be created. Go back to **Control Center** and, from the menu, select **View** and **Refresh**.

How it works...

DB2 will restore the database to the state of the specified backup. All containers from the current database will be deleted and the containers from the backup will be restored.

If you created a table space with a file container, since the previous backup, and you do a restore from a previous backup, this container will be deleted, as it's not recognized as being part of the database.

There's more...

Now, we do the actual restore (here, from the Linux command line); the following time stamp is part of DB2 backup file's naming convention:

```
[db2inst1@nodedb21 backups]$ db2 RESTORE DATABASE NAV FROM "/maint/
backups" TAKEN AT 20101114190028 WITH 2 BUFFERS BUFFER 1024 REPLACE
HISTORY FILE PARALLELISM 1 WITHOUT PROMPTING
DB20000I  The RESTORE DATABASE command completed successfully.
```

 One quick reminder—a backup performed on a Linux/Unix environment is not compatible with windows, so you can't just restore a Linux database on Windows.

Backups are not compatible between Windows and Linux/Unix; this is an example error message when attempting to restore a Windows database from a backup made on a Linux platform. Backups between Linux/Unix are compatible under certain conditions.

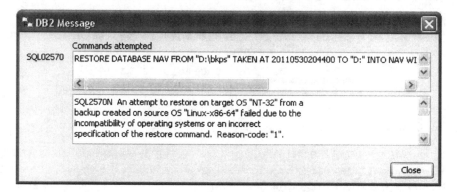

Roll-forward recovery

Roll-forward recovery lets you replay archived logs after a database recovery so you can recover the database to a specific moment, for example, just before a disk crash. We will cover this feature in *Chapter 7, DB2 Backup and Recovery*.

Redirected restore

Redirected restore lets you recover a database in a different location, for example if you want to create a QA environment from a prod database backup, so that they can coexist on the same server. We will cover this situation in *Chapter 7, DB2 Backup and Recovery*.

See also

Backup and recovery recipe in this chapter

Configuring automatic database maintenance

The automatic maintenance of the database involves tools to simplify your administration tasks. You can configure this option anytime after you create the database.

Basically, you define maintenance schedules:

▸ online: Period of low activity to allow for runstats
▸ offline: Period when there is no activity (no user connecting), for backups and reorgs

You also define maintenance activities:

▸ backups: DB2 determines if a backup is needed and schedules it during maintenance windows (offline)
▸ reorgs: Used to reorganize tables for optimal table space use (offline)
▸ runstats: Makes sure DB2 has a quantitative view of data for its optimizer to produce best results (online)

You can have configured notifications on maintenance jobs.

Getting ready

Identify the best time for maintenance windows, when there is low or no activity on this database. Choose which maintenance activities you want.

For backups, prepare your strategy first, between online or offline backups. In case you want online backups and have circular logging on this database, DB2 will offer to change this and will do an online backup, so you may want to plan ahead to allow time for the backup to complete.

Choose a destination for automatic backups. If it's on disk, have a separate directory for automatic backups. Choose people to be notified; for mail or pager mail notifications, you will have to obtain the SMTP server address. Make sure the server on which the database runs can send e-mails.

How to do it...

1. Choose the database you want to manage:

   Choose a database and right-click on it; select **Configure Automatic Maintenance**.

2. Select maintenance type:

   You can disable or change automation settings. Leave on **Change automation settings** and click **Next**.

3. Configure maintenance windows:

    We define here the maintenance windows and customize the schedules for online and offline maintenance. Click on **Change**; define here an online maintenance window outside of work hours from 9:00 a.m. till 6:00 p.m., from Monday through Friday then click **Ok**. You can also define here an offline maintenance window outside of work hours from 0:00 a.m. till 11:00 p.m., Saturday and Sunday and then click **Ok**. We'll be back in the maintenance windows definition, so click **Next**.

4. Manage your Notification List:

    The screen **Manage your Notification List** helps you set up your contact list for e-mails, or pagers. For the sake of brevity, I'll just give a quick description for these screens. Click on **Manage Contacts**, choose your SMTP server, and add your contacts manually or import them from another server. When you return to the **Notification list**, choose the contacts who will receive mails for *Database Health* notification, and click **Next**.

5. Select the maintenance activity.

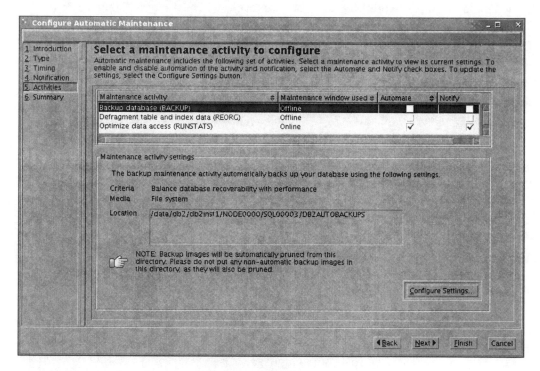

    You can select any activity and configure its settings.

▶ Backups:

You can let DB2 decide the frequency for backups or customize the settings yourself. You can choose the backup location in the same fashion as an ordinary backup and can choose whether you want an online or offline backup. We'll leave it off for now, until we discuss backups later on.

▶ Reorgs:

When you select **Configure Settings**, you can tell DB2 to include all tables, or select table scope by using the simple filter and fill in the conditions (such as name, schema, and so on), or by writing your own where clause with the custom filter. On the **Table scope** tab, just select **All tables** and do not include system tables.

Click on the **Reorganization options** tab, and check the following options:

Use a system temporary table space with a compatible page size

Keep, for the compression data dictionary

Offline Index reorganization mode.

Click on **Ok**.

▶ Runstats:

On the **Table scope** tab, just select **All tables**—do not include system tables. Click on **Ok**, and when back on Maintenance activity, click **Next**.

Review the automatic maintenance settings, and click **Finish**.

How it works...

DB2 automatically knows if maintenance is required and will do it in the next available maintenance window.

There's more...

You can obtain the same result by creating tasks in the task center. This is useful if you want to schedule specific hours for some tasks or make sure that, say, a backup is done without having DB2 evaluate if it's needed or not.

Backups

If you send backup to disks, you should have a separate directory for automatic maintenance backups. DB2 will automatically prune backup images, so, if you scheduled backups via the task center or other tools such as cron or other manual backups, make sure to save them in another directory, otherwise they will be deleted.

If you select an online backup and the database is configured with circular logging, DB2 will offer to change this and will do an online backup right away. Automatic backups results will be sent to `db2diag.log`. There are more advanced methods for backups; we will cover these in *Chapter 7, DB2 Backup and Recovery*.

Reorgs

DB2 Reorgs defragment table and index data. Automatic reorgs, before DB2 v9.7, were done in place. You needed to have enough space for a table and its copy on the same table space and could not tell DB2 to use a temporary table space. In DB2 v9.7, you now need to have a system temporary table space large enough for the largest table.

Reorg results are sent to `db2diag.log`.

Runstats

The Runstats utility gathers table and index statistics and information for the SQL optimizer. DB2 uses this information for its optimizer, and chooses the best path for each SQL query. With the automatic maintenance, you don't have to worry about being notified by development about new tables, and indexes, since they'll all be picked up for runstats (depending on the table scope you selected).

There is a downside to this. This utility is useful for small tables, since statistics are collected on the whole table. For large tables several Gigabytes in size, this could generate problems. You can override the default statistics settings for a table by setting a statistics profile. We'll discuss this in *Chapter 13, DB2 Tuning and Optimization*.

Runstat results are sent to `db2diag.log`.

See also

> ▸ *Chapter 13, DB2 Tuning and Optimization*

Managing federated databases—connecting to Oracle and MSSQL

A federated database allows client applications to see their data as a single database, even though the data itself can be located across different databases, or even databases created with another RDBMS such as Oracle or MSSQL.

Getting ready

IBM InfoSphere Federation Server must be installed. You can either choose to install a new copy of DB2 Enterprise Server Edition Version 9.7 or install Federation Server on top of an existing copy.

Since DB2 acts as a client for the remote databases, the client software for the databases you want to access must be installed on the same system as the federated server. For Oracle databases, you will need Oracle Net Client. Make sure you can do a `tnsping` and access your remote database with sqlplus.

```
[ora10g@nodedb21 ~]$ tnsping ERP10R2

TNS Ping Utility for Linux: Version 10.2.0.1.0 - Production on 19-JUN-
2011 15:34:00

Copyright (c) 1997, 2005, Oracle.  All rights reserved.

Used parameter files:

Used TNSNAMES adapter to resolve the alias

Attempting to contact (DESCRIPTION = (ADDRESS_LIST = (ADDRESS = (PROTOCOL
= TCP)(HOST = nodedb21)(PORT = 1521))) (CONNECT_DATA = (SERVICE_NAME =
ERP10R2)))

OK (0 msec)


[ora10g@nodedb21 ~]$ sqlplus robert@ERP10R2

SQL*Plus: Release 10.2.0.1.0 - Production on Sun Jun 19 15:31:29 2011

Copyright (c) 1982, 2005, Oracle.  All rights reserved.

Enter password:


Connected to:

Oracle Database 10g Enterprise Edition Release 10.2.0.1.0 - Production

With the Partitioning and Data Mining options

SQL>
```

For remote access to MSSQL Server databases, you need to install Unix ODBC driver on the federated server. Please refer to the documentation for the appropriate versions and supported databases. Check for the current configuration, and allow for a time slot in case you need to change the configuration and restart the instance.

How to do it...

1. Ensure the instance is configured for a federated server:

   Log in as the instance owner, and from the GUI, or at the command line, get the database manager configuration, and look for **Federated**; it should be set to yes, otherwise you need to change the configuration and restart the instance.

   ```
   db2 get dbm cfg
   ```

   Look for the following parameters:

   ```
   (FEDERATED) = NO
   (MAX_COORDAGENTS) = AUTOMATIC(200)
   (MAX_CONNECTIONS) = AUTOMATIC(MAX_COORDAGENTS)
   ```

   Change the parameters and restart the instance:

   ```
   db2 update dbm cfg using federated yes max_coordagents 200
     max_connections 200;
   ```

   If we configure the instance as a federated server, the concentrator has to be off. This is why we set MAX_COORDAGENTS = MAX_CONNECTIONS.

2. Set environment variables:

   You need to set environment variables in the db2dj.ini file, depending on the data sources you need. If it does not exist already, create db2dj.ini in the following path:

   - On Windows, you would find/create this file in :

     ```
     %DB2PATH%\cfg\db2dj.ini
     ```

   - In Linux:

     ```
     /home/db2instf/sqllib/cfg/db2dj.ini
     Add the following values depending on the data source you
     want to configure:
     ```

   - Oracle:

     ```
     ORACLE_HOME=/opt/oracle/product/10.2.0
     ```

   - SQL Server:

     ```
     DJX_ODBC_LIBRARY_PATH=/
     ```

Now, set DB2's registry so it knows where `db2gj.ini` is:

`db2set DB2_DJ_INI=/home/db2instf/sqllib/cfg/db2dj.ini`

3. Verify that library files have been linked correctly:

   Verify that library files have been linked correctly, and then proceed to step 5. Look for a message file, depending on the data source, in our example in `/opt/IBM/DB2/V9.7/lib64`:

   ❑ For Oracle, look for `dxjlinkOracle.out` and library file `libdb2net8.so`

   ❑ For Microsoft SQL Server, look for `djxlinkMssql.out` and library file `libdb2mssql3.so`

   If these files show errors or do not exist, relink manually, as seen in step 4.

4. Relink the library files:

   If you installed the client software after you installed Federation Server, or if you upgraded your client, you must manually relink the library files to the data source client software.

   Stop the instance:

   `db2stop force`

   For Oracle execute script:

   `export ORACLE_HOME=/opt/oracle/product/10.2.0`

   `cd /opt/IBM/DB2/v9.7.4P/bin`

   `./djxlinkOracle`

   For MSSQL execute script:

   `export DJX_ODBC_LIBRARY_PATH=/opt/IBM/WSII/odbc/lib`

   `./djxlinkMssql`

   In a multipartitioned instance, repeat this step for each instance.

   Now, log in as root, and update each instance:

   `cd /opt/IBM/DB2/v9.7.4P/instance`

   `./db2iupdt db2instf`

5. Create a database:

   Before you configure the federated server to access data sources, you must create a database. It can be a single or multipartitioned database. The current partition will become the catalog partition.

6. Create a wrapper:

   Choose or create a database to be used as the federated database. Then, you need to create a wrapper for each of the data sources you want. These wrappers encompass libraries used by the federated server to connect, as a client, to the target data sources. On the Linux command line, as the instance owner, issue the command:

   ❑ For Oracle:

   ```
   db2 create wrapper net8 library 'libdb2net8.so'
   ```

   ❑ For MSSQL:

   ```
   db2 create wrapper mssql3 library 'libdb2mssql3.so'
   ```

7. Locate the node name in the Oracle tnsnames.ora file:

   ```
   [ora10g@nodedb21 ~]$ cd $ORACLE_HOME/network/admin

   [ora10g@nodedb21 admin]$ more tnsnames.ora

   # tnsnames.ora Network Configuration File:
   /opt/oracle/product/10.2.0/network/admin/tnsnames.ora
   # Generated by Oracle configuration tools.

   ERP10R2 =
     (DESCRIPTION =
       (ADDRESS_LIST =
         (ADDRESS = (PROTOCOL = TCP)(HOST = 192.168.1.103)
           (PORT = 1521))
       )
       (CONNECT_DATA =
         (SERVICE_NAME = ERP10R2)
       )
     )
   ```

8. Create a server definition:

   Use the Oracle Service Name or Oracle SID as NODE name. You will need this so the connection can work.

   ```
   CREATE SERVER ERPFED TYPE oracle

   VERSION 10.2.0 WRAPPER net8

           OPTIONS (NODE 'ERP10R2')
   ```

9. Create user mappings:

   The user ID at the Oracle data source must be created by using the Oracle create user command:

   ```
   CREATE USER MAPPING FOR robert SERVER ERPFED
      OPTIONS (REMOTE_AUTHID 'robert', REMOTE_PASSWORD 'mypasswd') ;
   ```

   Test the connection (make sure user 'robert' has access to this table on the Oracle database):

   ```
   SET PASSTHRU ERPFED
   SELECT * FROM V$INSTANCE
   SET PASSTHRU RESET
   ```

10. Update data source stats:

    You need to have up-to-date statistics on the remote Oracle database.

11. Create nicknames:

    Statistics on the remote Oracle database are added to the system catalog in the federated database.

    ```
    CREATE NICKNAME N_GL
    FOR ERPFED."ERP"."GENERAL_LEDGER" ;
    ```

How it works...

A federated system is a DB2 instance that acts as a server and contains a database that is identified as the federated database. A client application accesses the server as if it were a DB2 database. DB2 accesses these data sources on behalf of these client applications.

See also

There is a lot of material for this matter that cannot be covered in detail, so please refer to the IBM Documentation, Configuration Guide for Federated Data Sources (SC19-1034-02) if you happen to have any difficulty with this setup.

Altering databases

This topic involves making changes to a database's characteristics. We will see this command from the DB2 point of view and from an Oracle point of view. This may help clear misunderstandings from one environment to the other.

How to do it...

As understood in DB2, ALTER DATABASE only has one function. Those of you coming from an Oracle DBA background should read on to *From Oracle to DB2...*, for further explanations.

The ALTER DATABASE command lets you add or remove storage paths from the list of storage paths used for automatic storage table spaces.

Add storage path:

```
[db2inst1@nodedb21 ~]$ db2 "ALTER DATABASE NAV ADD STORAGE ON
  '/data1/db2'"
```

DB20000I The SQL command completed successfully.

Remove storage path:

```
[db2inst1@nodedb21 ~]$ db2 "ALTER DATABASE NAV DROP STORAGE ON
  '/data1/db2'"
```

DB20000I The SQL command completed successfully.

How it works...

Adding a storage path to a manual storage database makes it an automatic storage database. Existing manual storage table spaces are not converted to automatic storage table spaces.

 ▸ Regular and large table spaces:

   Existing automatic storage table spaces will not use the new path in an initial phase.

 ▸ Temporary table spaces:

   The database must be restarted to enable use of new storage paths for temporary table spaces.

From Oracle to DB2

For those of you that have more of an Oracle background, the ALTER DATABASE is not the same. The following sections discuss Oracle ALTER DATABASE-related tasks and how to carry them out in DB2.

Startup/shutdown instance

Starting and stopping an instance (an instance = database) in Oracle is done with the ALTER DATABASE command, which is *NOT* the case with DB2. Make sure you want to shut down the instance, not just a database. This will shut down all databases in the instance.

1. Start instance:

   ```
   [db2inst1@nodedb21 ~]$ db2start
   SQL1063N  DB2START processing was successful.
   [db2inst1@nodedb21 ~]$
   ```

2. Stop instance:

   ```
   [db2inst1@nodedb21 ~]$ db2stop
   SQL1064N  DB2STOP processing was successful.
   ```

In DB2, a START DBM/STOP DBM is done at the instance level, so all databases from the instance are started/shut down.

Startup/shutdown database

Certain parameter changes necessitate rebouncing a database. Remember, in DB2 there may be more than one database per instance. If you need to start/stop a single database from an instance you use the activate/deactivate database command.

1. Start database:

   ```
   [db2inst1@nodedb21 ~]$ db2 connect reset
   DB20000I  The SQL command completed successfully.[db2inst1@
   nodedb21 ~]$ db2 activate database pos
   DB20000I  The ACTIVATE DATABASE command completed successfully.
   ```

2. Stop database:

   Make sure there are no connections first:

   ```
   [db2inst1@nodedb21 ~]$ db2 connect reset
   DB20000I  The SQL command completed successfully.[db2inst1@
   nodedb21 ~]$ db2 deactivate database pos
   DB20000I  The DEACTIVATE DATABASE command completed successfully.
   ```

Database file containers

Adding or dropping containers (Oracle datafile) is done with DB2's ALTER TABLESPACE command. However, you cannot rename a container.

1. Add container:

   ```
   db2 ALTER TABLESPACE NAV_TBLS ADD ( FILE
      '/data/db2/db2inst1/NODE0000/nav/nav_tbls_02.dbf' 2560 )
   ```

2. Drop container:

   ```
   db2 ALTER TABLESPACE NAV_TBLS DROP ( FILE
      '/data/db2/db2inst1/NODE0000/nav/nav_tbls.dbf' )
   ```

Log files

Log files are managed by the *get/update database configuration* command.

1. Change archiving mode:

   db2 update db cfg using logretain recovery deferred

2. Change archive log destination:

   **db2 update db cfg using newlogpath /data/db2/NODE0000/pos/
   db2logdir deferred**

A backup should be made after changing the logging mode. Within the control center, you will be prompted to make a backup after changing the logging mode.

How it works...

For those having more of a DB2 background, Oracle's ALTER DATABASE command will have a broader scope of activity than its DB2 counterpart.

There's more...

Other functionalities from Oracle's ALTER DATABASE command are also specific to DB2 and will be covered in subsequent chapters.

Control files

There is no equivalent to Oracle's control files in DB2, so there is no replacement to manipulate those kinds of files in DB2.

Quiesce instance/database

You can also issue QUIESCE INSTANCE and all databases will be in quiesced mode. Only users having SYSADM, SYSMAINT, or SYSCTRL authorization can access the databases and their objects. In the same fashion, UNQUIESCE INSTANCE restores access at the instance level and all its databases to regular users.

However, you can use the QUIESCE DATABASE command to quiesce a single database. The *force connections* option allows disconnecting users from the database. When the database is in a quiesced mode, you can still perform administrative tasks on it. You need to issue the UNQUIESCE DATABASE command, which restores user access to the database.

Backup and recovery

DB2's RESTORE DATABASE command is used to recover from a backup. It covers all the recovery aspects of Oracle's recover database command.

Standby databases

HADR is DB2's counterpart of Oracle's Data Guard technology. It enables to have a secure copy of a database in a remote location, so in case a disaster occurs, the remote site can take over data processing for this database. It works in the same way with regards to sending transaction logs to a remote server and applying the logs on another database. It has its own set of commands and is not part of the alter database syntax.

See also

> ▸ *Chapter 7, DB2 Backup and Recovery*

> ▸ *Chapter 4, Storage—Using DB2 Table Spaces*

Dropping databases

Dropping a database is an easy task compared to Oracle. You select the database you want to drop, and all its objects, containers, and files will be deleted.

Getting ready

The database must not be used, so all users have to be disconnected. I recommend you take a backup at this point. For many reasons, it could have been the wrong database to drop.

How to do it...

1. Select the database:

   Select the databases folder on the left pane of the control center; or, you can list databases:

   ```
   [db2inst1@nodedb21 ~]$ db2 list database directory

    System Database Directory

    Number of entries in the directory = 1

   Database 1 entry:

    Database alias                       = NAV
    Database name                        = NAV
    Local database directory             = /data/db2
    Database release level               = d.00
    Comment                              = Aviation Geo Data
    Directory entry type                 = Indirect
    Catalog database partition number    = 0
    Alternate server hostname            =
    Alternate server port number         =
   ```

2. Drop the database:

   Right-click on the NAV database, and then select **Drop** option. This will drop the database and remove it from the database directories, or, from the command line:

   ```
   [db2inst1@nodedb21 ~]$ db2 drop database nav
   DB20000I  The DROP DATABASE command completed successfully.
   ```

How it works...

Directory /db2inst1/NODE0000/NAV, relative to your storage path, is deleted with all files in it. In this case, /data/db2/db2inst1/NODE0000/NAV/*.* will be cleared.

There's more...

Let's review some precautions before dropping a database.

Backup history

Be aware that all logs files and backup history will be deleted. If you expect to be doing roll-forward recovery after a restore, make sure you save all necessary log files in a safe place. An added precaution would be to ensure the backup's integrity.

Keep safe

We recommend you set time aside for this type of operation and avoid any pressure. If someone asked you to drop a database, take your time to make sure it's the right one. Sometimes people refer to a database by its role or alias, so misunderstandings can occur.

The Control Center's GUI is easy to use, so a right-click can have disastrous results. I would prefer to drop a database from the command-line after making sure I'm connected to the right one.

See also

▶ *Chapter 7, DB2 Backup and Recovery*

3
DB2 Multipartitioned Databases— Administration and Configuration

In this chapter, we will cover:

- Creating and configuring a multipartitioned database
- Adding database partitions
- Creating and configuring partition groups
- Managing database partition group data redistribution
- The table partition key and its role in a multipartitioned database
- Altering database partition groups—adding partitions to database partition groups
- Altering database partition groups—removing partitions from database partition groups
- Removing database partitions
- Converting a non-partitioned database to a multipartitioned database in MS Windows
- Configuring the Fast Communication Manager

Introduction

There could be many situations when a non-partitioned database is not an appropriate choice. Many organizations today have high performance demands from their database systems and want to gain more value from their hardware and software.

IBM DB2 EE comes with database partitioning as an alternative option to implement a very scalable and high performance system. Database partitioning is suitable for both **Online Transaction Processing (OLTP)** and **Decision Support Systems (DSS)** systems.

You may partition an existent database on a single system, in a shared-everything configuration, or you can use multiple standalone systems in a shared-nothing configuration. For a large SMP system, the first method is the recommended one, because the inter-partition communication can be conducted through shared memory, which is obviously one of the fastest communication methods on the planet.

A shared-nothing configuration is recommended in cases where we have many servers with fewer hardware resources and want to group or distribute tables by different processing type (OLTP or DSS), on these systems. Another benefit of multipartitioning is data segregation by database partition groups; here, we could enumerate: table collocation (tables are collocated when they are stored in the same database partition group with compatible distribution keys), table partitioning combined with database partitioning, and so on.

Another major benefit is the inter-partition parallelism that can effectively boost considerably, the performance of operations such as large batch processing, sorting operations, hash joins, parallel index creations, or rebuilds. However, database partitioning, like many complex systems, needs careful design and testing.

In the following recipes, we will cover the main administrative and functional aspects of database partitioning.

Creating and configuring a multipartitioned database

In this recipe, we will proceed to create the NAV database as a multipartitioned database.

Getting ready

We will use nodedb21 and nodedb22 for all recipes in this chapter. The NAV database will be created under instance db2instp, created and configured in the *Creating and configuring instances for a multipartitioned environments* recipe in *Chapter 1, DB2 Instance—Administration and Configuration*.

For database storage, we have defined a new Linux partition /data. The database storage path will reside on the /data/db2 directory.

How to do it...

1. Navigate to the /db2partinst/db2instp/sqllib directory. Here, open
   db2nodes.cfg with your preferred editor; you should find three nodes already
   configured in the *Creating and configuring an instance for multipartitioned
   environments* recipe, in *Chapter 1, DB2 Instance—Administration and Configuration*:

   ```
   [db2instp@nodedb21 sqllib]$ more db2nodes.cfg

   0 nodedb21 0

   1 nodedb22 0

   2 nodedb21 1
   ```

   These three nodes will host the initial NAV multipartitioned database.

 You can set the database path at database creation, or you
can set the database manager parameter DFTDBPATH to the
desired database path.

As user db2instp executes the following command to create the NAV multipartitioned
database:

```
[db2instp@nodedb21 ~]$ db2 "CREATE DATABASE NAV AUTOMATIC STORAGE YES
ON '/data/db2' DBPATH ON '/data/db2' USING CODESET UTF-8 TERRITORY US
COLLATE USING SYSTEM PAGESIZE 8192 RESTRICTIVE  WITH 'Aviation Geo Data'"
DB20000I  The CREATE DATABASE command completed successfully.
[db2instp@nodedb21 ~]$
```

How it works...

By creating the database using automatic storage option the containers belonging to
USERSPACE1 and TEMPSPACE1 table spaces are spanned on all partitions. No matter what
storage option we choose, the SYSCATSPACE catalog table space represents an exemption
from this rule. The containers of SYSCATSPACE table space are placed only on the partition
where the CREATE DATABASE command was executed. The partition which hosts the
SYSCATSPACE table space is named the catalog partition. In our case, the catalog
partition has been created on partition 0.

There's more...

The database can be created from any partition within the configuration. To set the current
node you should use the DB2NODE environment variable. A more detailed coverage about
using this variable can be found in *Removing database partitions* recipe in this chapter.

Within multipartitioned databases all table spaces are organized inside database partition groups. This subject will be covered in the *Creating database partition groups* recipe in this chapters.

Adding database partitions

One of the notable advantages of database partitioning is scalability. Let us suppose that we want to supplement the processing power by providing more CPUs and memory, or we intend to add a new server in the infrastructure to increase processing power. In any of these cases, we should add one or more partitions to our existent database proportionally with the supplementary processing power, in order to benefit from the scalability of the multipartitioned environment. It is recommended to allocate a minimum of one CPU per database partition.

Getting ready

In the following recipe, we will add two new partitions, one on `nodedb21` and one on `nodedb22`.

How to do it...

You can perform these operations with **Control Center** or using the command line.

Using Control Center

1. In **Control Center**, right-click to navigate to the **db2instp** instance, and then right-click and choose **Add Database Partitions...**.

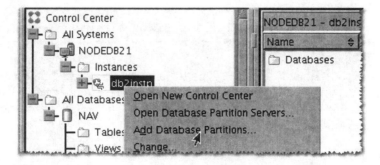

2. In the **Add Database Partitions Wizard** screen, click on the **Next** button, and next click the **Add** button to add partition **3** on **nodedb21**, with logical port **2**, and partition **4** on **nodedb22** with logical port **1**:

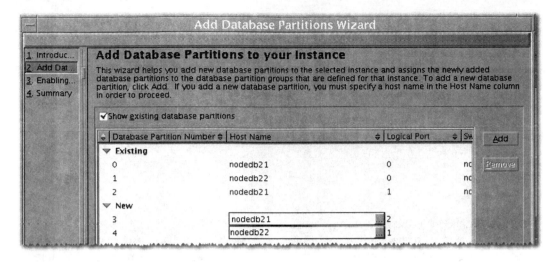

3. Follow the wizard through steps 3 and 4 and click **Finish**.

Using the command line

1. To add partition **3** on host **nodedb21** with logical port **2**, issue the following command:

```
[db2instp@nodedb21 ~]$ db2start dbpartitionnum 3 ADD
DBPARTITIONNUM HOSTNAME nodedb21 PORT 2 WITHOUT TABLESPACES
06/27/2011 18:14:38     3   0   SQL1489I  The add database
partition server  operation was successful. The new database
partition server "3" is active.
[db2instp@nodedb21 ~]$
```

2. To add partition **4** on host **nodedb22**, with logical port **1**, issue the following command:

```
[db2instp@nodedb21 ~]$ db2start dbpartitionnum 4 ADD
DBPARTITIONNUM HOSTNAME nodedb22 PORT 1 WITHOUT TABLESPACES
06/27/2011 18:15:18     4   0   SQL1489I  The add database
partition server  operation was successful. The new database
partition server "4" is active.
[db2instp@nodedb21 ~]$
```

All these operations will modify the db2nodes.cfg database partition configuration file. From version 9.7 database partitions can be added in online mode and are immediately visible to the instance. This behavior is controlled by DB2_FORCE_OFFLINE_ADD_PARTITION registry variable which in version 9.7 is by default set to FALSE. If it has a value of TRUE the instance might be restarted after adding partitions.

How it works...

After every new partition is added, a corresponding new entry is created in `db2nodes.cfg`.For example, after adding the two new partitions, `db2nodes.cfg` contains the following entries:

```
[db2instp@nodedb21 sqllib]$ more db2nodes.cfg
0 nodedb21 0
1 nodedb22 0
2 nodedb21 1
3 nodedb21 2
4 nodedb22 1
```

To add partition 3 and 4 we used the `WITHOUT TABLESPACES` option of `ADD DBPARTITIONNUM` command. Using this option no container is created for system temporary tables paces on partitions being added If this option is omitted the system temporary table space containers from the lowest numbered partition are used as models. However, there is an exemption from this rule in the case we use automatic managed storage, namely the containers for these type of table spaces are created regardless this option is used or not.

There's more...

In Linux and Unix the same operations can be made by editing the `db2nodes.cfg` database partition configuration file. For example, if we add one more partition entry, 5 nodedb22 2, in `db2nodes.cfg`, this operation is identical to issuing the `db2start dbpartitionnum 5 ADD DBPARTITIONNUM HOSTNAME nodedb22 PORT 2 WITHOUT TABLESPACES` command.

There is another option that can be used with `ADD DBPARTITIONNUM` command—`LIKE DBPARTITIONNUM <partition number>`. It should be used if we want to add system temporary table space containers, using as models those from `<partition number>`, to the new partition being created. For example:

db2start dbpartitionnum 3 ADD DBPARTITIONNUM HOSTNAME nodedb21 PORT 2 LIKE DBPARTITIONUM (1)

System temporary table space containers from partition 1 will be used as models for tables space containers created on partition 3.

Creating database partition groups

In a multipartitioned environment, we have a separation mechanism named partition groups. Inside partition groups, we can isolate tables, based on transaction type, or we can group tables that are frequently used in joins together. Data in partition groups are by default spread on all partitions on which they are defined, using a round-robin distribution method, unless you decide to spread data by your own rules using customdistribution maps. However remember that, not every table is a good candidate for spreading on all partitions, especially small tables or huge tables on which we are constantly involved in ad hoc queries. In these cases, the inter-partition communication mechanism used in multipartitioned environments could act as a performance bottleneck. Any complex environment comes with its advantages and disadvantages. Therefore, you have to take into consideration these aspects and be careful with the application design.

Getting ready

In the following recipe, will describe how to create a database partition group named NAVDATAGRP, which will contain the data and index table spaces of the NAV application.

How to do it...

In many organizations, it is prohibited to use graphical tools for administration; in these cases, you should probably rely only on the command line. Therefore, in almost all recipes, we try to present both administration methods.

Using Control Center

1. In **Control Center**, navigate to the **NAV** database, right-click on **Database partition groups**, and choose **Create....** Name the database partition group as NAVDATAGRP and comment with "NAV data partition group".

2. Next, move all partitions from the **Available database partitions** to the **Selected database partitions** listbox and click **OK**.

Using the command line

1. Create the NAVDATAGRP database partition group by executing the following command:

   ```
   [db2instp@nodedb21 ~]$ db2 "CREATE DATABASE PARTITION GROUP
   "NAVDATAGRP" ON DBPARTITIONNUMS (0,1,2) COMMENT ON DATABASE
   PARTITION GROUP "NAVDATAGRP" IS 'NAV data partition group'"
   [db2instp@nodedb21 ~]$
   ```

2. To increase separation from other partition groups, we first need to create the table spaces and define the NAV_BPT8k and NAV_BPI8k. To increase separation from other partition groups in terms of memory caching, we will create and assign first NAV_BPT8k and NAV_BPI8k buffer pools on the NAVDATAGRP database partition group. These two buffer pools will be assigned to table spaces NAV_TBLS and NAV_INDX, as in the non-partitioned counterpart.

Using Control Center

1. In **Control Center**, navigate to the **NAV** database, right-click on **Buffer pools**, and choose **Create...** (place a checkmark next to **Enable self tuning** (automatic memory management for buffer pools is not mandatory in multipartitioned enviorments, you can set your own values for buffer pool size) and move **NAVDATAGRP** to **Selected database partition groups**).

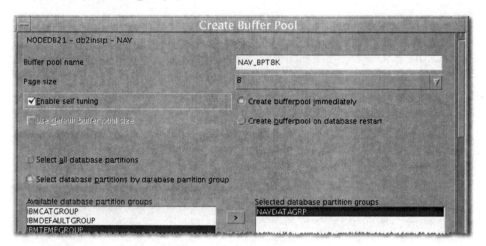

2. Create the NAV_BPI8k buffer pool identically.

Using the command line

1. To create the NAV_BPT8K buffer pool, execute the following command:

   ```
   [db2instp@nodedb21 ~]$ db2  "CREATE BUFFERPOOL NAV_BPT8K IMMEDIATE
   DATABASE PARTITION GROUP "NAVDATAGRP" SIZE 1000 AUTOMATIC PAGESIZE
   8 K "
   [db2instp@nodedb21 ~]$
   ```

2. To create the `NAV_BPI8k` buffer pool, execute the following command:

```
[db2instp@nodedb21 ~]$ db2 "CREATE BUFFERPOOL NAV_BPI8K IMMEDIATE
DATABASE PARTITION GROUP "NAVDATAGRP" SIZE 1000 AUTOMATIC PAGESIZE
8 K"

[db2instp@nodedb21 ~]$
```

Create the NAV application's table spaces

The next step is to create the data and index table spaces by using the MANAGED BY DATABASE option. One difference that you should notice between creating table spaces on non-partitioned and multipartitioned databases is that you can specify the partition number; in this way, you can implicitly define the host for containers.

1. To create the table space `NAV_TBLS` on partitions 0, 1, and 2, execute the following command:

```
[db2instp@nodedb21 ~]$ db2 "CREATE  LARGE  TABLESPACE NAV_TBLS IN
DATABASE PARTITION GROUP "NAVDATAGRP" PAGESIZE 8 K  MANAGED BY
DATABASE  USING ( FILE '/data/db2/db2instp/nav_tbls0p0.dbf' 2560
) ON DBPARTITIONNUM (0) USING ( FILE '/data/db2/db2instp/nav_
tbls0p1.dbf' 2560 ) ON DBPARTITIONNUM (1) USING ( FILE '/data/db2/
db2instp/nav_tbls0p2.dbf' 2560 ) ON DBPARTITIONNUM (2) EXTENTSIZE
16 OVERHEAD 10.5 PREFETCHSIZE 16 TRANSFERRATE 0.14 BUFFERPOOL
NAV_BPT8K"

[db2instp@nodedb21 ~]$
```

2. To create the table space `NAV_INDX` on partitions 0, 1, and 2, execute the following command:

```
[db2instp@nodedb21 ~]$  db2 "CREATE  LARGE  TABLESPACE NAV_INDX
IN DATABASE PARTITION GROUP "NAVDATAGRP" PAGESIZE 8 K  MANAGED BY
DATABASE  USING ( FILE '/data/db2/db2instp/nav_indx0p0.dbf' 2560
) ON DBPARTITIONNUM (0) USING ( FILE '/data/db2/db2instp/nav_
indx0p1.dbf' 2560 ) ON DBPARTITIONNUM (1) USING ( FILE '/data/db2/
db2instp/nav_indx0p2.dbf' 2560 ) ON DBPARTITIONNUM (2) EXTENTSIZE
16 OVERHEAD 10.5 PREFETCHSIZE 16 TRANSFERRATE 0.14 BUFFERPOOL
NAV_BPI8K"

[db2instp@nodedb21 ~]$
```

 It is mandatory to create the table space containers on the same partitions as the associated buffer pool. Notice also that a buffer pool in a multipartitioned environment that can be defined on one or more partition groups.

How it works...

Consider database partition groups as logical containers for tables and indexes. Their definition influences how the tables are spread among partitions. If a partition group has two partitions, the table is spread across these two partitions; if you have four partitions; tables are spread implicitly on four partitions, and so on. This might be considered as the implicit behavior.

You can control table spreading across partitions using custom distribution maps covered in the following recipes.

Implicitly, when a database is created, three database partition groups are defined, as follows:

▶ The `IBMDEFAULTGROUP` database partition group spreads on all existent partitions. The `USERSPACE1` table space is defined on this partition group. You cannot drop but you can alter this partition group.

▶ The `IBMCATGROUP` database partition group is defined on only one partition (the catalog partition). The `SYSCATSPACE1` table space is defined on this group. You cannot drop or alter this partition group.

▶ The `IBMTEMPGROUP` database partition group is defined on all partitions. The `TEMPSPACE1` temporary table space is defined on this group. You cannot drop but you can alter this partition group.

There's more...

If you define table spaces with automatic storage, they will spread automatically among all partitions defined in the database partition group assigned to them.

If you have tens or hundreds of partitions and use `MANAGED BY DATABASE` as storage option take in consideration the use of `$N` variable in container definition across the partitions.

Information about existent partition groups can be found in the following catalog views:

▶ `SYSCAT.DBPARTITIONGROUPS`

▶ `SYSCAT.DBPARTITIONGROUPDEF`

See also

▶ The *Creating and configuring table spaces in multipartitioned environment* recipe, in *Chapter 4, Storage—Using DB2 Table Spaces*

▶ The *Managing buffer pools in a multipartitioned database* recipe in *Chapter 5, DB2 Buffer Pools*

Altering database partition groups—adding partitions to database partition groups

At this point, we have finished adding the new partitions 3 and 4 to our database; in the following recipe, we will include them in our NAVDATAGRP database partition group.

Getting ready

In this recipe, we will demonstrate how to add the two newly created partitions, in the *Adding database partitions* recipe, into the NAVDATAGRP database using **Control Center** and the command line.

How to do it...

You can perform these operations with **Control Center** or using the command line.

Using Control Center

1. In **Control Center**, navigate to the NAV database, go to **Database partition groups**, and right-click on NAVDATAGRP; choose **Alter...**. Next, check **Assign available database partition groups to this partition group**.

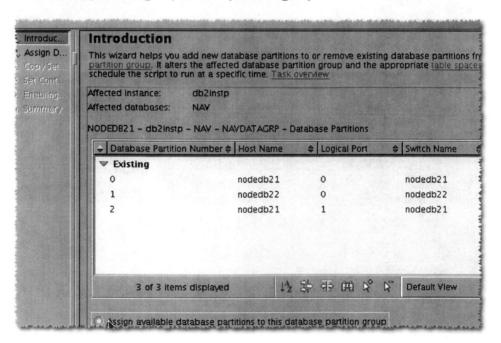

2. On the next screen, under **Available** nodes, check partitions **3** and **4**:

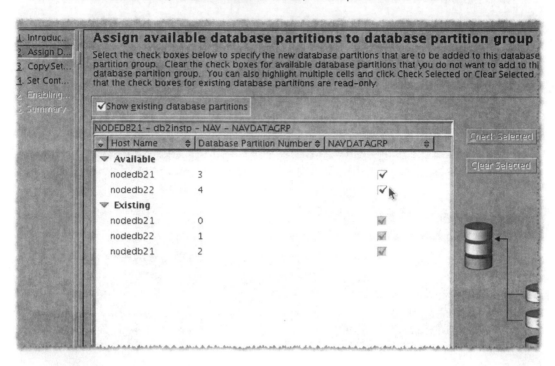

3. On the next screen, you get a dialog that asks to copy container settings from existent partitions by clicking the **...** button:

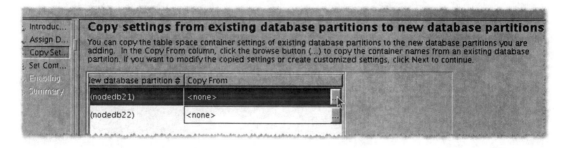

4. In the next step, choose the containers used as models for our new containers being created:

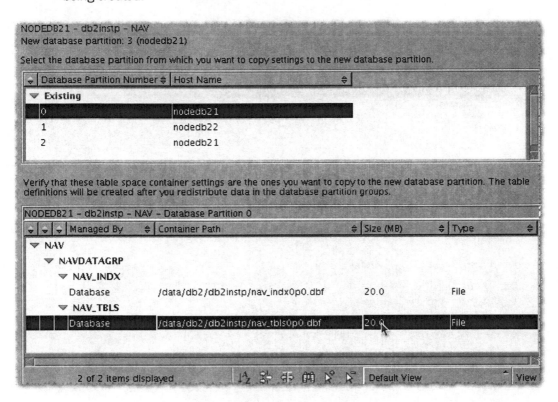

5. You must rename the files, suffix them with p3 and p4, according to the partition number on which they are to be defined:

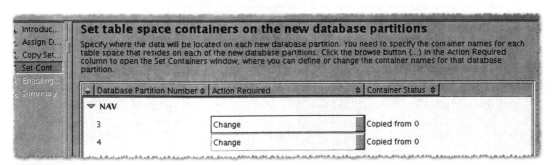

6. Click on **Change...** button and rename the files, adding p3 as suffix for partition 3; proceed similarly for partition 4:

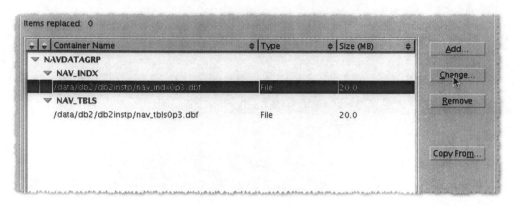

7. Navigate through the remaining step and click **Finish**.

Using the command line

1. To add partitions 3 and 4 to the database partition group NAVDATAGRP, issue the following command:

```
[db2instp@nodedb21 ~]$ db2 "ALTER DATABASE PARTITION GROUP
"NAVDATAGRP" ADD DBPARTITIONNUM (3,4) WITHOUT TABLESPACES"
SQL1759W  Redistribute database partition group is required to
  change database
partitioning for objects in database partition group "NAVDATAGRP"
  to include
some added database partitions or exclude some dropped database
  partitions.
SQLSTATE=01618
[db2instp@nodedb21 ~]$
```

2. To add a container to the NAV_TBLS table space on partition 3, issue the following command:

```
[db2instp@nodedb21 ~]$ db2 "ALTER TABLESPACE NAV_TBLS ADD (FILE '/
data/db2/db2instp/nav_tbls0p3.dbf' 20 M) ON DBPARTITIONNUM (3)"
SQL1759W  Redistribute database partition group is required to
  change database
partitioning for objects in database partition group "NAVDATAGRP"
  to include
some added database partitions or exclude some dropped database
  partitions.
SQLSTATE=01618
[db2instp@nodedb21 ~]$
```

3. To add a container to the NAV_TBLS table space on partition 4, issue the following command:

```
[db2instp@nodedb21 ~]$ db2 "ALTER TABLESPACE NAV_TBLS ADD (FILE '/
data/db2/db2instp/nav_tbls0p4.dbf' 20 M) ON DBPARTITIONNUM (4)"

SQL1759W  Redistribute database partition group is required to
   change database

partitioning for objects in database partition group "NAVDATAGRP"
   to include

some added database partitions or exclude some dropped database
   partitions.

SQLSTATE=01618

[db2instp@nodedb21 ~]$
```

4. To add a container to the NAV_INDX table space on partition 3, issue the following command:

```
[db2instp@nodedb21 ~]$ db2 "ALTER TABLESPACE NAV_INDX ADD (FILE '/
data/db2/db2instp/nav_indx0p3.dbf' 20 M) ON DBPARTITIONNUM (3)"

SQL1759W  Redistribute database partition group is required to
   change database

partitioning for objects in database partition group "NAVDATAGRP"
   to include

some added database partitions or exclude some dropped database
   partitions.

SQLSTATE=01618

[db2instp@nodedb21 ~]$
```

5. To add a container to the NAV_INDX table space on partition 4, issue the following command:

```
[db2instp@nodedb21 ~]$ db2 "ALTER TABLESPACE NAV_INDX ADD (FILE '/
data/db2/db2instp/nav_indx0p4.dbf' 20 M) ON DBPARTITIONNUM (4)"

SQL1759W  Redistribute database partition group is required to
   change database

partitioning for objects in database partition group "NAVDATAGRP"
   to include

some added database partitions or exclude some dropped database
   partitions.

SQLSTATE=01618

[db2instp@nodedb21 ~]$
```

How it works...

We previously used to add partitions 3 and 4 the `WITHOUT TABLESPACES` option. This option is similar with the `WITHOUT TABLESPACES` used before in `ADD DBPARTITIONNUM` command and instructs the `ALTER` command that container creation is defered for the database partition being added; and you should add them manually later. This command similarly does not have any effect in case we are using table spaces with automatic storage allocation.

There's more...

Similarly we have the `LIKE DBPARTITIONNUM <partition number>` option of `ADD DBPARTITIONNUM` command. It may be used if we want to use as models the containers found on `<partition number>` for containers being added.

For example the command:

```
ALTER DATABASE PARTITION GROUP "NAVDATAGRP" ADD DBPARTITIONNUM (3) LIKE
DBPARTITIONNUM (0)
```

Containers placed on partition 0 will be used as models for containers being added on partition 3.

See also

The *Creating and configuring table spaces in a multipartitioned environment* recipe in *Chapter 4, Storage—Using DB2 Table Spaces*.

Managing data redistribution on database partition groups

In this recipe, we will perform data redistribution on database partitions 3 and 4. For the method, we will use the default uniform distribution.

Getting ready

Now that we have added partitions 3 and 4 to partition group `NAVDATAGRP` and the corresponding containers to the `NAV_TBLS` and `NAV_INDX` table spaces, the next logical step should be to redistribute data on all existent partitions.

How to do it...

Internally, DB2 9.7 uses a distribution mechanism based on a partition map, which is actually an array containing 4,096 entries for backward compatibility. It can be extended to 32768 by setting the DB2_PMAP_COMPATIBILITY registry variable to OFF. The distribution map is generated and associated internally with a database partition group when is created. Every partition defined on a database partition group is mapped inside this array in a round-robin fashion.

We will generate a distribution map once before data redistribution for database partition group NAVDATAGRP and table COMM and once after data redistribution of table COMM, to give you an idea of how the partitions are remapped inside NAVDATAGRP database partition group.

In version 9.7, you may use larger distribution maps, using a maximum of 32,768 entries, by setting the registry variable DB2_PMAP_COMPATIBILITY to OFF. A larger distribution map will significantly reduce the data skew, especially when we have to deal with a larger number of partitions.

Using the command line

1. Execute the following command to generate the distribution map file for the NAVDATAGRP database partition group:

```
[db2instp@nodedb21 ~]$ db2gpmap -d NAV -m ~/beforerenavdatagrp.map
-g NAVDATAGRP
Connect to NAV.
Successfully connected to database.
Retrieving the partition map ID using nodegroup NAVDATAGRP.
The partition map has been sent to
/db2partinst/db2instp/beforerenavdatagrp.map.
[db2instp@nodedb21 ~]$
```

A short listing from the file generated /db2partinst/db2instp/beforenavdatagrp.map, to see the partition mapping before redistribution inside database partition group NAVDATAGRP:

```
........................................................................
1 1 0 1 1 0 1 1 0 1 1 0 1 1 0 1 1 0 1 1 0 1 1 0 1 1 0 1 1 0 1 1 0
1 1 0 1 1 0 1 2 0 2 2 0 2 2 0 2 2 0 2 2 0 2 2 0 2 2 0 2 2 0 2 2 0
2 2 0 2 2 0 2 2 0 2 2 0 2 2 0 2 2 0 2 2 0 2 2 0 2 2 0 2 2 0 2 2 0
........................................................................
```

0, 1, and 2 represent the partition numbers.

2. To generate the distribution map at the COMM table level, issue the following command:

```
[db2instp@nodedb21 ~]$ db2gpmap -d NAV -m ~/beforenavdatagrpCOMM.
map  -t NAV.COMM

Successfully connected to database.

Retrieving the partition map ID using table COMM.

The partition map has been sent to

/db2partinst/db2instp/beforenavdatagrpCOMM.map

[db2instp@nodedb21 ~]$
```

Short listing from the `beforenavdatagrpCOMM.map` file:

```
..................................................................... .
1 1 0 1 1 0 1 1 0 1 1 0 1 1 0 1 1 0 1 1 0 1 1 0 1 1 0 1 1 0 1 1 0
1 1 0 1 1 0 1 1 0 1 1 0 1 1 0 1 1 0 1 1 0 1 1 0 1 1 0 1 1 0 1 1 0
1 1 0 1 1 0 1 2 0 2 2 0 2 2 0 2 2 0 2 2 0 2 2 0 2 2 0 2 2 0 2 2 0
.................................................................. . .
```

3. To redistribute data on all the partitions in uniform mode, execute the following command:

```
[db2instp@nodedb21 ~]$ db2 "REDISTRIBUTE DATABASE PARTITION GROUP
NAVDATAGRP UNIFORM"

DB20000I  The REDISTRIBUTE NODEGROUP command completed
successfully.  [db2instp@nodedb21 ~]$
```

> Any redistribution operation generates a redistribution log file in the `<instance_owner_home>/sqllib/redist` directory. Here, you will find one or more files that contain the steps performed by the redistribution process having a generic format: `Databasename.Databasepartitiongroupname.yyyymmddhhmiss`.

4. Generate the distribution map for the table COMM, to see how the table data has been redistributed across database partitions:

```
[db2instp@nodedb21 ~]$ db2gpmap -d NAV -m ~/afternavdatagrpcomm.
map -t comm              Connect to NAV.

Successfully connected to database.

Retrieving the partition map ID using table COMM.
```

```
The partition map has been sent to
/db2partinst/db2instp/afternavdatagrpcomm.map.
```

A short listing from the map file is as follows:

```
..............................................................................

4 4 4 4 4 4 4 4 4 4 4 4 4 4 4 4 4 4 4 4 4 4 4 4 4 4 4 4 4 4 4 4
4 4 4 4 4 4 4 3 4 3 3 4 3 3 4 3 3 4 3 3 4 3 3 4 3 3 4 3 3 4 3 3 4
1 2 0 1 2 0 1 2 0 1 2 0 1 2 0 1 2 0 1 2 0 1 2 0 1 2 0 1 2 0 1 2

..............................................................................
```

We can see now, in the map file that the distribution of the COMM table also includes partitions 3 and 4.

5. Connnect to database NAV and collect statistics for all tables and indexes from NAV schema:

```
[db2instp@nodedb21 ~]$ RUNSTATS ON TABLE NAV.COMM ON ALL COLUMNS
AND INDEXES ALL ALLOW WRITE ACCESS"
DB20000I  The RUNSTATS command completed successfully.
```

 After data is redistributed across partition it is strongly recommend to collect statistics on the affected tables and indexes.

How it works...

The partition map is built up at database partition group creation. Any table created in NAVDATAGRP will be redistributed as the internal map directs it, by default, in round-robin fashion, as stated previously. The default redistribution method is UNIFORM. You can build and use, for redistribution, your own customized partition maps.

There's more...

We used a simple method to redistribute data. Generally if you want to redistribute a large volume of data preliminary resource analysis is required. DB2 provides a set of so called step-wise procedures for log space analysis and creating the best redistribution plan. These procedures are implemented in **Control Center** redistribute wizard.

In **Control Center**, right-click on the **NAVDATAGRP** database partition group and choose **Redistribute...**:

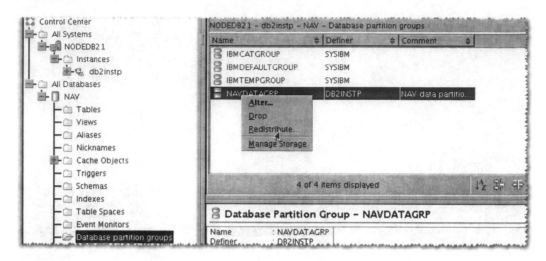

More information and examples with step wise procedures can be found at the following link:

```
http://publib.boulder.ibm.com/infocenter/db2luw/v9r7/index.
jsp?topic=%2Fcom.ibm.db2.luw.qb.server.doc%2Fdoc%2Ft0004714.html
```

For detailed usage and options of REDISTRIBUTE DATABASE PARTITION GROUP command consult the following link:

```
http://publib.boulder.ibm.com/infocenter/db2luw/v9r7/index.
jsp?topic=%2Fcom.ibm.db2.luw.qb.server.doc%2Fdoc%2Ft0004714.html.
```

The table distribution key and its role in a multipartitioned environment

The table distribution key is another element that can influence the distribution of table rows across existent partitions defined in a database partition group. Distribution keys can be created explicitly using DISTRIBUTION BY HASH (columns) directive inside table definition or they can be defined implicitly by DB2 using a series of column rules detailed in this recipe. Usually distribution column might be designed and used to improve query performance.

Getting ready

This recipe is strongly correlated with the preceding one; here, we will also use before and after pictures of how the data is distributed across database partitions.

How to do it...

For some of the queries, we will use **Command Editor**, because it offers better visibility.

Using the command line

1. To find the distribution key columns for the COMM table, issue the following command:

   ```
   [db2instp@nodedb21 ~]$ db2 "select name from sysibm.syscolumns
   where tbname='COMM' and partkeyseq !=0"
   ```

   ```
   NAME

   CKEY

     1 record(s) selected.
   [db2instp@nodedb21 ~]$
   ```

   Since we did not specify any distribution key at table creation, the primary key is used as the distribution key.

2. To find the distribution of rows on partitions, by row numbers, before performing redistribution of table COMM, issue the following command (for better visibility run this statement in **Command Center | Tools | Command Editor**):

   ```
   select dbpartitionnum(CKEY) as PARTITION_NUMBER,
       count(CKEY) as NUMBER_OF_ROWS
     from comm
     group by dbpartitionnum(CKEY)
     order by dbpartitionnum(CKEY)
   ```

Commands	Query Results	Access Plan

   Edits to these results are performed as positioned UPDATEs and DELETEs.

PARTITION_NUMBER ⇕	NUMBER_OF_ROWS ⇕
0	4876
1	5037
2	5113

3. After redistribution, issue the last statement again. Now we can see that rows are distributed slightly uniformly across partitions:

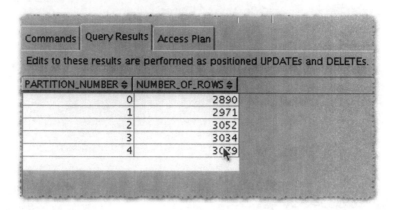

How it works...

Table rows partiticpating in distributed keys are assigned to partitions using a hashing algorithm that calculates their distribution across partitions. If you do not specify a distribution key at table creation, it will be created implicitly, as follows:

- ▸ If the table has a primary key, it will be used as a distribution key
- ▸ If the table does not have a primary key, the first column, whose data type is not LOB, LONG VARCHAR, LONG VARGRAPHIC, or XML, will be used as a partition key
- ▸ If the table columns are not in this category, it means that a partition key cannot be defined, and the table can only be created in a table space that has been created on a single-partition database partition group

Distribution keys should be created to improve query performance in the following conditions:

- ▸ Columns are frequently used in joins
- ▸ Columns are frequently used in group by clause
- ▸ Columns defined as primary keys or unique must be included in distribution keys
- ▸ Create distribution keys for column used mostly in equality conditions

Practically the key columns are hashed and divided in 4095 or 32768 buckets depending on the distribution map used. Every map entry indicates where a specific row on which partition might be found.

There's more...

You cannot change the distribution key by altering the table, unless the table is spread across only one partition. To change the partition key for tables spanned on multiple partitions you should follow these steps:

1. Export or copy table data in a staging table.
2. Drop and recreate the table, with the new distribution key defined.
3. Import or insert table data.

Table collocation

Distribution keys play a major role also in a method of table distribution called table collocation. Table collocation is another performance tuning technique found in multipartitioned database environments. A table is considered collocated when the following conditions are met:

> Tables are placed in the same table space and are in the same partition groups.

> The distribution keys have the same columns and same data types and are partition compatible.

Altering database partition groups— removing partitions from a database partition group

Usually, removing partitions from a database partition group is a seldom operation. It may be performed, for example, when a server containing the partitions is removed and commissioned from the configuration, or a partition is not placed optimally and induces performance problems. This is the first step if we want to drop the database partitions from the database.

Getting ready

In this recipe, we will remove partitions 3 and 4, added before to the NAVDATAGRP database partition group, and redistribute data on the remaining partitions.

How to do it...

It is highly recommended, before you begin, to drop a partition from a database partition group to perform a full database backup.

Using the command line

1. To remove partitions 3 and 4, execute the following command:

    ```
    [db2instp@nodedb21 ~]$ db2 "ALTER DATABASE PARTITION GROUP
    NAVDATAGRP DROP DBPARTITIONNUMS (3 TO 4)"
    ```

    SQL1759W Redistribute database partition group is required to
      change database

    partitioning for objects in database partition group "NAVDATAGRP"
      to include

    some added database partitions or exclude some dropped database
      partitions.

    SQLSTATE=01618

    ```
    [db2instp@nodedb21 ~]$
    ```

2. Initially, the partitions are just marked as removed; actually, we have to redistribute data from them as the warning message SQL179W instructs us. After the redistribution operation is finished, they are removed completely. To see the status of partition 3 and 4, run the following statement:

    ```
    [db2instp@nodedb21 ~]$db2" select * from sysibm.sysnodegroupdef
    where ngname='NAVDATAGRP'"
    ```

    NGNAME NODENUM IN_USE

    NAVDATAGRP   0 Y

    NAVDATAGRP   1 Y

    NAVDATAGRP   2 Y

    NAVDATAGRP   3 T

    NAVDATAGRP   4 T

    ```
    [db2instp@nodedb21 ~]$
    ```

    T -means that the distribution map is removed and no longer
    availaible

3. Now, redistribute data to the remaining partitions 0, 1, and 2:

    ```
    [db2instp@nodedb21 ~]$ db2 "REDISTRIBUTE DATABASE PARTITION GROUP
    NAVDATAGRP UNIFORM"
    ```

    DB20000I The REDISTRIBUTE NODEGROUP command completed
      successfully.

4. Now, we can see that the partitions 3 and 4 are completely removed and do not appear in catalog:

```
[db2instp@nodedb21 ~]$ db2  "select * from sysibm.sysnodegroupdef
where ngname='NAVDATAGRP'"

NGNAME   NODENUM IN_USE
NAVDATAGRP       0 Y
NAVDATAGRP       1 Y
NAVDATAGRP       2 Y
[db2instp@nodedb21 ~]$
```

 You can also use the LIST DATABASE PARTITION GROUPS SHOW DETAIL command to list detailed information about partition groups .

How it works...

Removing partitions from a database partition group is an operation similar to adding partitions in terms of internal processing.

There's more...

At this step do not remove database partitions that contain data by editing manually the db2nodes.cfg database partition configuration file.

Removing database partitions

Practically this recipe is linked with the previous one. Here, we will continue to remove the partitions 3 and 4 from the database.

Getting ready

Before deleting a partition, our first concern would be to make sure that the partition contains no data. Therefore, verification will be the first operation to be executed. If database partitions are empty, we can proceed further with removal. In this recipe, we will verify and remove the partitions 3 and 4, added previously, in the *Adding database partitions* recipe in this chapter.

How to do it...

You can perform these operations with **Control Center** or using the command line.

Using Control Center

1. In **Control Center**, navigate to instance **db2instp**, and right-click on **Open Database partition servers**. Next, right-click on the partition number and choose **Drop...**.

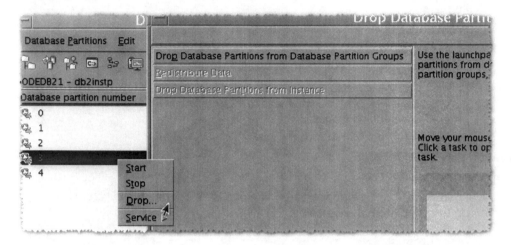

2. Follow these steps, as instructed by the wizard:

    ❑ **Drop Database Partition from Database Partition Groups**

    ❑ **Redistribute Data**

    ❑ **Drop Database Partitions from Instance**

Using the command line

In order to remove partitions, we have to switch the current partition to the one that we want to drop. We have the possibility to switch between partitions by setting the DB2NODE environment variable to the number of partitions. The main reason to use DB2NODE is that the drop dbpartitionnum verify command, used for verification, has no option to specify the partition number. Therefore, it must be used on the current node.

 Every time before you switch between partitions, use the terminate command to close the backend connection, otherwise you will get an error.

1. First, issue the `terminate` command to close any remaining backend connection:

   ```
   [db2instp@nodedb21 sqllib]$ db2 terminate
   DB20000I  The TERMINATE command completed successfully.
   [db2instp@nodedb21 sqllib]$
   ```

2. Set the current node planned for removal:

   ```
   [db2instp@nodedb21 sqllib]$ export DB2NODE=3
   [db2instp@nodedb21 sqllib]$
   ```

3. Now, verify that the database partition is empty:

   ```
   [db2instp@nodedb21 ~]$ db2 "drop dbpartitionnum verify"
   SQL6034W  Database partition "3" is not being used by any
   databases.
   [db2instp@nodedb21 ~]$
   ```

4. The database partition is clear, so we will proceed with dropping partition 3:

   ```
   [db2instp@nodedb21 ~]$ db2stop drop dbpartitionnum 3
   SQL6076W  Warning! This command will remove all database files
   on the node for this instance.  Before continuing, ensure that
   there is no user data on this node by running the DROP NODE VERIFY
   command.
   Do you want to continue ?  (y/n)y
   06/28/2011 16:08:54      2    0    SQL1064N  DB2STOP processing was
   successful.
   06/28/2011 16:08:54      1    0    SQL1064N  DB2STOP processing was
   successful.
   06/28/2011 16:08:55      4    0    SQL1064N  DB2STOP processing was
   successful.
   06/28/2011 16:09:05      3    0    SQL1064N  DB2STOP processing was
   successful
   [db2instp@nodedb21 ~]$
   ```

5. Start all the remaining partitions:

   ```
   [db2instp@nodedb21 sqllib]$ export DB2NODE=0
   [db2instp@nodedb21 sqllib]$ db2start
   ```

    Do not forget to switch the partition, now, to an existent one.

6. Repeat steps 1 to 4 to remove database partition 4.

7. Finally, the partitions 3 and 4 are removed:

```
[db2instp@nodedb21 sqllib]$ db2  list DBPARTITIONNUMS

DATABASE PARTITION NUMBER
-----------------------------
                           0
                           1
                           2
[db2instp@nodedb21 sqllib]$
```

How it works...

Dropping partitions is very similar to adding partitions. Corresponding entries are removed from db2nodes.cfg database partition configuration file.

There's more...

After you are sure that your partitions do not contain data you can remove partitions by editing db2node.cfg.

Converting a non-partitioned database to a multipartitioned database on MS Windows

The second method, besides creating a new multipartitioned database from scratch, is to convert an existent non-partitioned database to a multipartitioned one. In this recipe, we will convert the NAV database to multipartitioned, using a single server running the Windows 7 SP1 Enterprise Edition operating system, named node1. Also, we will cover some existent particularities of multipartitioned database systems available only on the MS Windows platforms.

Getting ready

In this recipe, we will add two new database partitions. In this way, we will have a total of three database partitions. A new database partition group, NAVDATAGRP, will be created and populated by using a particular method that involves data migration from the default IBMDEFAULTGROUP database partition group to NAVDATAGR database partition group.

How to do it...

In this recipe, we will use **Control Center** combined with the command line. For this recipe, we will use an instance named DB2.

1. Create the NAV database:

   ```
   E:\Program Files\IBM\SQLLIB\BIN>db2 " CREATE DATABASE NAV
   AUTOMATIC STORAGE YES  ON 'E:\' DBPATH ON 'E:\' USING

    CODESET UTF-8 TERRITORY US COLLATE USING SYSTEM PAGESIZE 8192"

   DB20000I  The CREATE DATABASE command completed successfully.

   E:\Program Files\IBM\SQLLIB\BIN>
   ```

2. Create the table spaces NAV_TBLS and NAV_INDX, according to the description found in the *Creating and configuring DB2 non-partitioned databases* recipe in *Chapter 2, Administration and Configuration of the DB2 Non-partitioned Database*; choose your own paths for table space containers.

3. Create buffer pools NAV_BPT8K and NAV_BPI8K, according to the description found in the *Creating and configuring DB2 non-partitioned databases* recipe in *Chapter 2, Administration and Configuration of the DB2 Non-partitioned Database*, or by using the provided scripts.

4. Create tables of the NAV application and load data into them using the provided scripts according to the description found in the *Creating and configuring DB2 non-partitioned databases* recipe in *Chapter 2, Administration and Configuration of the DB2 Non-partitioned Database*.

5. Add two new database partitions to the instance DB2. Navigate to the instance DB2, right-click and choose **Add Database Partitions** to open the **Add Database Partitions Launchpad**.

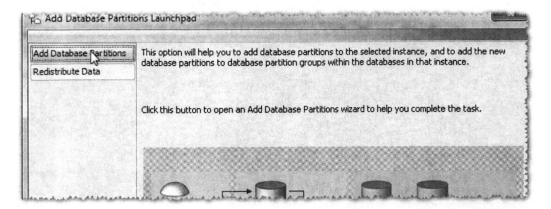

6. The launchpad can be also launched from **Control Center | Tools | Wizards | Add Database Partitions Launchpad**:

7. Add database partition **1** with logical port **1**, and database partition **2** with logical port **2**:

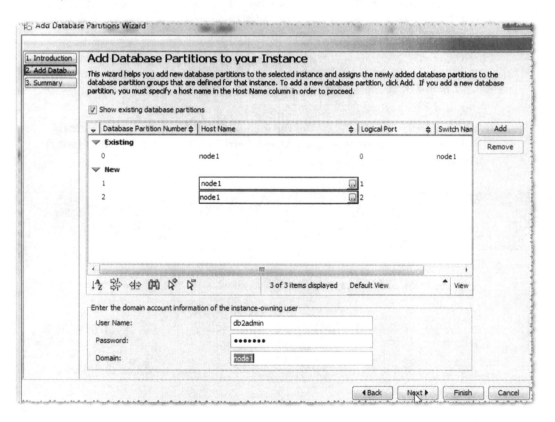

8. Review the actions and click **Finish**:

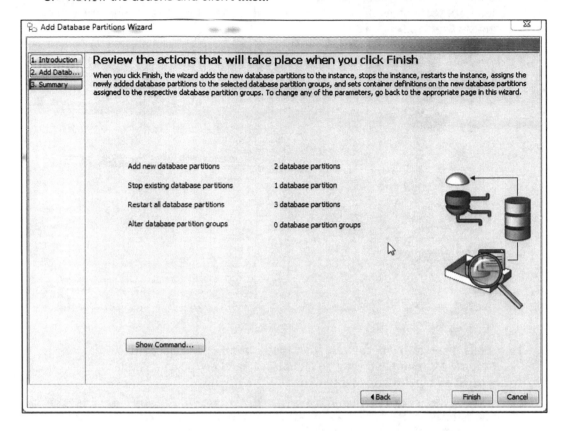

You should note that every database partition on MS Windows has its own service created and associated. These services have the startup mode set to **Manual**; if you want to start them at system startup, modify their startup mode to **Automatic**.

DB2 - DB2COPY1 - DB2-0	Allows appli...	Started	Automatic	.\db2admin
DB2 - DB2COPY1 - DB2-1	Allows appli...	Started	Manual	.\db2admin
DB2 - DB2COPY1 - DB2-2	Allows appli...	Started	Manual	.\db2admin

9. After the database partitions are successfully added, we create the NAVDATAGRDP database partition group. Navigate to **Database partition groups**, right-click, and choose **Create...**.

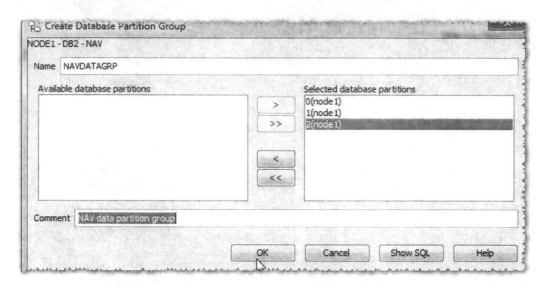

10. Create a new table space NAV_PART_TBS, which will be allocated to the NAVDATAGRP database partition group. This partition will contain the NAV application's tables after data move:

```
E:\Program Files\IBM\SQLLIB\BIN> db2 "CREATE  LARGE  TABLESPACE
NAV_PART_TBS IN DATABASE PARTITION GROUP "NAVDATAGRP" PAGESIZE
8 K  MANAGED BY AUTOMATIC STORAGE EXTENTSIZE 16 OVERHEAD 10.5
PREFETCHSIZE 16 TRANSFERRATE 0.14 BUFFERPOOL  NAV_BPT8K "

DB20000I  The SQL command completed successfully.

E:\Program Files\IBM\SQLLIB\BIN>
```

11. Create a new table space NAV_PART_INDX, which will be allocated to the NAVDATAGRP database partition group. This partition will contain the NAV application's indexes:

```
E:\Program Files\IBM\SQLLIB\BIN> db2 "CREATE  LARGE  TABLESPACE
NAV_PART_INDX IN DATABASE PARTITION GROUP "NAVDATAGRP"
PAGESIZE 8 K

 MANAGED BY AUTOMATIC STORAGE EXTENTSIZE 16 OVERHEAD 10.5
PREFETCHSIZE 16 TRANSFERRATE 0.14 BUFFERPOOL  NAV_BPI8K "

DB20000I  The SQL command completed successfully.

E:\Program Files\IBM\SQLLIB\BIN>
```

12. Create a table named COMMP, with identical definition as table COMM.
    For data table space, use NAV_PART_TBLS, and for index storage,
    use NAV_PART_INDX table space:

```
E:\Program Files\IBM\SQLLIB\BIN>db2 "set current schema nav"
DB20000I  The SQL command completed successfully.
E:\Program Files\IBM\SQLLIB\BIN>


E:\Program Files\IBM\SQLLIB\BIN>db2 "create table COMMP
(
 ckey        varchar(10) not null
,f2kaptkey   varchar(10) not null
,cnam        varchar(30)
,type        decimal(4)
,freq1       decimal(8,3)
,freq2       decimal(8,3)
,freq3       decimal(8,3)
,freq4       decimal(8,3)
,freq5       decimal(8,3)
,clat        decimal(8,2)
,clong       decimal(9,2)
,CONSTRAINT PK_COMMP PRIMARY KEY ( ckey ) )
in nav_part_tbls
index in nav_part_indx"
DB20000I  The SQL command completed successfully
E:\Program Files\IBM\SQLLIB\BIN>
```

13. Insert data from table COMM into table COMMP:

```
E:\Program Files\IBM\SQLLIB\BIN>db2 "insert into COMMP select *
from COMM"
DB20000I  The SQL command completed successfully
E:\Program Files\IBM\SQLLIB\BIN>db2 commit
DB20000I  The SQL command completed successfully
```

14. Rename table COMM:

```
E:\Program Files\IBM\SQLLIB\BIN>db2 "RENAME TABLE COMM TO COMM_
OLD"
DB20000I  The SQL command completed successfully
E:\Program Files\IBM\SQLLIB\BIN>
```

15. Rename table COMMP to COMM:

```
E:\Program Files\IBM\SQLLIB\BIN>db2 "RENAME TABLE COMMP TO COMM"
DB20000I  The SQL command completed successfully
E:\Program Files\IBM\SQLLIB\BIN>
```

16. Repeat steps 10, 11, 12, and 13. Create all the remaining tables with the NAV_ PART_TBS table space for data and the NAV_PART_INDX table space for indexes.

17. To find the distribution on partitions, by row numbers, for the table COMM, issue (for better visibility run this statement in **Command Center | Tools | Command Editor**):

```
select dbpartitionnum(CKEY) as PARTITION_NUMBER,
       count(CKEY) as NUMBER_OF_ROWS
   from comm
   group by dbpartitionnum(CKEY)
   order by dbpartitionnum(CKEY)
```

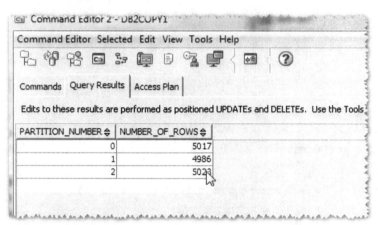

How it works...

When you add one or more partitions for an existent instance, one or more additional Windows services are created and assigned to every partition. All databases under the instance being partitioned are affected. Partition groups IBMDEFAULTGROUP, IBMCATGROUP, and IBMTEMPGROUP are created, and all table spaces are assigned to them, depending on their role. Catalog table space is assigned by default to IBMCATGROUP, temporary table spaces are assigned to IBMTEMPGROUP, and all other table spaces that contain data are allocated to IBMDEFAULTGROUP. The db2nodes.cfg file is modified, depending on the number of partitions allocated and on the corresponding host and port.

There's more...

Under MS Windows platforms, there are some command-line utilities that help us to add, drop, list, and modify database partitions, instead of modifying the db2nodes.cfg file manually, which is not really recommended anyway. These were summarized, also, in previous recipes. Here, we will give some example about how to use them. All these command-line utilities are making modifications in the db2nodes.cfg file.

1. To list current database partitions, issue the following command:

   ```
   E:\ Program Files\IBM\SQLLIB\BIN >db2nlist

   List of nodes for instance "DB2" is as follows:

   Node: "0" Host: "node1" Machine: "NODE1" Port: "0"

   Node: "1" Host: "node1" Machine: "node1" Port: "1"

   Node: "2" Host: "node1" Machine: "node1" Port: "2"

   E:\ Program Files\IBM\SQLLIB\BIN >db2nlist
   ```

2. To create database partition 3, with logical port 3, issue the following command:

   ```
   E:\Program Files\IBM\SQLLIB\BIN>db2ncrt /n:3 /u:node1\
   db2admin,test123 /p:3


   DBI1937W  The db2ncrt command successfully added the node. The
   node is

         not active until all nodes are stopped and started again.


   Explanation:


   The db2nodes.cfg file is not updated to include the new node until
   all

   nodes are simultaneously stopped by the STOP DATABASE MANAGER
   (db2stop)

   command. Until the file is updated, the existing nodes cannot

   communicate with the new node.


   User response:


   Issue db2stop to stop all the nodes. When all nodes are
   successfully

   stopped, issue db2start to start all the nodes, including the new
   node.

   E:\Program Files\IBM\SQLLIB\BIN>
   ```

```
E:\Program Files\IBM\SQLLIB\BIN>db2stop force
12/20/2011 00:13:05     1    0    SQL1032N  No start database
manager command was
issued.
12/20/2011 00:13:05     2    0    SQL1032N  No start database
manager command was
issued.
12/20/2011 00:13:06     0    0    SQL1064N  DB2STOP processing was
successful.
SQL6033W  Stop command processing was attempted on "3" node(s).
"1" node(s) wer
e successfully stopped.  "2" node(s) were already stopped.  "0"
node(s) could no
t be stopped.


E:\Program Files\IBM\SQLLIB\BIN>db2start
12/20/2011 00:16:15     1    0    SQL1063N  DB2START processing was
successful.
12/20/2011 00:16:15     3    0    SQL1063N  DB2START processing was
successful.
12/20/2011 00:16:16     0    0    SQL1063N  DB2START processing was
successful.
12/20/2011 00:16:16     2    0    SQL1063N  DB2START processing was
successful.
SQL1063N  DB2START processing was successful.
E:\Program Files\IBM\SQLLIB\BIN>
```

List partitions; actually, we have partition 3 added:

```
E:\Program Files\IBM\SQLLIB\BIN>db2nlist
List of nodes for instance "DB2" is as follows:
Node: "0" Host: "node1" Machine: "NODE1" Port: "0"
Node: "1" Host: "node1" Machine: "node1" Port: "1"
Node: "2" Host: "node1" Machine: "node1" Port: "2"
Node: "3" Host: "node1" Machine: "NODE1" Port: "3"
```

3. To drop database partition 3, issue the following command:

```
E:\Program Files\IBM\SQLLIB\BIN>


E:\Program Files\IBM\SQLLIB\BIN>db2stop dbpartitionnum 3
12/20/2011 00:17:13     3    0    SQL1064N  DB2STOP processing was
successful.
```

```
SQL1064N  DB2STOP processing was successful.

E:\Program Files\IBM\SQLLIB\BIN>db2ndrop /n:3
SQL2808W  Node "3" for instance "DB2" has been deleted.
```

4. List partitions again; in this listing, we can see that partition 3 has disappeared:

```
E:\Program Files\IBM\SQLLIB\BIN>db2nlist
List of nodes for instance "DB2" is as follows:
Node: "0" Host: "node1" Machine: "NODE1" Port: "0"
Node: "1" Host: "node1" Machine: "node1" Port: "1"
Node: "2" Host: "node1" Machine: "node1" Port: "2"
```

Configuring Fast Communication Manager

The **Fast Communication Manager** (**FCM**) is an internal component of DB2 that plays a crucial role in inter-partition communication and parallel execution. On non-partitioned databases, it is activated if the INTRA_PARALLEL database manager parameter is set to YES. Depending on the database partition configuration, it can use shared memory or socket communication. The first case is applicable if we have logical partitioning (every partition is located on the same server); socket communication is used if we have separated servers or physical partitions. It being an important performance factor, you should be careful with setting FCM-related parameters.

Getting ready

An important component of FCM is the FCM buffer. An FCM buffer is actually a structure that holds data that is going to be passed between agents. The communication ports used by FCM are defined in the /etc/services file. For example, in our case, we have defined a maximum of four logical ports:

```
DB2_db2instp               60008/tcp
DB2_db2instp_1             60009/tcp
DB2_db2instp_2             60010/tcp
DB2_db2instp_END           60011/tcp
```

How to do it...

FCM is controlled by the following parameters:

- FCM_NUM_BUFFERS: This parameter controls the number of FCM buffers
- FCM_NUM_CHANNELS: This parameter controls the number of channels used for communication

Both parameters have AUTOMATIC svalues assigned by default.

How it works...

FCM buffers are 4 KB memory structures that are allocated in instance shared memory. Internally, they have assigned priority levels, according to the type of messages they are handling on (failure messages have a higher priority than row passing messages between partitions).

There's more...

To set up a proper value for a number of buffers, it is recommended to monitor, from time to time, the values assigned to FCM_NUM_BUFFERS and FCM_NUM_CHANNELS, running in the AUTOMATIC mode, especially when the processing is at peak values.

To monitor FCM buffers and channels, issue the following command:

```
[db2instp@nodedb21 ~]$ db2 "get snapshot for database manager"
```

```
Node FCM information corresponds to      = 0
Free FCM buffers                         = 8049
Total FCM buffers                        = 8055
Free FCM buffers low water mark          = 8037
Maximum number of FCM buffers            = 1048940
Free FCM channels                        = 4475
Total FCM channels                       = 4475
Free FCM channels low water mark         = 4464
Maximum number of FCM channels           = 1048940
Number of FCM nodes                      = 5
```

See also

The *Monitoring and configuring FCM for optimal performance* recipe in *Chapter 11, Connectivity and Networking.*

4
Storage—Using DB2 Table Spaces

In this chapter, we will cover:

- ▶ Creating and configuring table spaces within automatic storage databases
- ▶ Creating and configuring SMS table spaces
- ▶ Creating and configuring DMS table spaces
- ▶ Using temporary table spaces
- ▶ Altering table spaces
- ▶ Dropping table spaces
- ▶ Creating and configuring table spaces in a multipartitioned environment

Introduction

Every database has a logical storage layout and must be mapped to its physical components. We will identify different database configurations and their major characteristics.

Table spaces are part of the logical components of a database and their physical implementation is subject to certain limitations and rules. We will guide you through the major storage definition aspects and show you how to avoid potential pitfalls.

Creating and configuring table spaces within automatic storage databases

Let's start by discussing the physical implementation of table spaces.

The way your data is structured, and its storage, should follow a well thought-out plan. In order to make this plan work for you, it is best to clearly understand what the underlying components are and how we can exploit them for reliability and performance.

Automatic Storage means the database takes charge of containers. Containers will be allocated and extended as needed, without intervention from the DBA. The table space type (SMS or DMS) is determined automatically.

Getting ready

Table spaces will be striped across storage paths, so you may need to have all storage paths ready.

How to do it...

1. Get current database parameters:

    ```
    db2 => connect to nav;


        Database Connection Information

     Database server        = DB2/LINUXX8664 9.7.4
     SQL authorization ID   = DB2INST1
     Local database alias   = NAV


    db2 => GET DB CFG;


        Database Configuration for Database

     Database configuration release level                = 0x0d00
     Database release level                              = 0x0d00
     ....
    ```

We'll look for specific items:

```
Database page size                                    = 8192
Degree of parallelism                (DFT_DEGREE) = 1
Changed pages threshold              (CHNGPGS_THRESH) = 80
Default prefetch size (pages)        (DFT_PREFETCH_SZ) = AUTOMATIC

Default number of containers                          = 1
Default tablespace extentsize (pages)  (DFT_EXTENT_SZ) = 32
```

2. Create proper buffer pool, if necessary:

   Determine the optimum page size for your table space. Create or choose a buffer pool with the corresponding page size. In the DB2 command center:

   ```
   [db2inst1@nodedb21 ~]$ db2 "CREATE BUFFERPOOL NAV_BPT8K IMMEDIATE
     SIZE 25600 PAGESIZE 8K"
   DB20000I  The SQL command completed successfully.
   ```

   We chose here to specify a fixed size. We'll discuss automatically sized buffer pools in the next chapter.

3. Create the table space:

   There is no need to define containers, since DB2 manages them. You still have to specify the page and the extent sizes. Remember that the page and extent size have to match those of the buffer pool. So, from the command center, or a script, run:

   ```
   [db2inst1@nodedb21 ~]$ db2 "CREATE TABLESPACE NAV_TBLS
               PAGESIZE 8 K
    BUFFERPOOL NAV_BPT8K"
   DB20000I  The SQL command completed successfully.
   ```

How it works...

The database manager will create either a **System-Managed Space** (**SMS**) or a **Database-Managed Space** (**DMS**) table space.

There's more...

We covered manually sized buffer pools, but we can also use an automatically sized buffer pool for a table space. We will also see where containers are created in an automatic storage database.

Using self tuning buffer pools

You can enable self tuning for this buffer pool by using the `AUTOMATIC` keyword. DB2 will allocate 25,600 pages as the initial size and will adjust the buffer pool's size depending on the workload. We recommend its use.

```
[db2inst1@nodedb21 ~]$ db2 "CREATE BUFFERPOOL NAV_BPT8K IMMEDIATE
  SIZE 25600 AUTOMATIC PAGESIZE 8K"
DB20000I  The SQL command completed successfully.
```

Physical implementation

Database files will be created automatically using the storage path you defined in the *default directory*. The new table space `NAV_TBLS` corresponds to the `T0000003` directory:

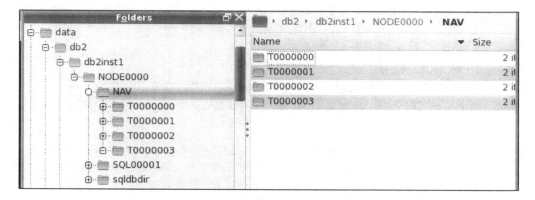

To better see how containers are related to the database, we can list all the table spaces (we show only an excerpt of the command's result), but we are only interested in the `NAV_TBLS` table space. We see, from the output, that the table space ID is `3`.

```
[db2inst1@nodedb21 ~]$ db2 list tablespaces
        Tablespace ID               = 3
        Name                        = NAV_TBLS
        Type                        = Database managed space
        Contents                    = All permanent data. Large table space.
        State                       = 0x0000
          Detailed explanation:
            Normal
```

With this table space ID, let's look at the containers defined for this table space:

```
[db2inst1@nodedb21 ~]$ db2 list tablespace containers for 3

                Tablespace Containers for Tablespace 3

    Container ID          = 0
    Name                  = /data/db2/db2inst1/NODE0000/
                            NAV/T0000003/C0000000.LRG
    Type                  = File
```

Adding a storage path to a manual storage database

Adding a storage path to a manual storage database makes it an automatic storage database. Existing manual storage table spaces are not converted to automatic storage table spaces.

   ▶ Regular and large table spaces:

   Existing automatic storage table spaces will not use the new path in an initial phase.

   ▶ Temporary table spaces:

   The database must be restarted to enable use of new storage paths for temporary table spaces.

Creating and configuring SMS table spaces

SMS is managed by the operating system, which means each table and/or index defined in this type of table space is implemented by at least one operating system file, depending on the number of containers for this table space. The space is limited by the amount of free space in the filesystem.

Getting ready

Make sure that the instance owner has write access to create a directory for the containers used in that table space. This will usually be under the same directory as specified in the storage path used to create the database.

Define all the containers you need for this table space type, since you cannot change this later. Containers should all have the same amount of available space.

Decide if you want to use a buffer pool or use filesystem caching. We recommend you use buffer pools with an AUTOMATIC size.

How to do it...

Use a script or, from the command center, execute the commands listed as follows:

1. Confirm write permissions in the storage path:

    In `/data/db2`, look for the write permissions for directory `db2inst1`; the permission has to be set to 750 (rwxr-x---) or 770 (rwxrwx---), so DB2 (`db2inst1`) can create the directory. Once the database is created, it is better to let DB2 manage the file and directory permissions.

    ```
    [db2inst1@nodedb21 ~]$ cd /data/db2/
    [db2inst1@nodedb21 db2]$ ls -al
    total 12
    drwxrwx--- 3 db2inst1  db2iadm1  4096 2011-06-20 17:08 ./
    drwxrwxrwx 4 root      root      4096 2011-06-20 17:08 ../
    drwxrwx--- 3 db2inst1  db2iadm1  4096 2011-06-20 13:04 db2inst1/
    ```

2. Create buffer pool:

    The following command creates a 200 Meg buffer pool (25600 X 8 KB = 204800 KB):

    ```
    [db2inst1@nodedb21 ~]$ db2 "CREATE BUFFERPOOL NAV_REFBPT8K
    IMMEDIATE SIZE 25600 PAGESIZE 8K"
    DB20000I  The SQL command completed successfully.
    ```

3. Create table space:

    The page size of the table space must match the buffer pool's page size:

    ```
    [db2inst1@nodedb21 ~]$ db2 "CREATE TABLESPACE NAV_REF_TBLS
    PAGESIZE 8K
        MANAGED BY SYSTEM USING ('/data/db2/db2inst1/NODE0000/NAV/
          nav_ref')
        BUFFERPOOL NAV_REFBPT8K"
    DB20000I  The SQL command completed successfully.
    [db2inst1@nodedb21 ~]$ db2 list tablespace containers for 5


            Tablespace Containers for Tablespace 5

    Container ID            = 0
    Name                    = /data/db2/db2inst1/NODE0000/NAV/nav_ref
    Type                    = Path
    ```

How it works...

You specify a directory name, and the operating system allocates space for each object in this table space. Unless the directory name is absolute, the directory is relative to the database directory. The database manager will create the directory if one does not exist.

There's more...

SMS table spaces have different space allocation behavior. We also have to take into account their limits, as compared to DMS table spaces, which we will cover next.

Space allocation

Space is allocated on demand, one page at a time, and is not preallocated, as in DMS table space. If the `multipage_alloc` database configuration parameter is set to `yes`, a full extent will be allocated when space is required.

When objects are deleted, the space is released to the filesystem. The database manager assigns names for each object created in this table space. Each object is spread on all containers, extents being allocated in round-robin fashion.

The SMS table space is considered full when one of the containers is full, so make sure all containers have the same space available on their respective filesystems.

Tables and objects

A table can be split into multiple table spaces by:

- ▶ Regular table data
- ▶ Indexes

Limits

- ▶ You cannot assign LONG or LOB data to an SMS table space
- ▶ You cannot define a large table space with SMS.

Filesystem caching

A SMS table space can make good use of filesystem caching. It is on by default, for SMS table spaces on all platforms. Let's not forget that, with filesystem caching, other O/S processes in the server will compete for this resource. We recommend that you use buffer pools, so that memory will be dedicated for your table space.

Limits

- ▶ You cannot define a large table space with SMS
- ▶ You cannot add or delete containers after the SMS table space is created
- ▶ You cannot specify `AUTORESIZE` on SMS table spaces

See also

The Creating and configuring buffer pools recipe in *Chapter 5, DB2 Buffer Pools*.

Creating and configuring DMS table spaces

With DMS, the database takes charge of space allocation for database objects, such as tables, indexes, and so on. The space is limited to the amount of space allocated for the container(s).

Benefits

In a nutshell, for large table spaces, DMS is the best choice:

- Since space is pre allocated, DMS table spaces yield better performance than SMS table spaces, on large volumes of data
- Container management is more flexible
- Space can be added by adding or extending containers

Getting ready

Determine the optimum page size for your table space. Create or choose a buffer pool with the corresponding page size. The following commands can be run through the command center or included in a script.

How to do it...

1. Get current database parameters:

```
db2 => connect to nav;


    Database Connection Information

  Database server      = DB2/LINUXX8664 9.7.4
  SQL authorization ID = DB2INST1
  Local database alias = NAV


db2 => GET DB CFG;


    Database Configuration for Database
```

```
Database configuration release level              = 0x0d00
Database release level                            = 0x0d00
....
```

We'll look for specific items:

```
Database page size                                = 8192
Degree of parallelism              (DFT_DEGREE) = 1
Changed pages threshold        (CHNGPGS_THRESH) = 80
Default prefetch size (pages)  (DFT_PREFETCH_SZ) = AUTOMATIC


Default number of containers                      = 1
Default tablespace extentsize (pages)  (DFT_EXTENT_SZ) = 32
```

2. Create proper buffer pool, if necessary:

Determine the optimum page size for your table space. Create or choose a buffer pool with the corresponding page size. In the DB2 command center:

```
[db2inst1@nodedb21 ~]$ db2 "CREATE BUFFERPOOL NAV_BPT8K IMMEDIATE
SIZE 25600 PAGESIZE 8K"
DB20000I  The SQL command completed successfully.
```

3. Create table space:

We need to define containers manually, since DB2 does not manage them:

```
[db2inst1@nodedb21 ~]$ db2 "drop tablespace NAV_TBLS"
DB20000I  The SQL command completed successfully.
[db2inst1@nodedb21 ~]$ db2 "CREATE  LARGE  TABLESPACE NAV_TBLS
PAGESIZE 8 K
>        MANAGED BY DATABASE USING
>        (FILE '/data/db2/db2inst1/NODE0000/nav/nav_tbls.dbf' 100 M)
>        EXTENTSIZE 32K AUTORESIZE YES MAXSIZE 500 M
>        BUFFERPOOL NAV_BPT8K
>        NO FILE SYSTEM CACHING"
DB20000I  The SQL command completed successfully.
```

How it works...

The initial space specified is allocated on table space creation and is immediately available. When not specified, DB2 creates a large table space, which means tables can be larger, and have more than 255 rows per data page. We recommend you leave the default setting.

There's more...

We've just covered basic commands, but there are many more aspects to discuss concerning the implementation, and some of these have an important performance impact.

Raw partitions

A container in this type of table space can be defined as a regular OS file or can be defined as a raw partition.

We do not recommend the use of raw partitions, since this adds complexity in disk and space management. A well-tuned DMS table space, that has containers defined as data files, will perform as well as containers defined as raw partitions.

Space allocation

Space is preallocated in the DMS table space. When multiple containers are defined, they are filled in round-robin fashion, one extent in each container. When `autoresize` is used, the containers will grow automatically, until `maxsize` value is reached, or until the filesystem is full, whichever comes first.

Tables and objects

A table can be split into multiple table spaces by:

- ▶ Regular table data
- ▶ Indexes
- ▶ Long field and LOB data

Filesystem caching

When using DMS table spaces, you may want to avoid double buffering, since you're already caching into a buffer pool. Use the **NO FILE SYSTEM CACHING** option, especially on Unix environments, such as AIX or HP-UX. The default is **FILE SYSTEM CACHING**, so you need to disable it specifically. On Linux or Windows platforms, **NO FILE SYSTEM CACHING** is the default option.

 Table spaces containing LOBs or LONG VARCHAR are not buffered by buffer pools, so you may consider filesystem caching on those table spaces.

AIX systems have some requirements concerning I/O serialization, so it's better to consult your system administrator before using this feature.

Extent size

DB2 will write a certain number of pages, called an extent, to each container before skipping to the next container in a table space. This is called the extent size.

If not specified, DB2 will use the default extent size provided, on database creation, by `dft_extent_sz`. If `dft_extent_sz` is not specified on database creation, the default extent size will be set to 32 pages.

If you have **RAID (Redundant Array of Independent Disks)** available, set extent size to RAID stripe size, so that reading an extent will access all disks.

Prefetch size

In order to satisfy a query, DB2 will have to read data. The goal of prefetching is to read as many pages as possible, so that the query will use most of the rows read from these pages. This means fewer I/O operations need to be performed.

The database default parameter, `dft_prefetch_sz` is AUTOMATIC when not specified at database creation. This database parameter can be changed later on. If you do not specify a prefetch size, the default database value will be used.

When the CPU is idle and waiting for I/O, increasing this value can help; so, it's likely the database will need the records contained in those pages.

If you want to configure the prefetch size for your table space, consider the number of containers, and if you are using RAID, the number of disks in the stripe set. With RAID devices, you should also set the `DB2_PARALLEL_IO` registry variable, to ensure DB2 knows you are using a RAID configuration.

Striping strategy

If you do not have RAID installed or available, you can create multiple containers for the same table space, ideally spreading them on multiple disks. DB2 will stripe data on all containers. When RAID is available, though, only one container will be sufficient. Check with your storage manager about your SAN/NAS configuration.

High water mark

The high water mark is the highest extent or page number allocated in this table space. This means that the high water mark may remain high, though there may be lots of free space. Reorganizing a table space will help set the water mark at the right level.

See also

- ▸ *Chapter 5, DB2 Buffer Pools*
- ▸ *Altering table spaces recipe in this chapter*
- ▸ *Chapter 13, DB2 Tuning and Optimization*

Using system temporary table spaces

Used mostly for sorts or joins, which are managed by DB2 (so there is no intervention necessary), a system temporary table space can also be used for reorganizations. This is what we'll discuss here.

Getting ready

Identify a system temporary table space that matches the page size of the table space containing the table you want to reorganize.

How to do it...

1. Connect to database:

   ```
   [db2inst1@nodedb21 ~]$ db2 connect to nav


      Database Connection Information

   Database server       = DB2/LINUXX8664 9.7.4
   SQL authorization ID  = DB2INST1
   Local database alias  = NAV
   ```

2. List table spaces:

   You will get the table space ID to manipulate the containers for this table space as well as the page size and other relevant information.

   ```
   [db2inst1@nodedb21 ~]$ db2 list tablespaces show detail
   ….
   Tablespace ID            = 3
   Name                     = NAV_TBLS
   Type                     = Database managed space
   Contents                 = All permanent data. Large table space.
   State                            = 0x0000
     Detailed explanation:
       Normal
   Total pages              = 6400
   Useable pages            = 6384
   Used pages               = 2416
   Free pages               = 3968
   ```

```
High water mark (pages)              = 2416
Page size (bytes)                    = 8192
Extent size (pages)                  = 16
Prefetch size (pages)                = 16
Number of containers                 = 1
```

3. Create temporary table space, if needed:

   Here, we chose to create a 200 M temporary table space on a manual storage database:

   ```
   CREATE SYSTEM TEMPORARY TABLESPACE TEMP8K  PAGESIZE 8K

   MANAGED BY DATABASE USING (
       FILE '/data/db2/db2inst1/NODE0000/nav/temp8k.dbf' 200 M )
       AUTORESIZE YES MAXSIZE 500 M;
   ```

4. Actual reorganization:

   ```
   REORG TABLE NAV.AIRPORT ALLOW NO ACCESS USE TEMP8K;
   ```

How it works...

DB2 will use this system temporary table space to process sorts or internal operations. In this case, DB2 will use the TEMP8K temporary table space to do its reorg for table NAV.AIRPORT. It allows for better performance and less space requirements.

There's more...

Consider space allocation of your tables in relation to page size.

Reorgs

For system temporary table spaces, find table spaces that have the same page size. You should consider allocating at least enough space to contain the largest table or partition for this page size.

Using user temporary table spaces

User temporary table spaces are used for storing temporary tables used by an application. Tables created within this table space are dropped when the application disconnects from the database.

Getting ready

Check whether there is any other user temporary table space with the same page size. Only one per page size is enough.

How to do it...

1. Connect to database:

```
[db2inst1@nodedb21 ~]$ db2 connect to nav


        Database Connection Information

 Database server        = DB2/LINUXX8664 9.7.4
 SQL authorization ID   = DB2INST1
 Local database alias   = NAV
```

2. List the table spaces:

   Let's see if there are any existing table spaces, but with the same page size; the *show detail* option is used to include the page size in the output.

   You will get the table space ID to manipulate the containers for this table space as well as the page size and other relevant information.

```
[db2inst1@nodedb21 ~]$ db2 list tablespaces show detail


             Tablespaces for Current Database

        Tablespace ID                       = 0
        Name                                = SYSCATSPACE
        ...
        Number of containers                = 1
```

TEMPSPACE1 is a system temporary table space, not a user temporary table space, so we leave it

```
Tablespace ID                       = 1
Name                                = TEMPSPACE1
Type                                = Database managed space
Contents                            = System Temporary data
State                               = 0x0000
  Detailed explanation:
    Normal
Total pages                         = 6400
```

```
Useable pages                        = 6368
Used pages                           = 64
Free pages                           = 6304
High water mark (pages)              = 64
Page size (bytes)                    = 8192
Extent size (pages)                  = 32
Prefetch size (pages)                = 32
Number of containers                 = 1
...
```

We created NAV_TBLS and NAV_INDX table spaces:

```
Tablespace ID                        = 3
Name                                 = NAV_TBLS
Type                                 = Database managed space
Contents                             = All permanent data. Large
table space.
State                                = 0x0000
  Detailed explanation:
     Normal
Total pages                          = 6400
Useable pages                        = 6384
Used pages                           = 2416
Free pages                           = 3968
High water mark (pages)              = 2416
Page size (bytes)                    = 8192
Extent size (pages)                  = 16
Prefetch size (pages)                = 16
Number of containers                 = 1

Tablespace ID                        = 4
Name                                 = NAV_INDX
Type                                 = Database managed space
Contents                             = All permanent data. Large
table space.
State                                = 0x0000
  Detailed explanation:
     Normal
Total pages                          = 6400
Useable pages                        = 6384
Used pages                           = 704
Free pages                           = 5680
```

```
High water mark (pages)              = 720
Page size (bytes)                    = 8192
Extent size (pages)                  = 16
Prefetch size (pages)                = 16
Number of containers                 = 1
```

. . .

3. Create temporary table space:

Since there are no user temporary table spaces, we'll use this command from the command editor to create a temporary table space with an 8 KB page size and an initial size of 100 MB, capable of growing up to a maximum size of 500 MB.

```
CREATE USER TEMPORARY TABLESPACE NAVTEMP8K  PAGESIZE 8K
MANAGED BY DATABASE USING (
   FILE '/data/db2/db2inst1/NODE0000/nav/navtemp8k.dbf' 100 M )
   AUTORESIZE YES MAXSIZE 500 M;
```

How it works...

Once the table space is created, users can use this table space to create their temporary tables.

When you list the table spaces again, you will see this entry:

```
Tablespace ID                        = 7
Name                                 = NAVTEMP8K
Type                                 = Database managed space
Contents                             = User Temporary data
State                                = 0x0000
  Detailed explanation:
    Normal
Total pages                          = 6400
Useable pages                        = 6368
Used pages                           = 64
Free pages                           = 6304
High water mark (pages)              = 64
Page size (bytes)                    = 8192
Extent size (pages)                  = 32
Prefetch size (pages)                = 32
Number of containers                 = 1
```

There's more...

Here's a tip or two for temporary table spaces and how to make the best choice between SMS and DMS table spaces.

Page size for temporary table space

Take the largest page size from your user table spaces, and define your temporary table space with that page size. You could also create as many temporary table spaces to match the different page sizes.

SMS or DMS?

If you expect to have heavy processing and sort large amounts of data, DMS is the best choice. SMS is better suited for small tables that expand and shrink a lot.

See also

▶ The *Creating and configuring buffer pools* in *Chapter 5, DB2 Buffer Pools*

▶ The *Using temporary tables* in *Chapter 6, Database Objects*

Altering table spaces and dropping table spaces

Altering a table space allows you to modify storage characteristics of a table space in the following ways:

▶ Container management

▶ Size management

▶ Physical characteristics

▶ Performance characteristics

Automatic storage table spaces have different sets of requirements and possibilities than manual storage table spaces. Please refer to the documentation for more details.

Getting ready

When dropping a table space, evaluate the impact on underlying objects and, ideally, arrange to be able to recover with a table space backup or with import/load utilities.

When altering a table space, obtain as much information as possible to evaluate the space or performance impact, if possible. This could be the filesystem sizes, the current space allocation for containers, or anything related to the characteristics you want to change.

How to do it...

To obtain useful information on table spaces and containers, you can use the following commands:

1. Connect to database:

```
[db2inst1@nodedb21 ~]$ db2 connect to nav


      Database Connection Information

   Database server        = DB2/LINUXX8664 9.7.4
   SQL authorization ID   = DB2INST1
   Local database alias   = NAV
```

2. List table spaces:

   You will get the table space ID to manipulate the containers for this table space as well as the page size and other relevant information.

```
[db2inst1@nodedb21 ~]$ db2 list tablespaces show detail
....
   Tablespace ID            = 3
   Name                     = NAV_TBLS
   Type                     = Database managed space
   Contents                 = All permanent data. Large table space.
   State                    = 0x0000
     Detailed explanation:
       Normal
   Total pages              = 6400
   Useable pages            = 6384
   Used pages               = 2416
   Free pages               = 3968
   High water mark (pages)  = 2416
   Page size (bytes)        = 8192
   Extent size (pages)      = 16
   Prefetch size (pages)    = 16
   Number of containers     = 1
```

3. Obtain container ID from the container list:

   With the table space ID, you can list its containers. With the container IDs, you will be able to manipulate the containers for this table space as well as the page size and other relevant information.

   ```
   [db2inst1@nodedb21 ~]$  db2 list tablespace containers for 3
   show detail
   ```

   ```
                Tablespace Containers for Tablespace 3


   Container ID                        = 0
   Name                                = /data/db2/db2inst1/
                                         NODE0000/nav/nav_tbls.dbf
   Type                                = File
   Total pages                         = 6400
   Useable pages                       = 6384
   Accessible                          = Yes
   ```

How it works...

When a table space is dropped, all objects are dropped and the corresponding containers and directories created by DB2 are deleted. Objects dependent on those contained in that table space will be dropped as well. Any packages that reference these objects will be invalidated.

There's more...

For non-automatic storage table spaces, you can manage the size, physical, or performance characteristics of its containers. This applies also to a database that has been converted to automatic storage but still has non-automatic storage table spaces.

In an automatic storage database, all the table spaces usually have automatic storage, so the following commands affecting size, containers, and characteristics, do not apply.

Container management

These commands are restricted to existing manual storage table spaces. You cannot rename a container.

► Adding a container:

   Here we add an additional 100 MB container to the table space.

   ```
   ALTER TABLESPACE NAV_TBLS ADD (
   FILE '/data/db2/db2inst1/NODE0000/nav/nav_tbls_02.dbf' 100 M );
   ```

▶ Dropping a container:

Here we drop this container from the table space. DB2 may complain if there are objects contained in this table space.

```
ALTER TABLESPACE NAV_TBLS DROP (
FILE '/data/db2/db2inst1/NODE0000/nav/nav_tbls_02.dbf' );
```

▶ Lower high water mark:

This will move the extents as low as possible, in the table space. It does not shrink the table space containers.

```
ALTER TABLESPACE NAV_TBLS LOWER HIGH WATER MARK;
```

Size management

You can operate on a single or all containers of a table space. We recommend having as many containers as possible, with the same size.

▶ Resize containers:

This command will bring all containers in this table space to a size of 2048 pages each, so, for an 8 KB page size, the total size will be 204800 X 8 KB = 1638400 KB = 1600 MB

```
ALTER TABLESPACE NAV_TBLS RESIZE ( ALL CONTAINERS 204800 );
```

▶ Extending:

This command will extend all containers in this table space by 100 MB each.

```
ALTER TABLESPACE NAV_TBLS EXTEND ( ALL CONTAINERS 100 M );
```

▶ Reducing:

This command will shrink all containers in this table space by 20 MB each. For non-automatic storage table spaces, DB2 will try first to reduce the high water mark before shrinking the containers. On automatic storage table spaces, the effect is different. This will reduce the high water mark to the new water mark.

```
ALTER TABLESPACE NAV_INDX REDUCE ( ALL CONTAINERS 20 M );
```

Physical characteristics

The physical disk characteristics of a table space influence DB2's optimizer. The reasons are as follows:

▶ Disk characteristics

The following command is just an example; it sets the I/O controller overhead, disk seek, and disk latency time. Please determine these numbers with the help of the Unix and Storage teams.

The transfer rate is the time it takes to read one page into memory. Times are in milliseconds and are used to determine I/O costs for DB2's query optimizer. We can use these numbers, for example, in a QA environment, to simulate production performance characteristics.

```
ALTER TABLESPACE NAV_TBLS OVERHEAD 10.5 TRANSFERRATE 0.14;
```

▶ **Table space storage configuration**

The next command modifies a regular DMS table space to a large table space. Certain restrictions apply for partitioned tables with partitions in different table spaces. The table space and its contents are locked during conversion, so this should be done in offline maintenance hours.

```
ALTER TABLESPACE NAV_TBLS CONVERT TO LARGE;
```

Performance characteristics

Caching configuration has an impact on performance. Automatic settings are recommended.

▶ **Set prefetch size**

It sets the prefetch size of a table space to be managed by DB2 automatically. DB2 will update the prefetch size when adding or removing containers.

```
ALTER TABLESPACE NAV_TBLS PREFETCHSIZE AUTOMATIC;
```

▶ **Disable filesystem caching**

Disables filesystem level cache for all I/O operations on this table space. It is disabled by default on Windows and Linux, but this is useful on Unix systems, where filesystem caching is enabled by default.

```
ALTER TABLESPACE NO FILE SYSTEM CACHING;
```

Dropping table space

This task is straightforward—from the db2 command line issue the following command:

```
DROP TABLESPACE NAV_TBLS;
```

See also

The Backing up table spaces recipe in *Chapter 7, DB2 Backup and Recovery*

The Altering databases recipe in *Chapter 2, Administration and Configuration of the DB2 Non-partitioned Database*

Table spaces in a multipartitioned environment

When you create a table space in a partition group with more than one partition, the tables will be distributed to each database partition. Normally, we would place large tables in those partition groups that span all or most of the partitions. This setup makes the best use of the hardware configuration.

For OLTP, you should consider using a partition group with one partition, while using multipartitioned groups for DSS tables. We will see here how to create tables spaces and discuss how to distribute data.

Getting ready

If you're not using automatic storage, ensure you have a naming convention that lets you correctly identify and manage database partitions. The database partition group must already exist.

How to do it...

This command creates a table space with one file container on each partition. We'll use the default partition group in this command.

```
CREATE   LARGE   TABLESPACE NAV_TBLS PAGESIZE 8 K
MANAGED BY DATABASE
USING ( FILE  '/data/db2/db2instp/NODE000 $N /NAV/nav_tbls_p $N .dbf'
 100 M )
AUTORESIZE YES MAXSIZE 500 M;
```

How it works...

DB2 will understand $N to mean the database partition number. Make sure you insert the blank before and after the $N. So, for a three-partition database, this command will create three file containers:

```
/data/db2/db2instp/NODE0001/NAV/nav_tbls_p1.dbf
/data/db2/db2instp/NODE0002/NAV/nav_tbls_p2.dbf
/data/db2/db2instp/NODE0003/NAV/nav_tbls_p2.dbf
```

There's more...

Partitioned databases need special attention paid to table space definitions. The distribution map and distribution key influence the table space distribution across partitions. Beware of changes affecting the table space state, as we'll see further.

Distribution maps

A distribution map is generated automatically by DB2, on table space creation, and ensures an even distribution of data across the partitions. A hashing algorithm based on the distribution key will determine the partition to use for storing each table row. In DB2 v9.7, the distribution map now has 32,768 entries (32 KB) instead of 4,096 (4KB).

Redistribution may be required when adding or removing partitions. Please refer to *Chapter 3, DB2 Multipartitioned Databases—Administration and Configuration*, for more details.

Distribution keys

A distribution key is defined when you create a table and is used by DB2 to determine into which partition each row will be stored. When not defined, DB2 will use the first column of the primary key.

Table space containers

If you have more than one partition on the same node, the same path cannot be used twice. Use a unique container for each partition.

Partition groups

When you are allocating the table space, you can associate it with a database partition group. This cannot be changed, once it is done.

When no partition group is specified, the table space will be assigned to the default group (IBMDEFAULTGROUP). This is for regular, large, or user temporary table spaces.

The IBMTEMPGROUP group will be used by default for system temporary table spaces.

Just for illustration purposes, suppose we have five partitions; we can create a partition group using only three partitions, in the following fashion.

1. Create partition group:

```
CONNECT TO NAV;
CREATE DATABASE PARTITION GROUP NAVDATAGRP ON DBPARTITIONNUMS
(0,1,2);
```

2. Create buffer pools for this partition group:

   Create a buffer pool for tables and the other one for indexes.

   ```
   db2 "CREATE BUFFERPOOL NAV_BPT8K IMMEDIATE DATABASE PARTITION
   GROUP "NAVDATAGRP" SIZE 1000 AUTOMATIC PAGESIZE 8 K "
   db2 "CREATE BUFFERPOOL NAV_BPI8K IMMEDIATE  DATABASE PARTITION
   GROUP "NAVDATAGRP" SIZE 1000 AUTOMATIC PAGESIZE 8 K
   ```

3. Create table space:

   ```
   db2 "CREATE  LARGE  TABLESPACE NAV_TBLS IN DATABASE PARTITION
   GROUP "NAVDATAGRP" PAGESIZE 8 K  MANAGED BY DATABASE
     USING ( FILE '/data/db2/db2instp/nav_tbls0p $N .dbf' 2560 )
   EXTENTSIZE 16 OVERHEAD 10.5 PREFETCHSIZE 16 TRANSFERRATE 0.14
   BUFFERPOOL  NAV_BPT8K"
   ```

   ```
   db2 "CREATE  LARGE  TABLESPACE NAV_INDX IN DATABASE PARTITION
   GROUP "NAVDATAGRP" PAGESIZE 8 K  MANAGED BY DATABASE
     USING ( FILE '/data/db2/db2instp/nav_indx0p $N .dbf' 2560 )
    EXTENTSIZE 16 OVERHEAD 10.5 PREFETCHSIZE 16 TRANSFERRATE 0.14
   BUFFERPOOL  NAV_BPI8K"
   ```

4. Create objects:

   We'll discuss creating tables in partitioned databases in *Chapter 6, Database Objects*.

Table space state

A REDISTRIBUTE DATABASE PARTITION GROUP command redistributes data across all partitions in a database partition group. When issued with the NOT ROLLFORWARD RECOVERABLE option, this will leave all its table spaces in BACKUP PENDING state. Tables will not be accessible until a backup has been made.

Storage paths in an automatic storage-partitioned database

When adding a storage path, as in our example, you can use the same naming convention for a partition using the NODE000 $N clause. You may then have filesystems configured for each partition, if you wish.

See also

- ▶ *The Creating and configuring a multipartitioned database* recipe in *Chapter 3, DB2 multi-partitioned databases—Administration and Configuration*
- ▶ *The Creating and configuring buffer pools* recipe in *Chapter 5, DB2 Buffer Pools*
- ▶ *The Implementing table partitioning* recipe in *Chapter 6, Database Objects*
- ▶ *The Database rollforward recovery* recipe in *Chapter 7, DB2 Backup and Recovery*
- ▶ *The I/O tuning* recipe in *Chapter 13, DB2 Tuning and Optimization*

5
DB2 Buffer Pools

In this chapter, we will cover:

- ► Creating and configuring buffer pools
- ► Configuring block-based area
- ► Managing buffer pools in a multipartitioned database
- ► Altering buffer pools
- ► Dropping buffer pools

Introduction

DB2 allows caching data read from disk into buffer pools. As reading from memory is faster than reading from disk, the buffer pools play an important part in database performance.

The block-based area is used to take advantage of prefetching—we'll see how to make the best use of it.

You may want to limit buffer pools to specific partitions or learn a little more about partitioning and managing buffer pools.

The actual maintenance of buffer pools themselves is relatively straightforward. We may need to alter or drop buffer pools, in the normal course of database evolution. We'll guide you through the steps and, together, see how it's done.

Creating and configuring buffer pools

A default buffer pool, IBMDEFAULTBP, is created when you create any database. As IBMDEFAULTBP is treated as a system object, it cannot be dropped. You may, and should create other buffer pools to optimize memory use.

Getting ready

A default buffer pool, IBMDEFAULTBP, is created when you create any database. As ' is treated as a system object, it cannot be dropped.

Each table space is associated with a buffer pool, when you create a table space. This IBMDEFAULTBP buffer pool will be used if you do not specify one.

> You should create the buffer pools first, before creating your table spaces.

Get your Operating System's memory configuration and database software's capacity. Determine if you want to use self memory tuning on this database, or manual memory tuning. As you will associate table spaces to buffer pools, it is important to match the buffer pool page size to the page size of the table space.

How to do it...

1. Get the database level:

   ```
   [db2inst1@nodedb21 ~]$ db2level
   DB21085I  Instance "db2inst1" uses "64" bits and DB2 code release
   "SQL09074"with level identifier "08050107".
   Informational tokens are "DB2 v9.7.0.4", "s110330", "IP23243", and
   Fix Pack"4".
   Product is installed at "/opt/IBM/DB2/v9.7.4".
   ```

   We have 64-bit database software. So, for a 64-bit system, the buffer pool can be set to practically any size you want. For an OLTP application, the buffer pool should not need more than 10 GB. If you have 32-bit database software, please consult the appropriate documentation to ensure proper limits and configuration.

2. Get the database configuration:

   ```
   [db2inst1@nodedb21 ~]$ db2 get db cfg
           Database Configuration for Database
   ```

   We'll be looking for parameters related to memory management.

   ```
   Database page size                                          = 8192
   ```

What is important here, from a memory standpoint, is that DB2 is using self-tuning memory, and that the memory is allocated dynamically to the database (DATABASE_MEMORY is set to AUTOMATIC).

```
 Self tuning memory                     (SELF_TUNING_MEM) = ON
 Size of database shared memory (4KB)   (DATABASE_MEMORY) =
AUTOMATIC(215120)
 Database memory threshold              (DB_MEM_THRESH) = 10
Skipping...
 Buffer pool size (pages)                      (BUFFPAGE) = 1000
```

3. See if other buffer pools exist:

    ```
    [db2inst1@nodedb21 ~]$ db2 "select substr(bpname,1,20)
    bpname,npages,pagesize from sysibm.sysbufferpools"
    BPNAME                   NPAGES       PAGESIZE
    -------------------- ----------- -----------
    IBMDEFAULTBP                1000        8192
    NAV_BPT8K                  25600        8192
    NAV_BPI8K                  12800        8192
      3 record(s) selected.
    ```

4. Create the buffer pool:

    ```
    [db2inst1@nodedb21 nav]$ db2 "create bufferpool nav_bpt32k
    immediate size automatic pagesize 32K"
    DB20000I  The SQL command completed successfully.
    ```

How it works...

In our NAV database, we already created 8 KB page size buffer pools. For our examples, let's assume that we'd like to create a future table space for other tables, with a page size of 32 KB.

We'll have to create a buffer pool to match this page size, as all other buffer pools have 8 KB page sizes. As the database has self memory tuning, we will let DB2 manage the number of pages by specifying automatic as the buffer pool size.

There's more...

Consider choosing between memory sizing and automatic memory management. Be aware of limits for AWE and ESTORE on Windows platforms.

Naming convention

We used the page size in our naming convention to easily identify the main characteristic of the buffer pools. Avoid using «IBM***» in buffer pool names; these should be reserved for the RDBMS only.

Specifying space size for the buffer pool

When you create a buffer pool and specify a size in terms of number of pages, DB2 will attempt to allocate space from the reserved space in the database shared memory. If it does not succeed, the created buffer pool is executed as DEFERRED, which means the buffer pool will be created when the database is deactivated.

If you specified the size to use, adding the AUTOMATIC keyword will set the initial space, and DB2 will manage the buffer pool's size.

Memory sizing

We recommend that you use automatic settings. However, if you define your buffer pools without self-tuning memory, you should make sure that the total space of buffer pools and database storage requirements does not exceed real memory storage; otherwise, you will induce memory swapping.

Windows 32-bit environments: Address Windowing Extensions (AWE) and Extended Storage (ESTORE)

Windows Address Windowing Extensions (AWE) and Extended Storage (ESTORE) have been discontinued. If you need more memory, you will have to upgrade to a 64-bit hardware Operating System, and DB2 software, too.

Hidden buffer pools

DB2 makes sure that an appropriate buffer pool is always available for a table space. When you create a database, DB2 creates a small buffer pool for each page size. These buffer pools—IBMSYSTEMBP4K, 8K, 16K, and 32K—are neither accessible nor visible from the system catalogs. They are strictly for internal use by DB2; for example, if a buffer pool is inactive or if there is insufficient memory, DB2 will remain functional, but the performance will decrease.

See also

> ▶ The *Creating and configuring DMS table spaces* recipe in Chapter 4, *Storage—Using DB2 Table Spaces*

> ▶ The *Operating system tuning* recipe in Chapter 13, *DB2 Tuning and Optimization*

Configuring the block-based area

Buffer pools are defined as having a large number of pages by default, so when DB2 issues a prefetch, the pages read from the disk may not be stored contiguously in the buffer pool.

The block-based area enhances prefetching performance by allowing a contiguous area of the buffer pool for this eventuality, named the block area, or block-based area. Each set of contiguous pages is called a block; the number of pages in a block is referred to as the blocksize.

Getting ready

Make sure the application uses sequential prefetching; otherwise the block area of the block buffer is useless. Allow a time frame for a possible database restart.

How to do it...

1. Get the database configuration:

   ```
   [db2inst1@nodedb21 ~]$ db2 get db cfg
           Database Configuration for Database
   ```

   We'll be looking for parameters related to prefetching.

   ```
    Default prefetch size (pages)         (DFT_PREFETCH_SZ) =
   AUTOMATIC
    Default table space extentsize (pages)   (DFT_EXTENT_SZ) = 32
   ```

2. Get current characteristics of the buffer pools:

   ```
   [db2inst1@nodedb21 nav]$  db2 "select substr(bpname,1,20)
     bpname,npages,pagesize,
     numblockpages,blocksize
     from sysibm.sysbufferpools"
   ```

BPNAME	NPAGES	PAGESIZE	NUMBLOCKPAGES	BLOCKSIZE
IBMDEFAULTBP	1000	8192	0	0
NAV_BPT8K	25600	8192	0	0
NAV_BPI8K	12800	8192	0	0
NAV_BPT32K	-2	32768	0	0

   ```
     4 record(s) selected.
   ```

3. Use an existing buffer pool (or you can create one).

   In this example, we chose to use an existing buffer pool. We could have created one from scratch; the syntax is almost the same.

   ```
   [db2inst1@nodedb21 nav]$ db2 "alter bufferpool nav_bpt32k
   numblockpages 20 blocksize 4"
   ```

```
SQL20149W  The buffer pool operation has been completed but will
not take
effect until the next database restart.  SQLSTATE=01649
```

How it works...

In buffer pool NAV_BPT32K, we created a block area of 20 pages (20 x 32 KB = 640 KB), with a 128 KB (4 x 32 KB) block size, which allows five blocks.

 The change has been made, but we need to restart the database, so that the changes take effect.

```
[db2inst1@nodedb21 nav]$ db2 "select substr(bpname,1,15)
   bpname,npages,pagesize,
   numblockpages,blocksize
   from sysibm.sysbufferpools"
BPNAME            NPAGES       PAGESIZE     NUMBLOCKPAGES BLOCKSIZE
---------------   -----------  -----------  ------------- -----------
IBMDEFAULTBP          1000         8192               0           0
NAV_BPT8K            25600         8192               0           0
NAV_BPI8K            12800         8192               0           0
NAV_BPT32K              -2        32768              20           4
   4 record(s) selected.
```

There's more...

You can make use of RAID architecture to your advantage by using extent size and block size.

Block size and table space extent size

Use the maximum possible space for the table space's extent size to help you configure the prefetch size and block area. In our database, the default prefetch size is automatic.

Suppose we have a RAID disk array with a stripe size of 1280 KB, for example.

The minimum size for the buffer pool's block should be equal to the RAID stripe size, 1280 KB (40 x 32 KB).

```
[db2inst1@nodedb21 ~]$ db2 "create bufferpool nav_bpt2_32k
   immediate size automatic pagesize 32K
   numblockpages 200 blocksize 40"
DB20000I  The SQL command completed successfully.
```

To define our new table space with a page size of 32 KB, we create the table space with an extent size of 1280 KB (40 x 32 KB) and match with the prefetch size so that prefetching will read all disks in one shot.

```
[db2inst1@nodedb21 ~]$ db2 "create  large  table space nav_tbls2
pagesize 32 k
 pagesize 32 k
  managed by database
  using ( file
  '/data/db2/db2inst1/node0000/nav/nav_tbls2.dbf' 6400 )
  autoresize yes maxsize 500 m
  extentsize 40 prefetchsize 40
  bufferpool  nav_bpt2_32k "
DB20000I  The SQL command completed successfully.
```

See also

Block-based buffer pools for improved sequential prefetching at `http://publib.boulder.ibm.com/infocenter/db2luw/v9r7/index.jsp?topic=/com.ibm.db2.luw.admin.perf.doc/doc/c0009651.html`

Managing buffer pools in a multipartitioned database

Managing buffer pools in a partitioned environment is practically the same as a single-partitioned database. If you wish, you can use the defaults and let DB2 create buffer pools in all partitions.

A multi-partitioned database can have partitions dedicated to specific functions. Let's say that we have a new POS database with the following architecture: one partition for Ad-Hoc Reporting and four for DSS, which makes five partitions.

Getting ready

In a partitioned database, a buffer pool is defined on all database partitions, unless database partition groups are specified when creating the buffer pool. In this example, we would create two partition groups—posp_ahr and posp_dss.

How to do it...

1. Create partition groups.

   In this example, we will create two partition groups:

   ```
   posp_ahr:
   [db2instp@nodedb21 ~]$ db2 "create database partition group
     posp_ahr on dbpartitionnums (0)"
   DB20000I  The SQL command completed successfully.
   posp_dss:
   [db2instp@nodedb21 ~]$ db2 "create database partition group
     posp_dss on dbpartitionnums (1,2,3,4)"
   DB20000I  The SQL command completed successfully.
   [db2instp@nodedb21 ~]$ db2 list database partition groups
   DATABASE PARTITION GROUP
   ----------------------------
   IBMCATGROUP
   IBMDEFAULTGROUP
   POSP_AHR
   POSP_DSS
     4 record(s) selected.
   ```

2. Create the buffer pools.

   Now, for the sake of this example, we create an 8 K page size buffer pool for each partition group:

   ```
   [db2instp@nodedb21 ~]$ db2 "create bufferpool bp_posp_ahr8k
     immediate database partition group posp_ahr
     size automatic pagesize 8 K"
   DB20000I  The SQL command completed successfully.
   [db2instp@nodedb21 ~]$ db2 "create bufferpool bp_posp_dss8k
     immediate database partition group posp_dss
     size automatic pagesize 8 K"
   DB20000I  The SQL command completed successfully.
   ```

   We will also create a 32 K page size buffer pool for each partition group:

   ```
   [db2instp@nodedb21 ~]$ db2 "create bufferpool bp_posp_ahr32k
     immediate database partition group posp_ahr
     size automatic pagesize 32 K"
   DB20000I  The SQL command completed successfully.
   [db2instp@nodedb21 ~]$ db2 "create bufferpool bp_posp_dss32k
     immediate database partition group posp_dss
     size automatic pagesize 32 K"
   DB20000I  The SQL command completed successfully.
   ```

3. Create table spaces.

DB2 interprets $N as the database partition number. Make sure you insert the blank before and after the $N in the container's path.

Create the table spaces for AHR (Ad-Hoc Reporting):

```
[db2instp@nodedb21 ~]$ db2 "create large table space posp_ahr_tb8k
  in database partition group posp_ahr
  pagesize 8 k
  managed by database
  using ( file
'/data/db2/db2instp/NODE000 $N /posp/posp_ahr_tb8k.dbf' 2000 )>
autoresize yes
  bufferpool  bp_posp_ahr8k "
DB20000I  The SQL command completed successfully.
[db2instp@nodedb21 ~]$ db2 "create large  table space posp_ahr_
tb32k
  in database partition group posp_ahr
  pagesize 32 k
  managed by database
  using ( file
'/data/db2/db2instp/NODE000 $N /posp/posp_ahr_tb32k.dbf' 2000 )
  autoresize yes
  bufferpool  bp_posp_ahr32k"
DB20000I  The SQL command completed successfully.
```

Create the table spaces for DSS:

```
[db2instp@nodedb21 ~]$ db2 "create large  table space
  posp_dss_tb8k
  in database partition group posp_dss
  pagesize 8 k
  managed by database
  using ( file '/data/db2/db2instp/NODE000 $N /posp/
  posp_dss_tb8k.dbf' 2000 )
  autoresize yes
  bufferpool  bp_posp_dss8k "
DB20000I  The SQL command completed successfully.
[db2instp@nodedb21 ~]$ db2 "create large  table space
  posp_dss_tb32k
  in database partition group posp_dss
  pagesize 32 k
  managed by database
  using ( file
'/data/db2/db2instp/NODE000 $N /posp/posp_dss_tb32k.dbf' 2000 )
  autoresize yes
  bufferpool  bp_posp_dss32k"
DB20000I  The SQL command completed successfully.
```

How it works...

We configured in this example two partition groups, one for ad-hoc reporting and one for DSS. Four partitions will host the DSS partition group, and the other will host the ad-hoc partition group. This configuration allows for DSS processing, without compromising ad-hoc reporting.

There's more...

Each partition group has its own sets of buffer pools and table spaces. When you create the tables in DSS table spaces, your DSS application will make use of tables created in those partition groups. The same goes with the ad-hoc applications.

See also

> ▸ The *Creating and configuring a multipartitioned database* recipe in *Chapter 3, DB2 Multipartitioned Databases—Administration and Configuration*

> ▸ The *Creating and configuring table spaces in a multipartitioned environment* recipe in *Chapter 4, Storage--Using DB2 Table Spaces*

Altering buffer pools

The characteristics of buffer pools that you can change are: the buffer's size, the automatic sizing, database partition groups, and block area. Other attributes cannot be changed, apart from dropping and recreating the buffer pool with the desired specifications.

Getting ready

Depending on what you want to change, you may need down time to restart the database.

How to do it...

In our last example, we wanted to use prefetching in this buffer pool. We defined only 20 pages (20 x 32 KB = 640 KB). We want to alter it to 1280 KB, which will give us 10 blocks:

```
[db2inst1@nodedb21 nav]$ db2 "alter bufferpool nav_bpt32k
  numblockpages 40 blocksize 4"
SQL20149W  The buffer pool operation has been completed but will
not take
effect until the next database restart.  SQLSTATE=01649
```

How it works...

Note here that the change has been made, but we need to restart the database so the change takes effect.

```
[db2inst1@nodedb21 nav]$ db2 "select substr(bpname,1,15)
   bpname,npages,pagesize,
   numblockpages,blocksize
   from sysibm.sysbufferpools"
BPNAME            NPAGES        PAGESIZE    NUMBLOCKPAGES BLOCKSIZE
---------------   -----------   ----------- ------------- -----------
IBMDEFAULTBP           1000          8192              0           0
NAV_BPT8K            25600          8192              0           0
NAV_BPI8K            12800          8192              0           0
NAV_BPT32K             -2         32768             24           4
   4 record(s) selected.
```

There's more...

Here are some things to consider before creating or altering buffer pools, as some settings cannot change after creation and other settings change the buffer pool's behavior.

Page size

You cannot alter the page size of a buffer pool once it's created. We suggest this recipe as a work around.

1. Create a new buffer pool, or pick an existing one as target buffer pool.
2. Alter your table space to use the new target buffer pool.
3. Drop or reuse the original buffer pool for another table space.

Buffer pool size

You can specify a new size for the buffer pool.

Self-tuning

The AUTOMATIC keyword enables self-tuning. DB2 will adjust the size, depending on the work load. If you specify a size for the buffer pool, then self-tuning will be deactivated.

Partitions

You can change the buffer pool size on all database partitions or on one partition only.

Partition groups

You can add a partition group to the list of applicable partition groups for this buffer pool. If any partition in the partition group does not already have a buffer pool defined, the buffer pool is created on that database partition, with the default size specified for the buffer pool.

See also

▶ *Chapter 3, DB2 Multipartioned Databases—Administration and Configuration*

▶ *Chapter 4, Storage—Using DB2 Table Spaces*

▶ *Chapter 13, DB2 Tuning and Optimization*

Dropping buffer pools

When you no longer need a buffer pool, you can drop it. Another alternative is to set it to automatic tuning, so it will not take up unneeded space.

Getting ready

Ensure no table spaces have been assigned to this buffer pool.

How to do it...

1. Create a fictitious buffer pool to be dropped later.

   In this example, this buffer pool should have been created in another database:

   ```
   [db2inst1@nodedb21 nav]$ db2 "create bufferpool pos_bpt32k
   pagesize 32 K"
   DB20000I  The SQL command completed successfully.
   ```

2. View the table space association list.

3. If the mistake has not been detected early enough, we may want to check if a table space has been associated with it:

   ```
   [db2inst1@nodedb21 nav]$ db2 "select
     substr(ts.tbspace,1,20),substr(bp.bpname,1,20)
     from sysibm.systable spaces ts right outer join
     sysibm.sysbufferpools bp
     on bp.bufferpoolid = ts.bufferpoolid"
   1                    2
   -------------------- --------------------
   SYSCATSPACE          IBMDEFAULTBP
   TEMPSPACE1           IBMDEFAULTBP
   USERSPACE1           IBMDEFAULTBP
   ```

```
NAV_TBLS              NAV_BPT8K
NAV_INDX              NAV_BPI8K
SYSTOOLSPACE          IBMDEFAULTBP
SYSTOOLSTMPSPACE      IBMDEFAULTBP
-                     POS_BPT32K
   8 record(s) selected.
Identify the buffer pool we want to delete, (POS_BPT32K)
```

The outer join is important, because it picks up the buffer pools without associations.

4. Drop the buffer pool:

```
[db2inst1@nodedb21 nav]$ db2 drop bufferpool nav_bpt32k
DB20000I  The SQL command completed successfully.
```

How it works...

Buffer pool memory is made immediately available to the database manager.

There's more...

Consider the following when dropping a buffer pool:

IBMDEFAULTBP

You cannot drop this buffer pool, as it is used as default. All table spaces must have a buffer pool assigned, so when a table space is created without specifying a buffer pool, DB2 will use this as default buffer pool.

Dependencies

DB2 keeps track of dependencies, so you can't drop a buffer pool if there's an associated table space.

```
[db2inst1@nodedb21 ~]$ db2 drop bufferpool NAV_BPI8K;
DB21034E  The command was processed as an SQL statement because it
was not a valid Command Line Processor command.  During SQL
processing it returned:
SQL0478N  DROP, ALTER, TRANSFER OWNERSHIP or REVOKE on object type
"BUFFERPOOL" cannot be processed because there is an object
"NAV_INDX", of type "TABLE SPACE", which depends on it.
SQLSTATE=42893
```

See also

- *The Creating and configuring a multipartitioned database recipe in Chapter 3, DB2 Multipartitioned Databases—Administration and Configuration*

- *The I/O tuning recipe in Chapter 13, DB2 Tuning and Optimization*

- *The Dropping table spaces recipe in Chapter 4, Storage—Using DB2 Table Spaces*

6
Database Objects

In this chapter, we will cover:

- ▸ Creating and using MDC tables and block-based indexes
- ▸ Creating and using materialized query tables
- ▸ Implementing table partitioning
- ▸ Using temporary tables

Introduction

Multidimensional Clustering (**MDC**), **Materialized Query Tables** (**MQT**), and **Partitioning** are the key techniques used for efficient data warehousing. We will elaborate on these topics in this chapter.

Since these are advanced topics, we will assume here that you have a basic knowledge of objects such as tables, indexes, and views, and their creation and maintenance as well. MDC is primarily intended for data warehousing and **Decision Support Systems** (**DSS**) environments, but can also be used in **Online Transaction Processing** (**OLTP**) situations. Combined with database partitioning, it delivers a scalable and effective solution, reduces performance problems and logging, and provides easier table maintenance.

Creating and using MDC tables and block-based indexes

MDC provides automatic and continuous data clustering on more than one dimension, simultaneously. This method results in significant performance enhancement of queries based on dimensions defined for a table.

Getting ready

We'll have to examine the database configuration for our table and determine the best way to cluster the data. We also have to ensure we have enough space for this table.

How to do it...

1. Determine dimension candidates:

   At the design stage, you might have to determine the dimensions with a data architect, to determine if an MDC is preferable.

   Good candidates for dimensions are columns with low cardinality, that is, the percentage of different values relative to the number of records. The columns should also have as much as possible a static value, and be used frequently in queries. For an existing table, you can do some research, using the RUNSTATS utility, as discussed further, in the *Using runstats to determine dimension candidates* recipe, in this chapter. For example, a timestamp would not be a good choice, since you will end up with one row per dimension. You can use a derived column, as in our case, based on the year and month of the sales date.

   Good candidates include:

   - Columns used for range queries
   - Roll-in or roll-out
   - Columns referenced in the group by or order by clauses

2. Identify dimensions:

   Each dimension will have its own block index and adds overhead to the process of inserting, updating, or deleting. It's less intensive than a regular index, though. Usually, three or four dimensions should be enough.

   Identify frequent queries that have the group by or order by clauses.

   The following SELECT will return the number of combinations of the dimensions, that is, Stores and Sales date (year and month only). Compared with the table's size, this should have a low cardinality, for example, 1-10 percent should provide a good base; if that is still too much, add another dimension, if applicable.

```
SELECT DISTINCT
   STORE, INTEGER(SALESDATE)/100
FROM POS.SALES
```

3. Estimate space:

An MDC table will use more space than a regular table, depending on the block size (extent size) used and number of cells. We estimate the number of cells by multiplying the cardinality of each dimension:

```
[db2inst1@ nodedb21 ~]$ db2 "select  card, avgrowsize

>        from    sysstat.tables

>        where   tabschema = 'POS'

>        and     tabname   = 'SALES'"


CARD                    AVGROWSIZE

-------------------- ----------

         133109108          88


 1 record(s) selected.
```

So, for 20 stores and a 10-year history, we can determine:

Stores (20) X Years (10) X Months (12). With a table of 135 million rows, we have an average of 56,250 rows per cell. For each 32K page we have 372 records per page:	
Stores (20) X Years (10) X Months (12)	2400 Cells
Cardinality 135,000,000 / Avg RowSz (88)	56,250 rows per cell
PageSize (32768) / Avg RowSz (88)	372 rows per page
Rows per cell (56,250) / Rows per page (372)	151 extents per cell
151 extents X 32 KB pagesize X 2400 cells	11,596,800 KB or 11.5 GB

We estimate this table to require at least 11.5 GB.

4. Create the table:

We create an MDC table using the ORGANIZE BY DIMENSIONS clause, as follows:

```
[db2inst1@nodedb21 ~]$ db2 "CREATE TABLE POS.MDC_SALES (
    salesdate     date          NOT NULL,
    store         decimal(6,0)  NOT NULL,
    sku           varchar(15)   NOT NULL,
    qty           decimal(15,2) NOT NULL,
    pxunit        decimal(15,2) NOT NULL,
    unit          varchar(2)    NOT NULL,
    categ         decimal(1,0)  NOT NULL,
    stotal        decimal(15,2) NOT NULL,
```

```
    year_month      generated as (integer(salesdate)/100)
)
    ORGANIZE BY DIMENSIONS ( store, year_month )
    IN pos_dss_tb32k"
DB20000I  The SQL command completed successfully.
```

How it works...

MDC's clustering is achieved by storing together rows with the same dimension, so that all rows in the same block have the same dimension. The main advantage of MDC is that clustering is always maintained, which results in query performance improvement and a significant reduction in maintenance overhead for operations such as insert, update, delete, reorganizations, and index maintenance.

When the table is created, a block index is created for each dimension, and another composite block index will contain all dimension key columns. Block indexes are the same as regular indexes but point to blocks instead of records. The index does not have to hold an index entry for every record, so this makes them much smaller than the regular index. This improves query performance, since fewer index pages have to be read.

There's more...

We'll see here how to address indexing for aggregate functions and combine MDC with a partitioned database.

Block indexes and aggregate functions in queries

There may be empty blocks in a dimension block index, so queries that have EXISTS, MIN, MAX, or DISTINCT will cause DB2 to perform physical reads on the table, in order to satisfy the request, which will degrade performance. Create regular indexes to enable index-only access in those cases.

Block size and extents

The terms **block** and **extent** mean the same thing and are interchangeable. You cannot alter the extent size after the table space is created.

Using runstats to determine dimension candidates

1. RUNSTATS on table: The RUNSTATS utility analyzes the POS.SALES table, computing distribution on potential dimension candidates, and stores in the SYSSTAT.COLDIST table, the 10 values that most frequently appear within the POS.SALES table, and the frequency for each of the 10 values.

   ```
   RUNSTATS ON TABLE POS.SALES ON ALL COLUMNS WITH DISTRIBUTION ON
   COLUMNS ( YEARMTH ) AND INDEXES ALL ALLOW WRITE ACCESS ;
   ```

2. Analyze data distribution: We see, in the following code, that the YEARMTH field covers much of the table. If the sum of the frequencies approaches the total number of rows, and they are evenly distributed, then this is an excellent dimension candidate.

```
[db2inst1@nodedb21 ~]$ db2 "select substr(colname,1,10) "colname",
>              type,seqno,
>              substr(colvalue,1,10) "colvalue",
>              valcount,distcount
>      from    sysstat.coldist
>      where   tabschema = 'POS'
>      and     tabname   = 'FACTURES'
>      and     colname   in ('YEARMTH')
>      and     type      = 'F'"
```

COLNAME	TYPE	SEQNO	COLVALUE	VALCOUNT	DISTCOUNT
YEARMTH	F	1	201007	829	
YEARMTH	F	2	201006	718	
YEARMTH	F	3	201008	561	
YEARMTH	F	4	201009	303	
YEARMTH	F	5	201105	202	
YEARMTH	F	6	201104	192	
YEARMTH	F	7	201010	127	
YEARMTH	F	8	201101	91	
YEARMTH	F	9	201011	88	
YEARMTH	F	10	201103	86	

```
10 record(s) selected.
```

Restrictions on dimensions

A dimension must be defined in the table and can appear only once. An XML column cannot be used as a dimension.

Loading an MDC for best performance, sort the data by the dimension columns before loading. To improve performance, consider increasing the values of the parameters UTIL_HEAP_SIZE, SORTHEAP, and SHEAPTHRES_SHR, because of the build clause for the dimension indexes.

The CREATE or REPLACE_CREATE commands are not valid for importing data into an MDC table.

Rollout

MDC simplifies rollout operations by using less log space and fewer index updates. Furthermore, when the MDC table has RID (regular) indexes, other than the block indexes on the dimensions, you can apply MDC rollout optimization by setting the current mdc rollout mode special register. This defers the RID (regular) index update operations until after the transaction is committed. The delete process is much faster and uses less log space.

```
[db2inst1@ nodedb21 ~]$ db2 "set current mdc rollout mode deferred"
DB20000I  The SQL command completed successfully.
[db2inst1@ nodedb21 ~]$ db2 "delete from pos.mdc_sales where year_month =
200901"
DB20000I  The SQL command completed successfully.
```

Partitioned database

We can create an MDC table; at the same time, the DISTRIBUTE BY HASH (store) command uses database partitions by storing the table in the table space we created in the last chapter. The distribution key we use for the partitions is the store ID.

```
[db2instp@nodedb21 ~]$ db2 "CREATE TABLE POSP.MDC_SALES (
  salesdate      date           NOT NULL,
  store          decimal(6,0)   NOT NULL,
  sku            varchar(15)    NOT NULL,
  qty            decimal(15,2)  NOT NULL,
  pxunit         decimal(15,2)  NOT NULL,
  unit           varchar(2)     NOT NULL,
  categ          decimal(1,0)   NOT NULL,
  stotal         decimal(15,2)  NOT NULL,
  year_month     generated as  (integer(salesdate)/100)
)
```

```
ORGANIZE   BY DIMENSIONS ( store, year_month )
DISTRIBUTE BY hash ( store )
IN posp_dss_tb32k"
```
DB20000I The SQL command completed successfully.

The distribution should not necessarily be an MDC dimension. Choose a key that will allow collocation with other tables in the database partition, in which the joins will be performed.

See also

The *Creating and configuring table spaces in multipartitioned environment* recipe in *Chapter 4, Storage—Using DB2 Table Spaces*

Creating and using materialized query tables

An MQT is based on a query and is much the same as a view, but the data retrieved from the query is stored in this MQT for later use. We can then query this table directly, as if it were a regular table.

An MQT can be defined as managed by the user, or by the system, which is the option we will use in our example. We'll discuss both the options later.

On table creation, you have to specify one of two refresh methods for this MQT:

- ▸ DEFERRED: Data in the MQT can be refreshed at any time with the REFRESH TABLE command. The refresh table will take a snapshot of the query's result set. Changes made on the underlying tables are not reflected until the next refresh.

- ▸ IMMEDIATE: Once the table is created, no other intervention is necessary. When changes are made to the underlying tables, the changes are applied to the MQT automatically, and any subsequent query will reflect the changes.

Getting ready

Estimate or get the actual number of records retrieved by your query, and allow sufficient space for data and indexes. Plan for an appropriate time to refresh this table from the underlying tables.

In our example, we will create underlying tables, in our partitioned database in the OLTP table spaces.

How to do it...

1. Create the tables:

   The first one is the invoices table:

```
[db2instp@nodedb21 ~]$ db2 "CREATE TABLE POSP.INVOICES (
>   INVID    DECIMAL(6,0) NOT NULL,
>   DATEINV  TIMESTAMP NOT NULL,
>   STOTAL   DECIMAL(15,2),
>   GST      DECIMAL(10,2),
>   PST      DECIMAL(10,2),
>   TOTAL    DECIMAL(15,2),
>   PAYM     VARCHAR(2) NOT NULL,
>   CHNG     DECIMAL(10,2),
>   NBITEMS  DECIMAL(2,0) NOT NULL,
>   CONSTRAINT PK_INVOICES PRIMARY KEY ( INVID )  )
>   IN POSP_TBLS
>INDEX
>   IN POSP_INDX"
DB20000I  The SQL command completed successfully.
```

   The second table is the invoice detail table:

```
[db2instp@nodedb21 ~]$ db2 "CREATE TABLE POSP.INVCDET (
>   INVID     DECIMAL(6,0)  NOT NULL,
>   ITEMID    DECIMAL(2,0)  NOT NULL,
>   SKU       VARCHAR(15)   NOT NULL,
>   QTY       DECIMAL(15,2) NOT NULL,
>   UNPRICE   DECIMAL(15,2) NOT NULL,
>   UNIT      VARCHAR(2)    NOT NULL,
>   CATEG     DECIMAL(1,0)  NOT NULL,
>   STOTAL    DECIMAL(15,2) NOT NULL,
>CONSTRAINT PK_INVCDET PRIMARY KEY ( INVID, ITEMID )  )
>   IN POSP_TBLS
>INDEX
>   IN POSP_INDX"
DB20000I  The SQL command completed successfully.
```

2. Load the data:

After we create the table, we can import some invoices:

```
[db2instp@nodedb21 partitioned]$ db2 -t -f import_invoices.db2


    Database Connection Information

 Database server        = DB2/LINUXX8664 9.7.4
 SQL authorization ID   = DB2INSTP
 Local database alias   = POSP




 Number of rows read        = 3309
 Number of rows skipped     = 0
 Number of rows inserted    = 3309
 Number of rows updated     = 0
 Number of rows rejected    = 0
 Number of rows committed   = 3309


SQL3107W  There is at least one warning message in the
  message file.
```

We now load the invoice detail table.

```
[db2instp@nodedb21 partitioned]$ db2 -t -f import_invcdet.db2


    Database Connection Information

 Database server        = DB2/LINUXX8664 9.7.4
 SQL authorization ID   = DB2INSTP
 Local database alias   = POSP




 Number of rows read        = 4595
 Number of rows skipped     = 0
 Number of rows inserted    = 4595
```

```
Number of rows updated     = 0
Number of rows rejected    = 0
Number of rows committed   = 4595


DB20000I  The SQL command completed successfully.
```

3. Create the materialized query table:

```
[db2instp@nodedb21 ~]$ db2 "CREATE TABLE POSP.DAILY_SALES AS (
> SELECT INV.DATEINV,
>         INV.INVID,
>         DET.ITEMID,
>         INV.STOTAL,
>         INV.GST,
>         INV.PST,
>         INV.TOTAL,
>         DET.SKU,
>         DET.UNPRICE,
>         DET.QTY
> FROM    POSP.INVOICES    INV,
>         POSP.INVCDET     DET
> WHERE   INV.INVID = DET.INVID )
> DATA INITIALLY DEFERRED
> REFRESH DEFERRED
> ENABLE QUERY OPTIMIZATION
> MAINTAINED BY SYSTEM
> IN POSP_DSS_TB8K"
DB20000I  The SQL command completed successfully.
```

4. Insert data into the materialized query table:

```
[db2instp@nodedb21 partitioned]$ db2 "refresh table
  posp.daily_sales"
DB20000I  The SQL command completed successfully.
```

How it works...

With DATA INITIALLY DEFERRED, the table is created as an empty shell. You have to issue the REFRESH TABLE command to insert data into the table. You can now query the new materialized query table as an ordinary table.

There's more...

Some restrictions apply. Please refer to the documentation if you have specific requirements for this task.

Refresh deferred

You can refresh this MQT at any time with the REFRESH TABLE command. The table is a snapshot of the query on actual data.

```
[db2instp@nodedb21 partitioned]$ db2 "refresh table posp.daily_sales"
DB20000I  The SQL command completed successfully.
```

Let's have a look now and see if there is data in the table:

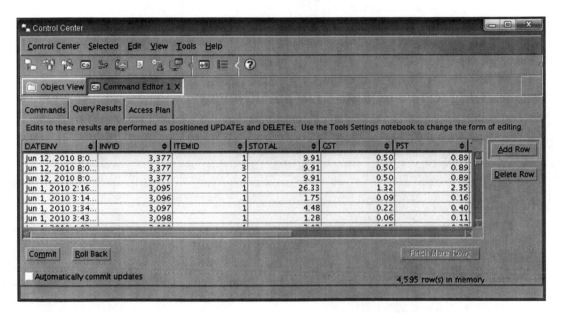

Maintained by system/user

- **SYSTEM**:

    When maintained by the system, data is maintained by DB2, refreshing from the underlying tables. You cannot perform INSERT, UPDATE, or DELETE operations on rows, in this type of MQT.

▶ **USER**:

You can also perform the INSERT, UPDATE, or DELETE operations on records, in this type of MQT.

You can only define the REFRESH DEFERRED option for this type of MQT. The REFRESH command is used only for MQTs managed by the system, so you have to rely on other means to manipulate data on this type of MQT. You can use load, insert, update, or delete.

Query rewrites

MQTs can improve the performance of complex queries. If the optimizer determines that a query can be resolved using an MQT, the query might be rewritten to take advantage of this MQT.

Combining with table partitioning

It is possible to build an MQT as a partitioned table. There are restrictions to consider for maintenance.

Replicated MQTs and database partitioning

You can create a replicated MQT on all database partitions, to enable collocation for queries running on multiple partitions. The performance benefit is worth the cost of replication. All you need to do is add this clause when you define the MQT:

```
db2 "CREATE TABLE POSP.MQT_REFTBLS AS ( ... )
 . . .
 MAINTAINED BY SYSTEM
 DISTRIBUTE BY REPLICATION"
```

See also

The *Implementing table partitioning* recipe that follows.

Implementing table partitioning

Table partitioning can be implemented on tables that have high volumes, usually in DSS environments. The typical configuration is to use the sales date for a range. Consider using a data partition for each period, either monthly or quarterly.

Getting ready

Decide on your partitioning range, and create table spaces/buffer pools to support this configuration.

How to do it...

1. Create buffer pools, one for each quarter:

   1st quarter:

   ```
   [db2instp@ nodedb21 posp]$ db2 "CREATE BUFFERPOOL BP_POSP_Q1_DSS8K
     IMMEDIATE DATABASE PARTITION GROUP POSP_DSS
     SIZE AUTOMATIC PAGESIZE 8 K"
   DB20000I  The SQL command completed successfully.
   ```

   2nd quarter:

   ```
   [db2instp@ nodedb21 posp]$ db2 "CREATE BUFFERPOOL BP_POSP_Q2_DSS8K
     IMMEDIATE DATABASE PARTITION GROUP POSP_DSS
     SIZE AUTOMATIC PAGESIZE 8 K"
   DB20000I  The SQL command completed successfully.
   ```

   3rd quarter:

   ```
   [db2instp@ nodedb21 posp]$ db2 "CREATE BUFFERPOOL BP_POSP_Q3_DSS8K
     IMMEDIATE DATABASE PARTITION GROUP POSP_DSS
     SIZE AUTOMATIC PAGESIZE 8 K"
   DB20000I  The SQL command completed successfully.
   ```

   4th quarter:

   ```
   [db2instp@ nodedb21 posp]$ db2 "CREATE BUFFERPOOL BP_POSP_Q4_DSS8K
     IMMEDIATE DATABASE PARTITION GROUP POSP_DSS
     SIZE AUTOMATIC PAGESIZE 8 K"
   DB20000I  The SQL command completed successfully.
   ```

2. Create table spaces:

   1st quarter:

   ```
   [db2instp@nodedb21 posp]$ db2 "create  large  tablespace
     POSP_DSS8K_2010_Q1
     in database partition group posp_dss
     pagesize 8 k
     managed by database
     using ( file '/data/db2/db2instp/node0000/posp/
       posp_dss8k_2010_q1.dbf' 6400 )
     autoresize yes maxsize 500 m
     extentsize 40 prefetchsize 40
     bufferpool  BP_POSP_Q1_DSS8K "
   DB20000I  The SQL command completed successfully.
   ```

2nd quarter:

```
[db2instp@nodedb21 posp]$ db2 "create   large   tablespace
  POSP_DSS8K_2010_Q2
  in database partition group posp_dss
  pagesize 8 k
  managed by database
  using ( file '/data/db2/db2instp/node0000/posp/
    posp_dss8k_2010_q2.dbf' 6400 )
  autoresize yes maxsize 500 m
  extentsize 40 prefetchsize 40
  bufferpool  BP_POSP_Q2_DSS8K "
DB20000I  The SQL command completed successfully.
```

3rd quarter:

```
[db2instp@nodedb21 posp]$ db2 "create   large   tablespace
  POSP_DSS8K_2010_Q3
  in database partition group posp_dss
  pagesize 8 k
  managed by database
  using ( file '/data/db2/db2instp/node0000/posp/
    posp_dss8k_2010_q3.dbf' 6400 )
  autoresize yes maxsize 500 m
  extentsize 40 prefetchsize 40
  bufferpool  BP_POSP_Q3_DSS8K "
DB20000I  The SQL command completed successfully.
```

4th quarter:

```
[db2instp@nodedb21 posp]$ db2 "create   large   tablespace
  POSP_DSS8K_2010_Q4
  in database partition group posp_dss
  pagesize 8 k
  managed by database
  using ( file '/data/db2/db2instp/node0000/posp/
    posp_dss8k_2010_q4.dbf' 6400 )
  autoresize yes maxsize 500 m
  extentsize 40 prefetchsize 40
  bufferpool  BP_POSP_Q4_DSS8K "
DB20000I  The SQL command completed successfully.
```

3. Create the partitioned table:

```
[db2instp@nodedb21 posp]$ db2 "CREATE TABLE POSP.QUARTERLYSALES (
     DATEINV   TIMESTAMP NOT NULL,
     INVID     DECIMAL(6,0) NOT NULL,
     STOTAL    DECIMAL(15,2),
     GST       DECIMAL(10,2),
     PST       DECIMAL(10,2),
     TOTAL     DECIMAL(15,2))
   PARTITION BY RANGE(DATEINV) (
    PARTITION Q1_2010
     STARTING FROM '1/1/2010' ENDING  AT  '3/31/2010' INCLUSIVE
       IN POSP_DSS8K_2010_Q1,
    PARTITION Q2_2010
     STARTING FROM '4/1/2010' ENDING  AT  '6/30/2010' INCLUSIVE
       IN POSP_DSS8K_2010_Q2,
    PARTITION Q3_2010
     STARTING FROM '7/1/2010' ENDING  AT  '9/30/2010' INCLUSIVE
       IN POSP_DSS8K_2010_Q3,
    PARTITION Q4_2010
     STARTING FROM '10/1/2010' ENDING  AT  '12/31/2010' INCLUSIVE
       IN POSP_DSS8K_2010_Q4 )"
  DB20000I  The SQL command completed successfully.
```

How it works...

Depending on the invoice date, records will be stored in the corresponding table space; this allows partitions to be deleted when no longer needed. New records are added to the latest table space.

Performance is improved since information pertaining to a single quarter is all grouped into one table space. The same goes for index access, as you will read later on.

There's more...

Partitioned tables are great for scalability, as we'll see. We'll discuss using indexes on partitioned tables for best performance and ease of maintenance. Performing rollin and rollout is straightforward, as well as adding or removing partitions.

Scalability

Creating a partitioned table adds scalability and allows you to create very large tables, while ensuring continued ease of use and maintenance.

This table has been created in a partitioned environment, so the added scalability of partitioned databases on this table becomes almost limitless, as you add more partitions to the table and database partitions to your database.

Non-partitioned indexes

Although it is preferable to create partitioned indexes on a partitioned table, you can create a non-partitioned index on a partitioned table.

```
[db2instp@nodedb21 posp]$ db2 "CREATE UNIQUE INDEX    POSP.IX_QTRLY_TAX
  ON POSP.QUARTERLYSALES ( INVID, DATEINV )
  NOT PARTITIONED
  IN POSP_DSS_TB8K
  INCLUDE  ( STOTAL, GST, PST, TOTAL )"
DB20000I  The SQL command completed successfully.
```

In this case, we needed an index to improve performance on category reports. We included the sales totals and tax amounts in the index so no table access would be required. Do not hesitate to experiment with your own settings.

 Remember that having reorgs on a non-partitioned index uses all of the tables as opposed to a partitioned index. A reorg may take more than six hours on a very large table, but could take just an hour using partitions.

Partitioned indexes

Partitioned indexes facilitate data maintenance by making `rollin` and `rollout` operations easier. They also improve performance, because you have less contention on index pages and on data pages, when you create an index partition.

You may want to have the partitioned indexes in separate table spaces from the table partitions.

1. Create buffer pools:

   1st quarter:

   ```
   [db2instp@ nodedb21 posp]$ db2 "CREATE BUFFERPOOL
     BP_POSP_Q1_DSI8K
       IMMEDIATE DATABASE PARTITION GROUP POSP_DSS
   ```

```
  SIZE AUTOMATIC PAGESIZE 8 K"
DB20000I  The SQL command completed successfully.
```

2nd quarter:

```
[db2instp@ nodedb21 posp]$ db2 "CREATE BUFFERPOOL
  BP_POSP_Q2_DSI8K
  IMMEDIATE DATABASE PARTITION GROUP POSP_DSS
  SIZE AUTOMATIC PAGESIZE 8 K"
DB20000I  The SQL command completed successfully.
```

3rd quarter:

```
[db2instp@ nodedb21 posp]$ db2 "CREATE BUFFERPOOL
  BP_POSP_Q3_DSI8K
  IMMEDIATE DATABASE PARTITION GROUP POSP_DSS
  SIZE AUTOMATIC PAGESIZE 8 K"
DB20000I  The SQL command completed successfully.
```

4th quarter:

```
[db2instp@ nodedb21 posp]$ db2 "CREATE BUFFERPOOL
  BP_POSP_Q4_DSI8K
  IMMEDIATE DATABASE PARTITION GROUP POSP_DSS
  SIZE AUTOMATIC PAGESIZE 8 K"
DB20000I  The SQL command completed successfully.
```

2. Create table spaces:

1st quarter index table space:

```
[db2instp@nodedb21 posp]$ db2 "create  large  tablespace
  POSP_DS8KI_2010_Q1
  in database partition group posp_dss
  pagesize 8 k
  managed by database
  using ( file '/data/db2/db2instp/node0000/posp/
    posp_ds8ki_2010_q1.dbf' 6400 )
  autoresize yes maxsize 500 m
  extentsize 40 prefetchsize 40
  bufferpool  BP_POSP_Q1_DSI8K "
DB20000I  The SQL command completed successfully.
```

2nd quarter:

```
[db2instp@nodedb21 posp]$ db2 "create   large   tablespace
  POSP_DS8KI_2010_Q2
  in database partition group posp_dss
  pagesize 8 k
  managed by database
  using ( file '/data/db2/db2instp/node0000/posp/
    posp_ds8ki_2010_q2.dbf' 6400 )
  autoresize yes maxsize 500 m
  extentsize 40 prefetchsize 40
  bufferpool  BP_POSP_Q2_DSI8K "
DB20000I  The SQL command completed successfully.
```

3rd quarter:

```
[db2instp@nodedb21 posp]$ db2 "create   large   tablespace
  POSP_DS8KI_2010_Q3
  in database partition group posp_dss
  pagesize 8 k
  managed by database
  using ( file '/data/db2/db2instp/node0000/posp/
    posp_ds8ki_2010_q3.dbf' 6400 )
  autoresize yes maxsize 500 m
  extentsize 40 prefetchsize 40
  bufferpool  BP_POSP_Q3_DSI8K "
DB20000I  The SQL command completed successfully.
```

4th quarter:

```
[db2instp@nodedb21 posp]$ db2 "create   large   tablespace
  POSP_DS8KI_2010_Q4
  in database partition group posp_dss
  pagesize 8 k
  managed by database
  using ( file '/data/db2/db2instp/node0000/posp/
    posp_ds8ki_2010_q4.dbf' 6400 )
  autoresize yes maxsize 500 m
  extentsize 40 prefetchsize 40
  bufferpool  BP_POSP_Q4_DSI8K "
DB20000I  The SQL command completed successfully.
```

3. Create the table, allowing for separate index table spaces:

```
[db2instp@nodedb21 posp]$ db2 "DROP    TABLE POSP.QUARTERLYSALES"
DB20000I  The SQL command completed successfully.
[db2instp@nodedb21 posp]$ db2 "CREATE TABLE POSP.QUARTERLYSALES (
  DATEINV   TIMESTAMP NOT NULL,
  INVID     DECIMAL(6,0) NOT NULL,
  STOTAL    DECIMAL(15,2),
  GST       DECIMAL(10,2),
  PST       DECIMAL(10,2),
  TOTAL     DECIMAL(15,2),
  PAYM      VARCHAR(2) NOT NULL,
  CHNG      DECIMAL(10,2),
  ITEMID    DECIMAL(2,0)  NOT NULL,
  SKU       VARCHAR(15)   NOT NULL,
  QTY       DECIMAL(15,2) NOT NULL,
  UNITPRICE DECIMAL(15,2) NOT NULL,
  UNIT      VARCHAR(2)    NOT NULL,
  CATEG     DECIMAL(1,0)  NOT NULL,
  ITEMTOTAL DECIMAL(15,2) NOT NULL)
PARTITION BY RANGE(DATEINV) (
 PARTITION Q1_2010
   STARTING FROM  '1/1/2010' ENDING  AT  '3/31/2010' INCLUSIVE
     IN POSP_DSS8K_2010_Q1   INDEX   IN POSP_DS8KI_2010_Q1,
 PARTITION Q2_2010
   STARTING FROM  '4/1/2010' ENDING  AT  '6/30/2010' INCLUSIVE
     IN POSP_DSS8K_2010_Q2   INDEX   IN POSP_DS8KI_2010_Q2,
 PARTITION Q3_2010
   STARTING FROM  '7/1/2010' ENDING  AT  '9/30/2010' INCLUSIVE
     IN POSP_DSS8K_2010_Q3   INDEX   IN POSP_DS8KI_2010_Q3,
 PARTITION Q4_2010
   STARTING FROM '10/1/2010' ENDING  AT '12/31/2010' INCLUSIVE
     IN POSP_DSS8K_2010_Q4   INDEX   IN POSP_DS8KI_2010_Q4 )"
DB20000I  The SQL command completed successfully.
```

4. Create the index:

```
[db2instp@nodedb21 posp]$ db2 "CREATE INDEX POSP.IX_QUARTERLYSALES
>    ON POSP.QUARTERLYSALES ( DATEINV ) PARTITIONED"
DB20000I  The SQL command completed successfully.
```

 By doing reorgs on specific partitions instead of the whole table, which save lots of time as well, you will need a smaller maintenance window.

Storage strategies

A partitioned table will need more storage than a normal table. The benefits, however, far outweigh the disadvantages. Explore the possibility of having many containers for each partition's table space, if you're not using RAID already.

Adding a partition to a table

When you want to create data for the new quarter, Q1, of 2011, you can create the table space with the same characteristics as the other partitions of this table. You alter the table to add this new table space, which will be a new partition of the partitioned table. The table is then ready for loading or inserting new data into this partition.

1. Create the table space for the new partition:

   You have to create the table space with the same characteristics as the other table spaces for other partitions of this table:

```
[db2instp@nodedb21 posp]$ db2 "create  large  tablespace
  POSP_DSS8K_2011_Q1
  in database partition group posp_dss
  pagesize 8 k
  managed by database
  using ( file '/data/db2/db2instp/node0000/posp/
    posp_dss8k_2011_q1.dbf' 6400 )
  autoresize yes maxsize 500 m
  extentsize 40 prefetchsize 40
  bufferpool  BP_POSP_Q1_DSS8K "
DB20000I  The SQL command completed successfully.
[db2instp@nodedb21 posp]$ db2 "create  large  tablespace
  POSP_DS8KI_2011_Q1
  in database partition group posp_dss
  pagesize 8 k
```

```
managed by database
using ( file '/data/db2/db2instp/node0000/posp/posp_ds8ki_2011_
q1.dbf' 6400 )
autoresize yes maxsize 500 m
extentsize 40 prefetchsize 40
bufferpool  BP_POSP_Q1_DSI8K "
DB20000I  The SQL command completed successfully.
```

2. Create the new partition:

```
[db2instp@nodedb21 posp]$ db2 "ALTER TABLE POSP.QUARTERLYSALES
 ADD PARTITION Q1_2011
 STARTING FROM ('1/1/2011') ENDING AT ('03/31/2011') INCLUSIVE
    IN POSP_DSS8K_2011_Q1   INDEX   IN POSP_DS8KI_2011_Q1"
DB20000I  The SQL command completed successfully.
```

In the **Control Center**, look for the POSP.QUARTERLYSALES table, right-click, and select **Open data partitions**:

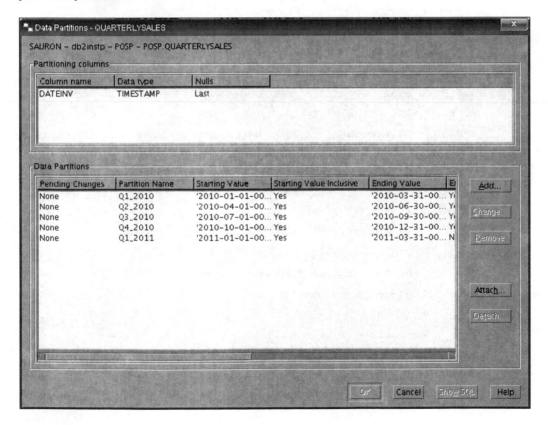

Detach a partition from a table

You cannot drop a partition. You need to detach it first, and then you can choose to drop it, archive it, or attach it to another partitioned table used as a history table.

1. Detach partition:

```
[db2instp@nodedb21 posp]$ db2 "ALTER TABLE POSP.QUARTERLYSALES
>  DETACH PARTITION Q1_2010 INTO POSP.QUARTERLYSALES_Q1_2010"
DB20000I  The SQL command completed successfully.
```

2. Drop the table created from the detached partition:

No data movement is necessary; the table partition's index is carried along and also detached, so there is no need to create an index for the detached table.

```
[db2instp@nodedb21 posp]$ db2 "DROP TABLE POSP.QUARTERLYSALES_
Q1_2010"
DB20000I  The SQL command completed successfully.
```

OR, attach the table created from the detached partition to a new table.

No data movement is necessary; you just need to follow the same guidelines we saw earlier for attaching a partition to a table.

```
[db2instp@nodedb21 partitioned]$ db2 "ALTER TABLE
  POSP.HISTORYSALES
  ATTACH PARTITION Q1_2010
  STARTING FROM  '1/1/2010' ENDING  AT  '3/31/2010' INCLUSIVE
  FROM POSP.QUARTERLYSALES_Q1_2010"
SQL3601W  The statement caused one or more tables to automatically
  be placed
 in the Set Integrity Pending state.  SQLSTATE=01586
```

All you need at this point is to check integrity for `historysales`; we will create a work table and reset integrity for this table.

```
[db2instp@nodedb21 partitioned]$ db2 "create table
  posp.historysales_chk like POSP.HISTORYSALES"
DB20000I  The SQL command completed successfully.
[db2instp@sauron partitioned]$ db2 "set integrity for
  posp.historysales
  immediate checked for exception in posp.historysales
  use posp.historysales_chk"
DB20000I  The SQL command completed successfully.
```

We will check here whether the operation is successful; we should have 0 records selected.

```
[db2instp@sauron partitioned]$ db2 "select
   substr(tabschema,1,15) "schema",
   substr(tabname,1,30)   "tabname", status
   from syscat.tables where status = 'C'"


SCHEMA           TABNAME                        STATUS
--------------- ------------------------------ ------

  0 record(s) selected.
```

See also

Chapter 4, Storage—Using DB2 Table Spaces

Using temporary tables

Temporary tables are used by applications that store results temporarily in a table.

There are two types of temporary tables, the *declared* global temporary table and the *created* global temporary table. The terms can appear confusing, so we'll explain, Declared Global temporary table

Also known as USER-DEFINED temporary table, a declared global temporary table is defined, or declared, for the current session and does not appear in the system catalog. This session has its own version, and this table is not visible to other sessions, hence the USER-DEFINED nickname. When the session ends, the table is dropped.

Getting ready

A user temporary table space must be present.

How to do it...

1. Create a user temporary table space, if it does not exist:

   ```
   [db2instp@nodedb21 posp]$ db2 "CREATE USER TEMPORARY TABLESPACE
   > POSP_TEMP8K  PAGESIZE 8K
   > MANAGED BY DATABASE USING (
   > FILE '/data/db2/db2instp/NODE0000/posp/posp_temp8k.dbf' 100 M )
   > AUTORESIZE YES MAXSIZE 500 M"
   DB20000I  The SQL command completed successfully.
   ```

2. Declare the temporary table:

   ```
   [db2instp@nodedb21 posp]$ db2 "DECLARE GLOBAL TEMPORARY TABLE TMP_
   INVCDET
   > LIKE POSP.INVCDET IN POSP_TEMP8K"
   DB20000I  The SQL command completed successfully.
   ```

How it works...

This statement defines a table `SESSION.TMP_INVCDET` with the same columns as table `POS.INVCDET` in tablespace `POSP_TEMP8K`. Other users cannot see or access this table. You can query, insert, update, or delete in this `SESSION.TMP_INVCDET` table. You can also create an index to improve query performance.

Created global temporary table

New in DB2 V9.7, the Created global temporary table is also known as GLOBAL temporary table. This type of table appears in the system catalog and is created once. Created temporary tables are used by applications that stores results temporarily in a table. The difference is that a created temporary table can be shared by applications, which is why it's called a GLOBAL temporary table. Each session does not have to create this table, and only the records created by the session are visible throughout the session. Once the session is done, the records are deleted.

How to do it...

1. Create a user temporary table space, if it does not exist:

    ```
    [db2instp@nodedb21 posp]$ db2 "CREATE USER TEMPORARY TABLESPACE
    > POSP_TEMP8K  PAGESIZE 8K
    > MANAGED BY DATABASE USING (
    > FILE '/data/db2/db2instp/NODE0000/posp/posp_temp8k.dbf' 100 M )
    > AUTORESIZE YES MAXSIZE 500 M"
    DB20000I The SQL command completed successfully
    ```

2. Create the temporary table:

    ```
    CREATE GLOBAL TEMPORARY TABLE TMP_INVCDET
    LIKE POSP.INVCDET
    ON COMMIT DELETE ROWS
    NOT LOGGED
    IN POSTEMP8K;
    ```

How it works...

This statement defines a table with the same columns as table `POS.INVOICE_DET`; however, indexes, unique constraints, foreign key constraints, and triggers are not defined.

When a `commit` or `rollback` is done, the table will be truncated. This is the default. If you want to have the same behavior as normal tables, use `LOGGED ON COMMIT PRESERVE ROWS`.

There's more...

Restrictions apply to field definitions, and recovery applies in certain conditions. Let's have a look at these now.

Restrictions

You cannot define columns with a user-defined type, long varchar, or XML columns in these types of tables.

Recovery

For Created (GLOBAL) tables, logging applies only when LOGGING is specified. Undo recovery is supported if LOGGING is applied. This means you can roll back your changes if LOGGING is specified. Database recovery does not apply here.

See also

Chapter 4, Storage—Using DB2 Table Spaces

7
DB2 Backup and Recovery

In this chapter, we will cover:

- ▸ Configuring database logging
- ▸ Performing an offline database backup
- ▸ Performing a full online database backup
- ▸ Performing an incremental delta database backup
- ▸ Performing an incremental cumulative database backup
- ▸ Backing up table spaces
- ▸ Crash recovery
- ▸ Full database recovery
- ▸ Database roll-forward recovery
- ▸ Incremental restore
- ▸ Recovering table spaces—full and `rollforward` recovery
- ▸ Redirected restore
- ▸ Recovering history file
- ▸ Configuring tape-based backup with IBM Tivoli Storage Manager
- ▸ `db2move` and `db2look` utilities as alternative backup methods

Introduction

We will discuss major aspects of backup and recovery as it is practiced industry-wide, what the preferred solutions are, and how we can implement some of these methods.

We will demonstrate some concepts, and we will walk you through different backup procedures and recovery techniques. We will also see other methods of saving data from the database for other purposes.

The first item we will cover is database logging, since it enables much more flexibility in your choice of backup solutions.

Configuring database logging

Normally, new databases are created by default with circular logging. However, their sole means of backup is an offline backup. This is fine for many types of use, but you may prefer to have other backup options.

Many backup solutions rely on archive logging. We have seen briefly in *Chapter 2, Administration and Configuration of the DB2 Non-partitioned Database*, how we can configure the database for automatic online backups and change the database logging method.

We will see here how to switch from a circular logging method to an archive logging mode. This will be used, as you will see in *Chapter 8, DB2 High Availability*, to set up *high availability* with log shipping, or anytime you may decide to switch from offline to online backups.

Getting ready

You will have to clear any sessions accessing the database. Allow for downtime and space for a full backup of the database, and allow a place to store archive logs.

How to do it...

1. Quiesce the database:

    As instance owner, these commands will disconnect any users connected to the database:

    ```
    [db2inst1@nodedb21 ~]$ db2 "CONNECT TO POS"

        Database Connection Information

      Database server        = DB2/LINUXX8664 9.7.4
      SQL authorization ID   = DB2INST1
    ```

```
    Local database alias    = POS
[db2inst1@nodedb21 ~]$ db2 "QUIESCE DATABASE IMMEDIATE FORCE
CONNECTIONS"
DB20000I  The QUIESCE DATABASE command completed successfully.

[db2inst1@nodedb21 ~]$ db2 "CONNECT RESET"
DB20000I  The SQL command completed successfully.
```

2. Change the configuration:

    We chose to send archive logs to disk. The directory has to exist and be writable for the instance owner. Since we disconnected, the next change will be effective right now.

    ```
    [db2inst1@nodedb21 ~]$ db2 "UPDATE DB CFG FOR POS
           USING logarchmeth1 "DISK:/logs/db2"
        logprimary 10 logsecond 5 logfilsiz 10240"
    DB20000I  The UPDATE DATABASE CONFIGURATION command completed
       successfully.
    ```

    Note that the update db placed the database in backup-pending state. If we try to connect, this is what happens:

    ```
    [db2inst1@nodedb21 ~]$ db2 connect to pos
    SQL1116N  A connection to or activation of database "POS" cannot
    be made because of BACKUP PENDING.   SQLSTATE=57019
    ```

3. Back up the database (offline):

    ```
    [db2inst1@nodedb21 ~]$ db2 "BACKUP DATABASE POS
            TO "/xchng/backups"
    WITH 2 BUFFERS
            BUFFER 1024 PARALLELISM 1 WITHOUT PROMPTING"

    Backup successful. The timestamp for this backup image is :
    20111125231153
    ```

How it works...

A full offline backup is required before accessing the database. With the DISK: log archive mode, DB2 will archive the logs from the active log directory to the directory we specified, /logs/db2. From this point on, certain options, such as online backups, table space backups, and high availability disaster recovery (HADR), can now figure in our backup and recovery scenarios.

There's more...

Now let's talk about some other options, or possibly some pieces of general information that are relevant to this task.

See also

- ▸ *Chapter 8, DB2 High Availability*
- ▸ *Configure tape-based backup with IBM Tivoli Storage Manager* recipe in this chapter

Performing an offline database backup

An offline backup is the sole option for backups on a circular logging database, and is used especially for small databases, such as a tools catalog database. This is different from a cold backup, since you have to connect to the database as instance owner, or a user that has database administration authority to perform the backup.

Getting ready

You will have to clear any sessions accessing the database. Allow for downtime and space for a full backup of the database.

How to do it...

1. Quiesce the database:

```
[db2inst1@nodedb21 ~]$ db2 "CONNECT TO POS"


     Database Connection Information

 Database server       = DB2/LINUXX8664 9.7.4
 SQL authorization ID  = DB2INST1
 Local database alias  = POS
[db2inst1@nodedb21 ~]$ db2 "QUIESCE DATABASE IMMEDIATE FORCE
CONNECTIONS"
DB20000I  The QUIESCE DATABASE command completed successfully.
[db2inst1@nodedb21 ~]$ db2 "CONNECT RESET"
DB20000I  The SQL command completed successfully.
```

2. Back up the database, offline:

```
[db2inst1@nodedb21 ~]$ db2 "BACKUP DATABASE POS
TO "/xchng/backups"
WITH 2 BUFFERS
BUFFER 1024 PARALLELISM 1 WITHOUT PROMPTING"

Backup successful. The timestamp for this backup image is :
20111125231153
```

3. Unquiesce the database:

The database will now be available for users.

```
[db2inst1@nodedb21 ~]$ db2 "UNQUIESCE DATABASE"
DB20000I  The UNQUIESCE DATABASE command completed successfully.
```

How it works...

The full offline backup will copy all files pertaining to the database into one single file, called the backup image, at the backup location. In our case, in /xchng/backups:

```
[db2inst1@nodedb21 backups]$ pwd
/xchng/backups
[db2inst1@ nodedb21 backups]$ ls -al POS.0*20111125231153*-rw-------
1 db2inst1 dba 268455936 2011-11-25 23:11 POS.0.db2inst1.NODE0000.
CATN0000.20111125231153.001
```

There's more...

When you need to restore a database, you must be aware of DB2's backup naming convention.

Backup naming convention

The filenames for backups should not be modified, since they contain information that is used by DB2 for recovery and the control center. A backup filename is composed of the following elements, separated by periods:

- ▸ Database alias
- ▸ Backup type (0-Full, 3-Table space, 4-Load ..copy to)
- ▸ Instance name
- ▸ Node number (always NODE0000 for non-partitioned databases)
- ▸ Catalog partition number (always CATN0000 for non-partitioned databases)
- ▸ Timestamp (YYYYMMDDHH24MISS)
- ▸ Sequence number

Partitioned database

For an offline backup, back up the catalog partition separately, and preferably before the other partitions. The backup operation on a partitioned database could require an exclusive connection to the catalog partition, and other database partitions cannot connect to the catalog partition.

Recovery from offline backup

Recovery is done on the whole database; executing rollforward is not possible, since the backup image does not contain log files. This is well-suited for small databases that can be backed up in an hour or less.

See also

Full database recovery recipe, later on in this chapter

Performing a full online database backup

This type of backup allows you to take a live backup, while users or processes are still connected to the database.

Getting ready

You do not need to schedule downtime for this task. Allow for sufficient space to hold backups and archived logs.

How to do it...

In this case we specify ONLINE, which tells DB2 to perform an online backup:

```
[db2inst1@nodedb21 ~]$ db2 "BACKUP DATABASE POS ONLINE
  TO "/xchng/backups"
  WITH 2 BUFFERS BUFFER 1024 PARALLELISM 1
  COMPRESS UTIL_IMPACT_PRIORITY 20
  INCLUDE LOGS WITHOUT PROMPTING"

Backup successful. The timestamp for this backup image is :
20111125231539
```

How it works...

As you perform the backup, db2 will store session operations in the online logs, so archive logging activity will be higher than usual until the backup is completed.

There's more...

You can throttle a backup operation to leave CPU resources available for other processes or users. Be aware there are restrictions to backups, and that certain other conditions may warrant an imperative backup.

Resource usage

The UTIL_IMPACT_PRIORITY 20 clause allows the backup to use only 20 percent of CPU resources for the backup task.

Restrictions

A database has to be in a normal or backup-pending state, otherwise you cannot perform a backup. A table space that is in a normal or backup-pending state can be backed up. In other cases, depending on certain conditions, a backup may or may not be permitted.

Backup pending

In an archive log mode database, certain conditions in a load may put a table space in backup-pending state. A backup is then mandatory, otherwise transactions cannot commit.

See also

Full database recovery recipe in this chapter

Performing an incremental delta database backup

Incremental database backups help reduce backup times, by tracking changes since the most recent backup. For example, a full backup is taken at noon. An incremental delta backup taken at 5:00 PM will include changes from noon to 5:00 PM. Another incremental delta backup taken at 10:00 PM will have changes from 5:00 PM till 10:00 PM. However, an incremental cumulative backup will cover changes from noon till 10:00 PM.

Getting ready

The database has to be in archive logging mode, and tracking database changes has to be enabled. Each of these will require a database restart if they are not set. Allow for downtime to do so. You also need a starting point, so a full database backup is required before proceeding to incremental backups.

How to do it...

If you are starting from a factory-installed database, you have to do steps 1 to 5, in order. Once you are set up for incremental backup, you only need to perform step 5.

1. Configure the database for archive logging mode:

   See the *Configuring database logging* recipe in this chapter.

2. Configure database to track changes:

   ```
   [db2inst1@nodedb21 ~]$ db2 "UPDATE DATABASE CONFIGURATION USING
   TRACKMOD Yes DEFERRED"
   DB20000I  The UPDATE DATABASE CONFIGURATION command completed
   successfully.
   ```

3. Perform a full online database backup:

   ```
   [db2inst1@nodedb21 ~]$ db2 "BACKUP DATABASE POS ONLINE
           TO "/xchng/backups"
           WITH 2 BUFFERS BUFFER 1024 PARALLELISM 1
           COMPRESS UTIL_IMPACT_PRIORITY 20
           INCLUDE LOGS WITHOUT PROMPTING"


   Backup successful. The timestamp for this backup image is :
   20111125231757
   ```

4. Restart database:

   ```
   [db2inst1@nodedb21 ~]$ db2stop force
   SQL1064N  DB2STOP processing was successful.
   [db2inst1@nodedb21 ~]$ db2start
   SQL1063N  DB2START processing was successful.
   ```

5. Prepare table space backup (we'll use this later in our demonstrations):

   ```
   [db2inst1@nodedb21 ~]$ db2 "BACKUP DATABASE POS
           TABLESPACE ( POS_TBLS )
           ONLINE TO "/xchng/backups" WITH 2
   ```

```
BUFFERS BUFFER 1024 PARALLELISM 1 WITHOUT PROMPTING"
```

```
Backup successful. The timestamp for this backup image is :
20111125232007
```

6. Allow for database activities:

   Here we should wait till we have user activity between the full database backup and the incremental backup. We provoke activity by creating a table.

```
[db2inst1@nodedb21 ~]$ db2 "CONNECT TO POS"
```

```
   Database Connection Information

 Database server        = DB2/LINUXX8664 9.7.4
 SQL authorization ID   = DB2INST1
 Local database alias   = POS
```

```
[db2inst1@nodedb21 ~]$ db2 "CREATE TABLE POS.PAYMENT (
  nofact    decimal(6,0) NOT NULL,
  nopaiem   decimal(6,0) NOT NULL,
  nolot     decimal(6,0),
  datepaim timestamp NOT NULL,
  total     decimal(15,2),
  paiem     varchar(2) NOT NULL,
  debit     decimal(15,2),
  visa      decimal(15,2),
  mv        decimal(15,2),
  remclnt   decimal(10,2)  )
  IN POS_TBLS
INDEX
  IN POS_INDX"
DB20000I  The SQL command completed successfully.
```

7. Perform incremental backup:

```
[db2inst1@nodedb21 ~]$ db2 "BACKUP DATABASE POS
        ONLINE INCREMENTAL DELTA
        TO "/xchng/backups"
```

```
                 WITH 2 BUFFERS BUFFER 1024 PARALLELISM 1
                 COMPRESS INCLUDE LOGS WITHOUT PROMPTING"
```

Backup successful. The timestamp for this backup image is :
20111125232127

8. Insert some records:

    We will insert some records here; we will see what happens in different
    restore scenarios:

    ```
    [db2inst1@nodedb21 ~]$ db2 "CONNECT TO POS"

        Database Connection Information

     Database server        = DB2/LINUXX8664 9.7.4
     SQL authorization ID   = DB2INST1
     Local database alias   = POS

    [db2inst1@nodedb21 ~]$ db2 "insert into POS.PAYMENT
    ( nofact    ,
      nopaiem   ,
      nolot     ,
      datepaim  ,
      total     ,
      paiem     ,
      debit     ,
      visa      ,
      mv        ,
      remclnt ) values
     (5193, 1, 78, to_date('201009191543','YYYYMMDDHH24MI'), 5.50,
    'DT', 6.00, null, null, null),
     (5196, 1, 78, to_date('201009191748','YYYYMMDDHH24MI'), 4.35,
    'DT', 4.85, null, null, null),
     (5203, 1, 78, to_date('201009202020','YYYYMMDDHH24MI'), 9.48,
    'DT', 9.98, null, null, null),
     (5207, 1, 78, to_date('201009211759','YYYYMMDDHH24MI'),10.00,
    'DT',10.50, null, null, null),
     (5215, 1, 78, to_date('201009221850','YYYYMMDDHH24MI'),25.00,
    'DT',25.50, null, null, 20.00)"
    DB20000I  The SQL command completed successfully.
    ```

How it works...

DB2 will do the incremental backup, by picking up changes since the last successful backup, and will write the operation in the recovery history file. Users can carry on their work while this is done. Transactions in # 8 will not figure in the incremental backup 20111125232127.

There's more...

Used particularly in warehouse databases in conjunction with an incremental restore, this type of recovery allows for faster recovery time, instead of full database and table space backups.

You can use it on complex migrations to ensure rollback points.

Table space name change

If you change a table space's name after an incremental backup and try to recover the table space from an automatic incremental restore, using the new name, an error will occur.

Recovery history file

These incremental types of backups and restores rely extensively on the recovery history file. Ensure this file is safe as well as other backups.

See also

Recovery history file recipe in this chapter.

Performing an incremental cumulative database backup

Incremental database backups help reduce backup times by tracking changes since the most recent full backup, in the case of an incremental cumulative backup.

Getting ready

Compared to an incremental delta backup, this backup may take a while longer to operate, since it picks up everything from the last full backup. Allow a larger maintenance window than for an incremental delta.

How to do it...

In our example, we created a table, POS.PAYMENT, since our last full backup, and we did an incremental delta backup. Now, let's add some data to the table, to have some activity on the database.

1. Database transactions:

```
[db2inst1@nodedb21 ~]$ db2 "insert into POS.PAYMENT
( nofact    ,
  nopaiem   ,
  nolot     ,
  datepaim  ,
  total     ,
  paiem     ,
  debit     ,
  visa      ,
  mv        ,
  remclnt ) values
 (5493, 1, 78, to_date('201010191543','YYYYMMDDHH24MI'), 5.50,
'DT', 6.00, null, null, null),
 (5496, 1, 78, to_date('201010191748','YYYYMMDDHH24MI'), 4.35,
'DT', 4.85, null, null, null),
 (5503, 1, 78, to_date('201010202020','YYYYMMDDHH24MI'), 9.48,
'DT', 9.98, null, null, null),
 (5507, 1, 78, to_date('201010211759','YYYYMMDDHH24MI'),10.00,
'DT',10.50, null, null, null),
 (5515, 1, 78, to_date('201010221850','YYYYMMDDHH24MI'),25.00,
'DT',25.50, null, null, 20.00)"
DB20000I  The SQL command completed successfully.
```

2. Perform backup:

```
[db2inst1@nodedb21 ~]$ db2 "BACKUP DATABASE POS
  ONLINE INCREMENTAL
  TO "/xchng/backups"
  WITH 2 BUFFERS BUFFER 1024 PARALLELISM 1
  COMPRESS INCLUDE LOGS WITHOUT PROMPTING"

Backup successful. The timestamp for this backup image is :
20111125233718
```

How it works...

The backup will pick up all the changes since the last full backup and store them in a file. Being an incremental cumulative backup, the changes included in this file will contain the `create` table for the POS.PAYMENT table, as well as this last `insert` command used in step 1.

There's more...

From our example, had this backup been an incremental delta, the backup file would have contained the results of the `insert` statement only.

See also

Recovery history file recipe in this chapter

Backing up table spaces

This type of backup allows you to back up single or multiple table spaces, while users are connected to the database.

Getting ready

DB2 can back up the table space with users connected, but it is always preferable to do it when nobody is connected.

How to do it...

There is no need to connect to the database; the backup utility will initiate the connection. This is the tablespace backup we made earlier:

```
[db2inst1@nodedb21 ~]$ db2 "BACKUP DATABASE POS
      TABLESPACE ( POS_TBLS )
      ONLINE TO "/xchng/backups" WITH 2
      BUFFERS BUFFER 1024 PARALLELISM 1 WITHOUT PROMPTING"


Backup successful. The timestamp for this backup image is :
20111125232007
```

How it works...

The table space will be backed up to this file: POS.3.db2inst1.NODE0000. CATN0000.20111125232007.001. Note the POS.3 at the beginning of the filename that indicates the backup type:

```
[db2inst1@nodedb21 ~]$ cd /xchng/backups
[db2inst1@nodedb21 backups]$ ls -al *20111125232007*
-rw------- 1 db2inst1 dba 12603392 2011-11-25 23:20 POS.3.db2inst1.
NODE0000.CATN0000.20111125232007.001
```

There's more...

Be aware of the following when scheduling table space backups.

Operations incompatible with online table space backups

Some operations have an impact on a table space as a whole entity and cannot be performed at the same time as a table space backup.

  ▸ Load
  ▸ Reorganization (online and offline)
  ▸ Drop table space
  ▸ Table truncation
  ▸ Index creation
  ▸ Not logged initially (used with the CREATE TABLE and ALTER TABLE statements)

See also

Recovering table spaces—full and rollforward recovery recipe in this chapter.

Crash recovery

A **crash** happens when the database is left in an inconsistent state, either by power or hardware failure, or other reasons. The recovery process, hence called crash recovery, will attempt to bring back the database to a consistent state.

The process is automatic when the database is started, but we do need to make sure that the database is recovered correctly, otherwise we may have to initiate other recovery procedures.

In this case, we deliberately provoke a crash in order to examine crash recovery. We encourage you to have a sandbox environment and test various scenarios.

Getting ready

You may want to try this on a test machine. Use a database for which you already made a backup, just in case. We will launch a transaction that will hopefully be long enough to allow us to shut the power and see the crash recovery results.

How to do it...

1. Start the database manager:

   ```
   [db2inst1@nodedb21 ~]$ db2start
   SQL1063N  DB2START processing was successful.
   ```

2. Connect to a database:

   ```
   [db2inst1@nodedb21 ~]$  db2 connect to pos


       Database Connection Information

    Database server       = DB2/LINUXX8664 9.7.4
    SQL authorization ID  = DB2INST1
    Local database alias  = POS
   ```

   Launch a command that will take a few moments. Choose a command that will do updates on the database; this will result in an inconsistent state.

   ```
   [db2inst1@nodedb21 ~]$ db2 "reorg table pos.factdet allow read
   access"
   ```

3. Stop the machine:

   Do not wait for the `reorg` command to finish; shut down the computer, or just pull the plug. This brings the machine to a halt, and the database will need crash recovery.

4. Restart the machine and start the database manager once again:

   ```
   [db2inst1@nodedb21 ~]$ db2start
   SQL1063N  DB2START processing was successful.
   ```

5. Examine the log and initiate recovery procedures if necessary:

   ```
   [db2inst1@nodedb21 ~]$ cd sqllib/db2dump/
   [db2inst1@nodedb21 db2dump]$ view db2diag.log
   ```

Look at the entries in the db2diag.log file; you should see Crash recovery completed. Otherwise, analyze the log entries, and check for media integrity and data corruption:

```
2011-08-30-22.29.59.657271-240 I768788E460         LEVEL: Warning
…..
EDUID    : 81                        EDUNAME: db2agent (POS)
FUNCTION: DB2 UDB, recovery manager, sqlpresr, probe:3170
MESSAGE : Crash recovery completed. Next LSN is 00000000060382C0
```

How it works...

The database initialized the crash recovery process when you started the database after the power failure.

You should see in the db2diag.log entries relative to the crash that happened and the recovery that took place:

```
2011-08-30-22.29.58.885448-240 I764490E432         LEVEL: Warning
PID      : 11157                     TID  : 140475818305808PROC : db2sysc
INSTANCE: db2inst1                   NODE : 000         DB    : POS
APPHDL   : 0-66                      APPID: *LOCAL.db2inst1.110831022958
AUTHID   : DB2INST1
EDUID    : 81                        EDUNAME: db2agent (POS)
FUNCTION: DB2 UDB, base sys utilities, sqledint, probe:30
MESSAGE : Crash Recovery is needed.
…
2011-08-30-22.29.59.305220-240 I765386E495         LEVEL: Warning
PID      : 11157                     TID  : 140475818305808PROC : db2sysc
INSTANCE: db2inst1                   NODE : 000         DB    : POS
APPHDL   : 0-66                      APPID: *LOCAL.db2inst1.110831022958
AUTHID   : DB2INST1
EDUID    : 81                        EDUNAME: db2agent (POS)
FUNCTION: DB2 UDB, recovery manager, sqlpresr, probe:410
MESSAGE : Crash recovery started. LowtranLSN 0000000005F40010
MinbuffLSN
         0000000005F40010
2011-08-30-22.29.59.600675-240 I767823E505         LEVEL: Warning
PID      : 11157                     TID  : 140475818305808PROC : db2sysc
INSTANCE: db2inst1                   NODE : 000         DB    : POS
APPHDL   : 0-66                      APPID: *LOCAL.db2inst1.110831022958
AUTHID   : DB2INST1
EDUID    : 81                        EDUNAME: db2agent (POS)
FUNCTION: DB2 UDB, recovery manager, sqlprecm, probe:4000
```

```
MESSAGE : DIA2051W Forward phase of crash recovery has completed.
Next LSN is
          "00000000060381E0".

2011-08-30-22.29.59.656348-240 E768329E458          LEVEL: Warning
PID     : 11157                  TID  : 140475818305808PROC : db2sysc
INSTANCE: db2inst1               NODE : 000          DB   : POS
APPHDL  : 0-66                    APPID: *LOCAL.db2inst1.110831022958
AUTHID  : DB2INST1
EDUID   : 81                     EDUNAME: db2agent (POS)
FUNCTION: DB2 UDB, recovery manager, sqlpresr, probe:3170
MESSAGE : ADM1531E  Crash recovery has completed successfully.
2011-08-30-22.29.59.657271-240 I768788E460          LEVEL: Warning
PID     : 11157                  TID  : 140475818305808PROC : db2sysc
INSTANCE: db2inst1               NODE : 000          DB   : POS
APPHDL  : 0-66                    APPID: *LOCAL.db2inst1.110831022958
AUTHID  : DB2INST1
EDUID   : 81                     EDUNAME: db2agent (POS)
FUNCTION: DB2 UDB, recovery manager, sqlpresr, probe:3170
MESSAGE : Crash recovery completed. Next LSN is 00000000060382C0
```

There's more...

You may want to make sure there is no corruption in the database in the wake of a system crash. Tools are available to help you determine the integrity of a database.

How crash recovery works to ensure database integrity

Since the DB2 processes may write dirty pages back to disk, all uncommitted transactions from the logs have to be rolled back. Changes that were committed but not written to the table spaces' containers are redone.

Inspect database

If you are not sure about the integrity of the database, you can inspect the database structure with the INSPECT command. The default behavior is to produce a report in the same directory as db2diag.log. If INSPECT is successful, the result file is deleted, so we can consider the database architecturally correct.

1. Launch INSPECT on the database:

    In order to demonstrate our case, we will perform an INSPECT operation, but we'll be telling DB2 to keep the result file so that we can browse through it.

    ```
    [db2inst1@nodedb21 pos]$ db2 "INSPECT CHECK DATABASE RESULTS KEEP
    20110917_POS_CHK.rpt"
    DB20000I  The INSPECT command completed successfully.
    ```

2. Format an output report from the result file:

```
[db2inst1@nodedb21 ~]$ cd sqllib/db2dump
[db2inst1@nodedb21 db2dump]$ ls -l 20110917_POS_CHK.rpt
-rw-r----- 1 db2inst1 dba 100858 2011-09-17 15:32 20110917_POS_
CHK.rpt
[db2inst1@nodedb21 db2dump]$ db2inspf 20110917_POS_CHK.rpt
20110917_POS_CHK.log
```

See also

Chapter 9, Problem Determination, Event Sources, and Files

Full database recovery

In the event a database is unusable or corrupted, this type of recovery, also known as version recovery, will recover the whole database from a backup. The database will be an exact image of itself at the time the backup was made. Transactions entered after the backup will be lost. Here, we will discuss a restore for an archive logging database.

Getting ready

Allow for downtime, since users cannot access a database during recovery. A restore is necessary before doing recovery.

How to do it...

1. Quiesce the database:

```
[db2inst1@nodedb21 ~]$ db2 "CONNECT TO POS"


    Database Connection Information

  Database server        = DB2/LINUXX8664 9.7.4
  SQL authorization ID   = DB2INST1
  Local database alias   = POS
[db2inst1@nodedb21 ~]$ db2 "QUIESCE DATABASE IMMEDIATE FORCE
CONNECTIONS"
DB20000I  The QUIESCE DATABASE command completed successfully.
[db2inst1@nodedb21 ~]$ db2 "CONNECT RESET"
DB20000I  The SQL command completed successfully.
```

2. Restore the database from a full online backup of when the database was in the archive logging state:

The database was in archive logging mode at 20111125231153.

```
[db2inst1@nodedb21 ~]$ db2 "RESTORE DATABASE POS
    FROM "/xchng/backups"
    TAKEN AT 20111125231153
    WITH 2 BUFFERS BUFFER 1024 PARALLELISM 1
    WITHOUT ROLLING FORWARD WITHOUT PROMPTING"
SQL2540W  Restore is successful, however a warning "2539" was
encountered during Database Restore while processing in No
Interrupt mode.
```

3. Unquiesce the database:

Now that the database is in a consistent state at the time of the full backup, we can put the database back online.

```
[db2inst1@nodedb21 pos]$ db2 CONNECT TO POS


    Database Connection Information

 Database server        = DB2/LINUXX8664 9.7.4
 SQL authorization ID   = DB2INST1
 Local database alias   = POS


[db2inst1@nodedb21 pos]$ db2 "UNQUIESCE DATABASE"
DB20000I  The UNQUIESCE DATABASE command completed successfully.
```

How it works...

In this case, the restore picked up all information from the backup and restored the database to the point where the backup was launched. Any transactions entered during the backup are lost.

There's more...

Sometimes, things don't always perform as expected.

Attempting to recover from a backup of database in another logging mode

You may encounter some difficulties restoring from a backup when the database was in a different logging configuration. We'll demonstrate the effects, here. The solution is to take an offline backup to remove the backup-pending state.

1. Restore database:

    Restoring a database, that is presently in archive logging mode, from a backup taken while the database was in circular logging mode will place the database in backup-pending state.

    ```
    [db2inst1@nodedb21 ~]$ db2 "RESTORE DATABASE POS
      FROM "/xchng/backups"
      TAKEN AT 20110805205335
      WITH 2 BUFFERS BUFFER 1024 PARALLELISM 1
      WITHOUT PROMPTING"
    SQL2540W  Restore is successful, however a warning "2539" was
    encountered during Database Restore while processing in No
    Interrupt mode.
    ```

2. Attempt to connect to database:

    Attempts to connect will fail, since DB2 will consider the database as if it changed state from circular logging to archive logging mode.

    ```
    [db2inst1@nodedb21 ~]$ db2 CONNECT TO POS
    SQL1116N  A connection to or activation of database "POS" cannot
    be made
     because of BACKUP PENDING.   SQLSTATE=57019
    ```

3. See configuration:

    Verify that the LOGARCHMETH1 variable is not set to OFF, because the database has remained in archive logging mode:

    ```
    [db2inst1@nodedb21 ~]$ db2 get db cfg for pos
    Backup pending                                          = YES

    All committed transactions have been written to disk    = YES
    Rollforward pending                                     = NO
    Restore pending                                         = NO
    ```

```
       First log archive method                (LOGARCHMETH1) = DISK:/
logs/db2/
       Options for logarchmeth1                 (LOGARCHOPT1) =
       Second log archive method                (LOGARCHMETH2) = OFF
```

4. If we try an online full backup:

   An online full backup won't clear the backup-pending state, since the database was in circular logging state, at that point.

```
[db2inst1nodedb21 backups]$ db2 "BACKUP DATABASE POS ONLINE
        TO "/xchng/backups"
        WITH 2 BUFFERS BUFFER 1024 PARALLELISM 1
        UTIL_IMPACT_PRIORITY 20 WITHOUT PROMPTING"
SQL2413N  Online backup is not allowed because the database is
 not recoverable
 or a backup pending condition is in effect.
```

5. If we try an offline full backup:

   An offline full backup will clear the backup-pending state.

```
[db2inst1nodedb21 backups]$ db2 "BACKUP DATABASE POS
        TO "/xchng/backups"
        WITH 2 BUFFERS BUFFER 1024 PARALLELISM 1 WITHOUT PROMPTING"


Backup successful. The timestamp for this backup image is :
20111125143013


[db2inst1nodedb21 backups]$ db2 CONNECT TO POS


    Database Connection Information

 Database server        = DB2/LINUXX8664 9.7.4
 SQL authorization ID   = DB2INST1
 Local database alias   = POS
```

See also

Performing full online database backup recipe in this chapter

Database rollforward recovery

This type of recovery allows for a restore of the database, as well as all transactions recorded in the logs since the backup. All transactions, from backup to the point of failure, can be recovered by this process.

Getting ready

We will have to quiesce the database and perform a database restore first. Make sure all necessary archived logs are available for recovery. When that is done, we'll be ready to roll forward the archived logs.

How to do it...

1. Connect to the database:

```
[db2inst1@nodedb21 pos]$ db2 CONNECT TO POS


    Database Connection Information

 Database server       = DB2/LINUXX8664 9.7.4
 SQL authorization ID  = DB2INST1
 Local database alias  = POS
```

2. Quiesce the database:

```
[db2inst1@nodedb21 pos]$ db2 "QUIESCE DATABASE IMMEDIATE FORCE
CONNECTIONS"
DB20000I  The QUIESCE DATABASE command completed successfully.
```

3. Restore the database:

When you are restoring to an existing database, DB2's restore will issue a warning to indicate that you are overwriting the existing database. Since we specified WITHOUT PROMPTING, the RESTORE operation just continued and displayed the warning. We will use the incremental cumulative backup we took earlier.

```
[db2inst1@nodedb21 pos]$ db2 "RESTORE DATABASE POS
  INCREMENTAL AUTOMATIC
  FROM "/xchng/backups"
  TAKEN AT 20111125232127
  WITH 2 BUFFERS BUFFER 1024 PARALLELISM 1 WITHOUT PROMPTING"
```

OR (works with either one of these backups):

```
db2 "RESTORE DATABASE POS
   FROM "/xchng/backups"
   TAKEN AT 20111125231757
   WITH 2 BUFFERS BUFFER 1024 PARALLELISM 1 WITHOUT PROMPTING"
SQL2540W  Restore is successful, however a warning "2539" was
encountered during Database Restore while processing in No
Interrupt mode.
```

4. Roll forward to the end of the logs:

   This command will replay all logs since the backups, until it reaches the end. The database will then be available.

```
[db2inst1@nodedb21 pos]$ db2 "ROLLFORWARD DATABASE POS TO END OF
LOGS AND COMPLETE"


                              Rollforward Status

  Input database alias                 = POS
  Number of nodes have returned status = 1

  Node number                          = 0
  Rollforward status                   = not pending
  Next log file to be read             =
  Log files processed                  = S0000001.LOG - S0000007.
LOG
   Last committed transaction          = 2011-11-26-
04.37.21.000000 UTC


DB20000I  The ROLLFORWARD command completed successfully.
[db2inst1@nodedb21 pos]$ db2 CONNECT TO POS

     Database Connection Information

  Database server      = DB2/LINUXX8664 9.7.4
  SQL authorization ID = DB2INST1
  Local database alias = POS


[db2inst1@nodedb21 pos]$ db2 "UNQUIESCE DATABASE"
DB20000I  The UNQUIESCE DATABASE command completed successfully.
```

How it works...

The database is restored from the last incremental-cumulative backup, and all logs were redone, to the last operation we performed, when we created the PAYMENT table and inserted records. You won't see the PAYMENT records we inserted for Sept 2010 (201009) but those that were done after the backup with the empty table. So, we'll see data inserted for Oct 2010 (201010).

There's more...

You can specify a point in time, if you want to restore the database to a specific time.

Database state after restore

After the restore, the database will be put in rollforward pending mode. You may either ROLLFORWARD the database to a point in time or till the end of logs. The complete or stop command turns off the rollforward pending state of the database.

Point-in-time recovery on a partitioned database

Point-in-time recovery is used, which will require all database partitions in the system to be in rollforward pending state. You need to ROLLFORWARD all partitions to make sure they are all consistent.

The ROLLFORWARD DATABASE command has to be run on the catalog partition.

History of restore operations

You can see the result of this operation by listing rollforward operations:

```
[db2inst1@nodedb21 pos]$

db2 list history rollforward all for pos

                    List History File for pos

Number of matching file entries = 2

 Op Obj Timestamp+Sequence Type Dev Earliest Log Current Log  Backup ID
 -- --- ------------------ ---- --- ------------ ------------ -----------
 ---
  F   D   20111125233439      P        S0000004.LOG S0000005.LOG
20111125232131000000
 ------------------------------------------------------------------------
 ----
```

```
----------------------------------------------------------------
----
    Comment: 20111126043441GMT
 Start Time: 20111125233439
   End Time: 20111125233441
     Status: A
 ----------------------------------------------------------------
----
   EID: 24


Op Obj Timestamp+Sequence Type Dev Earliest Log Current Log  Backup ID
-- --- ----------------- ---- --- ------------ ------------ -----------
---
 F  D   20111125235720    E        S0000001.LOG S0000007.LOG
 ----------------------------------------------------------------
----


 ----------------------------------------------------------------
----
    Comment: 20111126045728GMT
 Start Time: 20111125235720
   End Time: 20111125235728
     Status: A
 ----------------------------------------------------------------
----
   EID: 41
```

See also

Recovery history file recipe in this chapter

Incremental restore

Used particularly in warehouse databases in conjunction with an incremental restore, this type of recovery allows for faster recovery time, instead of full database and table space backups. You can use it on complex migrations to ensure rollback points.

An incremental restore can be run in automatic mode.

Getting ready

The database has to be in archive logging mode, and tracking database changes has to be enabled, as explained in the *Performing an incremental delta database backup* recipe in this chapter.

How to do it...

1. Quiesce database:

    ```
    [db2inst1@nodedb21 pos]$ db2 "QUIESCE DATABASE IMMEDIATE FORCE
    CONNECTIONS"
    DB20000I  The QUIESCE DATABASE command completed successfully.
    [db2inst1@nodedb21 pos]$ db2 CONNECT RESET
    DB20000I  The SQL command completed successfully.
    ```

2. Check restore:

    This command will generate a list of timestamps required for the incremental restore till the timestamp you provide; the commands to use (with a simplified syntax) are also generated:

    ```
    [db2inst1@nodedb21 pos]$ db2ckrst -d pos -t 20111125232127 -r
    database


    Suggested restore order of images using timestamp 20111125232127
    for
      database pos.
    ====================================================================
      restore db pos incremental taken at 20111125232127
      restore db pos tablespace ( SYSCATSPACE, USERSPACE1,
    SYSTOOLSPACE, POS_INDX ) incremental taken at 20111125231757
      restore db pos incremental taken at 20111125232007
      restore db pos incremental taken at 20111125232127
    ====================================================================
    ```

3. Restore the database from the incremental backup:

    We now restore the database using the timestamps provided. Note the warning telling us we are overwriting an existing database. The WITHOUT PROMPTING option allows the operation to continue without having to confirm by entering *yes* or *no*.

    ```
    [db2inst1@nodedb21 pos] $ db2 "RESTORE DATABASE POS
      INCREMENTAL AUTOMATIC
      FROM "/xchng/backups"
    ```

```
TAKEN AT 20111125232127
WITH 2 BUFFERS BUFFER 1024 PARALLELISM 1 WITHOUT PROMPTING"

SQL2540W  Restore is successful, however a warning "2539" was
encountered
 during Database Restore while processing in No Interrupt mode.
```

4. Stop rollforward mode:

The database is now in rollforward pending mode, so for now, let's just stop the rollforward.

```
[db2inst1@nodedb21 pos]$ db2 "ROLLFORWARD DATABASE POS TO END OF
BACKUP AND COMPLETE"


                         Rollforward Status

Input database alias                   = POS
Number of nodes have returned status   = 1


Node number                            = 0
Rollforward status                     = not pending
Next log file to be read               =
Log files processed                    = S0000004.LOG - S0000005.
LOG
Last committed transaction             = 2011-11-26-
04.21.31.000000 UTC


DB20000I  The ROLLFORWARD command completed successfully.
```

5. Unquiesce the database:

Now, the database is in a consistent state, at the time of the incremental backup. We can put the database back online.

```
[db2inst1@nodedb21 pos]$ db2 CONNECT TO POS

   Database Connection Information

Database server      = DB2/LINUXX8664 9.7.4
SQL authorization ID = DB2INST1
Local database alias = POS
[db2inst1@nodedb21 pos]$ db2 "UNQUIESCE DATABASE"
DB20000I  The UNQUIESCE DATABASE command completed successfully.
```

6. Open the PAYMENT table:

    The table was empty at the time of the backup, so now you can open the PAYMENT table and confirm it is empty.

    ```
    [db2inst1@nodedb21 pos]$ db2 "select * from POS.PAYMENT"

    NOFACT    NOPAIEM  NOLOT    DATEPAIM                    TOTAL
    PAIEM DEBIT                 VISA              MV
    REMCLNT
    -------- -------- -------- -------------------------- -------------
    ----- ----- ---------------- ---------------- -----------------
    -----------

        0 record(s) selected.
    ```

How it works...

DB2's restore command will identify the primary full backup and apply the incremental backup, depending on the timestamp you supply.

There's more...

There may be issues with current logs.

Archive log file not associated with the current log sequence

While rolling forward, you may encounter this message:

```
[db2inst1@ nodedb21 backups]$ db2 "ROLLFORWARD DATABASE POS TO END OF
BACKUP AND COMPLETE"
SQL1265N  The archive log file "S0000005.LOG" is not associated with the
current log sequence for database "POS" on node "0".
```

Perform the following steps to remedy the situation:

1. Get the current configuration for the logs:

    ```
    [db2inst1@ nodedb21 backups]$ db2 get db cfg for pos | grep -i
    path
     Changed path to log files               (NEWLOGPATH) =
     Path to log files                                    = /logs/
    db2/
     Overflow log path                   (OVERFLOWLOGPATH) =
     Mirror log path                      (MIRRORLOGPATH) =
     Failover log archive path             (FAILARCHPATH) =
    ```

2. See what logs are there, and move or delete the unnecessary logs:

```
[db2inst1nodedb21 backups]$ cd /logs/db2/db2inst1/POS/NODE0000
[db2inst1nodedb21 NODE0000]$ ls -la
total 24
drwxr-x--- 6 db2inst1 dba 4096 2011-11-25 20:43 ./
drwxr-x--- 3 db2inst1 dba 4096 2011-11-25 00:55 ../
drwxr-x--- 2 db2inst1 dba 4096 2011-11-25 21:18 C0000000/
drwxr-x--- 2 db2inst1 dba 4096 2011-11-25 20:15 C0000001/
drwxr-x--- 2 db2inst1 dba 4096 2011-11-25 17:21 C0000002/
drwxr-x--- 2 db2inst1 dba 4096 2011-11-25 20:43 C0000003/
[db2inst1nodedb21 NODE0000]$ ls -l *
C0000000:
total 84
-rw-r----- 1 db2inst1 dba 12288 2011-11-25 20:59 S0000000.LOG
-rw-r----- 1 db2inst1 dba 12288 2011-11-25 21:07 S0000001.LOG
-rw-r----- 1 db2inst1 dba 12288 2011-11-25 21:10 S0000002.LOG
-rw-r----- 1 db2inst1 dba 24576 2011-11-25 21:14 S0000003.LOG
-rw-r----- 1 db2inst1 dba 12288 2011-11-25 21:15 S0000004.LOG
-rw-r----- 1 db2inst1 dba 12288 2011-11-25 21:18 S0000005.LOG

C0000001:
total 7380
-rw-r----- 1 db2inst1 dba 6987776 2011-11-25 14:26 S0000000.LOG
-rw-r----- 1 db2inst1 dba   12288 2011-11-25 01:28 S0000003.LOG
-rw-r----- 1 db2inst1 dba   12288 2011-11-25 01:33 S0000004.LOG
-rw-r----- 1 db2inst1 dba   12288 2011-11-25 01:33 S0000005.LOG
-rw-r----- 1 db2inst1 dba   12288 2011-11-25 01:35 S0000006.LOG
-rw-r----- 1 db2inst1 dba  503808 2011-11-25 20:15 S0000008.LOG

C0000002:
total 6544
-rw-r----- 1 db2inst1 dba 6688768 2011-11-25 17:21 S0000007.LOG

C0000003:
total 0
```

3. From the timestamps, S0000003 to S0000006.LOG have been modified at around 1:30 a.m. and are from an obsolete version of the database, so we can safely delete them. Run the rollforward command again:

```
[db2inst1nodedb21 C0000001]$ db2 "ROLLFORWARD DATABASE POS TO END
OF BACKUP AND COMPLETE"
```

```
                               Rollforward Status

   Input database alias                = POS
   Number of nodes have returned status = 1

   Node number                         = 0
   Rollforward status                  = not pending
   Next log file to be read            =
   Log files processed                 = S0000004.LOG - S0000005.
LOG
   Last committed transaction          = 2011-11-26-
02.15.03.000000 UTC

DB20000I  The ROLLFORWARD command completed successfully.
```

See also

Recovery history file recipe in this chapter

Recovering table spaces—full and rollforward recovery

This procedure allows us to restore only part of a database. This can be useful in recovering from many types of failure scenarios, such as year-end batch jobs or monthly data migration, when they affect only tables confined into specific table spaces.

Getting ready

Identify the table space and the backup you want to use for this operation. Make sure users are not connected.

How to do it...

1. Full (version) recovery:

    We will first perform a full (version) recovery of a single table space:

    ```
    [db2inst1@nodedb21 ~]$ db2 "QUIESCE DATABASE IMMEDIATE FORCE
    CONNECTIONS"
    DB20000I  The QUIESCE DATABASE command completed successfully.
    [db2inst1@nodedb21 ~]$ db2 CONNECT RESET
    DB20000I  The SQL command completed successfully.[db2inst1@
    nodedb21 ~]$ db2 "RESTORE DATABASE POS
      TABLESPACE (POS_TBLS) ONLINE
      FROM "/xchng/backups"
      TAKEN AT 20111125013459
      WITH 2 BUFFERS BUFFER 1024 PARALLELISM 1
      WITHOUT ROLLING FORWARD WITHOUT PROMPTING"
    SQL2537N  Roll-forward is required following the Restore.
    ```

2. Connect to database:

    ```
    [db2inst1@nodedb21 ~]$ db2 connect to pos


        Database Connection Information

     Database server        = DB2/LINUXX8664 9.7.4
     SQL authorization ID   = DB2INST1
     Local database alias   = POS
    ```

3. Examine table space state:

    Note that a `State` value of `0x0000` indicates that the table space is in a normal state and is no longer in `rollforward` pending mode.

    ```
    [db2inst1@nodedb21 ~]$ db2 list tablespaces


            Tablespaces for Current Database

     Tablespace ID                   = 5
     Name                            = POS_TBLS
     Type                            = Database managed space
    ```

```
      Contents                           = All permanent data. Large
    table space.
      State                              = 0x0000

        Detailed explanation:

        Normal
```

4. Now, we'll prepare the database for the next scenario:

    We'll start by recovering the whole database, without forgetting to quiesce the database first. We ignore the warning, as discussed earlier. The reason for this is we avoid having log sequence conflicts resulting in the `SQL2154N` error message.

```
[db2inst1@nodedb21 ~]$ db2 "QUIESCE DATABASE IMMEDIATE FORCE
CONNECTIONS"
DB20000I  The QUIESCE DATABASE command completed successfully.
[db2inst1@nodedb21 ~]$ db2 CONNECT RESET
DB20000I  The SQL command completed successfully.
[db2inst1@nodedb21 ~]$ db2 "RESTORE DATABASE POS
      FROM "/xchng/backups"
      TAKEN AT 20111125231757
      WITH 2 BUFFERS BUFFER 1024 PARALLELISM 1 WITHOUT PROMPTING"
SQL2540W  Restore is successful, however a warning "2539" was
encountered
   during Database Restore while processing in No Interrupt mode.
```

5. We run the `rollforward` command now:

```
[db2inst1@nodedb21 ~]$ db2 "ROLLFORWARD DATABASE POS TO
      END OF LOGS AND COMPLETE"


                                 Rollforward Status

  Input database alias               = POS
  Number of nodes have returned status = 1


  Node number                        = 0
  Rollforward status                 = not pending
  Next log file to be read           =
  Log files processed                = S0000001.LOG - S0000007.
LOG
```

```
    Last committed transaction              = 2011-11-26-
04.37.21.000000 UTC


    DB20000I  The ROLLFORWARD command completed successfully.
```

6. Now we can try the restore with recovery:

```
[db2inst1@nodedb21 ~]$ db2 "RESTORE DATABASE POS
        TABLESPACE (POS_TBLS) ONLINE
        FROM "/xchng/backups"
        TAKEN AT 20111125232007
        WITH 2 BUFFERS BUFFER 1024 PARALLELISM 1
        WITHOUT PROMPTING"
DB20000I  The RESTORE DATABASE command completed successfully.
```

7. ROLLFORWARD the table space:

```
[db2inst1@nodedb21 ~]$ db2 "ROLLFORWARD DATABASE POS
        TO END OF LOGS AND COMPLETE
        TABLESPACE (POS_TBLS) ONLINE"


                              Rollforward Status

    Input database alias              = POS
    Number of nodes have returned status   = 1


     Node number                       = 0
    Rollforward status                = not pending
    Next log file to be read          =
    Log files processed               = -
    Last committed transaction        = 2011-11-26-
04.37.21.000000 UTC


    DB20000I  The ROLLFORWARD command completed successfully.
```

How it works...

When you restore a table space, you have to roll forward the table space to apply the logs. You can choose to roll forward to a point in time, or you can apply all logs to the end.

There's more...

The following present different cases applying to table space recovery.

Backup image

You can use a full database backup image to restore a single table space, or you can choose a table space backup image.

Table space with system catalog

A table space in error containing system catalog tables must be restored by restoring the SYSCATSPACE table space and performing a rollforward recovery until the end of logs.

Partitioned database

In a partitioned database environment, the rollforward command for a table space extends to all database partitions. If you do not want to roll forward a table space in all partitions, you have to supply a list of database partitions you want to roll forward.

Partitioned table

In case you want to recover a table space containing a part of a partitioned table, you need to consider this: if you want to roll the table space forward to a point in time, this implies all other table spaces containing this table must be rolled forward to the same point in time, as well.

You can rollforward a table space containing part of a partitioned table to the end of logs.

See also

▸ The *Database partitioning* recipe in *Chapter 3, DB2 Multipartitioned Databases—Administration and Configuration*

▸ The *Table partitioning* recipe in *Chapter 6, Database Objects*

Redirected restore

A redirected restore allows you to restore a database to a different physical location than its original location. For example, a software supplier provides you with a database for test or demo purposes. The drawback is they don't follow the same file naming conventions and don't store the files in the same directories.

Let's take an example from a real-life situation; I changed the names to preserve confidentiality for this site.

Getting ready

List the table spaces and containers from the source databases, and map the containers to their respective destinations for the new database. All the commands have to be issued in the same window or CLP session.

How to do it...

1. List source tablespace and containers:

   List the table spaces and containers from the source databases, and map the containers to their respective destination for the new database.

   ```
   connect to marcustrn;
   list tablespaces show detail;
   list tablespace containers for 0;
   list tablespace containers for 1;
   list tablespace containers for 2;
   ...
   ```

2. Initiate restore redirect:

   We will attach to the instance. (The redirected restore is done on a Windows XP server).

   ```
   ATTACH TO DB2
   ```

   ```
        Instance Attachment Information

    Instance server       = DB2/NT 8.2.4
    Authorization ID      = RPELLETI...
    Local instance alias  = DB2
   ```

   This command will output a warning about table space state; this is normal.

   ```
   RESTORE DATABASE MARCUSTRN FROM 'D:\webApps\TrainingGold'
   TAKEN AT 20110217165613
   INTO MARCUS_TS WITH 2 BUFFERS BUFFER 1024
   REDIRECT PARALLELISM 1
   WITHOUT ROLLING FORWARD
   WITHOUT PROMPTING
   SQL1277N  Restore has detected that one or more table space
   containers are
   ```

```
inaccessible, or has set their state to 'storage must be defined'.
```

```
DB20000I  The RESTORE DATABASE command completed successfully.
```

3. Set new path for containers:

   We need to set the new path for each table space container:

   ```
   set tablespace containers for 0 using ( path 'D:\MARCUS_TS\
   SQLT0000.0' )
   ```

   ```
   DB20000I  The SET TABLESPACE CONTAINERS command completed
     successfully.
   ```

   ```
   set tablespace containers for 1 using ( path 'D:\MARCUS_TS\
   SQLT0001.0' )
   ```

   ```
   DB20000I  The SET TABLESPACE CONTAINERS command completed
     successfully.
   ```

   ```
   set tablespace containers for 2 using ( path 'D:\MARCUS_TS\
   SQLT0002.0' )
   ```

   ```
   DB20000I  The SET TABLESPACE CONTAINERS command completed
     successfully.
   ```

   ```
   set tablespace containers for 3 using ( path 'D:\MARCUS_TS\MARCUS_
   TSL' )
   ```

   ```
   DB20000I  The SET TABLESPACE CONTAINERS command completed
     successfully.
   ```

   ```
   set tablespace containers for 4 using ( path 'D:\MARCUS_TS\MARCUS_
   TST' )
   ```

   ```
   DB20000I  The SET TABLESPACE CONTAINERS command completed
     successfully.
   ```

   ```
   set tablespace containers for 5 using ( path 'D:\MARCUS_TS\
   SYSTOOLSPACE' )
   ```

   ```
   DB20000I  The SET TABLESPACE CONTAINERS command completed
     successfully.
   ```

   ```
   set tablespace containers for 6 using ( path 'D:\MARCUS_TS\
   SYSTOOLSTMPSPACE' )
   ```

   ```
   DB20000I  The SET TABLESPACE CONTAINERS command completed
     successfully.
   ```

4. Launch actual restore redirect:

   This command will output a warning about table space state; this is normal:

   ```
   RESTORE DATABASE MARCUSTRN CONTINUE
   DB20000I  The RESTORE DATABASE command completed successfully.
   ```

How it works...

The `REDIRECT` clause will direct DB2 to first place the table space containers in a **storage must be defined** state. Once the containers are all set to their new path/location, the `CONTINUE` launches the restore itself.

There's more...

If you need to stop the redirected restore, you have the option below.

ABORT

The `ABORT` clause will stop the redirected restore. This command is useful, if you have to step back and correct an error. You will have to start over with the `RESTORE DATABASE REDIRECT` command:

```
RESTORE DATABASE MARCUSTRN ABORT.
```

See also

▸ The *Database partitioning* recipe in *Chapter 3, DB2 Multipartitioned Databases—Administration and Configuration*

Recovery history file

This file is created at database creation time. It is updated automatically when `backup` or `restore` operations occur on the database, or on a table space. Table space operations, such as, `creation`, `quiesce`, `rename`, or `drop`, among others, also will have an impact on this file.

In our recipe, we will deliberately corrupt a history file and recover using an existing backup.

Getting ready

Please use a sandbox environment to duplicate this experience. Allow for the downtime to restart the instance.

We will *corrupt* the recovery history file by copying something else into this file. We already made a backup, so we're fine. Perhaps you would like to make a precautionary copy of this file first.

How to do it...

1. Make a precautionary copy of the recovery history file:

    ```
    [db2inst1@nodedb21 ~]$ pwd
    /home/db2inst1
    [db2inst1@nodedb21 ~]$ cd /data/db2/db2inst1/NODE0000/SQL00001
    [db2inst1@nodedb21 SQL00001]$ ls -l db2rhist.asc
    -rw-r----- 1 db2inst1 dba 15362 2011-08-05 20:08 db2rhist.asc
    [db2inst1@nodedb21 SQL00001]$ mv db2rhist.asc db2rhist.asc.bkp
    ```

2. Induce corruption into the recovery history file:

    We just copy something that is not compatible, to the db2rhist.asc. When the database is restarted, the startup is normal.

    ```
    [db2inst1@nodedb21 SQL00001]$ echo "Ne sarugi necogad etey lo sig
    lube pedeset. Ram cohece xico copu osimiv rud fama;" > db2rhist.
    asc
    [db2inst1@nodedb21 SQL00001]$ db2stop
    SQL1064N  DB2STOP processing was successful.
    [db2inst1@nodedb21 SQL00001]$ db2start
    SQL1063N  DB2START processing was successful.
    ```

3. Verify whether we indeed have corruption:

    When we attempt to list the history for backups the file's content is not recognized.

    ```
    [db2inst1@nodedb21 SQL00001]$ db2 list history backup all for pos
    SQL1224N  The database manager is not able to accept new requests,
    has

     terminated all requests in progress, or has terminated the
    specified request because of an error or a forced interrupt.
    SQLSTATE=55032
    ```

4. Recover the recovery history file:

    Get a list of backup files, and restore the history file from the most recent backup.

    ```
    [db2inst1@nodedb21 SQL00001]$ db2 "RESTORE DATABASE POS
            HISTORY FILE
            FROM  /xchng/backups
    ```

TAKEN AT 20110905153815"

DB20000I The RESTORE DATABASE command completed successfully.

5. Check if the backup history is ok:

```
[db2inst1@nodedb21 SQL00001]$ db2 list history backup all for pos
| more

                    List History File for pos

Number of matching file entries = 12


 Op Obj Timestamp+Sequence Type Dev Earliest Log Current Log
Backup ID
 -- --- ------------------ ---- --- ------------ ------------ ----
----------
  B   D   20110805205335001    F    D   S0000000.LOG S0000000.LOG
 ...
```

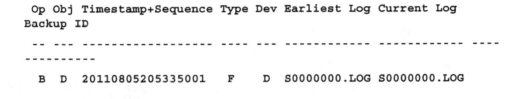

How it works...

DB2 will read the backup you specified and rebuild the history file from the backup.

There's more...

If you have made a precautionary copy using the operating system utility, you can just copy the db2rhist.asc.bkp back to the db2rhist.asc file and restart the database.

Location

db2rhist.asc is located in the same directory as the database configuration file.

```
[db2inst1@nodedb21 SQL00001]$ pwd
/data/db2/db2inst1/NODE0000/SQL00001
[db2inst1@nodedb21 SQL00001]$ ls -l db2rhist.asc
-rw-r----- 1 db2inst1 dba 15362 2011-08-05 20:08 db2rhist.asc
```

List history

View the history for all the database and table space operations cited earlier. In this case, we are using the LIST HISTORY command. In the report, you will see three important fields:

Op	OperationB - Backup	
	R - Restore	
	F - Roll-forward	
Obj	Object	D - Database
		P - Table space

PRUNE

You can use this command to remove old backup entries from the history file.

Drop database

All backups will include a copy of the recovery history file, so dropping a database also deletes the history file.

Restore database

The recovery history file is part of the backup file. If a recovery history file does not exist, it will be restored with the backup.

Configuring tape-based backup with IBM Tivoli Storage Manager

Tivoli Storage Manager (TSM) is a storage management application you can use across your network. Backup and restores, archiving are available by means of a server usually dedicated to this task. DB2 has an interface that uses the TSM Application program interface (API), which integrates tape backup/restore facilities. Please refer to the documentation for your platform.

Getting ready

Since DB2 V9.7 comes only in 64-bit version, make sure Tivoli Storage Manager is also a 64-bit version. We will assume the TSM server is ready and configured and that the TSM client is installed. DB2 supports TSM, so the only step required is installing and configuring the API for TSM. If the .profile is not set, allow for an instance restart.

How to do it...

1. Install Tivoli Storage Manager API:

   Install as per operating instructions.

2. Create the `dsm.opt` configuration file for TSM:

   Replace `TSM_DB2` with your server name, and save in `/usr/tivoli/tsm/client/api/bin64/dsm.opt`

   ```
   servername TSM_DB2
   ```

3. Create the `dsm.sys` configuration file for TSM:

   Replace `xxx.xxx.xxx.xxx` with `TSM_DB2`'s IP address and save in `/usr/tivoli/tsm/client/api/bin64/dsm.sys`

   ```
   servername TSM_DB2
   commmethod TCPIP
   tcpserveraddress xxx.xxx.xxx.xxx
   nodename DB2TSM
   passwordaccess GENERATE
   ```

4. Register the node `DB2 TSM` on the Tivoli Storage Manager Server:

   It is recommended to create a new `DOMAIN` on the TSM server for this node. You just need to create one management class. It will have a **copy group** configured as follows:

   ```
   VEREXIST=1
   VERDELETED=0
   RETEXTRA=0
   RETONLY=0
   ```

5. Run `dsmapipw` as root and follow the indications.

   This command will allow you to change TSM's password.

   ```
   cd /opt/IBM/DB2/v9.7.4/adsm
   ./dsmapipw
   ```

6. Update `.profile` for each instance owner on your server:

   In Linux or Unix, add to the instance owner's `.profile`, the following entries, log out and log in again, and restart the instance:

   ```
   export DSMI_CONFIG=/usr/tivoli/tsm/client/api/bin64/dsm.opt
   export DSMI_LOG=$HOME/logs
   export DSMI_DIR=/usr/tivoli/tsm/client/api/bin64
   ```

7. You can now perform a backup using TSM.

How it works...

DB2 supports TSM, but we do need to set the environment, to make DB2 aware of TSM. You can use the TSM client command line to query the TSM server.

There's more...

There is much more to discuss than these few lines. We suggest you read more on the subject before implementing tape backups.

Partitioned environment

In a large partitioned database environment, however, it might not be practical to have a tape device dedicated to each database partition server. You can connect the tape devices to one or more TSM servers, so that access to these tape devices is provided to each database partition server.

See also

Refer to the following link:
http://www.redbooks.ibm.com/redbooks/pdfs/sg246247.pdf.

db2move and db2look utilities as alternative backup methods

Sometimes backups may not be transportable to another operating system, or you may have to copy only a subset of a database, or perhaps just a schema. Since the backup command does not support these operations, we can still use db2move and db2look for alternate backups.

db2look is useful with extracting DDL, or data definition language, so we can recreate database objects, if need be. db2move will take care of data movement.

Getting ready

Allow for sufficient space and time for data extraction. We suggest you have a separate drive or filesystem for these, especially if you intend to have huge tables copied this way.

How to do it...

1. Choose a proper directory:

   ```
   [db2inst1@nodedb21 ~]$ cd /xchng/exports/pos/
   ```

2. Check if enough space is available:

   ```
   [db2inst1@nodedb21 pos]$ df .
   Filesystem             Size  Used Avail Use% Mounted on
   /dev/sdb1              459G   64G  372G  15% /xchng
   ```

3. Do the export:

   In this case, we chose to export all the POS schema's tables. Perform experiment with other settings, to do table exports, table space exports, and so on.

   ```
   [db2inst1@nodedb21 pos]$ db2move pos export -sn pos

   Application code page not determined, using ANSI codepage 1208


   *****   DB2MOVE   *****

   Action:  EXPORT

   Start time:  Mon Sep 12 22:33:00 2011


   All schema names matching:  POS;

   Connecting to database POS ... successful!  Server : DB2 Common
   Server V9.7.4

   EXPORT:   4595 rows from table "POS     "."FACTDET"
   EXPORT:   3309 rows from table "POS     "."FACTURES"
   EXPORT:      5 rows from table "POS     "."PAYMENT"
   EXPORT:     86 rows from table "POS     "."PRODUITS"
   EXPORT:      0 rows from table "POS     "."RECONCV"

   Disconnecting from database ... successful!

   End time:  Mon Sep 12 22:33:02 2011
   ```

4. Extract the DDL for these tables:

    We are using db2look to extract all DDLs from the POS database with table space creation DDLs. We'll be sending all normal and error stream output to DB2LOOK.out.

    ```
    [db2inst1@nodedb21 pos]$ db2look -d pos -e -l > DB2LOOK.out 2>&1
    ```

How it works...

db2move will store table information into a file called db2move.lst. This file can be used later on to load the tables into the same database, if you want to roll back on a complex migration, for example.

```
[db2inst1@nodedb21 pos]$ ls -l
total 736
-rw-r--r-- 1 db2inst1 dba    207 2011-09-12 22:33 db2move.lst
-rw-r--r-- 1 db2inst1 dba    539 2011-09-12 22:33 EXPORT.out
-rw-r--r-- 1 db2inst1 dba 313092 2011-09-12 22:33 tab1.ixf
-rw-r--r-- 1 db2inst1 dba    144 2011-09-12 22:33 tab1.msg
-rw-r--r-- 1 db2inst1 dba 321739 2011-09-12 22:33 tab2.ixf
-rw-r--r-- 1 db2inst1 dba    144 2011-09-12 22:33 tab2.msg
-rw-r--r-- 1 db2inst1 dba  10987 2011-09-12 22:33 tab3.ixf
-rw-r--r-- 1 db2inst1 dba    141 2011-09-12 22:33 tab3.msg
-rw-r--r-- 1 db2inst1 dba  21562 2011-09-12 22:33 tab4.ixf
-rw-r--r-- 1 db2inst1 dba    142 2011-09-12 22:33 tab4.msg
-rw-r--r-- 1 db2inst1 dba  37913 2011-09-12 22:33 tab5.ixf
-rw-r--r-- 1 db2inst1 dba    141 2011-09-12 22:33 tab5.msg
```

There's more...

Feel free to browse through db2move.lst and EXPORT.out files. You can use the EXPORT.out file to check row counts.

Using db2move to load data

You can now use these files to reimport into the same database, or on another database. db2move will use the db2move.lst to map the files back to the proper table name. If it's a different database, the tables have to be created with the REPLACE_CREATE option.

```
[db2inst1@nodedb21 pos]$ db2move pos import -io REPLACE

Application code page not determined, using ANSI codepage 1208
```

```
*****  DB2MOVE  *****

Action:  IMPORT

Start time:  Mon Sep 12 23:19:46 2011


Connecting to database POS ... successful!  Server : DB2 Common Server
V9.7.4

* IMPORT:  table "POS      "."FACTDET"
  -Rows read:          4595
  -Inserted:           4595
  -Rejected:              0
  -Committed:          4595

* IMPORT:  table "POS      "."FACTURES"
  -Rows read:          3309
  -Inserted:           3309
  -Rejected:              0
  -Committed:          3309

* IMPORT:  table "POS      "."PAYMENT"
  -Rows read:             5
  -Inserted:              5
  -Rejected:              0
  -Committed:             5

* IMPORT:  table "POS      "."PRODUITS"
  -Rows read:            86
  -Inserted:             86
  -Rejected:              0
  -Committed:            86

* IMPORT:  table "POS      "."RECONCV"
  -Rows read:             0
  -Inserted:              0
  -Rejected:              0
```

```
 -Committed:              0
```

`Disconnecting from database ... successful!`

`End time:  Mon Sep 12 23:19:50 2011`

LOAD with care

We suggest strongly that you use the LOAD utility with the NONRECOVERABLE option. With the default LOAD behavior, the first commit places a table space in backup-pending state; no other operations are allowed on each table space that has been loaded, until a backup has been done.

For example:

```
Load from d:\webapps\marcus\exp_imp\users.ixf
of ixf method N (
      userid,
      username,
      statuscode,
      role )
replace into marcus.users (
      userid,
      username,
      statuscode,
      role )
nonrecoverable without prompting data buffer 4000 sort buffer 2048;
```

Consider this carefully with production DBAs if you're in charge of migrating data to a critical production environment, to avoid unplanned downtime.

This NONRECOVERABLE option allows the load to be done, without being forced to take a backup immediately because of backup-pending conditions. If a problem happens during this type of LOAD operation, the table will be marked as corrupted and it must be dropped and recreated; you can't roll forward a database through a non-recoverable load without losing the table.

Once the table is loaded, we recommend you make a backup. Recovery and rolling forward is then possible.

See also

Backing up table spaces recipe in this chapter

8
DB2 High Availability

In this chapter, we will cover:

- ▸ Setting up HADR by using the command line
- ▸ Setting up HADR by using Control Center
- ▸ Changing HADR synchronization modes
- ▸ Performing takeover and takeover by force
- ▸ Using automated client rerouting with HADR
- ▸ Opening the standby database in read-only mode
- ▸ Using the DB2 fault monitor

Introduction

IBM DB2 comes and integrates a multitude of high-availability solutions, that can employ and increase the availability of databases. There are software high availability solutions, such as SQL Replication, Q Replication, HADR, DB2 ACS, and IBM TSA, and hardware-based solutions, such as IBM PPRC, HACMP, FlashCopy, or hybrid such as the new clustering solution provided by DB2 pureScale technology, covered in *Chapter 14, IBM pureScale Technology and DB2*. Obviously, we can choose to implement one solution or use a virtually unlimited number of combinations to ensure that we are highly protected from any type of disaster. In the following recipes, we will cover how to set up and and DB2 fault monitor as high availability solutions as a high availability solution.

HADR is a high availability software solution provided by IBM for DB2 database protection in the case of disaster or critical database failure. HADR is an abbreviation for **High Availability Disaster Recovery**. The technology itself can be classified as a replication solution. Basically, this technology replicates data by sending and replaying logs from a source database to a destination database. The source database, by convention, is called the primary database; the destination database is called the standby database.

Some important benefits of HADR:

- ▸ Transparent takeover (switchover) or takeover by force (failover) for clients connected
- ▸ Automatic client reroute capabilities
- ▸ It is a very fast method in terms of recoverability
- ▸ It has a negligible impact on transaction performance
- ▸ The cost is low compared with a hardware replication solution

Some restrictions with using HADR:

- ▸ Backup operations are not supported on standby databases
- ▸ HADR cannot be implemented with multipartitioned databases
- ▸ The primary and standby database must be run on the same operating system (same bit size) and the same version of the DB2 database system
- ▸ The system clock must be synchronized on both primary and standby servers

Operations replicated using HADR:

- ▸ Data definition language (DDL)
- ▸ Data manipulation language (DML)
- ▸ Buffer pool operations
- ▸ Table space operations
- ▸ Online reorganization
- ▸ Offline reorganization
- ▸ Metadata for stored procedures and user-defined functions

Operations that do not replicate using HADR:

- ▸ Tables created with the NOT LOGGED INITIALLY option
- ▸ Non-logged LOB columns are not replicated
- ▸ Updates to database configuration
- ▸ Database configuration and database manager configuration parameters
- ▸ Objects external to the database-related objects and library files
- ▸ The recovery history file (db2rhist.asc) and changes made to it

Setting up HADR by using the command line

Setting up HADR is straightforward. You can use a variety of methods to set up HADR, using the command line or **Control Center**, and IBM Optim Database Administrator HADR setup wizards. In the following recipe, we will set up HADR using the command line.

Getting ready

In this recipe, `nodedb21` will be used for the initial primary database, and `nodedb22` for the initial standby database. We use the term initially, because in the following recipes, we will initiate takeover and takeover by force operations, and the databases will exchange and change their roles. All operations will be conducted on the non-partitioned `NAV` database, under instance `db2inst1` on `nodedb21`, and `db2inst1` on `nodedb22`.

How to do it...

To set up a HADR configuration, we will use the following steps:

- Install IBM DB2 9.7 ESE in location `/opt/ibm/db2/ V9.7_01, on nodedb22`
- Creating additional directories for log archiving, backup, and mirror log locations, on both nodes
- Setting proper permissions on new directories
- Configuring log archiving and log mirroring
- Configuring the `LOGINDEXBUILD` and `INDEXREC` parameters
- Backing up the primary database
- Copying primary database backup to `nodedb22`
- Setting up HADR communication ports
- Configuring HADR parameters on both databases
- Configuring client reroute on both databases
- Initiating HADR on the standby database
- Initiating HADR on the primary database

Install IBM DB2 ESE on nodedb22

Install IBM DB2 9.7 Enterprise Server Edition in location `/opt/ibm/db2/V9.7_01`, on `nodedb22`; create users `db2inst1` and `db2fenc1`, and instance `db2inst1`, during installation.

Creating additional directories for table space containers, archive logs, backup, and mirror logs

1. Create one directory for table space containers of the NAV application on nodedb22:

   ```
   [root@nodedb22 ~]# mkdir -p /data/db2/db2inst1/nav
   [root@nodedb22 ~]#
   ```

2. Create directories for the archive logs location on both servers:

   ```
   [root@nodedb22 ~]# mkdir -p /data/db2/db2inst1/logarchives
   [root@nodedb22 ~]#
   [root@nodedb21 ~]# mkdir -p /data/db2/db2inst1/logarchives
   [root@nodedb22 ~]#
   ```

3. Create directories for the database backup location on both servers:

   ```
   [root@nodedb21 ~]# mkdir -p /data/db2/db2inst1/backup
   [root@nodedb21 ~]#
   [root@nodedb21 ~]# mkdir -p /data/db2/db2inst1/backup
   [root@nodedb21 ~]#
   ```

4. Create directories for the mirror log location on both servers:

   ```
   [root@nodedb21 ~]# mkdir -p /data/db2/db2inst1/mirrorlogs
   [root@nodedb21 ~]#
   [root@nodedb22 ~]# mkdir -p /data/db2/db2inst1/mirrorlogs
   [root@nodedb22~]#
   ```

    This is just an example; usually, the mirror logs should be stored in a safe location. If it is possible use an NFS mount exported from another server.

Setting permissions on the new directories

1. Set db2inst1 as owner for the directories where we will configure archive log and log mirrors, and restore the NAV application table space containers on both servers:

   ```
   [root@nodedb21 ~]# chown -R db2inst1:db2iadm1 /data/db2/db2inst1
   [root@nodedb21 ~]#
   [root@nodedb22 ~]# chown -R db2inst1:db2iadm1 /data/db2/db2inst1
   [root@nodedb22 ~]#
   ```

Configuring archive log and mirror log locations

1. Connect to the NAV database:

   ```
   [db2inst1@nodedb21 ~]$ db2 "CONNECT TO NAV"


      Database Connection Information

    Database server      = DB2/LINUXX8664 9.7.4
    SQL authorization ID = DB2INST1
    Local database alias = NAV
   ```

2. Quiesce the NAV database:

   ```
   [db2inst1@nodedb21 ~]$ db2 "QUIESCE DATABASE IMMEDIATE"
   DB20000I  The QUIESCE DATABASE command completed successfully.
   [db2inst1@nodedb21 ~]$
   ```

3. Set the log archive location:

   ```
   [db2inst1@nodedb21 ~]$ db2 "UPDATE DB CFG FOR NAV USING
      logarchmeth1 'DISK:/data/db2/db2inst1/logarchives'"
   DB20000I  The UPDATE DATABASE CONFIGURATION command completed
      successfully.
   [db2inst1@nodedb21 ~]$
   ```

4. Set the number of primary logs; usually, in a HADR configuration, it should be set to a greater value than in a normal database:

   ```
   [db2inst1@nodedb21 ~]$ db2 "UPDATE DB CFG FOR NAV USING
      LOGPRIMARY 20"
   DB20000I  The UPDATE DATABASE CONFIGURATION command completed
      successfully.
   [db2inst1@nodedb21 ~]$
   ```

5. Set the number of secondary logs:

   ```
   [db2inst1@nodedb21 ~]$ db2 "UPDATE DB CFG FOR NAV USING
      LOGSECOND 5"
   DB20000I  The UPDATE DATABASE CONFIGURATION command completed
      successfully.
   [db2inst1@nodedb21 ~]$
   ```

6. Set log file size; it is also recommended to be bigger than in a normal database:

```
[db2inst1@nodedb21 ~]$  db2 "UPDATE DB CFG FOR NAV USING
   LOGFILSIZ 2048 "

DB20000I  The UPDATE DATABASE CONFIGURATION command completed
   successfully.

[db2inst1@nodedb21
```

7. Set a mirror log location in the case where the primary log's host fails (these logs will be needed for replaying on the standby database):

```
[db2inst1@nodedb21 ~]$ db2 "UPDATE DATABASE CONFIGURATION USING
   MIRRORLOGPATH /data/db2/db2inst1/mirrorlogfiles"

DB20000I  The UPDATE DATABASE CONFIGURATION command completed
   successfully.

[db2inst1@nodedb21 ~]$
```

8. Set log buffer size. Use a log buffer size on both the primary and standby databases, bigger than in a normal database, to overcome log buffer full events:

```
[db2inst1@nodedb21 ~]$ db2 "UPDATE DB CFG FOR NAV USING
   LOGBUFSZ 1024 "

DB20000I  The UPDATE DATABASE CONFIGURATION command completed
   successfully.

db2inst1@nodedb21 ~]$
```

9. Unquiesce the NAV database:

```
[db2inst1@nodedb21 ~]$  db2 "UNQUIESCE DATABASE"

DB20000I  The UNQUIESCE DATABASE command completed successfully.

[db2inst1@nodedb21 ~]$
```

> LOGBUFSZ should be correlated with network tuning; try to set TCP tunables (receive and send buffer) to appropriate values.

Configuring LOGINDEXBUILD and INDEXREC parameters

1. The LOGINDEXBUILD parameter specifies if operations as create index, rebuild index, and reorganize table generates log when it has a value of ON or not if it is OFF, rebuild or table reorganization; usually, this parameter in a HADR configuration should be configured to ON. If you plan to use the standby database for reporting, then it is mandatory to set the parameter to ON.

2. If it is set to OFF, then there is not enough log information for building the indexes on the standby database. Therefore, the new indexes created or rebuilt in a HADR configuration are marked as invalid on the standby database.

3. In case you have slow network bandwidth, you can set it to OFF, but the amount of time needed to activate the standby database will increase considerably, because the invalid indexes have to be rebuilt. You can also control index logging at table level by setting the table option LOG INDEX BUILD to ON or OFF.

```
[db2inst1@nodedb21 ~]$ db2 "UPDATE DATABASE CONFIGURATION FOR NAV
   USING LOGINDEXBUILD ON "

DB20000I  The UPDATE DATABASE CONFIGURATION command completed
   successfully.

[db2inst1@nodedb21 ~]$
```

4. The parameter INDEXREC controls the rebuild of invalid indexes on database startup. In HADR configurations, it should be set to RESTART, on both databases.

```
[db2inst1@nodedb21 ~]$ db2 "UPDATE DATABASE CONFIGURATION FOR NAV
   USING INDEXREC RESTART"

DB20000I  The UPDATE DATABASE CONFIGURATION command completed
   successfully.

[db2inst1@nodedb21 ~]$
```

Backing up the primary database

1. Back up the database with the compress option, to save space; it is useful to compress the backup piece, especially when you have a very large database:

```
[db2inst1@nodedb21 ~]$ db2 terminate

DB20000I  The TERMINATE command completed successfully.

[db2inst1@nodedb21 ~]$ db2 "BACKUP DATABASE NAV TO "/data/backup"
   COMPRESS"

Backup successful. The timestamp for this backup image is :
   20110707150659

[db2inst1@nodedb21 ~]$
```

Copying the database backup to nodedb22

1. Copy the database backup to location /data/db2/db2inst1/backup on nodedb22:

```
[db2inst1@nodedb21 ~]$ scp /data/db2/db2inst1/backup/
NAV.0.db2inst1.NODE0000.CATN0000.
   20110707150659.001 nodedb22:/data/db2/db2inst1/backup

db2inst1@nodedb22's password:

NAV.0.db2inst1.NODE0000.CATN0000.20110707150659.001

[db2inst1@nodedb21 ~]$
```

Restoring the database NAV on nodedb22

1. Restore the database on the standby location:

```
[db2inst1@nodedb22 ~]$ db2 "RESTORE DATABASE NAV FROM /data/db2/
db2inst1/backup TAKEN AT 20110707150659 REPLACE
  HISTORY FILE"
DB20000I  The RESTORE DATABASE command completed successfully.
[db2inst1@nodedb22 ~]$
```

Setting up HADR communication ports

1. Add the following two entries to /etc/services, on both locations:

```
DB2_HADR_NAV1        55006/tcp
DB2_HADR_NAV2        55007/tcp
```

Setting up HADR parameters on the primary database

1. To specify the active hosts, we have to configure the following parameters:

    ❑ HADR_LOCAL_HOST – Specifies the local host; this parameter can either have the IP address or the hostname as values.

    ```
    [db2inst1@nodedb21 ~]$ db2 "UPDATE DATABASE CONFIGURATION
    FOR NAV USING HADR_LOCAL_HOST nodedb21"
    DB20000I  The UPDATE DATABASE CONFIGURATION command
    completed successfully.
    [db2inst1@nodedb21 ~]$
    ```

    ❑ HADR_REMOTE_HOST – Specifies the remote host; this parameter can either have the IP address or the hostname as values. On the primary database, it specifies the standby database host, and on the standby database, it specifies the primary database host.

    ```
    [db2inst1@nodedb21 ~]$ db2 "UPDATE DATABASE CONFIGURATION
    FOR NAV
      USING HADR_REMOTE_HOST nodedb22"
    DB20000I  The UPDATE DATABASE CONFIGURATION command
    completed
      successfully.;

    [db2inst1@nodedb21 ~]$
    ```

2. To specify the communication services, we have to configure the following parameters:

   ❑ HADR_LOCAL_SVC – Specifies the local HADR service name or port.

   ```
   [db2inst1@nodedb21 ~]$ db2 "UPDATE DATABASE CONFIGURATION
   FOR NAV
     USING HADR_LOCAL_SVC DB2_HADR_NAV1 "

   DB20000I  The UPDATE DATABASE CONFIGURATION command
   completed
     successfully.

   [db2inst1@nodedb21 ~]
   ```

   ❑ HADR_REMOTE_SVC – Specifies the remote HADR service name or port.

   ```
   [db2inst1@nodedb21 ~]$ db2 "UPDATE DATABASE CONFIGURATION
   FOR NAV
     USING HADR_REMOTE_SVC DB2_HADR_NAV2 DEFERRED"

   DB20000I  The UPDATE DATABASE CONFIGURATION command
   completed
     successfully.

   [db2inst1@nodedb21 ~]$
   ```

3. Specify the remote instance, on the primary it has as value the instance of the standby database:

   ❑ HADR_REMOTE_INST – Used to specify the remote instance.

   ```
   [db2inst1@nodedb21 ~]$ db2 "UPDATE DATABASE CONFIGURATION
   FOR NAV
     USING HADR_REMOTE_INST db2inst1 "

   DB20000I  The UPDATE DATABASE CONFIGURATION command
   completed
     successfully.

   [db2inst1@nodedb21 ~]$
   ```

4. To specify the synchronization mode, we have to configure the following parameter:

   ❑ HADR_SYNCMODE – Determines how the primary log writes are synchronized with the standby database. It can have the following values: SYNC, NEARASYNC, and SYNC.

   ```
   [db2inst1@nodedb21 ~]$ db2 "UPDATE DATABASE CONFIGURATION
   FOR NAV
     USING HADR_SYNCMODE ASYNC DEFERRED"

   DB20000I  The UPDATE DATABASE CONFIGURATION command
   completed
     successfully.

   [db2inst1@nodedb21 ~]$
   ```

5. Restart the database to activate the HADR parameters:

    ```
    [db2inst1@nodedb21 ~]$ db2 "DEACTIVATE DATABASE NAV"
    ```

    SQL1496W Deactivate database is successful, but the database was not activated.

    ```
    [db2inst1@nodedb21 ~]$ db2 "ACTIVATE DATABASE NAV"
    ```

    DB20000I The ACTIVATE DATABASE command completed successfully.

    ```
    [db2inst1@nodedb21 ~]$
    ```

Setting up HADR parameters on the standby database

1. Set the local and remote hosts:

    ```
    [db2inst1@nodedb22 ~]$ db2 "UPDATE DATABASE CONFIGURATION FOR NAV
        USING HADR_LOCAL_HOST nodedb22 "
    ```

    DB20000I The UPDATE DATABASE CONFIGURATION command completed successfully.

    ```
    [db2inst1@nodedb22 ~]$
    ```

    ```
    [db2inst1@nodedb22 ~]$ db2 "UPDATE DATABASE CONFIGURATION FOR NAV
        USING HADR_REMOTE_HOST nodedb21 "
    ```

    DB20000I The UPDATE DATABASE CONFIGURATION command completed successfully.

    ```
    [db2inst1@nodedb22 ~]$
    ```

2. Set the local and remote communication services:

    ```
    [db2inst1@nodedb22 ~]$ db2 "UPDATE DATABASE CONFIGURATION FOR NAV
        USING HADR_LOCAL_SVC DB2_HADR_NAV2 "
    ```

    DB20000I The UPDATE DATABASE CONFIGURATION command completed successfully.

    ```
    [db2inst1@nodedb22 ~]$ db2 "UPDATE DATABASE CONFIGURATION FOR NAV
        USING HADR_REMOTE_SVC DB2_HADR_NAV1 "
    ```

    DB20000I The UPDATE DATABASE CONFIGURATION command completed successfully.

3. Set the synchronization mode, identically:

    ```
    [db2inst1@nodedb22 ~]$ db2 "UPDATE DATABASE CONFIGURATION FOR NAV
        USING HADR_SYNCMODE ASYNC "
    ```

    DB20000I The UPDATE DATABASE CONFIGURATION command completed successfully.

    ```
    [db2inst1@nodedb22 ~]$
    ```

4. Set the remote instance, in this case, the instance of the primary database:

```
[db2inst1@nodedb22 ~]$ db2 "UPDATE DATABASE CONFIGURATION FOR NAV
   USING HADR_REMOTE_INST db2inst1 "

DB20000I  The UPDATE DATABASE CONFIGURATION command completed
   successfully. [db2inst1@nodedb22 ~]$
```

Starting HADR on standby database

1. The first step to activate HADR is to start HADR on the standby database:

```
[db2inst1@nodedb22 ~]$ db2 "START HADR ON DATABASE NAV AS STANDBY"

DB20000I  The START HADR ON DATABASE command completed
   successfully.

[db2inst1@nodedb22 ~]$
```

2. Activate the database, if necessary:

```
[db2inst1@nodedb22 ~]$ db2 "ACTIVATE DATABASE NAV"

DB20000I  The ACTIVATE DATABASE command completed successfully.

[db2inst1@nodedb22 ~]$
```

3. The parameter hadr_role should now change its value to STANDBY:

```
[db2inst1@nodedb22 ~]$ db2 "GET DB CFG FOR NAV" | grep "HADR
   database role"

HADR database role                         = STANDBY

[db2inst1@nodedb22 ~]$
```

Starting HADR on primary database

1. Activate HADR on the primary database:

```
[db2inst1@nodedb21 ~]$ db2 "START HADR ON DATABASE NAV AS PRIMARY"

DB20000I  The START HADR ON DATABASE command completed
   successfully.

[db2inst1@nodedb21 ~]$
```

2. The parameter hadr_role will have the value changed to PRIMARY:

```
[db2inst1@nodedb21 ~]$ db2 "GET DB CFG FOR NAV" | grep "HADR
   database role"

HADR database role                         = PRIMARY

[db2inst1@nodedb21 ~]$
```

Monitoring HADR

1. To monitor the status of HADR, you can use the db2pd command:

```
[db2inst1@nodedb21 ~]$ db2pd -d NAV -hadr
```

How it works...

The mechanism used by HADR to protect against data loss consists of transmitting data changes continually from the primary database to the standby database. Actually, the primary database sends the contents of its log buffer to be replayed on standby. The transmission is realized between two special edu processes; on the primary, `db2hadrp` is used, and on standby, `db2hadrs`.

The health and integrity of HADR is monitored continuously by a mechanism named heartbeats, in which the primary database and standby database send messages to each other or ping each other from time to time, or to be more precise, a message occurs every quarter of the `hard_timeout` value, which is specified in seconds.

HADR tries all the time to keep the standby database synchronized; with the primary database. In HADR, there are three levels of synchronization implemented that are explained in more detail in the recipes that follow: `ASYNC`, `NEARSYNC`, and `SYNC`.

There could be situations when the databases are not synchronized, for example, we could experience a network failure or another unpredicted event, which can influence the log record transmission. To resolve log desynchronizations, HADR uses a mechanism named **log catchup**. It is based on reading the log records that are not yet applied on the standby database, from archive log files generated on the primary database. This is the first reason why the primary database has to be in archive logs mode. The log replay process on the standby database is very similar to a database recovery (the standby database is in continuous rollforward pending state).

If the databases are synchronized, then they are in peer state.

The database roles are interchangeable: the primary may become standby, and vice versa, in the case of initiating a takeover operation. In the case that the primary database is no longer available, we should initiate a takeover by force or a failover operation. In this case, we can restore the database from the standby site or reinitialize the former primary, if it is possible.

There's more...

Before you plan to set up a HADR configuration, you have to meet some requirements regarding table spaces:

- Table space type must be the same on both servers
- Table space container paths must be the same on both servers
- Table space container sizes must be the same
- Table space container types (raw or file) must be the same

The hadr_timeout and hadr_peer_window database configuration parameters

There are two more important parameters which can influence the behavior and response of HADR connection failure:

- ▶ HADR_TIMEOUT – Specified in seconds, the amount of time to wait before HADR considers the communication lost between database pairs. When HADR detects a network disconnect, all transactions running on primary will hang for the amount of time specified by this parameter.

- ▶ HADR_PEER_WINDOW – Specified in seconds, the amount of time in which the primary database suspends a transaction after the database pairs have entered disconnect state.

Set these in conformance with your internal MTTR.

See also

Chapter 9, Problem Determination, Event Sources, and Files, for monitoring HADR; you can also use the db2top or GET SNAPSHOT ON DATABASE NAV commands.

Setting up HADR by using Control Center

In this recipe, we will cover how to set up HADR using the wizard provided by **Control Center**.

Getting ready

In this recipe, we will set up the same HADR configuration build-up, using the command line. But, there are some differences; we will skip the configuration of archive log and mirror logging and focus just on the HADR part itself.

- ▶ Install IBM DB2 ESE according to the *Install IBM DB2 ESE on nodedb22* subsection under the *Setting up HADR by using the command line* recipe.

- ▶ Create directories according to the *Creating additional directories for table space containers, archive log, backup, and mirror logs* subsection under the *Setting up HADR by using the command line* recipe.

- ▶ Set permission on directories according to the *Setting proper permissions on the new directories* subsection under the *Setting up HADR by using the command line* recipe.

- ▶ Configure archive log and log mirroring according to the *Configuring log archiving and mirror logging* subsection under the *Setting up HADR by using the command line* recipe.

▶ Catalog the admin `nodedb22` node (you can catalog the admin nodes using the setup provided by the wizard at step 3):

```
[db2inst1@nodedb21 ~]$ db2 "CATALOG ADMIN TCPIP NODE NODEDB22
   REMOTE nodedb21 SYSTEM  nodedb22 OSTYPE  LINUXX8664"
DB20000I  The CATALOG ADMIN TCPIP NODE command completed
   successfully.
DB21056W  Directory changes may not be effective until the
   directory cache is
refreshed.[db2inst1@nodedb21 ~]$
```

▶ Catalog instance `db2inst1` under the admin node:

```
[db2inst1@nodedb21 ~]$ db2 "CATALOG TCPIP NODE node22 REMOTE
   NODEDB22 SERVER 50001 REMOTE_INSTANCE  db2inst1 SYSTEM  NODEDB22
   OSTYPE  LINUXX8664"DB20000I  The CATALOG TCPIP NODE command
   completed successfully.
DB21056W  Directory changes may not be effective until the
   directory cache is Refreshed
[db2inst1@nodedb21 ~]$
```

How to do it...

1. Right-click on the database `NAV` and choose **High Availability Disaster Recovery | Set Up...**.

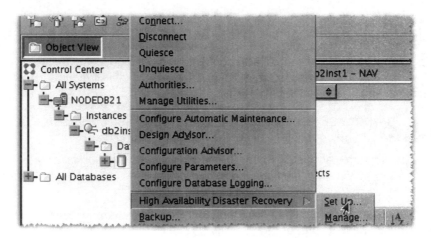

2. Skip the introduction; next, we can see that our database is in archive log mode and enabled for log shipping to a standby location:

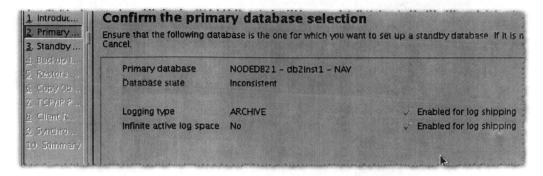

3. In the next step, we are asked to identify the standby database:

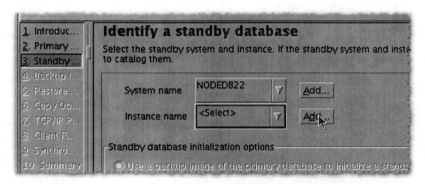

4. Next, we'll do a full database backup, which will be used for restoring NAV database on nodedb22:

5. Choose /data/db2/db2inst1/backup as the backup location:

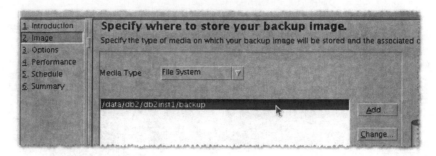

6. Next, select the backup made previously. It is recommended to choose the most recent backup; in this way, fewer log archives need to be replayed on the standby database.

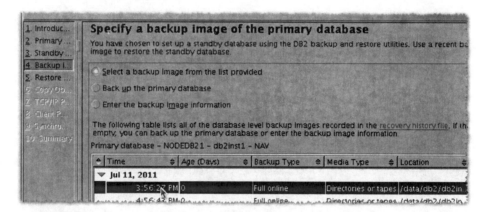

7. Select the same location for nodedb22, for the database backup location:

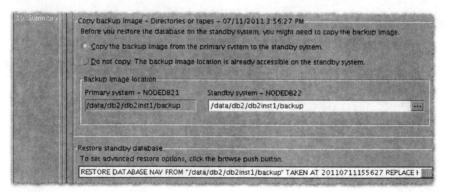

8. Set the hostname, HADR service name, and HADR port number. You can choose new values or use existing ones. The service name and port number will be added to `/etc/services`, on both hosts:

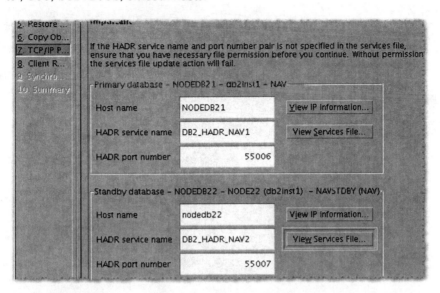

9. Set the automatic client reroute; for `NAV` on `nodedb21`, the alternative will be `NAVSTDBY` from host `nodedb22`, and vice versa:

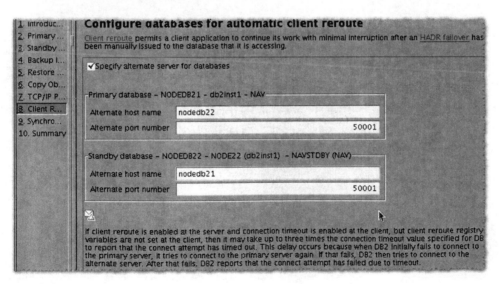

10. Set the synchronization mode to **Asynchronous**. We'll delve into more detail about synchronization modes and related parameters, later.

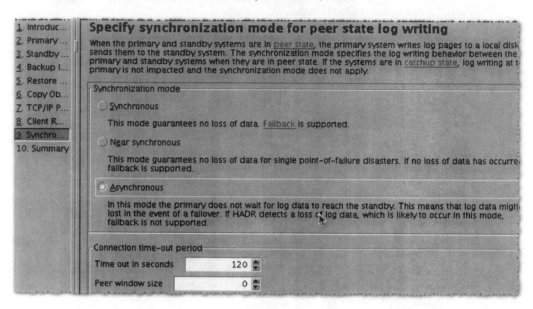

11. Next, on the summary screen, you can review the steps and the command lines used to implement HADR:

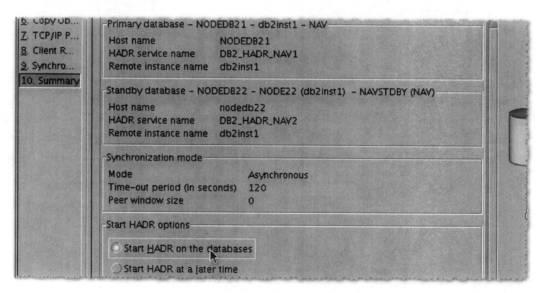

12. Click on **Finish**, to start the implementation of HADR; next, we'll see a progress box showing the steps as follows:

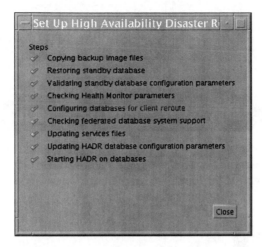

13. If the setup was successful, we should now be able to manage and monitor our HADR configuration. Right-click on the NAV database and go to **High Availability Disaster Recovery | Manage...**.

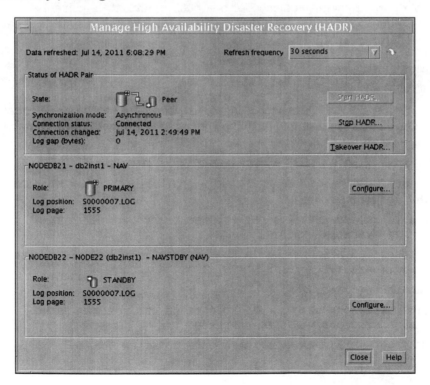

How it works...

The main difference between using the **Control Center** and the command line is that you need to additionally catalog admin nodes on both sides.

You can also use the HADR wizard provided by IBM Optim Administrator if you are familiar with this tool.

Changing HADR synchronization modes

Synchronization modes determine how primary logs are propagated and synchronized with the standby database when the systems are in peer state. The stricter the synchronization mode, the more influenced the performance on the primary database. There are three synchronization modes: SYNC, NEARSYNC, and ASYNC.

Getting ready

In this recipe, we will switch first to NEARSYNC mode, then to SYNC synchronization mode, and then back to ASYNC mode.

The HADR_SYNCMODE parameter mentioned previously controls the synchronization mode of HADR. Since this parameter is not dynamic after any modification, a HADR and database restart is needed.

How to do it...

The parameter HADR_SYNCMODE is not dynamic, so every change to the synchronization mode requires a database restart for both the primary database and standby database.

Changing to NEARSYNC synchronization mode

1. Change the value of HADR_SYNCMODE, on both the databases, to NEARSYNC synchronization mode:

```
[db2inst1@nodedb22 ~]$ db2 "UPDATE DB CFG FOR NAV USING
  HADR_SYNCMODE NEARSYNC "

DB20000I  The UPDATE DATABASE CONFIGURATION command completed
  successfully.

[db2inst1@nodedb22 ~]$

[db2inst1@nodedb21 ~]$ db2 "UPDATE DB CFG FOR NAV USING
  HADR_SYNCMODE NEARSYNC DEFERRED"

DB20000I  The UPDATE DATABASE CONFIGURATION command completed
  successfully.

[db2inst1@nodedb21~]$
```

2. Stop the HADR process on the NAV standby database:

```
[db2inst1@nodedb22 ~]$ db2 "DEACTIVATE DATABASE NAV"
DB20000I   The DEACTIVATE DATABASE command completed successfully.
[db2inst1@nodedb22 ~]$
[db2inst1@nodedb22 ~]$ db2 "STOP HADR ON DATABASE NAV"
DB20000I   The STOP HADR ON DATABASE command completed
  successfully.
[db2inst1@nodedb22 ~]$
```

3. Also stop HADR on the NAV primary database:

```
[db2inst1@nodedb21 ~]$ db2 "STOP HADR ON DATABASE NAV"
DB20000I   The STOP HADR ON DATABASE command completed
  successfully.
[db2inst1@nodedb21 ~]$
```

4. Now, start HADR on the NAV standby database, first:

```
[db2inst1@nodedb22 ~]$ db2 "START HADR ON DATABASE NAV AS STANDBY"
DB20000I   The START HADR ON DATABASE command completed
  successfully.
[db2inst1@nodedb22 ~]$
```

5. Start HADR on the NAV primary, too:

```
[db2inst1@nodedb21 ~]$ db2 "START HADR ON DATABASE NAV AS PRIMARY"
DB20000I   The START HADR ON DATABASE command completed
  successfully.
[db2inst1@nodedb21 ~]$
```

6. To see the current synchronization mode, you can take a database snapshot on the primary database :

```
[db2inst1@nodedb21 ~]$ db2 "get snapshot for database on NAV"
..........................................................................

HADR Status
  Role                = Primary
  State               = Peer
  Synchronization mode  = Nearsync
  Connection status   = Connected, 07/11/2011 15:02:46.823678
  Heartbeats missed   = 0
  Local host          = NODEDB21
  Local service       = DB2_HADR_NAV1
  Remote host         = nodedb22
```

```
Remote service          = DB2_HADR_NAV2
Remote instance         = db2inst1
timeout(seconds)        = 120
Primary log position(file, page, LSN) = S0000003.LOG, 37,
0000000005F6554D
Standby log position(file, page, LSN) = S0000003.LOG, 37,
0000000005F6554D
Log gap running average(bytes) = 0
```

Changing to SYNC synchronization mode

1. Change the value of HADR_SYNCMODE, on both the databases, to SYNC synchronization mode:

   ```
   [db2inst1@nodedb22 SQL00001]$ db2 "UPDATE DB CFG FOR NAV USING
     HADR_SYNCMODE SYNC "
   ```

   DB20000I The UPDATE DATABASE CONFIGURATION command completed successfully.

   ```
   [db2inst1@nodedb21 ~]$ db2 "UPDATE DB CFG FOR NAV USING
     HADR_SYNCMODE RSYNC"
   ```

   DB20000I The UPDATE DATABASE CONFIGURATION command completed successfully.

2. Repeat steps 2 to 5 in the *Change to NEARSYNC mode* subsection.

Changing back to ASYNC synchronization mode

1. Change the value of HADR_SYNMODE on both the databases to ASYNC synchronization mode:

   ```
   [db2inst1@nodedb22 SQL00001]$ db2 "UPDATE DB CFG FOR NAV USING
     HADR_SYNCMODE ASYNC DEFERRED"
   ```

   DB20000I The UPDATE DATABASE CONFIGURATION command completed successfully.

   ```
   [db2inst1@nodedb21 ~]$ db2 "UPDATE DB CFG FOR NAV USING
     HADR_SYNCMODE ASYNC DEFERRED"
   ```

   DB20000I The UPDATE DATABASE CONFIGURATION command completed successfully.

2. Repeat steps 2 to 5 in the *Changing to NEARSYNC mode* subsection.

How it works...

A brief description of synchronization modes:

> ▸ SYNC – Synchronous transmission provides the greatest protection and influences the transaction speed the most. When running the HADR synchronization in this mode, log writes are considered to be successful only when log records have been written to the log files on the primary database. Next, the standby database will send an acknowledgment to the primary database that the standby database logs have also been written to disk. When the primary database receives the acknowledgment from the standby database, the running transaction is accepted as committed. In this mode, there is no data loss.

> ▸ NEARSYNC – Meaning near-synchronous, this is an intermediate level between synchronous and asynchronous transmission. In this mode, the primary database receives acknowledgment in the case when the log records have also been written to log buffer on the standby side. Running in this mode ensures minimal transaction loss.

> ▸ ASYNC – In this mode, you have the shortest transaction response, but the highest chance of transaction loss. The primary does not wait for acknowledgement from the standby database to commit the running transaction.

There's more...

To see the current synchronization mode you can also query the system administrative view `sysibmadm.snaphadr`.

A new synchronization mode has been added in fixpack level 5—SUPERASYNC. In this mode, we may have the best performance because it is less restrictive in terms of transaction commit acknowledgement (transactions might be considered committed when they are still on their way to the standby), and as a disadvantage, we also have the highest probability for losing transactions in this synchronization mode.

Performing takeover and takeover by force

Performing a takeover operation simply means the primary database and the standby database will exchange their roles. Usually, a role switching is appropriate during a database upgrade or other planed operation, such as server maintenance, operating system upgrades, and so on.

A takeover by force is suitable in the case that the primary host is no longer available for some reason.

Getting ready

In this recipe, we will perform a takeover from NAV primary to NAV standby, and vice versa. We'll also proceed to do a takeover by force, simulating a host failure.

How to do it...

Using Control Center

1. Right-click on the NAV database and select **High availability disaster recovery | Manage**, and then click on the **Takeover HADR** button:

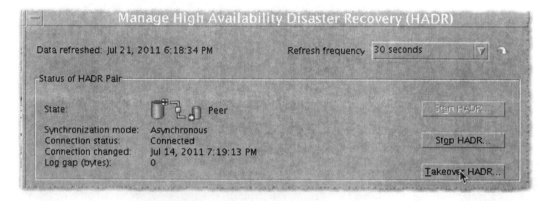

2. Next, we get the following dialog box; choose **Takeover** and click **OK**:

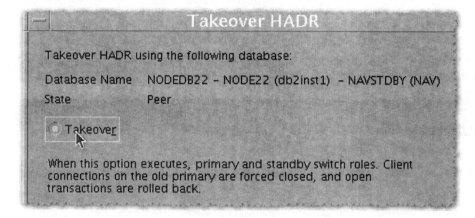

3. Now, we can observe that the database roles are changed:

4. Repeat steps 1 to 4 to switch back the NAV standby database to primary role.

Using the command line to perform a takeover

1. On nodedb22, issue the following command:

    ```
    [db2inst1@nodedb22 ~]$ db2 "TAKEOVER HADR ON DATABASE NAV USER
    db2inst1 USING db2inst1"DB20000I  The TAKEOVER HADR ON DATABASE
      command completed successfully.

    [db2inst1@nodedb22 ~]$
    ```

2. After the takeover command is completed successfully, go on nodedb21,
    to switch back:

    ```
    [db2inst1@nodedb21 ~]$  db2 "TAKEOVER HADR ON DATABASE NAV USER
      db2inst1 USING db2inst1"

    DB20000I  The TAKEOVER HADR ON DATABASE command completed
      successfully.

    [db2inst1@nodedb21 ~]$
    ```

Using the command line to perform a takeover by force

Remember that after you perform a takeover by force you have to try to reintegrate the former primary as standby or recreate the standby database and rebuild the HADR configuration.

1. Shut down the primary host (`nodedb21`); wait and monitor to see that no connection is available and issue the following command:

```
[db2inst1@nodedb22 ~]$ db2 "TAKEOVER HADR ON DATABASE NAV USER
   db2inst1 USING db2inst1 BY FORCE"

DB20000I  The TAKEOVER HADR ON DATABASE command completed
   successfully.

[db2inst1@nodedb22 ~]$
```

How it works...

When a takeover operation is initiating, the standby database sends a message to the primary database to indicate that a takeover operation is ready to start. Next, the primary database disconnects all connections and refuses any new connections; it `rollback` any current transaction and ships the remaining log to the standby database. Next, the standby database replays the received log and the databases switch their roles; the primary becomes standby, and vice versa.

In the takeover by force operation, the standby database does not cooperate with the primary database as in the takeover operation. The standby database sends a confirmation message to the primary database to shut down, but it does not wait for any acknowledgment.

There's more...

The takeover by force operation can be used with the peer window state option.

Using automated client rerouting with HADR

The client reroute mechanism is based on transferring the client application requests from a failed server to one that is available and running. After we initiate a takeover or takeover by force, the primary database is no longer available to handle requests from clients, and all connections will be redirected to the new primary database.

Getting ready

All connections will be established from the DB2 client installed in *Chapter 1, DB2 Instance— Administration and Configuration*. In the meantime, we'll initiate a takeover and see how the client connections are reestablished to the standby site. The rerouting capability was set up during HADR implementation using **Control Center**.

How to do it...

1. First, we have to catalog `nodedb21`, `db2inst1`, and the NAV database, on the client.

2. Connect to the NAV primary database:

   ```
   [db2clnt1@nodedb22 ~]$ db2 "connect to NAV user db2inst1 using
       db2inst1"


       Database Connection Information

   Database server        = DB2/LINUXX8664 9.7.4
   SQL authorization ID   = DB2INST1
   Local database alias   = NAV
   ```

3. Next, perform a database takeover on `nodedb21`:

   ```
   [db2inst1@nodedb21 ~]$  db2 "TAKEOVER HADR ON DATABASE NAVSTDBY
       USER db2inst1 USING db2inst1"

   DB20000I  The TAKEOVER HADR ON DATABASE command completed
       successfully.

   [db2inst1@nodedb21 ~]$
   ```

4. Try to run a query, a simple count from table `comm`, on the primary database:

   ```
   [db2inst1@nodedb21 ~]$  db2 "select count(*) from nav.comm"

   SQL30108N  A connection failed but has been re-established.
   The hostname or IP address is "nodedb22" and the service name or
       port number is "50001".

   Special register settings might have been replayed.

   (Reason code = "1").

   SQLSTATE=08506

   [db2inst1@nodedb21 ~]$
   ```

5. After a short time, the connection is reestablished, and if we again issue our query, it works:

   ```
   [db2inst1@nodedb21 ~]$  db2 select count(*) from nav.comm


   1
   -----------
         15026

     1 record(s) selected.
   [db2inst1@nodedb21 ~]$
   ```

6. We will observe that our connection is reestablished on the former standby database, which now has a primary database role. Verify the current active connections by executing the following command:

```
[db2inst1@nodedb21 ~]$  db2 list applications


Auth Id  Application     Appl.       Application Id
DB        # of
          Name            Handle
Name     Agents
-------- -------------- ---------- ------------------------------
------------------------------ -------- -----
DB2INST1 db2bp    247       *LOCAL.db2inst1.110711163243      NAV  1
DB2INST1 db2bp    231       10.231.56.118.50308.11071116302   NAV  1
[db2inst1@nodedb21 ~]$
```

How it works...

The automatic client reroute is totally automatic, as its name suggests. When a communication failure occurs, the connection is terminated and the client retries to connect to any available node that is defined as an alternative. The alternative location is stored in the system database directory.

There's more...

We can control or tune client reroute by setting some related DB2 registry variables, such as the following:

- DB2TCP_CLIENT_CONTIMEOUT
- DB2TCP_CLIENT_RCVTIMEOUT
- DB2_MAX_CLIENT_CONNRETRIES
- DB2_CONNRETRIES_INTERVAL

Opening the standby database in read-only mode

One of the biggest achievements of using HADR is that the standby database can be opened in read-only mode and used for reporting purposes. For example, in some hardware replication solutions, it is not possible to open the standby/replicated database. In this way, you can release the primary database from additional processing effort induced by possible intensive reports. Issuing read-only queries on the standby database does not interfere with the log replay mechanism, so it has no impact on data synchronization.

Getting ready...

For this recipe, we will run some simple queries on the standby database to demonstrate how to use the standby database in read-only mode.

How to do it...

1. To enable read-only mode for the standby database, we need to modify the `DB2_HADR_ROS` registry variable to `ON`.

   [db2inst1@nodedb22 ~]$ db2set DB2_HADR_ROS=ON

2. Restart the instance.

    Try to use a different IP address for connecting to the standby database in read-only mode, enable a virtual IP address, or add a physical Ethernet card to your standby host. The client rerouting mechanism cannot differentiate between the primary and standby databases, when it is activated as read-only.

3. Connect to the `NAV` standby database:

   [db2inst1@nodedb22 ~]$ db2 "connect to nav"

   ```
      Database Connection Information

    Database server        = DB2/LINUXX8664 9.7.4
    SQL authorization ID   = DB2INST1
    Local database alias   = NAV
   ```

4. Next, we will execute some queries on the standby database. Get the synchronization mode by issuing the following query:

   [db2inst1@nodedb22 ~]$ db2 "select HADR_SYNCMODE from sysibmadm.snaphadr"

   ```
   HADR_SYNCMODE
   -------------
   ASYNC

     1 record(s) selected.
   ```

5. Here is another query, but this time on a regular table. For example, we want to know how many rows the comm table has:

```
[db2inst1@nodedb22 ~]$ db2 "select count(*) from nav.comm"


1

-----------

SQL1773N  The statement or command requires functionality that is
   not supported on a read-enabled HADR standby database.
Reason code = "1".
If we issue
```

6. The query was not executed. The reason is that we are not using the supported isolation level on read-only standby databases:

```
[db2inst1@nodedb22 ~]$ db2 "? SQL1773N"
SQL1773N  The statement or command requires functionality that is
   not supported on a read-enabled HADR standby database.
Reason code = "<reason-code>".


Explanation:


The explanation corresponding to the reason code is:


1


         An isolation level other than UR is used and the
         DB2_STANDBY_ISO registry variable is turned off.
```

7. Set the DB2_STANDBY_ISO registry variable to the recommended value:

```
[db2inst1@nodedb22 ~]$ db2set DB2_STANDBY_ISO=UR
```

8. Stop HADR on the standby database:

```
[db2inst1@nodedb22 ~]$ db2 "deactivate database nav"
DB20000I  The DEACTIVATE DATABASE command completed successfully.
[db2inst1@nodedb22 ~]$ db2 "stop hadr on database nav"
DB20000I  The STOP HADR ON DATABASE command completed
   successfully.
```

9. Restart the instance:

```
[db2inst1@nodedb22 ~]$ db2stop
07/23/2011 23:36:20     0   0   SQL1064N  DB2STOP processing was
  successful.
SQL1064N  DB2STOP processing was successful.
[db2inst1@nodedb22 ~]$ db2start
07/23/2011 23:36:25     0   0   SQL1063N  DB2START processing was
  successful.
SQL1063N  DB2START processing was successful.
```

10. Start HADR:

```
[db2inst1@nodedb22 ~]$ db2 "start hadr on database nav as standby"
DB20000I  The START HADR ON DATABASE command completed
  successfully.
```

11. Connect to the NAV standby database and repeat the query:

```
[db2inst1@nodedb22 ~]$ db2 "connect to nav"


    Database Connection Information

 Database server        = DB2/LINUXX8664 9.7.4
 SQL authorization ID   = DB2INST1
 Local database alias   = NAV


[db2inst1@nodedb22 ~]$ db2 "select count(*) from nav.comm"


1
-----------
      15026


  1 record(s) selected.
```

How it works...

To open a standby database, it must be in a peer state with the primary. A connection to the standby database cannot be established until it is in catch-up phase or in replay-only window state (replaying DDL statements or performing maintenance operations).If the standby database enters the replay-only window, existent connections will be disconnected. Therefore, it is recommended to minimize these types of operations or execute them in a reserved time window. On the standby database, you will see only the committed transactions. Therefore, it is recommended to increase the number of commits on the primary database, to have a more consistent view of the standby database. Since there are no writes possible, the only isolation level permitted is uncommitted read (anyway, you don't have uncommitted transactions in the standby database either uncommitted transactions).

There's more...

Some restriction that applies to read-only standby databases:

- No operations that result in log generation can be executed
- Declared temporary tables cannot be created and accessed
- Created temporary tables are not accessible and cannot be created
- Sort operations or any operation that needs temporary segments are possible just in SMS temporary table spaces
- A read-only standby database cannot be quiesced
- Database backups and archive logs are not supported
- Queries that are using other isolation levels than Uncommitted Read (UR) will not be executed

Be sure to tune the memory and I/O parameters, to run your reports optimally. Generally, use the same settings as on the primary database at operating system, instance and database level.

Using the DB2 fault monitor

The main role of DB2 fault monitor is to keep the instances running all the time. In the case where an instance fails because of an unpredicted event, such as a software bug or an accidental close, the fault monitor will try to restart it.

Getting ready

In the following recipe, we will cover the parameters that control the fault monitor and how it works.

How to do it...

Every instance has a fault monitor registry file located in `<instance user home>/sqllib/`. This file has the format `fm.machinename.reg` and contains the parameters that control the behavior of the fault monitor. Usually, this file is updated using the corresponding switches of the `db2fm` command. For example, our fault monitor registry, for `db2inst1` on `nodedb21`, has the following parameters or keywords:

```
[db2inst1@nodedb21 sqllib] more fm.nodedb21.reg
FM_ON = no # default
FM_ACTIVE = yes # default
START_TIMEOUT = 600 # default
STOP_TIMEOUT = 600 # default
STATUS_TIMEOUT = 20 # default
STATUS_INTERVAL = 20 # default
RESTART_RETRIES = 3 # default
ACTION_RETRIES = 3 # default
```

The following are the descriptions of the Fault monitor parameters:

- ▶ `FM_ON` – If it is `ON`, the fault monitor is started. If is set to `OFF`, the fault monitor does not start at system boot and stops if it has already been started (value can be set using the `-f` switch, thus: `db2fm -f on`/.`db2fm -f off`).

- ▶ `FM_ACTIVE` – If `YES`, the fault monitor is active. If it is set to `NO`, the fault monitor is not active, so it does not take any action if the instance is shut down abnormally (the value can be set using the `-a` switch, thus: `db2fm -a on/off`).

- ▶ `START_TIMEOUT` – The value is specified in seconds. It specifies the amount of time within which it must start the instance (the value can be set by using the `db2fm -T T1` switch).

- ▶ `STOP_TIMEOUT` – The value is specified in seconds and represents the amount of time within which it must bring down the monitored service (the value can be set by using the `db2fm -T /T2` switch).

- ▶ `STATUS_TIMEOUT` – The value is specified in seconds and represents the amount of time needed to get the status of the monitored service (the value can be set by using the `db2fm -l /T2` switch).

- ▶ `STATUS_INTERVAL` – The value is specified in seconds and represents the value between two consecutive calls to obtain the status of service (the value can be set by using the `db2fm -l T1` switch).

- ▶ `RESTART_RETRIES` – Specifies the number of times the fault monitor will try to obtain the status of the service being monitored after a failed attempt. Once this number is reached, the fault monitor will take action to bring the service back online (the value can be set by using the `db2fm -R  R1` switch).

- ► `ACTION_RETRIES` – Specifies the number of times fault monitoring will attempt to start the service (value can be set by using the db2fm –R /R2 switch).

- ► `NOTIFY_ADDRESS` – Represents the mail address for sending notifications to (value can be set by using db2fm –n).

For exemplification set some Fault monitor parameters and simulate an instance crash:

1. Set `START_TIMEOUT` to 10 seconds:

   db2fm –T 10

2. To turn on the fault monitor daemon, issue:

   Db2fm –f on

3. Now, find the db2sys process and kill it, or issue the db2_kill operation. Wait more than 10 seconds and you should see the instance db2inst1 up.

How it works...

The fault monitor is actually coordinated by a daemon that is started at boot. If you have more than one instance on your server, then you will have one fault monitor, for every instance, with its own set of rules. The daemon process will try to ensure the continuity of availability for each fault monitor.

There's more...

The fault monitor will become inactive in the case where you bring down the instance with db2stop or its variants (STOP DATABASE MANAGER). In any other cases, it will try to bring up the instance online.

9
Problem Determination, Event Sources, and Files

In this chapter, we will cover:

- ▸ Using `db2mtrk`—DB2 memory tracker
- ▸ Using `db2pd`—DB2 problem determination tool
- ▸ Using `db2dart`—DB2 database analysis and reporting tool command
- ▸ Using `db2ckbkp`—DB2 check backup tool for backup integrity
- ▸ Using `db2support` to collect diagnostic data

Introduction

There could be many situations where you might encounter different performance problems, physical corruption, or bugs. In reality, the list of problems could be huge, especially when we administer a complex system. In order to detect and solve these types of problems, DB2 comes with plenty of diagnostic and problem determination tools.

To inspect memory consumption at instance and database-level, you can use the DB2 memory tracker. For more diagnostics, almost at any level, IBM provides a complex tool named DB2 problem determination. To analyze the database structure and solve space issues, or to extract data from unrecoverable databases, you may use the DB2 database analysis and reporting tool. To trace different problematic operations and to find bottlenecks, you may use application or process tracing, facilitated by DB2 trace.

For ensuring that we have consistent backup files, we have at our disposal the DB2 check backup tool for backup integrity. Another very helpful tool for detecting performance problems is db2top. This tool inherits its structure and functionality from top utility found in almost all Linux distros and nmon utility found in AIX.

In the following recipes, we'll cover and describe how to use some of these helpful tools.

Using db2mtrk—DB2 memory tracker

With the help of this tool we can monitor agents, applications, databases, and instance memory structures. It is very useful for monitoring memory consumption at peak times or to gather information about memory utilization during data processing.

Getting ready

In this recipe, we will gather information about memory consumption at instance and database level.

How to do it...

1. To see how memory is allocated per component for the current instance, issue the following command:

    ```
    [db2inst1@nodedb21 ~]$ db2mtrk -i

    Tracking Memory on: 2011/08/09 at 21:38:07


    Memory for instance


        other       fcmbp       monh
        17.2M       832.0K      640.0K
    [db2inst1@nodedb21 ~]$
    ```

    Here, the -i option is used for showing the memory used by the current instance. The truth is that the previous listing appears a little cryptic. For more detailed information regarding the memory usage use the -v switch. With this option, we can display verbose memory usage information.

2. Now reissue the command using the -v option to obtain a more detailed output:

```
[db2inst1@nodedb21 ~]$ db2mtrk -i -v
Tracking Memory on: 2011/08/09 at 21:40:39

Memory for instance

   Other Memory is of size 18087936 bytes
   FCMBP Heap is of size 851968 bytes
   Database Monitor Heap is of size 655360 bytes
   Total: 19595264 bytes
[db2inst1@nodedb21 ~]$
```

FCMBP is the **Fast Communication Manager Buffer Pool** (FCM buffers and channels). Other Memory is the memory associated with the overhead of operating the database management system.

3. To see the memory allocated for the NAV database, issue the following command:

```
[db2inst1@nodedb21 ~]$ db2mtrk -d  -v
Tracking Memory on: 2011/08/09 at 22:20:20

Memory for database: NAV

   Backup/Restore/Util Heap is of size 262144 bytes
   Package Cache is of size 8454144 bytes
   Other Memory is of size 196608 bytes
   Catalog Cache Heap is of size 851968 bytes
   Buffer Pool Heap (3) is of size 107151360 bytes
   Buffer Pool Heap (2) is of size 214171648 bytes
   Buffer Pool Heap (1) is of size 182910976 bytes
   Buffer Pool Heap (System 32k buffer pool) is of size 851968
     bytes
   Buffer Pool Heap (System 16k buffer pool) is of size 589824
     bytes
   Buffer Pool Heap (System 8k buffer pool) is of size 458752 bytes
   Buffer Pool Heap (System 4k buffer pool) is of size 393216 bytes
   Shared Sort Heap is of size 196608 bytes
   Lock Manager Heap is of size 24576000 bytes
   Database Heap is of size 20840448 bytes
   Application Heap (46652) is of size 65536 bytes
   Application Heap (31) is of size 65536 bytes
   Application Heap (30) is of size 65536 bytes
```

```
     Application Heap (29) is of size 65536 bytes
     Application Heap (28) is of size 196608 bytes
     Application Heap (27) is of size 65536 bytes
     Application Heap (26) is of size 65536 bytes
     Application Heap (25) is of size 65536 bytes
     Applications Shared Heap is of size 1638400 bytes
     Total: 564199424 bytes
  [db2inst1@nodedb21 ~]$
```

4. You can combine the options or use just one option at a time. One of the `-i`, `-d`, `-a`, or `-p` options must be specified when you issue the `db2mtrk` command. For a summary description of all options, issue the following command:

```
  [db2inst1@nodedb21 ~]$ db2mtrk -h
  Usage: db2mtrk -i | -d | -a | -p [-m | -w] [-v] [-r interval
     [count]] [-h]
```

```
     -i  Display instance level memory usage
     -d  Display database level memory usage
     -a  Display application level memory usage
     -p  Display agent private memory usage
     -m  Display maximum usage information
     -w  Display watermark usage information
     -v  Display verbose memory usage information
     -r  Run in repeat mode
          interval  Amount of seconds to wait between reports
          count     Number of reports to generate before quitting
     -h  Display this help screen


  Notes:


     1. One of -i -d -a -p must be specified.
     2. The -w and -m flags are optional.  An invocation of the
        application is invalid if both flags are specified.
     3. The -m flag reports the maximum allowable size for a given
        heap while the -w flag reports the largest amount of memory
        allocated from a given heap at some point in its history.
     ...................................................................... .

  [db2inst1@nodedb21 ~]$
```

How it works...

When `db2mtkr` is executed, it provides a snapshot with memory consumption. However, the information provided is not too accurate during intense database utilization. Therefore, it is better to monitor memory usage using time intervals. Static memory information applies better to see consumption watermarks or maximum memory limits.

There's more...

To monitor maximum memory consumption represented by a watermark, use the `-w` option. For example, to see the maximum memory allocated by the current instance, since startup, issue the following command:

```
[db2inst1@nodedb21 ~]$ db2mtrk -i -w -v
Tracking Memory on: 2011/08/09 at 13:36:14


Memory for instance

    Other Memory has watermark of 17563648 bytes

    FCMBP Heap has watermark of 851968 bytes

    Database Monitor Heap has watermark of 655360 bytes

    Total: 19070976 bytes
[db2inst1@nodedb21 ~]$
```

You also have the ability to gather memory information at intervals, adding the `-r` (interval, count) option to the `db2mtkr` command.

For example, to monitor database memory every 3 seconds, with a count of 4, and save the output to a file, issue the following command:

```
[db2inst1@nodedb21 ~]$ db2mtrk -d -v -r 3 4 > dbnavmonitor.out
[db2inst1@nodedb21 ~]$
```

Using db2pd—DB2 problem determination tool

`db2pd` is an abbreviation for the DB2 problem determination tool. It is very useful for detecting various problems and has almost negligible impact on the database and instance, because it does not rely on memory latches for inspection. It inspects the memory structures without interfering with the database engine.

Getting ready

db2pd has plenty of options used for retrieving information about operating systems, dynamic SQL, table statistics, database partitions, and also including information about storage, configuration, recovery processes, HADR status, and many more. There are two possible methods to use db2pd, in interactive mode or executing from the command line with options.

How to do it...

1. Further, we will cover some common options and diagnostics. To gather information about the operating system using db2pd, execute the following command:

```
[db2inst1@nodedb21 ~]$ db2pd -osinfo


Operating System Information:


OSName:    Linux
NodeName:  nodedb21
Version:   2
Release:   6
Machine:   x86_64


CPU Information:
TotalCPU   OnlineCPU   ConfigCPU   Speed(MHz)   HMTDegree   Cores/
Socket
2          2           2           3332         1
1


Physical Memory and Swap (Megabytes):
TotalMem   FreeMem     AvailMem    TotalSwap    FreeSwap
3950       584         n/a         4096         4096


Virtual Memory (Megabytes):
Total      Reserved    Available   Free
8046       n/a         n/a         4680


Message Queue Information:
MsgSeg     MsgMax      MsgMap      MsgMni       MsgTql      MsgMnb
MsgSsz
n/a        65536       65536       4096         65536       65536
16
```

```
Shared Memory Information:
ShmMax                   ShmMin                    ShmIds      ShmSeg
68719476736              1                         4096        4096


Semaphore Information:
SemMap        SemMni        SemMns        SemMnu        SemMsl        SemOpm
SemUme        SemUsz        SemVmx        SemAem
256000        1024          256000        256000        250           32
n/a           20            32767         32767


CPU Load Information:
Short       Medium      Long
0.070000    0.030000    0.000000


CPU Usage Information (percent):
Total       Usr         Sys         Wait        Idle
3.500000    n/a         n/a         n/a         96.500000
[db2inst1@nodedb21 ~]$
```

2. To gather information about current HADR status, execute the following command:

```
[db2inst1@nodedb21 ~]$ db2pd -hadr -db NAV


Database Partition 0 -- Database NAV -- Active -- Up 17 days
22:37:54 -- Date 08/09/2011 15:43:28


HADR Information:
Role     State               SyncMode HeartBeatsMissed
LogGapRunAvg (bytes)
Primary Peer                 Async    0                            0


ConnectStatus ConnectTime                             Timeout
Connected     Sat Jul 23 23:37:58 2011 (1311453478) 120


LocalHost                             LocalService
NODEDB21                              DB2_HADR_NAV1


RemoteHost                            RemoteService
RemoteInstance
nodedb22                              DB2_HADR_NAV2
db2inst1
```

```
        PrimaryFile  PrimaryPg  PrimaryLSN
        S0000018.LOG 1197       0x000000000DBED574


        StandByFile  StandByPg  StandByLSN
        S0000018.LOG 1197       0x000000000DBED574
        Showing information about storage paths
        [db2inst1@nodedb21 ~]$ db2pd -storagepath -db NAV


        Database Partition 0 -- Database NAV -- Active -- Up 17 days
        22:40:50 -- Date 08/09/2011 15:46:24


        Database Storage Paths:
        Number of Storage Paths       1


        Address             PathID    PathState    PathName
        0x00002B2E9FF81BE0 0          InUse        /data/db2
        [db2inst1@nodedb21 ~]$
```

How it works...

db2pd attaches directly to memory structures. It does not acquire latches or locks on the database, which means that you can use this tool for diagnosing, even if the database is hanged.

There's more...

To obtain the complete list of options, use the -help switch. Also you can use db2pd, as mentioned previously, in interactive mode. In this mode, you will get a prompt where you will able to use the same options as in the command line mode:

```
[db2inst1@nodedb21 ~]$ db2pd -interactive
db2pd> You are running db2pd in interactive mode.
db2pd> If you want command line mode, rerun db2pd with valid options.
db2pd> Type -h or -help for help.
db2pd> Type q to quit.
db2pd> -d NAV
```

Using db2dart—DB2 database analysis and reporting tool command

This tool inspects structural and architectural correctness of databases and the objects within them. Since this tool reads the data directly from the disk, it is highly recommended to run it after all applications and users are disconnected (it is more desirable to effectively close the database). The main reason for this is that db2dart cannot read committed pages (dirty pages) from memory and the diagnostics will not be accurate.

The granularity of db2dart can be classified in levels, as database, table space, and table. You can also dump and format table data, index data, and mark indexes as invalid to be eligible for rebuild. Also you can get information about table high watermarks and how to lower them.

Getting ready

In this recipe, we will verify the entire NAV database and use some analysis options, such as dump and formatting.

How to do it...

1. First, close the NAV database to have consistent data, before you run the db2dart utility:

   ```
   [db2inst1@nodedb21 ~]$ db2 "deactivate database NAV"
   DB20000I  The DEACTIVATE DATABASE command completed successfully.
   ```

2. Now, run the utility to diagnose the NAV database:

   ```
   [db2inst1@nodedb21 ~]$ db2dart NAV


           The requested DB2DART processing has completed
   successfully!

                           Complete DB2DART report found in:
   /home/db2inst1/sqllib/db2dump/DART0000/NAV.RPT
   ```

   At the end of the report, we get the status (in our case it has not found any error):

   ```
   [db2inst1@nodedb21 ~]$ tail -f /home/db2inst1/sqllib/db2dump/
   DART0000/NAV.RPT


           The requested DB2DART processing has completed
   successfully!
   ```

```
                    All operation completed without error;
                    no problems were detected in the database.


                    Complete DB2DART report found in:
       /home/db2inst1/sqllib/db2dump/DART0000/NAV.RPT


          _____    D A R T   P R O C E S S I N G    C O M P L E T E  _____
```

3. To check all table spaces, execute the following command:

```
[db2inst1@nodedb21 db2]$ db2dart NAV /DTSF /RPT /data/db2/db2inst1


        The requested DB2DART processing has completed
successfully!
                    Complete DB2DART report found in:
/data/db2/db2inst1/DART0000/NAV.RPT


Where /RPT is to point to the directory where to put the report.
```

4. To export in a dump COMM table, issue the following command:

```
[db2inst1@nodedb21 DART0000]$ db2dart NAV /DDEL


FYI: An active connection to the database has been detected.
     False errors may be reported.
     Deactivate all connections and re-run to verify.



   Table object data formatting start.
   Please enter
Table ID or name, tablespace ID, first page, num of pages:
COMM,4,0,2000


   11 of 11 columns in the table will be dumped.
   Column numbers and datatypes of the columns dumped:
        0   VARCHAR() -VARIABLE LENGTH CHARACTER STRING
        1   VARCHAR() -VARIABLE LENGTH CHARACTER STRING
        2   VARCHAR() -VARIABLE LENGTH CHARACTER STRING
        3   DECIMAL
        4   DECIMAL
        5   DECIMAL
```

```
        6  DECIMAL
        7  DECIMAL
        8  DECIMAL
        9  DECIMAL
       10  DECIMAL
```

Default filename for output data file is TS4T5.DEL,
do you wish to change filename used? y/n
n

....

```
    Dumping Page 165 ....
    Dumping Page 166 ....
    Dumping Page 167 ....
    Dumping Page 168 ....
    Dumping Page 169 ....
    Dumping Page 170 ....
    Dumping Page 171 ....
    Dumping Page 172 ....
    Dumping Page 173 ....
    Table object data formatting end.
```

        The requested DB2DART processing has completed
successfully!
                        Complete DB2DART report found in:
/home/db2inst1/sqllib/db2dump/DART0000/NAV.RPT

5. A short listing from the resulting table dump:

    [db2inst1@nodedb21 DART0000]$ more TS4T5.DEL

    "3EA697B9","CA13372","MIDLAND TRAFFIC",+0256.,+00122.700,
    +00126.700,+00000.000,+00000.000,+00000.000,+160860.00,+10082
    58.00

    "3EA697F1","CA18519","COLLINGWOOD TRAFFIC",+0256.,+00122.800,
    +00000.000,+00000.000,+00000.000,+00000.000,+160017.00,+1
    007430.00

    "3EA698B7","CA31334","BUTTONVILLE RDO",+0286.,+00122.300,
    +00126.700,+00000.000,+00000.000,+00000.000,+161909.00,+10105
    08.00

....

How it works...

`db2dart` reads data and metadata directly from disk; actually, it reads data directly from the table space containers.

There's more...

`db2dart` has high watermark lowering capacities. For more information about the existent options and their usage, issue the following command:

```
[db2inst1@nodedb21 backup]$ db2dart -h
```

Using db2ckbkp—DB2 check backup tool for backup integrity

This utility is used for checking the backup file integrity to determine if the backup file image is eligible for restore. Also, with the help of this tool, we can read the backup image header information. In this area, various descriptions are stored (if logs are included, if the backup image is compressed, and so on).

Getting ready

Next, we will perform a full database backup. We will perform a check of the backup image. These operations are followed by corrupting the backup image to see what the tool reports after.

How to do it...

1. Back up the NAV database:

   ```
   [db2inst1@nodedb21 ~]$ db2 "BACKUP DATABASE NAV ONLINE TO "/
   data/backup" WITH 2 BUFFERS BUFFER 1024 PARALLELISM 1 WITHOUT
   PROMPTING"


   Backup successful. The timestamp for this backup image is :
   20110809161456
   ```

2. List the available backups:

   ```
   [db2inst1@nodedb21 backup]$ db2 "list history backup since
   20110809172151 for NAV"


                       List History File for NAV
   ```

```
Number of matching file entries = 1


  Op Obj Timestamp+Sequence Type Dev Earliest Log Current Log
Backup ID
  -- --- ------------------ ---- --- ------------ ------------ ----
- ---------
   B   D   20110809172151001   N     D   S0000021.LOG S0000021.LOG
   -----------------------------------------------------------------
- ---------
   Contains 5 tablespace(s):

   00001 SYSCATSPACE
   00002 USERSPACE1
   00003 SYSTOOLSPACE
   00004 NAV_TBLS
   00005 NAV_INDX
   -----------------------------------------------------------------
- ---------
     Comment: DB2 BACKUP NAV ONLINE
  Start Time: 20110809172151
    End Time: 20110809172154
      Status: A
   -----------------------------------------------------------------
- ---------
   EID: 98 Location: /data/backup [db2inst1@nodedb21 ~]$
```

3. Check the integrity of the backup file:

   ```
   [db2inst1@nodedb21 backup]$ db2ckbkp NAV.0.db2inst1.NODE0000.
   CATN0000.20110809172151.001


   [1] Buffers processed:  #######################################
   ##################################


   Image Verification Complete - successful.
   ```

4. Next, we'll corrupt the backup file and run a check again:

```
[db2inst1@nodedb21 backup]$ sed -i '1 a\ corrupt123$$'
NAV.0.db2inst1.NODE0000.CATN0000.20110809172151.001
```

5. Now, check the backup image, again:

```
[db2inst1@nodedb21 backup]$ db2ckbkp NAV.0.db2inst1.NODE0000.
CATN0000.20110809172151.001


[1] Buffers processed:  #########################################
##################################
        ERROR!  No history file found!
        ERROR!  No DATA.POOL.TABLE!
        ERROR!  No DB configuration!
        ERROR!  No BUFFER.POOL.FILE found!
        ERROR!  No LOG.FILE.HEADER found!
        ERROR!  No MIRRORLOG.FILE.HEADER found!
        ERROR!  No END.OF.INITIAL.DATA found!
        ERROR!  No backup tail found!


Image Verification Complete - ERRORS DETECTED:  8
```

How it works...

Every backup file has a header where it stores the information about the backup file. The DB2 check backup tool inspects the header first and then verifies if the backup file corresponds as structure and data with the header information.

There's more...

To display the header information and verify the image use the -h option:

```
[db2inst1@nodedb21 backup]$ db2ckbkp -h NAV.0.db2inst1.NODE0000.
CATN0000.20110809225356.001


=====================
MEDIA HEADER REACHED:
=====================
        Server Database Name            -- NAV
        Server Database Alias           -- NAV
        Client Database Alias           -- NAV
```

```
            Timestamp                            -- 20110809225356
            Database Partition Number            -- 0
            Instance                             -- db2inst1
            Sequence Number                      -- 1
            Release ID                           -- D00
            Database Seed                        -- 7F3848D2
            DB Comment's Codepage (Volume)       -- 0
            DB Comment (Volume)                  --
            DB Comment's Codepage (System)       -- 0
            DB Comment (System)                  --
            Authentication Value                 -- -1
            Backup Mode                          -- 1
            Includes Logs                        -- 1
            Compression                          -- 0
            Backup Type                          -- 0
            Backup Gran.                         -- 0
            Merged Backup Image                  -- 0
            Status Flags                         -- 20
            System Cats inc                      -- 1
            Catalog Partition Number             -- 0
            DB Codeset                           -- ISO8859-1
            DB Territory                         --
            LogID                                -- 1309789578
            LogPath                              -- /data/db2/db2inst1/logfiles/
NODE0000/
            Backup Buffer Size                   -- 4194304
            Number of Sessions                   -- 1
            Platform                             -- 1E

  The proper image file name would be:
NAV.0.db2inst1.NODE0000.CATN0000.20110809225356.001


[1] Buffers processed:  ##############################################
###########################

Image Verification Complete - successful..
[db2inst1@nodedb21 backup]$
```

With the help of db2ckbkp you may find if log files are included in the backup image (in report Include Logs has a status of 1) or the backup image is compressed(in report Compression has a status of 1).

Using db2support to collect diagnostic data

db2support is a tool mainly used to collect extensive information for a running problem. By using this tool, you no longer need to manually collect traces, dumps, or other files requested by IBM DB2 technical support. The collected data is generated and held organized to be easier to study by IBM support. It can also be used for internal use, to diagnose various performance problems.

Getting ready

This tool has many options; there is also the possibility of use in interactive mode, based on questions and answers. In this recipe, we will execute db2support by mainly using general options and will give one example of how to use it in interactive mode.

How to do it...

1. To get a summary description about the possible options, issue the following command:

   ```
   [db2inst1@nodedb21 ~]$ db2support -help
   ```

2. To collect information for the NAV database, issue the following command:

   ```
   [db2inst1@nodedb21 backup]$ db2support /data/support/NAV -d NAV
   ```

3. To start db2support in interactive mode, issue the following command:

   ```
   [db2inst1@nodedb21 backup]$ db2support d:\data\support -d NAV -q
   ,,,,,,,,,,,,,,,,,,,,,,,,,,,,,,,,,db2support Interactive Mode

   ...................................................................
   ................................................

    What type of DB2 problem is occurring?
   POSSIBLE ANSWERS:

   1) Performance
   2) Recovery, Logging, or Backup and Restore
   3) Hang or Crash
   4) Application Development
   5) Installation or migration
   6) Administration tools
   7) Client, connectivity, or authentication
   8) DB2 utilities
   ```

```
9) Data integrity
10) Locking or concurrency
Enter the number corresponding to your answer.


or press 'q' to quit
1


 Describe the problem with the query including:,
      What is the intended function of this statement?,
      Are your statements generated by a query generator (3rd
party product)?,
       What is the name of the query generator?,
      Are you having problems with a particular query plan?,
      Have you recently rerun runstats or reorg?,
      anything else?



Enter your response.
Anything else
.........................................................
.........................
q
[db2inst1@nodedb21 backup]$
```

How it works...

The db2support tool collects diagnostic files in specific directories under the destination directory. It also generates a file named db2support.html, which contains a table of contents organized according to the analyzed information.

There's more...

You can direct db2support to collect information about statements that have performance problems, using the following options:

```
db2support output_directory -d database_name -sf sql_file
```

10
DB2 Security

In this chapter, we will cover:

- ► Managing instance-level authorities
- ► Managing database-level authorities and privileges
- ► Managing object privileges
- ► Creating roles
- ► Using encryption
- ► Using **label-based access control (LBAC)** to strengthen data privacy
- ► Auditing DB2

Introduction

Today, we live in a world where there seems to be an equal proportion between defense and attack methods. We can have the most calibrated and well-designed database in the world; all is in vain if it can be compromised at any time.

Most companies that develop and sell database systems tend to allocate a lot of effort to developing security products within and around their products. This field can make a difference in today's fierce competition. These companies, including IBM, have invested heavily in tools and methods for securing DB2. In the following recipes, we will cover some of them, such as authorizations, roles, encryption, LBAC, and auditing.

Managing instance-level authorities

We can define an authority as a predefined role with privileges at instance or database level. In DB2, there are two types of authority: instance level and database level. In this chapter, we will cover instance-level authorities.

Getting ready

We have four instance-level authorities: SYSADM (system administration authority), SYSCTRL (system control authority), SYSMAINT (system maintenance authority), and SYSMON (system monitoring authority). Assignment to these authorities is managed through operating system groups.

SYSADM is the highest level authority in DB2. It has full access to data and utilities, has implicit DBADM authority within any database under instance, and can grant and revoke SECADM.

SYSCTRL is the highest level of system control authority. It is mainly an exclusive instance-level authority; it has no privileges to query data from a database unless it has been granted them explicitly. With this authority, it is possible to drop and create databases, restore databases, start and stop instances, and reorganize tables.

The SYSMAINT authority is the second-highest level of system control authority at instance-level. Mainly, it is assigned to groups that are responsible for instance and database maintenance; it has no rights to query data unless explicitly granted.

SYSMON is the lowest authority for system control. This authority is granted for users who perform database and instance monitoring (instance and database snapshots, and event monitoring).

In this recipe, we will create three groups and three users corresponding to each instance control authority, excluding SYSADM (this authority is granted to db2iadm1 at installation). We'll assign authorities to all of these groups and cover some of the operations that they are able to perform.

How to do it...

1. Get our current instance level authority assignments:

```
[db2inst1@nodedb21 ~]$ db2 "get dbm cfg " | grep SYS
    SYSADM group name                   (SYSADM_GROUP) = DB2IADM1
    SYSCTRL group name                  (SYSCTRL_GROUP) =
    SYSMAINT group name                 (SYSMAINT_GROUP) =
    SYSMON group name                   (SYSMON_GROUP) =
```

2. Next, create three new operating groups and three new users:

```
[root@nodedb21 ~]# groupadd sysctrl
[root@nodedb21 ~]#
[root@nodedb21 ~]# groupadd sysmaint
[root@nodedb21 ~]#
[root@nodedb21 ~]# groupadd sysmon
[root@nodedb21 ~]#
[root@nodedb21 ~]# useradd instctrl -g sysctrl
[root@nodedb21 ~]#
[root@nodedb21 ~]# useradd instmant -g sysmaint
[root@nodedb21 ~]#
[root@nodedb21 ~]# useradd instmon -g sysmon
[root@nodedb21 ~]#
```

3. Set passwords identically with usernames.

4. Next, assign the new groups to each instance-level authority:

```
[db2inst1@nodedb21 ~]$ db2 "update dbm cfg using sysctrl_group
sysctl  sysmaint_group sysmaint sysmon_group sysmon "
DB20000I  The UPDATE DATABASE MANAGER CONFIGURATION command
completed

successfully.

[db2inst1@nodedb21 ~]$
```

5. User instctrl, belonging to group sysctrl, now has SYSCTRL authorization. Next, we will attach to instance db2inst1 and perform some system control operations:

```
[db2inst1@nodedb21 ~]$ db2 "attach to db2inst1 user instctrl using
instctrl"


    Instance Attachment Information

Instance server        = DB2/LINUXX8664 9.7.4
Authorization ID       = INSTCTRL
Local instance alias   = DB2INST1
```

6. One of the privileges this authority has is to bounce the instance:

```
[db2inst1@nodedb21 ]db2stop
```

```
01/23/2012 23:40:56     0   0   SQL1064N  DB2STOP processing was
successful.
```

```
SQL1064N  DB2STOP processing was successful.
```

```
[db2inst1@nodedb21 ] db2start
```

```
01/23/2012 23:41:00     0   0   SQL1063N  DB2START processing was
successful.
```

```
SQL1063N  DB2START processing was successful.
```

```
[db2inst1@nodedb21 ]
```

7. Perform a backup of table spaces NAV_TBLS and NAV_INDX:

```
[db2inst1@nodedb21 ]db2 "BACKUP DATABASE NAV TABLESPACE ( NAV_
INDX, NAV_TBLS ) ONLINE TO "/data/db2/db2inst1/backup" WITH 2
BUFFERS BUFFER 1024 PARALLELISM 1 UTIL_IMPACT_PRIORITY 50 WITHOUT
PROMPTING"
```

```
Backup successful. The timestamp for this backup image is :
20120123234846
```

```
[db2inst1@nodedb21 ]
```

8. Connect to the NAV database:

```
[db2inst1@nodedb21 ~]$ db2
```

```
"connect to nav user instctrl using instctrl"
```

```
   Database Connection Information

 Database server        = DB2/LINUXX8664 9.7.4

 SQL authorization ID   = INSTCTRL

 Local database alias   = NAV
[db2inst1@nodedb21 ~]$
```

9. To demonstrate that this authority has no access rights in the database, issue the following query:

```
[db2inst1@nodedb21 ~]$ db2 "select count(*) from nav.comm"
```

```
SQL0551N  "INSTCTRL" does not have the required authorization or
privilege to
```

```
perform operation "SELECT" on object "NAV.COMM".
SQLSTATE=42501[db2inst1@nodedb21 ~]$
```

10. You need to grant table access explicitly to instctl. Connect with the SYSADM or DBADM authorities and grant select on table COMM from schema nav to instctrl:

```
[db2inst1@nodedb21 ~]$ db2 "connect to nav"


   Database Connection Information

   Database server        = DB2/LINUXX8664 9.7.4
   SQL authorization ID   = DB2INST1
   Local database alias   = NAV


   b2inst1@nodedb1:~> db2 "grant select on nav.comm to instctrl"
   DB20000I  The SQL command completed successfully.
```

11. To see authorizations for user instctrl, connect to the NAV database as user instctrl, and issue the following command:

```
[db2inst1@nodedb21 home]$ db2 "get authorizations"


   Administrative Authorizations for Current User

   Direct SYSADM authority                        = NO
   Direct SYSCTRL authority                       = NO
   Direct SYSMAINT authority                      = NO
   Direct DBADM authority                         = NO
   Direct CREATETAB authority                     = NO
   Direct BINDADD authority                       = NO
   Direct CONNECT authority                       = NO
   Direct CREATE_NOT_FENC authority               = NO
   Direct IMPLICIT_SCHEMA authority               = NO
   Direct LOAD authority                          = NO
   Direct QUIESCE_CONNECT authority               = NO
   Direct CREATE_EXTERNAL_ROUTINE authority       = NO
   Direct SYSMON authority                        = NO

   Indirect SYSADM authority                      = NO
   Indirect SYSCTRL authority                     = YES
   Indirect SYSMAINT authority                    = NO
   Indirect DBADM authority                       = NO
```

```
Indirect CREATETAB authority                    = YES

Indirect BINDADD authority                      = YES

Indirect CONNECT authority                      = YES

Indirect CREATE_NOT_FENC authority              = NO

Indirect IMPLICIT_SCHEMA authority              = YES

Indirect LOAD authority                         = NO

Indirect QUIESCE_CONNECT authority              = NO

Indirect CREATE_EXTERNAL_ROUTINE authority = NO

Indirect SYSMON authority                       = NO.

[db2inst1@nodedb21 ~]$
```

12. Attach to db2inst1 as user instmant who has SYSMAINT authority:

```
[db2inst1@nodedb21 ~]$ db2 "attach to db2inst1 user instmant using
instmant"


    Instance Attachment Information

Instance server         = DB2/LINUXX8664 9.7.4
Authorization ID        = INSTMANT
Local instance alias    = DB2INST1
[db2inst1@nodedb21 ~]$
```

13. Connect to the NAV database:

```
[db2inst1@nodedb21 ~]$ db2 "connect to nav user instmant using
instmant"


    Database Connection Information

Database server         = DB2/LINUXX8664 9.7.4
SQL authorization ID    = INSTMANT
Local database alias    = NAV


[db2inst1@nodedb21 ~]$
```

14. To see authorizations for user `instmant`, issue the following command:

```
[db2inst1@nodedb21 ~]$ db2 "get authorizations"


Administrative Authorizations for Current User

Direct SYSADM authority                      = NO
Direct SYSCTRL authority                     = NO
Direct SYSMAINT authority                    = NO
Direct DBADM authority                       = NO
Direct CREATETAB authority                   = NO
Direct BINDADD authority                     = NO
Direct CONNECT authority                     = NO
Direct CREATE_NOT_FENC authority             = NO
Direct IMPLICIT_SCHEMA authority             = NO
Direct LOAD authority                        = NO
Direct QUIESCE_CONNECT authority             = NO
Direct CREATE_EXTERNAL_ROUTINE authority     = NO
Direct SYSMON authority                      = NO


Indirect SYSADM authority                    = NO
Indirect SYSCTRL authority                   = NO
Indirect SYSMAINT authority                  = YES
Indirect DBADM authority                     = NO
Indirect CREATETAB authority                 = YES
Indirect BINDADD authority                   = YES
Indirect CONNECT authority                   = YES
Indirect CREATE_NOT_FENC authority           = NO
Indirect IMPLICIT_SCHEMA authority           = YES
Indirect LOAD authority                      = NO
Indirect QUIESCE_CONNECT authority           = NO
Indirect CREATE_EXTERNAL_ROUTINE authority = NO
Indirect SYSMON authority                    = YES
[db2inst1@nodedb21 ~]$
```

15. Attach to `db2inst1` as user `instmon`, who has the `SYSMON` authority:

```
[db2inst1@nodedb21 ~]$ db2 "attach to db2inst1 user instmon using
instmon"


            Instance Attachment Information


 Instance server        = DB2/LINUXX8664 9.7.5
 Authorization ID       = INSTMON
 Local instance alias   = DB2INST1
[db2inst1@nodedb21 ~]$
```

16. Collect information about the instance by getting a snapshot for the database manager:

```
[db2inst1@nodedb21 ~]$ db2 "get snapshot for database manager "


            Database Manager Snapshot


Node type                                = Enterprise Server
Edition with local and remote clients
Instance name                            = db2inst1
Number of database partitions in DB2 instance = 1
Database manager status                  = Active
...........................................................
.......................................................
Node number                          = 0
    Memory Pool Type                     = Database Monitor
Heap
        Current size (bytes)             = 65536
        High water mark (bytes)          = 65536
        Configured size (bytes)          = 393216
...........................................................
.......................................................
[db2inst1@nodedb21 ~]$
```

17. Next, include user `instmant` in the group `SYSCTRL`:

```
[root@nodedb21 ~]# usermod  -G sysctrl instmant
[root@nodedb21 ~]#
```

18. Again, issue the `get authorizations` command to see if there are changes at authority levels :

```
[db2inst1@nodedb21 ~]$ db2 "get authorizations"


Administrative Authorizations for Current User


Direct SYSADM authority                       = NO
Direct SYSCTRL authority                      = NO
Direct SYSMAINT authority                     = NO
Direct DBADM authority                        = NO
Direct CREATETAB authority                    = NO
Direct BINDADD authority                      = NO
Direct CONNECT authority                      = NO
Direct CREATE_NOT_FENC authority              = NO
Direct IMPLICIT_SCHEMA authority              = NO
Direct LOAD authority                         = NO
Direct QUIESCE_CONNECT authority              = NO
Direct CREATE_EXTERNAL_ROUTINE authority      = NO
Direct SYSMON authority                       = NO


Indirect SYSADM authority                     = NO
Indirect SYSCTRL authority                    = YES
Indirect SYSMAINT authority                   = YES
Indirect DBADM authority                      = NO
Indirect CREATETAB authority                  = YES
Indirect BINDADD authority                    = YES
Indirect CONNECT authority                    = YES
Indirect CREATE_NOT_FENC authority            = NO
Indirect IMPLICIT_SCHEMA authority            = YES
Indirect LOAD authority                       = NO
Indirect QUIESCE_CONNECT authority            = NO
Indirect CREATE_EXTERNAL_ROUTINE authority    = NO
Indirect SYSMON authority                     = NO
```

19. Now user `instmant` has inherited SYSCTRL authority from secondary group sysctrl. This demonstrates how the group assignment can add other authorization levels to users in that group.

How it works...

Generally these authorities are granted to specialized administrators in backup and maintenance. Any user that belongs to a group has the same rights as the others, unless you assign it to another group, defined as a secondary group, or grant explicitly a different database authority or privilege.

There's more...

You have mentioned probably the indirect `authorization` assigned to every instance-level authority in the get authorizations listings. An indirect authority can be given by granting rights to a group authorization ID to which the user belongs or if the authority or privilege has been granted to `PUBLIC`. In our case, these authorities are inherited from `PUBLIC`. You may restrict public rights by creating the database with the `RESTRICTIVE` option or by revoking them manually.

IBM recommends, instead of using the `get authorizations` command (discontinued), that you use the `AUTH_LIST_AUTHORITIES_FOR_AUTHID` table function.

Managing database-level authorities and privileges

Database-level authorities can be assigned directly to users or groups. The only exception is the `SECADM` authority, which can be granted only to users.

The following table lists the database-level authorities and their privileges:

Database authority	Description
DBADM	It is the highest database authority and has access to all the data. If this authority is revoked, the implicit database authorities remain in place. Therefore, these must be revoked explicitly. They can be granted to users and groups, but not to the public.
SECADM	Security administrator. It has the ability to manage LBAC and to transfer ownership of objects, but has no access to data. It is a special user created to implement advanced security at database level. It can only be granted to users.
CONNECT	Allows users to connect to database. Can be granted to users and groups. This is a privilege.

Database authority	Description
BINDADD	It allows users to create packages. This is a privilege.
CREATETAB	It allows users to create new tables in the database. This is a privilege.
BINDADD	It allows users to create packages. This is a privilege.
CREATE_EXTERNAL_ROUTINES	It allows users rights to create external routines. This is a privilege.
CREATE_NOT_FENCED_ROUTINE	It allows users rights to create NOT FENCED routines (these routines will run in the agent address space). This is a privilege.
IMPLICIT_SCHEMA	It allows users the ability to create schemas that do not exist. This is a privilege.
LOAD	It allows users to use the LOAD utility. This is a privilege.
QUIESCE_CONNECT	Users with this authority can connect to databases in quiesced state. This is a privilege.
DATAACCESS	Users with this authority have rights to query tables in the database.
WLMADM	It grants the workload administrator role. In particular, the holder of the WLMADM authority can create and drop workload manager objects, grant and revoke workload manager privileges, and execute workload manager routines.
SQLADM	It allows users to monitor and tune SQL statements.
ACCESSCTRL	It allows granting and revoking all object privileges within the database. A user with this authority has no access to data, excepting catalog tables and views. It can be granted and revoked exclusively by users with SECADM authority.

Getting ready

In this recipe, we will create a user group named db2dba; a user named dba, belonging to this group, will get the DBADM authority, and a user dac, also assigned to this group, will get the DATAACCES authority. In this chapter, we will also introduce and create a user with the security administrator (SECADM) authority, named db2secad.

How to do it...

1. Create a new group db2dba, and a new user dba belonging to this group, by issuing the following commands:

   ```
   [root@nodedb21 ~]# groupadd db2dba
   [root@nodedb21 ~]#
   [root@nodedb21 ~]# useradd dba -g db2dba
   [root@nodedb21 ~]#
   ```

2. Set the username and password to the same value for user dba.

3. Connect to the NAV database and grant DBADM database-level authority to user dba:

   ```
   [db2inst1@nodedb21:~] db2 "connect to nav"


       Database Connection Information

   Database server        = DB2/LINUXX8664 9.7.4
   SQL authorization ID   = DB2INST1
   Local database alias   = NAV
   [db2inst1@nodedb21 ~]$ db2 "grant dbadm on database to dba"
   DB20000I  The SQL command completed successfully.
   [db2inst1@nodedb21:~]
   ```

4. Connect to database NAV, with user dba:

   ```
   [db2inst1@nodedb21 ~]$ db2 "connect to nav user dba using dba"


       Database Connection Information

   Database server        = DB2/LINUXX8664 9.7.4
   SQL authorization ID   = DBA
   Local database alias   = NAV
   [db2inst1@nodedb21:~]
   ```

5. To see authorizations for user dba on database NAV, issue the following command :

   ```
   [db2inst1@nodedb21 ~]$ db2 "get authorizations"


   Administrative Authorizations for Current User


   Direct SYSADM authority                      = NO
   ```

```
Direct SYSCTRL authority                         = NO
Direct SYSMAINT authority                        = NO
Direct DBADM authority                           = YES
Direct CREATETAB authority                       = NO
Direct BINDADD authority                         = NO
Direct CONNECT authority                         = NO
Direct CREATE_NOT_FENC authority                 = NO
Direct IMPLICIT_SCHEMA authority                 = NO
Direct LOAD authority                            = NO
Direct QUIESCE_CONNECT authority                 = NO
Direct CREATE_EXTERNAL_ROUTINE authority         = NO
Direct SYSMON authority                          = NO

Indirect SYSADM authority                        = NO
Indirect SYSCTRL authority                       = NO
Indirect SYSMAINT authority                      = NO
Indirect DBADM authority                         = NO
Indirect CREATETAB authority                     = YES
Indirect BINDADD authority                       = YES
Indirect CONNECT authority                       = YES
Indirect CREATE_NOT_FENC authority               = NO
Indirect IMPLICIT_SCHEMA authority               = YES
Indirect LOAD authority                          = NO
Indirect QUIESCE_CONNECT authority               = NO
Indirect CREATE_EXTERNAL_ROUTINE authority       = NO
Indirect SYSMON authority                        = NO
```

6. Create a new user dac, by issuing the following command:

   ```
   [root@nodedb21 ~]# useradd dac -g db2dba
   ```

7. Connect to the NAV database and grant DATAACCESS database-level authority to user dac:

   ```
   [db2inst1@nodedb21:~] db2 "connect to nav"


      Database Connection Information

   Database server        = DB2/LINUXX8664 9.7.4
   ```

```
 SQL authorization ID    = DB2INST1
 Local database alias    = NAV
[db2inst1@nodedb21 ~]$ db2 "grant dbadm to dba"
[db2inst1@nodedb21:~]
[db2inst1@nodedb21:~] db2 "grant dataaccess on database to dac"
DB20000I  The SQL command completed successfully.
```

8. Retrieve database-level authorities and privileges for user `dac`, by executing the following query:

```
[db2inst1@nodedb21 ~]$  db2 "SELECT varchar(AUTHORITY,27)as auth,
D_USER as USER, D_GROUP as GROUP, D_PUBLIC as PUBLIC
   FROM TABLE (SYSPROC.AUTH_LIST_AUTHORITIES_FOR_AUTHID ('DAC',
'U') ) AS T
   ORDER BY AUTHORITY"
```

AUTH	USER	GROUP	PUBLIC		
ACCESSCTRL	N	N	N		
BINDADD	N	N	Y		
CONNECT	N	N	Y		
CREATE_EXTERNAL_ROUTINE	N	N	N		
CREATE_NOT_FENCED_ROUTINE	N	N	N		
CREATETAB	N	N	Y		
DATAACCESS	Y	N	N		
DBADM	N	N	N		
EXPLAIN	N	N	N		
IMPLICIT_SCHEMA	N	N	Y		
LOAD	N	N	N		
QUIESCE_CONNECT	N	N	N		
SECADM	N	N	N		
SQLADM	N	N	N		
SYSADM	*	N	*		
SYSCTRL	*	N	*		
SYSMAINT	*	N	*		
SYSMON	*	N	*		
WLMADM	N	N	N		
SYSMAINT	*	N	*	*	*

```
*              *
SYSMON
*      N       *       *       *       *       *
WLMADM
N      N       N       N       N       N       *
```

```
    19 record(s) selected.
[db2inst1@nodedb21 ~]$
```

9. Finally, create the security administrator user db2secad, by executing the following commands:

```
[root@nodedb21 ~]# groupadd db2sec
[root@nodedb21~]#
[root@nodedb21 ~]# useradd db2secad -g db2sec
[root@nodedb21~]#
```

10. Connect to database NAV and grant SECADM authority to user db2secad:

```
[db2inst1@nodedb21 ~]$ db2 "connect to nav"


    Database Connection Information

    Database server        = DB2/LINUXX8664 9.7.4
    SQL authorization ID   = DB2INST1
    Local database alias   = NAV
[db2inst1@nodedb21 ~]$
[db2inst1@nodedb21 ~]$ db2 "grant secadm on database to db2secad"
DB20000I  The SQL command completed successfully.
[db2inst1@nodedb21 ~]$
```

How it works...

The assignment is similar to instance-level authorities. The only difference is that database-level authorities can be assigned directly to users.

There's more...

In production environments, try to use strong passwords. Also, try to enforce password rules, such as password aging, locking, and expiration, by using proprietary methods specific to the operating system used. One example could be to use PAM, on Linux operating systems, for password and user management. Also, at network level use security and hardening methods, such as closing unused services and ports, using firewalls to filter access to your servers, and not allowing direct remote root logins.

Security administrator authority

This is a special database-level authority designed to allow special users to configure advanced security such as LBAC and ownership transfer.

The tasks that are allowed to be performed by having the SECADM authority are, briefly, as follows:

> ▸ Creating and dropping security labels, policies, and components
>
> ▸ Granting and revoking security labels from individual users
>
> ▸ Granting and revoking LBAC rule exemptions
>
> ▸ Granting and revoking setsessionuser privileges
>
> ▸ Transfering ownership of any object from one user to another

Managing object privileges

Object privileges determine the ability to perform operations on database objects:

Object	Privilege
Tablespace	USE – allows the users to create tables and indexes in the table space.
Schema	CREATEIN – allows the users to create objects within the schema.
	ALTERIN – allows the users to alter objects within the schema.
	DROPIN – allows the users to drop any object within the schema.

Object	Privilege
Table	CONTROL – provides a user with with all table privileges. Also provides the user the ability to grant or revoke more privileges on the table, excluding CONTROL.
	ALTER – allows a user to alter a table.
	SELECT – allows a user to issue SELECT statements against the table.
	INSERT – allows a user to issue INSERT statements against the table.
	UPDATE- allows a user to execute UPDATE statements against the table.
	DELETE – allows a user to execute DELETE statements against the table.
	INDEX – permits the creation of indexes for the table.
	REFERENCES – allows a user to create and drop foreign key constraints that reference the table in a parent relationship.
View	CONTROL – provides a user with with all table privileges. Also provides the user the ability to grant or revoke more privileges on the view, excluding CONTROL.
	SELECT – gives rights to issue SELECT statements against the view.
	INSERT – allows user to execute INSERT statements against the view.
	UPDATE – gives rights to update the view at entire level or column level.
	DELETE –give rights to execute DELETE statements against the view.
INDEX	CONTROL – allows the user to drop the index from the database. The index owner has this privilege granted implicitly.
SEQUENCE	USAGE – grants the use of PREVIOUS VALUE and NEXT VALUE to a user.
	ALTER – grants right to restart the sequence from its initial value, change the increment, and add comments about sequence.

Object	Privilege
PACKAGE	CONTROL – grants the possibility to drop and the ability to grant EXECUTE and BIND privileges to other users.
	BIND – allows a user to rebind or add new package versions to package that have already been bound to the database.
	EXECUTE – grants a user to execute a package.
SERVER (Federated priviledges)	PASSTHRU – allows a user to execute DDL and DML statements directly on federated servers (Oracle, MS SQL, and so on).
LBAC	SETSESSIONUSER – can change the session authorization ID.

Getting ready

In this recipe, we will create a group named db2users, designed for regular database users. All the object privileges from here on will be granted to this group. Privileges will be granted using the db2secad security administrator user created in the previous recipe. We will also cover a special operation, called **transfer ownership**, that can be performed only by users with the SECADM authority.

How to do it...

1. Create a group db2users and user db2user, by executing the following commands:

   [root@nodedb21 ~]# groupadd db2users

   [root@nodedb21 ~]#

   [root@nodedb21 ~]# useradd db2user -g db2users

   [root@nodedb21 ~]#

2. Set the username and password to the same value for user db2user.

3. Connect to database NAV and grant the CONNECT database-level authority to the group db2users, by executing the following command:

   [db2inst1@nodedb21 ~]$ db2 "grant connect on database to db2users"

   DB20000I The SQL command completed successfully.

   [db2inst1@nodedb21 ~]$

4. Grant the SELECT privilege, on table NAV.COMM, to user db2user:

   [db2inst1@nodedb21 ~]$ db2 "GRANT SELECT ON TABLE NAV.COMM TO USER db2user"

   DB20000I The SQL command completed successfully.

5. Granting the CONNECT authority to user group db2users will grant the CONNECT database authority to all users within this group. Connect to the NAV database as db2user:

```
[db2inst1@nodedb21 ~]$ db2 "connect to nav user db2user using
db2user"

    Database Connection Information

 Database server        = DB2/LINUXX8664 9.7.4
 SQL authorization ID   = DB2USER
 Local database alias   = NAV
```

6. Now, by having the SELECT privilege on table nav.comm, we can issue a select count(*) command against table nav.comm:

```
[db2inst1@nodedb21 ~]$ db2 "select count(*) from nav.comm"


1
-----------
      15026


  1 record(s) selected.
```

7. List user db2user authorizations:

```
[db2inst1@nodedb21 ~]$ db2 "get authorizations"


Administrative Authorizations for Current User

 Direct SYSADM authority                   = NO
 Direct SYSCTRL authority                  = NO
 Direct SYSMAINT authority                 = NO
 Direct DBADM authority                    = NO
 Direct CREATETAB authority                = NO
 Direct BINDADD authority                  = NO
 Direct CONNECT authority                  = NO
 Direct CREATE_NOT_FENC authority          = NO
 Direct IMPLICIT_SCHEMA authority          = NO
 Direct LOAD authority                     = NO
 Direct QUIESCE_CONNECT authority          = NO
 Direct CREATE_EXTERNAL_ROUTINE authority  = NO
```

```
Direct SYSMON authority                            = NO


Indirect SYSADM authority                          = NO
Indirect SYSCTRL authority                         = NO
Indirect SYSMAINT authority                        = NO
Indirect DBADM authority                           = NO
Indirect CREATETAB authority                       = YES
Indirect BINDADD authority                         = YES
Indirect CONNECT authority                         = YES
Indirect CREATE_NOT_FENC authority                 = NO
Indirect IMPLICIT_SCHEMA authority                 = YES
Indirect LOAD authority                            = NO
Indirect QUIESCE_CONNECT authority                 = NO
Indirect CREATE_EXTERNAL_ROUTINE authority = NO
Indirect SYSMON authority                          = NO
```

8. To find out the owner of table `nav.comm`, execute the following query:

   [db2inst1@nodedb21 ~]$ db2 "select owner from syscat.tables where tabname='COMM'"

   OWNER

   -DB2INST1

   ` 1 record(s) selected.`

   [db2inst1@nodedb21 ~]$

9. Connect as user `db2secad` and transfer the ownership of table `nav.comm` to user `db2user`:

   [db2inst1@nodedb21 ~]$ db2 "transfer ownership of table nav.comm to user db2users preserve privileges"

   DB20000I   The SQL command completed successfully.

10. Now, the `nav.comm` table has the ownership transferred to user `db2user`:

    [db2inst1@nodedb21 ~]$ db2 "select owner from syscat.tables where tabname='COMM'"

    OWNER

    DB2USERS

    ` 1 record(s) selected.`

    [db2inst1@nodedb21 ~]$

When you transfer ownership for different types of objects, from one user to another user, take into consideration any object-related dependencies. To check object dependencies, query `syscat.*deps` system views.

How it works...

Object privileges can also be granted to users or groups. If you grant object privileges to a group, all users within that group will have that object privilege.

There's more...

As a best practice, if you have to grant many privileges for many objects to several users, try to group this by granting those privileges to roles. We will cover roles in the next recipe.

As a best practice for security, try to regularly audit user and group object privileges, using the `db2audit` facility. You can find more information about authorities granted at object level by querying the `syscat.*auth` system views.

```
[db2inst1@nodedb21 ~]$
db2 "select varchar(viewschema,20) as schema,varchar(viewname,25) as name
from syscat.views where viewname like '%AUTH'"
```

SCHEMA	NAME
-SYSCAT	COLAUTH
SYSCAT	DBAUTH
SYSCAT	INDEXAUTH
SYSCAT	LIBRARYAUTH
SYSCAT	MODULEAUTH
SYSCAT	PACKAGEAUTH
SYSCAT	PASSTHRUAUTH
SYSCAT	ROLEAUTH
SYSCAT	ROUTINEAUTH
SYSCAT	SCHEMAAUTH
SYSCAT	SEQUENCEAUTH
SYSCAT	TABAUTH
SYSCAT	TBSPACEAUTH
SYSCAT	VARIABLEAUTH
SYSCAT	WORKLOADAUTH
SYSCAT	XSROBJECTAUTH

```
  16 record(s) selected.
[db2inst1@nodedb21 ~]$
```

Or, to find all privileges granted at schema-level NAV, you can execute the following query:

```
SELECT AUTHID, PRIVILEGE, OBJECTNAME, OBJECTSCHEMA, OBJECTTYPE
    FROM SYSIBMADM.PRIVILEGES where objectschema='NAV'
```

Using roles

A **role** can be defined as a database object that has the capability to hold a collection of privileges and authorities that can be assigned to a user or a group. Using roles considerably simplifies the management of privileges and authorities to be granted, especially if you have a large user base in your organization.

Getting ready

In this recipe, we will create two roles, named db2rlus and db2rinh. We will grant the CONNECT and SELECT privileges on tables NAV.COMM and NAV.WAYPOINT, to role db2rlus. We will grant this role to group db2users. Next, we will grant role db2rlus to role db2rihn. Next, we will revoke role db2rlus from the db2users group and re-grant db2rlus role to this group, to demonstrate how roles inherit rights from other roles.

1. Connect to database NAV as user db2secad:

   ```
   [db2inst1@nodedb21 ~]$ db2 "connect to nav user db2secad using
   db2secad"


        Database Connection Information

    Database server        = DB2/LINUXX8664 9.7.4
    SQL authorization ID   = DB2SECAD
    Local database alias   = NAV
   ```

2. Revoke the CONNECT authority on database NAV from db2users group:

   ```
   [db2inst1@nodedb21 ~]$ db2 "revoke connect on database from
   db2users"
   DB20000I  The SQL command completed successfully.
   [db2inst1@nodedb21 ~]$
   ```

3. Create roles db2rlus and db2rinh, by executing the following commands:

   ```
   [db2inst1@nodedb21 ~]$ db2 "create role db2rlus"
   DB20000I  The SQL command completed successfully.
   [db2inst1@nodedb21 ~]$ db2 "create role db2rihn"
   DB20000I  The SQL command completed successfully.
   ```

4. Grant the CONNECT authority on database NAV and select privilege on the nav.comm table to the db2rlus role:

```
[db2inst1@nodedb21 ~]$ db2 "grant connect on database to db2rlus"
DB20000I  The SQL command completed successfully.
[db2inst1@nodedb21 ~]$ db2 "grant select on nav.comm  to db2rlus"
DB20000I  The SQL command completed successfully.
```

5. Grant role db2rlus to the db2users group:

```
[db2inst1@nodedb21 ~]$  db2 "grant db2rlus to db2users"
DB20000I  The SQL command completed successfully.
[db2inst1@nodedb21 ~]$
```

6. Connect with user db2user to database NAV:

```
[db2inst1@nodedb21 ~]$ db2 "connect to nav user db2user using
db2user"


   Database Connection Information

 Database server        = DB2/LINUXX8664 9.7.4
 SQL authorization ID   = DB2USER
 Local database alias   = NAV
[db2inst1@nodedb21 ~]$
```

7. Now, issue a count against table nav.comm with user db2user:

```
[db2inst1@nodedb21 ~]$ db2 "select count(*) from nav.comm"


1
-----------
      15026

  1 record(s) selected.
[db2inst1@nodedb21 ~]$
```

8. Connect with user db2secad and grant the SELECT privilege, on table NAV. WAYPOINT, to role db2rlus:

```
[db2inst1@nodedb21 ~]$ db2 "connect to nav user db2secad using
db2secad"


    Database Connection Information

 Database server        = DB2/LINUXX8664 9.7.4

 SQL authorization ID   = DB2SECAD

 Local database alias   = NAV
[db2inst1@nodedb21 ~]$


[db2inst1@nodedb21 ~]$ db2 "grant select on nav.waypoint to
db2rlus"
DB20000I  The SQL command completed successfully.
```

9. Now, db2user has the SELECT privilege on NAV.WAYPOINT, inherited from role db2rlus:

```
[db2inst1@nodedb21 ~]$ db2 "connect to nav user db2user using
db2user"


    Database Connection Information

 Database server        = DB2/LINUXX8664 9.7.4

 SQL authorization ID   = DB2USER

 Local database alias   = NAV


[db2inst1@nodedb21 ~]$ db2 "select count(*) from nav.waypoint"


1
-----------
      65565


  1 record(s) selected.
```

10. Connect as user db2secad and grant the db2rlus role to db2rihn:

```
[db2inst1@nodedb21 ~]$ db2 "grant db2rlus to db2rihn"
DB20000I  The SQL command completed successfully.
[db2inst1@nodedb21 ~]$
```

11. Revoke role db2rlus from db2users and grant role db2rihn to db2users:

```
[db2inst1@nodedb21 ~]$db2 "revoke db2rlus from db2users"
DB20000I  The SQL command completed successfully.
[db2inst1@nodedb21 ~]$ db2 "grant db2rihn to db2users"
DB20000I  The SQL command completed successfully.
```

12. Connect to database NAV with user db2user, to test that we have the CONNECT authority granted back from role db2rihn:

```
[db2inst1@nodedb21 ~]$db2 connect to nav user db2user using
db2user


   Database Connection Information

Database server        = DB2/LINUXX8664 9.7.5
SQL authorization ID   = DB2USER
Local database alias   = NAV
```

How it works...

Granting or revoking privileges and authorities to and from roles is the same as granting them to users and groups. The only difference is that you can grant or revoke a role to and from another role. All the roles are enabled by default, when a user establishes a connection to the database.

There's more...

To see privileges granted to roles on schema NAV, you can use the following query:

```
SELECT p.AUTHID, p.PRIVILEGE, p.OBJECTNAME, p.OBJECTSCHEMA, p.OBJECTTYPE
   FROM SYSIBMADM.PRIVILEGES p, syscat.roles r where objectschema='NAV'
and p.authid=r.rolename
```

Creating roles using the WITH ADMIN OPTION

Because roles do not have owners with this option, roles can be delegated to a user to grant membership to other users.

SECAD exception

All authorities and privileges can be granted to a role, except the SECAD authority.

Using table encryption

In DB2, we may use encryption in two areas: network communication and table data encryption. Regarding network communication, also named data in transit, we can enforce the encryption of just the authorization identifiers, such as the username and password, by setting database manager parameter AUTHENTICATION or SRVCON_AUTH to SERVER_ENCRYPT, SERVER_ENCRYPT, GSS_SERVER_ENCRYPT, KRB_SERVER_ENCRYPT or to encrypt authentication and data sent over the network between clients and servers by setting to DATA_ENCRYPT or DATA_ENCRYPT_CMP values. Here, we can also enumerate SSL as encryption method for data in transit. Table data encryption is used, in general, to hide sensitive data from users who have access to those tables and it also offers protection against physical theft.

Getting ready

In this recipe, we will encrypt the CNAM column of the NAV.COMM table to demonstrate how to use data encryption.

How to do it...

The function used to encrypt columns is encrypt. For decryption, you can use the decrypt_char or decrypt_bin functions.

To encrypt data using the ENCRYPT function, you should include it in INSERT or UPDATE statements. Because the ENCRYPT function has as the return value varchar for bit data, and decrypt_bin and decrypt_char have the input argument also as varchar for bit data, we must change first the CNAM column's data type to this data type. Also, we will increase the length of the column, because the password used for encryption and the password hint, if you use one, will also be stored in this field and requires additional space. For data encrypted without using hints, increase the field length to *maximum length of non-encrypted data + 8 bytes + number of bytes to next 8-byte boundary*. For example, if unencrypted column length is 35, then increase to 35+8=43, and round it up to the next 8-byte boundary; the result is 48. For data encrypted with hints, add 32 bytes. So, if for an encrypted column without hints, we calculated that a length of 35 has to be increased to 48, with hints we will have 48+32=90.

1. Change the data type for column **CNAM** of table COMM to **VARCHAR** for bit data and increase the column length to **100**:

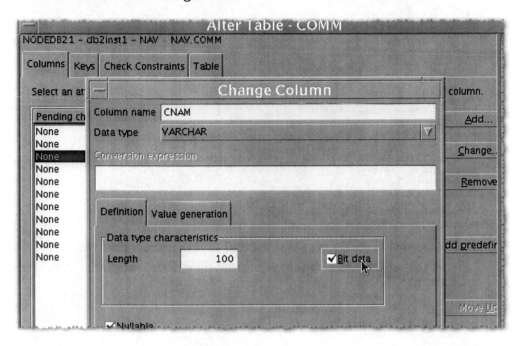

2. Set NAV as the current schema:

    ```
    [db2inst1@nodedb21 ~]$ "set current schema nav"
    DB20000I  The SQL command completed successfully.
    [db2inst1@nodedb21 ~]$
    ```

3. Encrypt column CNAM by providing a password and a hint in function encrypt, as follows :

    ```
    [db2inst1@nodedb21 ~]$ db2 "update comm set cnam=encrypt(cnam,'rut
    e456','route')"
    DB20000I  The SQL command completed successfully.
    [db2inst1@nodedb21 ~]$db2 commit
    DB20000I  The SQL command completed successfully.
    ```

4. If you accidentally forget the password, you may get the password hint that is stored in the column. To get the password hint, use the `gethint` function, as follows :

```
[db2inst1@nodedb21 ~]$ db2 "select gethint(cnam) as hint from comm
fetch first 1 rows only"
HINT
-------------------------------
route
[db2inst1@nodedb21 ~]$
```

5. If you want to see how the encrypted data actually looks, issue the following query:

```
[db2inst1@nodedb21 ~]$ db2 "select varchar(cnam,50) as
cnamencrypted from comm fetch first 2 rows only"
CNAMENCRYPTED
------------------------------------------------------------------
--------------------------------------------
x'09BB4505B804A4D5726F757465DD5AF5C86D8F1B7C4D57BB12268BB822'
x'09D72905B804B8D5726F75746589BDDEF3060B6BDB71F82D53BCD72A051ADEEB
DF14D039CD'

2 record(s) selected
```

6. Retrieve column CNAM in decrypted format, using the `decrypt_char` function:

```
[db2inst1@nodedb21 ~]$ db2 "select decrypt_char(cnam,'rute456')
from comm fetch first 2 rows only"
CNAM
------------------------------------------------------------------
---------------------------
MIDLAND TRAFFIC
COLLINGWOOD TRAFFIC

  2 record(s) selected.
```

7. Revert column CNAM in decrypted format, giving the password by using the `set encryption password` command at session-level, as follows:

```
[db2inst1@nodedb21 ~]$ db2 "set encryption password='rute456'"
DB20000I  The SQL command completed successfully.
[db2inst1@nodedb21 ~]$ db2 " update comm set cnam=decrypt_
char(cnam)"
[db2inst1@nodedb21 ~]$ db2 commit
[db2inst1@nodedb21 ~]$
```

How it works...

The algorithm used to encrypt the data is an RC2 block cipher with a 128-bit secret key. The 128-bit secret key is derived from the password using an MD5 message digest. The encrypted data can be decrypted only by using `decrypt_char` and `decrypt_bin` functions; no other method is allowed.

There's more...

The encryption of numeric and date data types is indirectly supported via casting, using `varchar`, `char`, and `to_char` functions. Data type casting should also be used when performing decryption.

If you want to implement advanced data encryption by using policies check IBM InfoSphere Guardium Encryption Expert. `http://www-01.ibm.com/software/data/guardium/encryption-expert/` and `http://www.ibm.com/developerworks/data/library/techarticle/dm-0907encryptionexpert/`.

Using label-based access control (LBAC) to strengthen data privacy

LBAC implements data safety to a higher level of granularity. In many organizations, there are requirements that stipulate that sensitive data will not be visible to anyone but nominated persons. Another problem that may arise regarding visibility is that users with authorities such as `SYSADM`, `DBADM`, and `DATAACCES` have read access on all tables within the database. By defining security policies, labels, and components that are part of LBAC, access to sensitive data can be greatly restricted. In the past, this was implemented by creating custom views and stored procedures. However, this method did not solve the entire table access problem for database administrators.

Getting ready...

In this recipe, we'll create five new users with control privilege on table `navaid` within the `NAV` schema. We will divide this recipe in a way that will cover every LBAC object being created, step-by-step. Next, we'll apply LBAC securitization on two different tables, using tree and array security components.

How to do it...

1. Create five new users within the group db2users, by executing the following commands:

    ```
    [root@nodedb21 ~]# useradd andrew -g db2users
    [root@nodedb21 ~]#
    [root@nodedb21 ~]# useradd cristian -g db2users
    [root@nodedb21 ~]#
    [root@nodedb21 ~]# useradd pilot -g db2users
    [root@nodedb21 ~]#
    [root@nodedb21 ~]# useradd tom -g db2users
    [root@nodedb21 ~]#
    [root@nodedb21 ~]# useradd peter -g db2users
    [root@nodedb21 ~]#
    ```

2. As user db2secad, create a role named navrole, and grant connect and control privileges on table NAV.NAVAID:

    ```
    [db2inst1@nodedb21 ~]$ db2 "connect to nav user db2secad using db2secad"


    [db2inst1@nodedb21 ~]$ db2 "create role navrole"
    DB20000I  The SQL command completed successfully.
    [db2inst1@nodedb21 ~]$


     [db2inst1@nodedb21 ~]$ db2 "grant control on nav.navaid to navrole"
    DB20000I  The SQL command completed successfully.
    [db2inst1@nodedb21 ~]$
    ```

3. Next, grant role navrole to all users by granting it to the group db2users:

    ```
    [db2inst1@nodedb21 ~]$ db2 "grant navrole to db2users"
    DB20000I  The SQL command completed successfully.
    ```

Creating security label components

A security label component defines a criterion that regulates how data will be accessed. In LBAC, there exist three security component types: set, array, and tree.

set represents a collection of unordered elements. In the set security label components, hierarchy does not exist, so every element is equal in terms of security implementation. It is used mainly in enforcing column-level security.

`array` represents a collection of ordered elements where the first element has the higher value, and the last the lower. This type of security label component implements a hierarchical view of data in terms of security. Like the `set` security label component, it is used mainly in column-level security.

`tree` elements are arranged in a tree hierarchy. This security component is mainly used to enforce row-level security.

Next, create three different security label components:

1. Create a `set` security label component named `Continents`:

```
[db2inst1@nodedb21 ~]$ db2 " create security label component
Continents set {'Asia','Europe','North America','Australia','South
America','Africa','Antartica'}"
DB20000I  The SQL command completed successfully.
[db2inst1@nodedb21 ~]$
```

2. Create an `array` security label component named `Routes`:

```
[db2inst1@nodedb21 ~]$ db2 "create security label component Routes
array['Top Secret routes','Secret routes','Public routes']"
DB20000I  The SQL command completed successfully.
[db2inst1@nodedb21 ~]$
```

3. Create a `tree` security label named `Levels`:

```
[db2inst1@nodedb21 ~]$  db2 "create security label component
Levels tree ('Pilot' root,'Grade I' under 'Pilot','Grade II '
under 'Grade I')"
DB20000I  The SQL command completed successfully.
[db2inst1@nodedb21 ~]$
```

Defining security policies

Security policies are objects that actually contain information about what security label's rules and exemptions are used and determine who has read or write access to data. There is a limit of one security policy per table.

1. Create security policy `table_access`, which contains all three security labels defined before:

```
[db2inst1@nodedb21 ~]$ db2 "create security policy table_access
components Continents,Routes,Levels with db2lbacrules"
DB20000I  The SQL command completed successfully.
```

Creating security labels

Security labels define a set of criteria used to secure data. Security labels are granted to users. Every security label is part of exactly one security policy and includes one value for each component in that existing security policy.

1. Create three security labels by using the `tree` security label component:

   ```
   [db2inst1@nodedb21 ~]$ db2 "create security label table_access.
   Pilot component Levels 'Pilot'"
   DB20000I  The SQL command completed successfully.
   [db2inst1@nodedb21 ~]$ db2 "create security label table_access.
   PilotGradeI component Levels 'Grade I'"
   DB20000I  The SQL command completed successfully.
   [db2inst1@nodedb21 ~]$ db2 "create security label table_access.
   PilotGradeII component Levels 'Grade II'"
   DB20000I  The SQL command completed successfully.
   ```

2. Create a new table `nav.navaidsec` with the `table_access` security policy:

   ```
   [db2inst1@nodedb21 ~]$ db2 "connect to nav user db2inst1 using
   db2inst1"


       Database Connection Information

    Database server        = DB2/LINUXX8664 9.7.4
    SQL authorization ID   = DB2INST1
    Local database alias   = NAV


   [db2inst1@nodedb21 ~]$ db2 "create table nav.navaidsec (nkey
   varchar(10) not null, ident varchar(7), nman varchar(40), grade
   db2securitylabel) security policy table_access in nav_tbls index
   in nav_indx"
   DB20000I  The SQL command completed successfully.
   ```

3. Now grant CONTROL privilege on table `nav.navaidsec`, through role `navrole`, to all users from `db2users` group:

   ```
   [db2inst1@nodedb21 ~]$ db2 "grant control on nav.navaidsec to
   navrole"
   DB20000I  The SQL command completed successfully.
   ```

4. User andrew will be granted read and write rights only on his inserted data. Grant security-label access according to user level for andrew:

```
[db2inst1@nodedb21 ~]$ db2 "grant security label table_access.
PilotGradeI to user andrew for all access"
DB20000I  The SQL command completed successfully.
```

5. Next, as user andrew, insert data from table navaid and enforce the security policy using the seclabel_by_name function:

```
[db2inst1@nodedb21 ~]$ db2 "connect to nav user andrew using
andrew"


    Database Connection Information

 Database server        = DB2/LINUXX8664 9.7.4

 SQL authorization ID    = ANDREW

 Local database alias    = NAV


[db2inst1@nodedb21 ~]$ db2 "insert into nav.navaidsec  select
nkey,ident,nnam,seclabel_by_name('TABLE_ACCESS','PILOTGRADEI')
from nav.navaid where ident like 'A%' or ident like '%M'"
DB20000I  The SQL command completed successfully.
[db2inst1@nodedb21 ~]$ db2 "commit"
DB20000I  The SQL command completed successfully.
```

6. Grant security label access according to user level for cristian:

```
 [db2inst1@nodedb21 ~]$ db2 "grant security label table_access.
PilotGradeII to user cristian for all access"
DB20000I  The SQL command completed successfully.
```

7. As user cristian, insert data from table navaid and apply the security policy using the seclabel_by_name function:

```
[db2inst1@nodedb21 ~]$ db2 "connect to nav user cristian using
cristian"


    Database Connection Information

 Database server        = DB2/LINUXX8664 9.7.4

 SQL authorization ID    = CRISTIAN

 Local database alias    = NAV
```

```
[db2inst1@nodedb21 ~]$  db2 "insert into nav.navaidsec  select
nkey,ident,nnam,seclabel_by_name('TABLE_ACCESS','PILOTGRADEII')
from nav.navaid where ident like 'N%' or ident like 'Z%'"
DB20000I  The SQL command completed successfully.
[db2inst1@nodedb21 ~]$ db2 "commit"
DB20000I  The SQL command completed successfully.
```

8. Grant the security label access according to user level for `Pilot`:

```
[db2inst1@nodedb21 ~]$ db2  "grant security label table_access.
Pilot to user Pilot for all access"
DB20000I  The SQL command completed successfully.
[db2inst1@nodedb21 ~]$
```

9. As user `andrew`, issue a simple count on criteria `like '%O'`. We can observe that the query returns `0` rows. Actually, this data is not visible to `andrew`, because it belongs to `cristian`:

```
[db2inst1@nodedb21 ~]$ db2 "connect to nav user andrew using
andrew"


    Database Connection Information

 Database server        = DB2/LINUXX8664 9.7.4
 SQL authorization ID   = ANDREW
 Local database alias   = NAV


[db2inst1@nodedb21 ~]$ db2 "select count(*) from nav.navaidsec
where ident like 'O%'"


1
-----------
          0
```

10. Again, run the query using `like 'M%'`. This fits the criteria in which `andrew` has rights:

```
[db2inst1@nodedb21 ~]$ db2 "select count(*) from nav.navaidsec
where ident like 'M%'"


1
-----------
        757


  1 record(s) selected.
```

11. Connect as user `Pilot` and issue a count on table `nav.navaidsec`. This user has full read rights, as the returned value demonstrates:

```
db2 "select count(*) from nav.navaidsec"
```

```
1
-----------
        1984
```

12. Now, use the `select` command with criteria `like '%A'` and `'%Z'`:

```
[db2inst1@nodedb21 ~]$ db2 "select ident, nman from nav.navaidsec
where ident='AJF' or ident='ZF'"
```

```
IDENT   NMAN
-------  -----------------------------------------
AJF      AL JOUF
ZF       YELLOWKNIFE
ZF       TIMIKA
ZF       HEKOU
   4 record(s) selected..
```

Modifying read and write access rules by using exemptions

Access rules enforce read or write data to comply with the security labels defined on rows and columns. However, these rules can be changed by imposing exemptions that will permit the bypass of current access rules regarding read and write.

Every security label component has corresponding rules that can be the subject of exemption.

Security label component	Exemption	What it does
set	db2lbacreadset	User's value is lower than the protected value. By granting this exemption, user will be able to read all data
	db2lbacwriteset	There are one or more protecting values that the user does not hold. By granting this exemption, user will be able to write in other columns.

Security label component	Exemption	What it does
array	db2lbacreadarray	User's value is lower than the protecting value. By granting this exemption, user will be able to read data that is protected with higher levels.
	db2lbacwritearray	It has two variants, write-up and write-down. By granting this exemption, user will be able to write to higher levels with write-up, or to lower levels with write-down.
tree	db2lbacreadtree	By granting this value, user will be able to read the ancestor's data
	db2lbacwritetree	By granting this exemption, user will be able to write ancestor's data

1. As user db2secad, grant db2lbacreadtree exemption to user cristian:

   ```
   [db2inst1@nodedb21 ~]$ db2 "grant exemption on rule
   db2lbacreadtree for table_access to cristian"
   DB20000I  The SQL command completed successfully.
   ```

2. In this way, user cristian has rights to see the records of user andrew:

   ```
   [db2inst1@nodedb21 ~]$ db2 "connect to nav user cristian using
   cristian"


       Database Connection Information

    Database server        = DB2/LINUXX8664 9.7.4
    SQL authorization ID    = CRISTIAN
    Local database alias    = NAV
   [db2inst1@nodedb21 ~]$db2 "select count(*) from nav.navaidsec
   where ident like 'M%'"


   1
   -----------
           757


     1 record(s) selected.
   ```

One more example using the ARRAY security component label

Generally, `set` and `array` component labels are used mainly to secure data at column level. Actually, you may combine `tree` with `set` or `array` to enforce your custom rules of accessing data from tables.

1. Connect to the NAV database as user db2secad:

    ```
    [db2inst1@nodedb21 ~]$ db2 "connect to nav user db2secad using
    db2secad"


        Database Connection Information

     Database server        = DB2/LINUXX8664 9.7.4
     SQL authorization ID   = DB2SECAD
     Local database alias   = NAV
    ```

2. Create security labels TOPSECROUTES, SECROUTES, and PUBROUTES:

    ```
    [db2inst1@nodedb1:~/Desktop> db2 "create security label table_
    access.TOPSECROUTES component Routes 'Top Secret routes'"

    DB20000I  The SQL command completed successfully.

    [db2inst1@nodedb21 ~]$ db2 "create security label table_access.
    SECROUTES component Routes  'Secret routes'"

    DB20000I  The SQL command completed successfully.

    [db2inst1@nodedb21 ~]$ db2 "create security label table_access.
    PUBROUTES component Routes  'Public routes'"

    DB20000I  The SQL command completed successfully.
    ```

3. Grant security labels to users tom and peter, according to their desired level of access:

    ```
    [db2inst1@nodedb21 ~]$ db2 "grant security label table_access.
    TOPSECROUTES to user tom for all access"

    DB20000I  The SQL command completed successfully.

    [db2inst1@nodedb21 ~]$ db2 "grant security label table_access.
    SECROUTES to user peter for read access"

    DB20000I  The SQL command completed successfully.

    [db2inst1@nodedb21 ~]$ db2 "grant security label table_access.
    PUBROUTES to user db2user for read access"

    DB20000I  The SQL command completed successfully.
    ```

4. Connect to NAV database and create a new table named `nav.navaidsecarray` with security policy `data_access`:

```
[db2inst1@nodedb21 ~]$ db2 connect to nav

   Database Connection Information

Database server        = DB2/LINUXX8664 9.7.5

SQL authorization ID   = DB2INST1

Local database alias   = NAV


[db2inst1@nodedb21 ~]$ db2 "create table nav.navaidsecarray
(nkey varchar(10) not null , ident varchar(7), nnan varchar(40))
security policy table_access in nav_tbls index in nav_indx"
```

5. As user `db2secad`, grant `CONTROL` privilege on `nav.navaidsecarray` to role `navrole`:

```
[db2inst1@nodedb21 ~]$ db2 connect to nav user db2secad using
db2secad

   Database Connection Information


Database server        = DB2/LINUXX8664 9.7.5

SQL authorization ID   = DB2SECAD

Local database alias   = NAV


DB20000I  The SQL command completed successfully.


[db2inst1@nodedb21 ~]$ db2 "grant control on table nav.
navaidsecarray to navrole"

DB20000I  The SQL command completed successfully.
```

6. Grant exemption `db2lbacwritearray` write-down to user `tom`. Without this exemption, `tom` has no right to insert in columns `ident` and `nnan` and to alter the table `nav.navaidsecarray`:

```
[db2inst1@nodedb21~]$ db2 "grant exemption on rule
db2lbacwritearray writedown for table_access to user tom"

DB20000I  The SQL command completed successfully.
```

7. User `tom` now has rights to secure columns on table `nav.navaidsecarray`. Connect to database `NAV` with user `tom` and secure every column:

```
[db2inst1@nodedb21 ~]$ db2 connect to nav user tom using tom


    Database Connection Information

  Database server        = DB2/NT 9.7.5
  SQL authorization ID   = TOM
  Local database alias   = NAV
```

```
[db2inst1@nodedb21 ~]$ db2 "alter table nav.navaidsecarray  Alter
column ident secured with SECROUTES alter column nkey secured with
TOPSECROUTES Alter column nnan secured  with PUBROUTES "
DB20000I  The SQL command completed successfully
.[db2inst1@nodedb21 ~]$
```

8. Populate table `nav.navaidsecarray`:

```
[db2inst1@nodedb21 ~]$ "db2 insert into nav.navaidsecarray select
nkey,ident,nnam from nav.navaid"
DB20000I The SQL command completed successfully.
[db2inst1@nodedb21 ~]$ db2 commit
DB20000I  The SQL command completed successfully.
```

9. As user `tom`, issue the following query on table `nav.navaidsecarray`:

```
[db2inst1@nodedb21 ~]$ db2 select nkey,ident,nnan from nav.
navaidsecarray where nkey in('ZI5CP1','ZI5WO1','ZA5KS1')


NKEY        IDENT   NNAN
----------  ------- ------------------------------------------
ZA5KS1      KS      KASAMA
ZI5CP1      CP      HARARE CHARLES PRINCE
ZI5WO1      WO      BULAWAYO

  3 record(s) selected.
```

10. Now try the same `select` command as user `peter`:

    ```
    [db2inst1@nodedb21 ~]$ db2 connect to nav user peter using peter


        Database Connection Information


     Database server        = DB2/LINUXX8664 9.7.4
     SQL authorization ID   = PETER
     Local database alias   = NAV
    ```
    ```
    [db2inst1@nodedb21 ~]$ db2 "select nkey,ident,nnan from nav.
    navaidsecarray where nkey in('ZI5CP1','ZI5WO1','ZA5KS1')"
    ```
    ```
    SQL20264N  For table "NAV.NAVAIDSECARRAY", authorization ID
    "PETER" does not
    ```
    ```
    have "READ" access to the column "NKEY".  SQLSTATE=42512
    ```

11. If user `peter` selects his authorized columns the query works:

    ```
    [db2inst1@nodedb21 ~]$ db2 "select ident,nnan from nav.
    navaidsecarray where ident in('CP')"


    IDENT   NNAN

    ------- ----------------------------------------
    CP      CONSTABLE PYNT
    CP      PARDUC
    CP      CAPARICA
    CP      MAGNITOGORSK
    CP      BREST
    CP      CAMOPI
    CP      SHANGRAO
    CP      JOHNO
    CP      ACORE
    CP      CHIPATA
    CP      HARARE CHARLES PRINCE


      11 record(s) selected.
    ```

How it works...

When a table is accessed, the LBAC rules enforce access restriction by comparing the security label with the security label that is granted through the security policy defined on tables for the user. There could be read and write security labels for each security policy. When a user attempts to access protected data, the LBAC rules enforce access restriction. db2lbacrules is provided to enforce LBAC.

There's more...

When LBAC is implemented, you should take care about the additional storage per secured column or table. You can obtain information about LBAC components created in the database by querying the related `syscat.security*` system views:

```
db2 "select varchar(viewschema,20) as schema,varchar(viewname,25) as name
from syscat.views where viewname like 'SECURITY%'"
```

SCHEMA	NAME
SYSCAT	SECURITYLABELACCESS
SYSCAT	SECURITYLABELCOMPONENTELEMENTS
SYSCAT	SECURITYLABELCOMPONENTS
SYSCAT	SECURITYLABELS
SYSCAT	SECURITYPOLICIES
SYSCAT	SECURITYPOLICYCOMPONENTRULES
SYSCAT	SECURITYPOLICYEXEMPTIONS

Auditing DB2

No matter how strong our database security is, there is always a possibility of it being penetrated. In case of penetration attempts or other malicious intentions, early detection is crucial.

Therefore, we need to implement auditing to trace and overcome these types of events or other suspicious operations against the database. Auditing is also useful to detect and monitor operations performed in a certain period of time

Getting ready

In this recipe, we will cover how to configure the db2audit facility for different auditing scopes. Also we will cover how to implement audit policies using the AUDIT statement.

How to do it...

We will next introduce the main elements of the db2audit facility.

Configuring auditing scopes

An audit scope is a category of operations related to specific database objects, authorities, and privileges.

In the following table, we have summarized the audit scopes:

Scope	Description
AUDIT	This scope defines auditing of the audit facility. Records are generated when the audit facility settings are changed or the logs are accessed.
CHECKING	Carries out Authorization checking. Records are generated during authorization check of operations, such as access attempted against database objects or functions (for example, SELECT, UPDATE, and INSERT).
OBJMAINT	Object maintenance operations are audited. Records object creation, dropping alter statements against objects.
SECMAINT.	Carries out Security maintenance. It records any grant or revoke operation on object privileges or database authorities, and security labels or exemptions. Also, any modification related to SYSADM_GROUP, SYSCTRL_ GROUP, SYSMAINT_GROUP, or SYSMON_GROUP configuration parameters is recorded.
SYSADMIN	It has as scope operation performed that requires SYSADM, SYSMAINT, or SYSCTRL are performed
VALIDATE	It has as scope user validation. Records are generated when users authenticate or when system security information is retrieved.
CONTEXT	It generates records for a group of operations in a specific context. This category allows for better interpretation of the audit log file. It generates a correlator field, this field helps to associate different kind of linked operations (performed by a package or by a dynamic query).

The audit facility uses a configuration file named db2audit, which has entries for every AUDIT scope and paths for logs and archives. It stores the configuration for status and error types, applicable for every auditing scope. This file is usually located in INST_HOME/ sqllib/security directory; in our case, the complete path is /home/db2inst1/sqllib/ security/db2audit.cfg.

1. To see what options are activated, their scope, and also the running status of db2audit facility, issue the following command:

```
[db2inst1@nodedb21 security]$ db2audit describe
DB2 AUDIT SETTINGS:

Audit active: "FALSE "
Log audit events: "FAILURE"
Log checking events: "FAILURE"
Log object maintenance events: "FAILURE"
Log security maintenance events: "FAILURE"
Log system administrator events: "FAILURE"
Log validate events: "FAILURE"
Log context events: "FAILURE"
Return SQLCA on audit error: "FALSE "
Audit Data Path: ""
Audit Archive Path: ""
AUD0000I  Operation succeeded.
```

2. From this output, we can see that the db2audit facility is not started and all auditing scope values have the auditing status set on failure. To configure, for example, the auditing for specific operations performed by users with secadm authority, we may issue the following command:

```
[db2inst1@nodedb21 security]$ db2audit configure scope secmaint
status both errortype normal
AUD0000I  Operation succeeded.
[db2inst1@nodedb21 security]$
```

3. You have also the ability to extend the scope to record both failure and success events for every auditing scope, by using the all option:

```
[db2inst1@nodedb21 security]$ db2audit configure scope all status
both errortype normal

AUD0000I  Operation succeeded.
[db2inst1@nodedb21 security]$
```

Configure audit data path and archive path:

Audit logs are classified into database-level and instance-level logs. All log files generated by the audit facility have to be archived before analysis.

1. For database-level logs, the format is as follows:

    db2audit.dbdatabase.log.partition.YYYYMMDDHHMMSS.

    In our case, partition will be 0

2. For instance-level logs, the format is as follows:

    db2audit.instance.log.partition.YYYYMMDDHHMMSS.

3. To configure the active audit log path, execute the following commands:

    [db2inst1@nodedb21 security]$ mkdir -p /data/db2/activeauditlogs

    [db2inst1@nodedb21 security

    [db2inst1@nodedb21 security]$ db2audit configure datapath /data/db2/activeauditlogs

    AUD0000I Operation succeeded.

    [db2inst1@nodedb21 security]$

    The audit log storage locations you set, using db2audit, apply to all databases in the instance.

4. To configure the archived audit log path, execute the following commands:

    [db2inst1@nodedb21 security]$ mkdir -p /data/db2/archivedauditlogs

    [db2inst1@nodedb21 security]$ db2audit configure archivepath /data/db2/archivedauditlogs

    AUD0000I Operation succeeded.

    [db2inst1@nodedb21 security]$

5. Now that we have configured everything, we can start the audit facility by issuing the following command:

    [db2inst1@nodedb21 security]$db2audit start

    AUD0000I Operation succeeded.

    [db2inst1@nodedb21 security]$

Archiving, formatting, and extracting the audit data:

To generate archive audit log files for analysis, you should first indentify the active audit logs, archive them, and then extract and format the audited scope of interest.

1. Configure the AUDIT buffer:

    ```
    [db2inst1@nodedb21 security]$ db2 "update dbm cfg using audit_buf_
    sz 4000"
    DB20000I  The UPDATE DATABASE MANAGER CONFIGURATION command
    completed successfully.
    [db2inst1@nodedb21 security]$
    ```

2. AUDIT_BUF_SZ is not dynamic, so bounce the instance:

    ```
    [db2inst1@nodedb21 security]$ db2stop force; db2start
    01/26/2012 23:22:51     0    0    SQL1064N  DB2STOP processing was
    successful.
    SQL1064N  DB2STOP processing was successful.
    01/26/2012 23:22:52     0    0    SQL1063N  DB2START processing was
    successful.
    SQL1063N  DB2START processing was successful.
    ```

3. To list the active database audit logs being used in the data path, issue the following command:

    ```
    [db2inst1@nodedb21 security]$db2 "SELECT varchar(FILE,30),size
    FROM TABLE(SYSPROC.AUDIT_LIST_LOGS('/data/db2/activeauditlogs'))
    AS U"

    1                                SIZE
    ------------------------------   -------------------
    db2audit.db.NAV.log.0                       8297

        1 record(s) selected.
    ```

4. Archive current audit data by executing the following function:

    ```
    [db2inst1@nodedb21 security]$ db2  "CALL SYSPROC.AUDIT_ARCHIVE( '/
    data/db2/auditarchivedlogs', -2 )"

        Result set 1
        --------------
    ```

```
          DBPARTITIONNUM PATH


FILE


SQLCODE        SQLSTATE SQLERRMC
-------------- -------------------
-                    0 /data/db2/auditarchivedlogs


db2audit.db.NAV.log.0.20120126233624335657.bk
```

5. Create a new directory `extractformaud`, and then extract and format the archive generated, by issuing the following function:

```
[db2inst1@nodedb21 security]$

mkdir -p /data/db2/extractedformaud


[db2inst1@nodedb21 security]$

db2 "CALL SYSPROC.AUDIT_DELIM_EXTRACT( '|','/data/db2/
extractedformaud','/data/db2/archivedauditlogs', 'db2audit.db.NAV.
log.0.20120126233624335657.bk',NULL)"


   Return Status = 0
```

6. Files are generated for every scope, because we do not specify one:

```
db2inst1@nodedb1:/data/db2/extractedformaud> ls -al
total 12
drwxr-xr-x 2 db2inst1 db2iadm1 4096 2012-01-26 23:50 .
drwxr-xr-x 6 db2inst1 db2iadm1 4096 2012-01-26 23:48 ..
-rw-rw-rw- 1 db2inst1 db2iadm1    0 2012-01-26 23:50 audit.del
-rw-rw-rw- 1 db2inst1 db2iadm1    0 2012-01-26 23:50 auditlobs
-rw-rw-rw- 1 db2inst1 db2iadm1    0 2012-01-26 23:50 checking.del
-rw-rw-rw- 1 db2inst1 db2iadm1  136 2012-01-26 23:50 context.del
```

```
-rw-rw-rw- 1 db2inst1 db2iadm1    0 2012-01-26 23:50 execute.del
-rw-rw-rw- 1 db2inst1 db2iadm1    0 2012-01-26 23:50 objmaint.del
-rw-rw-rw- 1 db2inst1 db2iadm1    0 2012-01-26 23:50 secmaint.del
-rw-rw-rw- 1 db2inst1 db2iadm1    0 2012-01-26 23:50 sysadmin.del
-rw-rw-rw- 1 db2inst1 db2iadm1    0 2012-01-26 23:50 validate.del
```

7. Next, create a new user, belonging to group db2users, named sam:

    ```
    nodedb1:~ # useradd -g db2users sam
    ```

8. Connect as user db2secad and grant security label table_access.PUBROUTES to user sam:

    ```
    [db2inst1@nodedb21 security]$

     db2 "grant security label table_access.PUBROUTES to user sam for
    read access"
    DB20000I  The SQL command completed successfully.
    ```

9. Flush any pending audit records by issuing the following command:

    ```
    [db2inst1@nodedb21 security]$ db2audit flush


    AUD0000I  Operation succeeded.
    ```

10. Archive current audit data:

    ```
    [db2inst1@nodedb21 security]$ db2  "CALL SYSPROC.AUDIT_ARCHIVE( '/
    data/db2/auditarchivedlogs', -2 )"
    ```

    --..

    ```
    db2audit.db.NAV.log.0.20120127000447675401.bk
    ```

11. Extract and format the archive generated, by limiting the scope to just secadm operations:

    ```
    [db2inst1@nodedb21 security]$

    db2 "CALL SYSPROC.AUDIT_DELIM_EXTRACT( '|','/data/db2/
    extractedformaud','/data/db2/archivedauditlogs', 'db2audit.db.NAV.
    log.0.20120126233624335657.bk','category secmaint')"


     Return Status = 0
    ```

Using audit policies

You can limit the objects to be audited by using audit policies. Policies are created using the CREATE POLICY statement and are implemented using the AUDIT statement. Remember that a policy is not activated until a commit command is issued. The AUDIT statement can be used at: DATABASE, TABLE, TRUSTED CONTEXT, USERS, GROUPS, and ROLES levels and SYSADM, SYSCTRL, SYSMAINT, SYSMON, SECADM, and DBADM authorities.

1. Connect as db2secad and create a policy named SENSDATA, using the CHECKING and EXECUTE scopes:

   ```
   [db2inst1@nodedb21 security]$db2 "CREATE AUDIT POLICY SENSDATA
   CATEGORIES CHECKING STATUS BOTH, EXECUTE WITH DATA STATUS BOTH
   ERROR TYPE AUDIT"
   DB20000I  The SQL command completed successfully.
   [db2inst1@nodedb21 security]$ db2 commit
   DB20000I  The SQL command completed successfully.


   Next apply policy to table NAV.NAVAID:[db2inst1@nodedb21
   security]$db2 "audit table nav.navaid using policy sensdata"
   DB20000I  The SQL command completed successfully.
   [db2inst1@nodedb21 security]$
   ```

2. As user tom, issue a simple count on table NAV.NAVID:

   ```
    [db2inst1@nodedb21 security]$db2 "select count(*) from nav.
   navaid"


   1
   -----------
         11184


    1 record(s) selected.
   ```

3. Next, archive, extract, and format audit data, and limit the scope to execute the following command:

   ```
   [db2inst1@nodedb21 security]$ db2  "CALL SYSPROC.AUDIT_ARCHIVE( '/
   data/db2/auditarchivedlogs', -2 )"
   ..............................................................
   db2audit.db.NAV.log.0.20120127125826.bk
   [db2inst1@nodedb21 security]$ db2 "CALL SYSPROC.AUDIT_
   DELIM_EXTRACT( '|','/data/db2/extractedformaud','/data/db2/
   archivedauditlogs', ' db2audit.db.NAV.log.0.20120127125826.
   bk','category execute')"


   Return Status = 0
   ```

4. Now go to directory `/data/db2/extractedformaud` and inspect files `execute.del` and `auditlobs`, which contain the last statement, issued by `tom`.

5. As user `db2secad`, remove policy `SENSDATA` from table `nav.navaid`:

    ```
    [db2inst1@nodedb21 security]$ db2 "audit table nav.navaid remove
    policy sensdata"
    DB20000I  The SQL command completed successfully.
    [db2inst1@nodedb21 security]$
    ```

How it works...

`db2audit` is implemented as an independent utility, it is not dependent on instance availability; therefore, if you stop the instance, `db2audit` continues to run.

Here, status refers to what type of events should be audited; you can specify to audit at failure, success, or both. We have chosen both.

You can also configure the way you want the audit facility to handle errors, using the `ERRORTYPE` clause in the `db2audit` command. You have the ability to specify whether audit facility errors are returned to the user (`AUDIT`) or ignored (`NORMAL`). In the former case, all errors, including errors occurring within the audit facility, are managed by DB2 and all negative SQLCODEs are reported back to the application. In the latter case, any errors generated by the audit facility are ignored and only the SQLCODEs for the errors associated with the operation being performed are returned to the application.

Configuring the audit buffer is helpful in case we have to produce a large amount of audit records. If this parameter is not set (has a value of 0), writing of the audit log file is performed in synchronous mode and can have a significant impact on database I/O performance. After a value is assigned, all writes performed to the audit log file are made in asynchronous batch mode without waiting for write confirmation and are triggered by a buffer full event.

There's more...

Every audit event has a special record layout inside audit log files. You may find these layouts described in the **IBM** documentation found at this link: `http://publib.boulder.ibm.com/infocenter/db2luw/v9r7/index.jsp?topic=%2Fcom.ibm.db2.luw.admin.sec.doc%2Fdoc%2Fc0005483.html`.

To implement fine-grained auditing, vulnerability assessments, user monitoring and many more use a advanced tool as IBM InfoSphere Guardium Database Security: `http://www-01.ibm.com/software/data/guardium/`.

11
Connectivity and Networking

In this chapter, we will cover:

- ▶ Configuring network communications
- ▶ Cataloging and uncataloging instances and databases
- ▶ Using DB2 discovery
- ▶ Communications with DRDA servers (z/OS and i/OS)
- ▶ Monitoring FCM for optimal performance

Introduction

In large organizations, the application systems are usually implemented on different layers. There may exist different types of clients, from application servers to simple clients, and all these applications need to communicate somehow with a database or several database servers. All the clients must be configured to know about the database servers. The configuration is made at server-level and client-level and is about what type of protocol is used and its related specifics and the type of database server where the clients connect (DB2 LUW, i/OS, or z/OS). DB2 supports and comes with a lot of utilities and wizards to set up a reliable network communication. In the next series of recipes, we'll cover a lot of aspects related to how to set up network communications.

Configuring network communications

Nowadays, almost every organization is using a server/client model for accessing data stored in a central location. In order to communicate with a server, clients must use network communication protocols recognized by the servers to perform inbound requests. The configuration of the communication stack used by the database servers, necessary to establish connections from clients, is the main subject of the following recipe.

Getting ready

In this recipe, we'll create a new instance db2inst3 and configure the communication protocol (TCP/IP) and ports by using the command line and **Control Center**.

How to do it...

1. Create the fenced user, db2fenc3:

    ```
    [root@nodedb21 instance]# useradd db2inst3 -g db2iadm1
    [root@nodedb21 instance]#
    ```

2. Create to be a fenced user for instance db2inst3:

    ```
    [root@nodedb21 home]# useradd db2fenc3 -g db2iadm1
    [root@nodedb21 instance]#
    ```

3. Set password identical to the username for both users.

4. Create instance db2inst3:

    ```
    [root@nodedb21 ~]# /opt/ibm/db2/V9.7/instance/db2icrt -u db2fenc3
      db2inst3
    DBI1070I  Program db2icrt completed successfully.
    [root@nodedb21 ~]#
    ```

5. Set the DB2COMM variable to TCPIP as communication port:

    ```
    [db2inst3@nodedb21 ~]$ db2set DB2COMM=TCPIP
    ```

     DB2COMM registry variable can be set to TCPIP or SSL as communication protocols.

6. Assign a port number and service to instance db2inst3 in the /etc/services file:

    ```
    [root@nodedb21 ~]#  cat >> /etc/services

    db2c_db2inst3 50004/tcp

    Ctrl+D

    [root@nodedb21 ~]#
    ```

7. Update SVCNAME instance parameter with the service name defined previously. As db2inst3 instance owner, execute the following command:

    ```
    [db2inst3@nodedb21 ~]$  db2 "update dbm cfg using SVCENAME
      db2c_db2inst3 "

    DB20000I  The UPDATE DATABASE MANAGER CONFIGURATION command
      completed successfully.

    [db2inst3@nodedb21 ~]$
    ```

8. If you are planning to use the SVCENAME port numbers instead of service names then the service file does not need to be updated. Stop and start the instance (SVCENAME is not a dynamic parameter):

    ```
    [db2inst3@nodedb21 ~]$ db2stop; db2start

    10/03/2011 12:36:51     0   0   SQL1064N  DB2STOP processing was
      successful.

    SQL1064N  DB2STOP processing was successful.

    10/03/2011 12:36:53     0   0   SQL1063N  DB2START processing was
      successful.

    SQL1063N  DB2START processing was successful.

    [db2inst3@nodedb21 ~]$
    ```

Using Control Center

1. To set DB2COMM to TCPIP with CA use **Tools | Configuration Assistant | Configure | Registry** (or start it with the db2ca command):

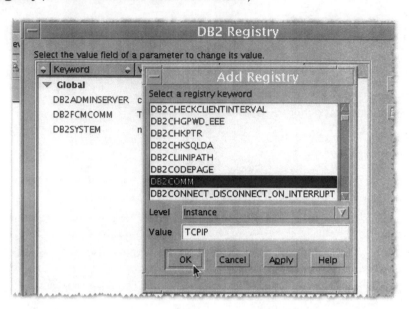

2. You can stop the instance by right-clicking on **db2inst3**, and then selecting **Stop**. In order to start the instance right-click on db2inst3 and select **Start**:

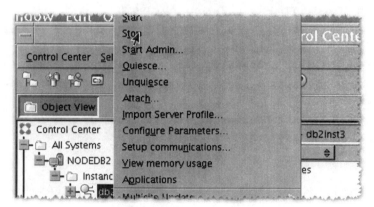

3. If you are running DB2 on Linux or Unix, edit the `/etc/service` file as `root`:

    ```
    [root@nodedb21 ~]#  cat >> /etc/services
    db2c_db2inst3 50004/tcp
    Ctrl+D
    [root@nodedb21 ~]#
    ```

4. To set up the communication, right-click on **db2inst3** and select **Setup communications...**:

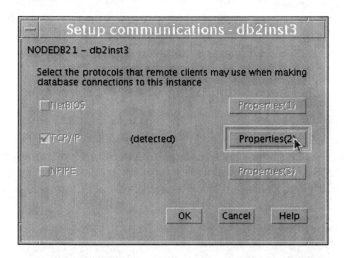

5. Click on the **Properties(2)** button that's applicable to the protocol we're going to use, in this case we've selected the TCP/IP configuration settings:

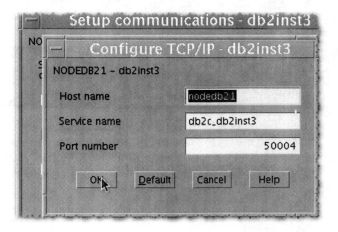

6. Stop and start the instance by right-clicking on **db2inst3** and selecting **Stop** and then again right-click on **db2inst3** and select **Start**.

Using this method for configuring communications in MS Windows will automatically update the service file with the values provided. Therefore, you should use an unallocated service name and port, otherwise you will get an error message.

In Linux and Unix, you have to edit `/etc/services` as `root` as listed previously.

How it works...

TCPIP and SSL are using protocol managers to implement the communication protocols. If `DB2COMM` is not set, no protocol manager is started and you might not be able to connect to the instance from a client. However, you can use the system locally.

There's more...

Setting `DB2COMM` to SSL may have a slight impact on network performance. Therefore, it is not a good idea to use it when you have large sets to return from database servers, found especially in DSS, unless you are dealing with very sensitive data. Instead, use `DATA_ENCRYPT` as the authentication mode to encrypt network transmission.

See also

See the following recipes in *Chapter 1, DB2 Instance—Administration and Configuration*:

- ▶ *Creating and Configuring instances for non-partitioned environments Starting and stopping instances*

- ▶ *Configuring SSL for client-server instance communication*

Cataloging and uncataloging instances and databases

In the previous recipe, we covered how to set up communication for a newly created instance. Cataloging instances and databases is the next important task after you install and configure a DB2 client or DB2 Connect product. It is very important to ensure that you have correctly cataloged a remote or a local system to be able to connect and work with it.

Getting ready

For this recipe, we'll create a new database under instance db2inst3, and further we'll catalog the instance and the database at the DB2 client installed in the *Creating and configuring a client instance* recipe in *Chapter 1, DB2 Instance—Administration and Configuration*.

How to do it...

1. As a db2inst3 instance owner, create a sample database using db2sample script:

   ```
   [db2inst3@nodedb21 ~]$ db2sampl

       Creating database "SAMPLE"...
       Connecting to database "SAMPLE"...
       Creating tables and data in schema "DB2INST3"...
       Creating tables with XML columns and XML data in schema
   "DB2INST3"...

       'db2sampl' processing complete.
   [db2inst3@nodedb21 ~]$
   ```

2. Since we want to use DB2 **Control Center** for database administration then the first step should be to catalog the admin node. On the db2clnt1 client instance that resides on nodedb22, execute the following command:

   ```
   [db2clnt1@nodedb22 ~]$ db2 "CATALOG ADMIN TCPIP NODE nodedb21
   REMOTE nodedb21 SYSTEM  NODEDB21 OSTYPE  LINUXX8664"
   DB20000I  The CATALOG ADMIN TCPIP NODE command completed
   successfully.
   DB21056W  Directory changes may not be effective until the
   directory cache is
   refreshed.
   [db2clnt1@nodedb22 ~]$
   ```

3. Catalog the instance db2inst3 under client instance db2clnt1 using the following command:

   ```
   [db2clnt1@nodedb22 ~]$ db2 "CATALOG TCPIP NODE NODE21 REMOTE
   nodedb21 SERVER 50004 REMOTE_INSTANCE  db2inst3 SYSTEM  NODEDB21
   OSTYPE  LINUXX8664"
   DB20000I  The CATALOG TCPIP NODE command completed successfully.
   DB21056W  Directory changes may not be effective until the
   directory cache is
   refreshed.
   [db2clnt1@nodedb22 ~]$
   ```

For IP6 addresses use TCPIP6 instead of TCPIP in the CATALOG TCPIP ADMIN NODE and CATALOG TCPIP NODE commands.

4. Next, catalog database Sample in the previous cataloged instance node:

    ```
    [db2clnt1@nodedb22 ~]$ db2 "CATALOG DATABASE SAMPLE AS SAMPLE AT
    NODE  NODE21"
    DB20000I  The CATALOG DATABASE command completed successfully.
    DB21056W  Directory changes may not be effective until the
    directory cache is refreshed.
    ```

5. Verify if the instance is cataloged correctly and if it is available by using the following command:

    ```
    [db2clnt1@nodedb22 ~]$ db2 "attach to node21 user db2inst3 using
    db2inst3 "


        Instance Attachment Information

    Instance server          = DB2/LINUXX8664 9.7.4
    Authorization ID         = DB2INST3
    Local instance alias     = NODE21
    ```

6. Verify if the database is cataloged correctly and if it is available by trying to connect:

    ```
    [db2clnt1@nodedb22 ~]$ db2 "connect to sample user db2inst3 using
    db2inst3"


        Database Connection Information

    Database server          = DB2/LINUXX8664 9.7.4
    SQL authorization ID     = DB2INST3
    Local database alias     = SAMPLE
    ```

7. To see the admin nodes and details about them, issue the following command:

    ```
    [db2clnt1@nodedb22 ~]$ db2 "list admin node directory show detail"
    Node Directory
    Number of entries in the directory = 1
    Node 1 entry:
    Node name                       = NODEDB21
    Comment                         =
    Directory entry type            = LOCAL
    Protocol                        = TCPIP
    ```

```
Hostname                      = NODEDB21

Service name                  = 523

Remote instance name          =

System                        = NODEDB21

Operating system type         = LINUXX8664
[db2clnt1@nodedb22 ~]$
```

8. To see the `node21` instance node details, issue the following command:

```
[db2clnt1@nodedb22 ~]$ db2 "list node directory show detail"
Node Directory
Number of entries in the directory = 1

Node 1 entry:
Node name                     = NODE21
Comment                       =
Directory entry type          = LOCAL
Protocol                      = TCPIP
Hostname                      = nodedb21
Service name                  = 50004
Remote instance name          = db2inst3
System                        = NODEDB21
Operating system type         = LINUXX8664
[db2clnt1@nodedb22 ~]$
```

9. Finally, uncatalog the admin node `nodedb21` and instance node `NODE21`:

```
[db2clnt1@nodedb22 ~]$ db2 "UNCATALOG NODE nodedb21"
DB20000I  The UNCATALOG NODE command completed successfully.
DB21056W  Directory changes may not be effective until the
directory cache is refreshed.
[db2clnt1@nodedb22 ~]$
[db2clnt1@nodedb22 ~]$ db2 "UNCATALOG NODE NODE21"
DB20000I  The UNCATALOG NODE command completed successfully.
DB21056W  Directory changes may not be effective until the
directory cache is refreshed.
[db2clnt1@nodedb22 ~]$
```

Using Control Center

1. On `nodedb22` start **Control Center**. Catalog the admin node by right-clicking on **All systems** and selecting **Add**:

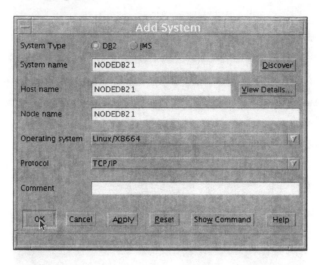

2. Catalog the instance node using **All systems | NODEDB21** then right-click on **Instances** and select **Add**:

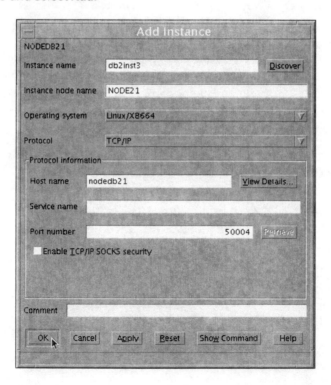

3. Catalog the sample database at node `NODE21` using **All systems | NODEDB21 | Instances | NODE21(db2inst3) | Databases**:

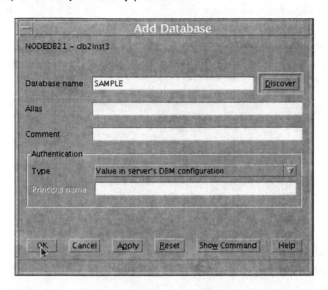

4. To uncatalog `NODE21` instance node use **All Systems | NODEDB21 | NODE21(db2inst3) | Remove**:

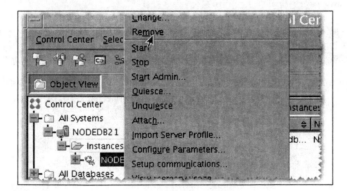

How it works...

After a node is cataloged the information is stored in structures called **directories**. We have the following directories depending on what we have cataloged:

▶ **Node directory** – this contains information about remote and local instances. It is created when an instance is cataloged. Its content can be listed by using the `LIST NODE DIRECTORY` command and its variants.

- ▸ **Local database directory** – this is used for keeping information about local databases. We can have several local database directory files depending on how many local databases we have created. Its contents can be listed by using `LIST DATABASE DIRECTORY` command.

- ▸ **System database directory** – this is stored in a file `~/sqllib/sqldbdir/sqldbdir`. It stores information about local databases and remote databases cataloged. Its contents can be viewed by using `LIST DB DIRECTORY <ON [Location] >` command.

- ▸ **Database Connection Services directory** – this is used by DB2 Connect products for storing information about DRDA hosts databases. Its contents can be listed using the `LIST DCS DIRECTORY` command.

See also

Communications with DRDA servers (z/OS and i/OS) recipe in this chapter

There's more...

You may also use **Configuration Assistant (CA)** for cataloging or uncataloging instances and databases. When you want to use SSL as communication protocol you should catalog the server instance by using the command line on the client. Configuration Assistant or **Control Center** wizards have no option to specify Security SSL.

Using DB2 Discovery

DB2 Discovery is very useful in large networks where you don't know all the characteristics of the database servers such as the listening port numbers, the operating system, or other information used at cataloging.

Getting ready

In the following recipe, we'll discuss the discovery process and its related parameters at instance and database-level. We'll discover and catalog `db2inst3` and the sample database created in the previous recipes at DB2 client instance.

How to do it...

1. On `nodedb22`, start **Control Center**. Catalog the admin node by right-clicking on **All systems** and selecting **Add**:

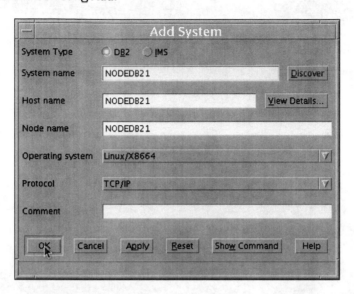

2. Discover the instances on `nodedb21` using **Configuration Center** | **All Systems** | **NODEDB21** | **Instance** | **Add**:

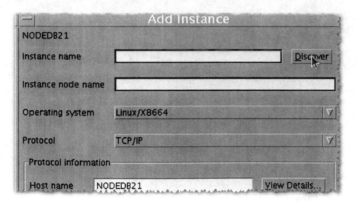

3. In the instances discovered on `nodedb21`, choose `db2inst3`:

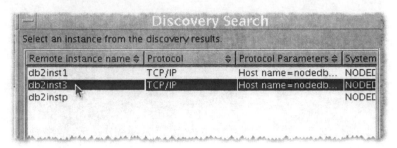

4. The **Add Instance** window is auto completed, the only one box that needs completion is instance node name. Name it **NODE21**:

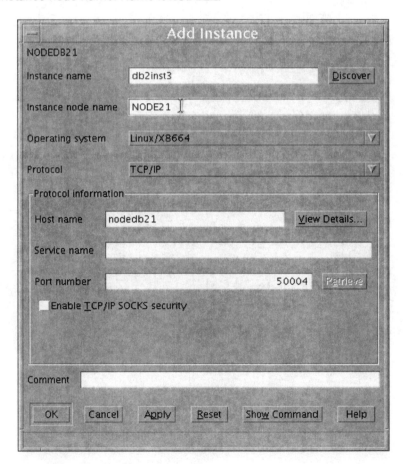

5. Next, discover the Sample database under instance `db2inst3`:

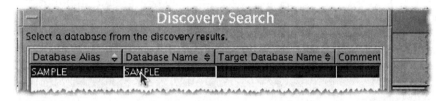

6. After short time database Sample is discovered.

7. The window is auto completed with all information related to sample database:

How it works...

Configuration Assistant broadcasts messages all over the network to identify the instances and databases. The instances and the databases will respond with their related information.

The instance parameters that control the discovery process for the instance are DISCOVER and DISCOVER_INST. The DISCOVER parameter can be set to DISABLE, SEARCH, or KNOWN and it is working at DAS level. The DISCOVER_INST parameter has two possible values: ENABLE and DISABLE. At database-level we have the DISCOVER_DB parameter, which is similar to DISCOVER_INST with the same possible states ENABLE and DISABLE.

If the DISCOVER parameter has a SEARCH value then a search discovery is performed. Using this method you don't need to provide anything such as communication information or server names; the discovery is totally automatic. If it has a value of KNOWN, then a known discovery type is performed; in this way you have to provide the server names, and any other information will be returned by the discovery process. Setting this parameter to DISABLE will suspend any respond to a discovery broadcast, in this way we can hide a server in the network. Similarly, setting DISCOVER_INST and DISCOVER_DB to ENABLE or DISABLE will determine their response to the discovery process.

There's more...

It is a good method to use when you work with large networks with hundreds of database servers. However, using the search discovery method, it can take a long time to identify every server. The Discovery process will only operate on TCP/IP protocol.

On MS Windows operation systems you can use the DB2DISCOVERYTIME registry variable to increase the amount of time that SEARCH discovery will search for DB2 systems.

Communications with DRDA servers (z/OS and i/OS)

There are some big shops which are running critical applications on DB2 on z/OS or i/OS. The reason to use these systems is that they are very reliable and provide unsurpassed scalability. Usually you need to connect and extract database from these systems. IBM provides a tool or an add-on named DB2 Connect for connecting to these systems. Next we'll show you how to catalog and establish connection to an i/OS DB2 database.

Getting ready

In the following recipe, we'll install DB2 Connect Server Edition product and establish a connection to a DB2 i/OS system and database.

How to do it...

After you have installed DB2 Connect, perform the following steps:

1. Launch Configuration Assistant from its installation home **Configuration Assistant | Add Database Using Wizard...**:

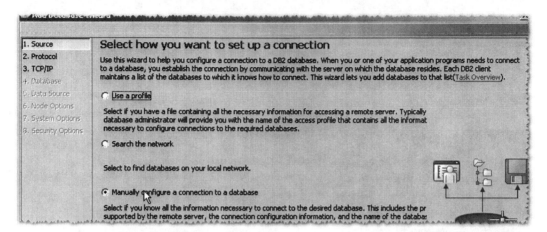

2. Select TCP/IP as the communication protocol.

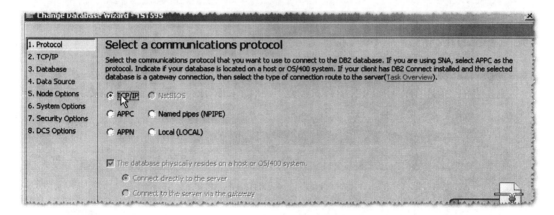

3. Specify **Host name** and **Service name**:

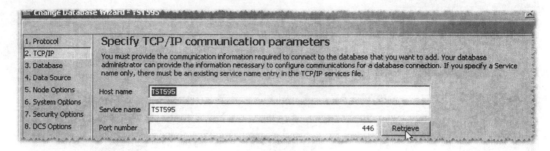

4. Usually the database name in i/OS is identical to the host name:

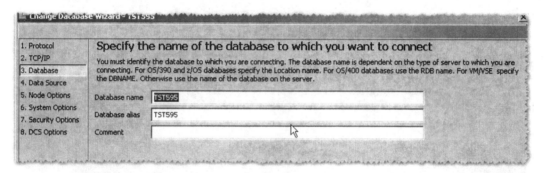

5. Specify the instance; this will be used just for cataloging purposes:

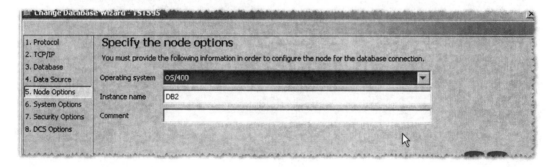

6. Fill system options such as **System name**, **Host name**, and **Operating system**:

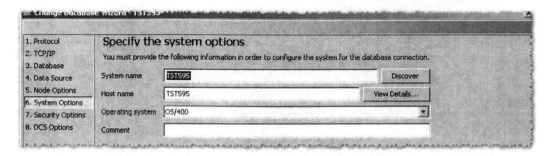

7. Set the authentication type to **SERVER**:

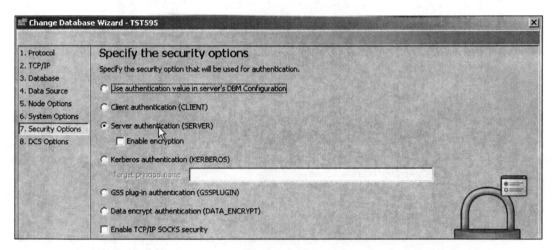

8. The next step is to verify the connection to database **TST595** is configured and running correctly:

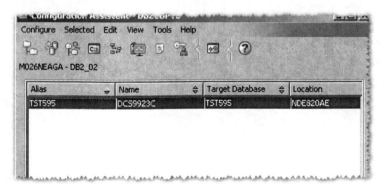

9. Next choose a connection method and provide a username and password:

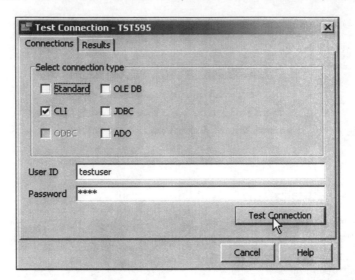

10. The connection test has succeeded:

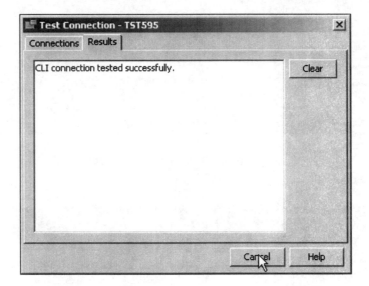

11. We have successfully cataloged the i/OS **TST595** database in DB2 Connect. The database is catalogued as a DCS entry:

```
db2 => list dcs directory


    Database Connection Services (DCS) Directory


    Number of entries in the directory = 1


 DCS 1 entry:


    Local database name              = DCS9923C
    Target database name             = TST595
    Application requestor name       =
    DCS parameters                   =
    Comment                          =
    DCS directory release level      = 0x0100
 db2 =>
```

12. Try a connection to database using the command line:

```
db2 => connect to tst595 user testuser2 using test


    Database Connection Information

 Database server        = OS/400 5.4.0
 SQL authorization ID   = T7026H01
 Local database alias   = TST595
 db2 =>
```

How it works...

The catalog information related to DCS databases is stored in a special directory structure named DCS directory. For i/OS and z/OS you don't have to catalog instances first; instead you have to catalog the system database. On z/OS operating systems databases are located in subsystems.

There's more...

After you catalog a DCS database you should bind the applications and utilities. This will enable using export/import or the command line processor with DCS databases. Binding can be initiated from Configuration Assistant or by the command line using the BIND command.

Monitoring and configuring FCM for optimal performance

FCM is an abbreviation for Fast Communication Manager. It is activated if you are using intra-partition parallelism or multipartitioned databases. The Fast Communication Manager as structure is composed by FCM buffers and FCM channels. It has a very important role in ensuring the communication between database partitions and between query slaves (subagents) and the coordinator agent when using intra-partition or inter-partition query parallelism.

Getting ready

In this recipe, we'll try to figure out the main components of FCM functionality. We'll cover some methods used for determining the performance of FCM in our NAV partitioned database created in *Chapter 2, Administration and Configuration of the DB2 Non-partitioned Database*.

How to do it...

Let's activate FCM usage for the NAV non-partitioned database:

1. To see the FCM buffers currently allocated for the db2inst1 instance, issue the following query:

    ```
    db2 "SELECT member, buff_free, buff_free_bottom
       FROM TABLE (MON_GET_FCM (-2))"
    ```

    ```
    MEMBER BUFF_FREE             BUFF_FREE_BOTTOM
    ------ -------------------- --------------------
        0                  128                  128
    ```

2. To enable FCM on a non-partitioned database you have to change the database
   manager configuration parameter INTRA_PARALLELISM to YES:

   ```
   [db2inst1@nodedb21 ~]$ db2 "update dbm cfg using intra_parallel
   yes"

   DB20000I  The UPDATE DATABASE MANAGER CONFIGURATION command
   completed

   successfully.
   ```

3. Bounce the instance :

   ```
   [db2inst1@nodedb21 ~]$ db2stop; db2start

   10/05/2011 15:40:17     0    0    SQL1064N  DB2STOP processing was
   successful.

   SQL1064N  DB2STOP processing was successful.

   10/05/2011 15:40:19     0    0    SQL1063N  DB2START processing was
   successful.

   SQL1063N  DB2START processing was successful.

   [db2inst1@nodedb21 ~]$
   ```

4. Set the query parallelism degree to 2 at database-level:

   ```
   [db2inst1@nodedb21 ~]$ db2 "update db cfg for nav using dft_degree
   2"

   DB20000I  The UPDATE DATABASE CONFIGURATION command completed
   successfully.

     [db2inst1@nodedb21 ~]$ db2stop; db2start

   10/05/2011 15:40:17     0    0    SQL1064N  DB2STOP processing was
   successful.

   SQL1064N  DB2STOP processing was successful.

   10/05/2011 15:40:19     0    0    SQL1063N  DB2START processing was
   successful.

   SQL1063N  DB2START processing was successful.
   ```

    Generally, the parallel degree should be adjusted proportionally
   with the number of cores/CPUs.

5. Now run a simple query to see if parallelism is really enabled and FCM is used for
   parallel execution:

   ```
   [db2inst1@nodedb21 ~]$ db2 "select * from nav.comm where
   ckey='VE85242TW'"

   .........................................................................

   [db2inst1@nodedb21 ~]$
   ```

6. Now, we should observe an increase in the number of FCM buffers and their usage. Again, monitor the number of buffers and channels allocated:

```
[db2inst1@nodedb21 ~]$ db2 "SELECT member, buff_free, buff_free_
bottom,ch_total,ch_free
    FROM TABLE (MON_GET_FCM (-1))"


MEMBER BUFF_FREE                 BUFF_FREE_BOTTOM      CH_TOTAL
CH_FREE
------ --------------------      --------------------  -----------------
--- --------------------
     0                 1790                     1777
895                894
    1 record(s) selected.

[db2inst1@nodedb21 ~]$
```

7. To inspect the number of buffers sent and received, issue the following query:

```
[db2inst1@nodedb21 ~]$ db2 "select member,remote_member,TOTAL_
BUFFERS_SENT,TOTAL_BUFFERS_rcvd from TABLE (MON_GET_FCM_
CONNECTION_LIST(-1))"


MEMBER REMOTE_MEMBER TOTAL_BUFFERS_SENT    TOTAL_BUFFERS_RCVD
------ ------------- --------------------  --------------------
     0             0                 1051                   891


    1 record(s) selected.


[db2inst1@nodedb21 ~]$
```

8. Enable intra-parallelism on the NAV multipartitioned database too. As user db2instp, execute the following command:

```
[db2instp@nodedb21 ~]$ db2 "update dbm cfg using intra_parallel
yes"
DB20000I  The UPDATE DATABASE MANAGER CONFIGURATION command
completed successfully.
```

9. Bounce instance *db2instp*.

10. Connect to the NAV multipartitioned database:

```
[db2instp@nodedb21 ~]$ db2 "connect to nav"


    Database Connection Information
```

```
Database server        = DB2/LINUXX8664 9.7.4

SQL authorization ID   = DB2INSTP

Local database alias   = NAV


[db2instp@nodedb21 ~]$
```

11. To see the FCM buffers currently allocated for the db2instp instance for each partition, issue the following query:

```
[db2instp@nodedb21 ~]$ db2 "select member,remote_member,TOTAL_
BUFFERS_SENT,TOTAL_BUFFERS_rcvd from TABLE (MON_GET_FCM_
CONNECTION_LIST(-2))"
```

MEMBER	REMOTE_MEMBER	TOTAL_BUFFERS_SENT	TOTAL_BUFFERS_RCVD
0	0	10	10
0	1	11	8
0	2	11	8
0	3	11	8
0	4	11	8

```
 5 record(s) selected.
```

12. Now run a simple query to see if parallelism is really enabled and FCM is used for parallel execution on partitions:

```
[db2inst1@nodedb21 ~]$ db2 "select * from nav.comm where
ckey='VE85242TW'"

..........................................................................................

[db2inst1@nodedb21 ~]$
```

13. Now, we should observe an increase in the number of FCM buffers and channels and their usage on each partition if it is the case. Again, monitor the number of buffers and channels allocated:

```
[db2instp@nodedb21 ~]$  db2 "select member,remote_member,TOTAL_
BUFFERS_SENT,TOTAL_BUFFERS_rcvd from TABLE (MON_GET_FCM_
CONNECTION_LIST(-2))"
```

MEMBER	REMOTE_MEMBER	TOTAL_BUFFERS_SENT	TOTAL_BUFFERS_RCVD
3	0	1590	982
3	1	20	20

3	2	20	20
3	3	1066	1066
3	4	20	20
0	0	3324	2833
0	1	880	822
0	2	871	812
0	3	1229	1590
0	4	872	813

```
[db2instp@nodedb21 ~]$
```

How it works...

The FCM is controlled by two parameters: `fcm_num_buffers` and `fcm_num_channels`.

`fcm_num_buffers` determines the maximum number of FCM buffers available. The FCM buffers hold data which is passed between agents. The data is passed through FCM channels. It has an integer value, and the maximum value depends on the operating system; for a 32-bit operating system the maximum value is 120 000 and for a 64-bit operating system the maximum value is 524 288. IBM recommends leaving this value on AUTOMATIC.

`fcm_num_channels` determines the maximum numbers of FCM channels available. An FCM channel represents a logical communication end point between EDUs. It has an integer value. The maximum value depends on the operating system; for a 32-bit operating system the maximum value is 120 000 and for a 64-bit operating system the maximum value is 524 288. IBM recommends leaving this value on AUTOMATIC.

On single databases, FCM is used to broadcast data between subagents and the coordinator agent.

Internally, FCM buffers have a priority assignment: low, medium, and high.. The priority is established depending on the operation performed; error messages have a higher priority than data handling between agents.

For monitoring you can also use the db2pd –fcm command or db2top.

There's more...

Usually, setting `fcm_num_buffers` and `fcm_num_channel` to AUTOMATIC is appropriate for many environments. In this mode, buffers and channels are usually allocated on demand. If nothing happens in 30 minutes they are released. If you have to execute some very intensive operations concurrently with a high degree of parallelism it is a good idea to start with higher values because dynamic allocation and deallocation could impose some performance penalty.

On Linux operating systems you may use the DB2_FCM_SETTINGS environment variable. This variable has two possible values that may help in tuning optimal FCM memory allocation for consuming tasks. One is FCM_MAXIMIZE_SET_SIZE, which if has a value of TRUE preallocates 4 GB of memory for the FCM when instance is started, and FCM_CFG_BASE_ AS_FLOOR applicable if we use automatic allocation. This variable when is activated mark the initial values for FCM_NUM_BUFFERS and FCM_NUM_CHANNELS as boundaries that cannot be lowered by automatic tuning processes.

To set 4 GB of memory to be preallocated for the FCM:

[db2instp@nodedb21 ~]$ db2set DB2_FCM_SETTINGS=FCM_MAXIMIZE_SET_SIZE:NO

Bounce the instance to activate this option.

To set the lower boundaries for FCM_NUM_BUFFERS to 10000 pages and for FCM_NUM_CHANNELS to 5600 pages issue the following commands:

[db2instp@nodedb21 ~]$ db2 update dbm cfg using fcm_num_buffers 10000 fcm_num_channels 5600

DB20000I The UPDATE DATABASE MANAGER CONFIGURATION command completed successfully.

[db2instp@nodedb21 ~]$

[db2instp@nodedb21 ~]$ db2set DB2_FCM_SETTINGS=FCM_CFG_BASE_AS_FLOOR:YES

[db2instp@nodedb21 ~]$ db2 update dbm cfg using fcm_num_buffers automatic fcm_num_channels automatic

DB20000I The UPDATE DATABASE MANAGER CONFIGURATION command

12
Monitoring

In this chapter, we will cover the following topics:

- ▶ Configuring and using system monitoring
- ▶ Configuring and using snapshot monitoring
- ▶ Configuring and using event monitoring
- ▶ Using Memory Visualizer
- ▶ Using Health Monitor

Introduction

Monitoring your database means you ensure that the database is available and nothing hinders its functionality. We can divide all the monitoring activities into the following three aspects:

1. System monitoring: In this, we monitor the overall system availability and use
2. Snapshot monitoring: This aspect is in fact a picture or snapshot of the actual state of the database at a specific time
3. Event monitoring: This is triggered on certain events, which gather statistics based on the event that is monitored

 There are many excellent tools available. One of my favorite tools is Toad for DB2, which is available as a freeware (certain restrictions apply). The commercial version has many more options for DBAs.

The Memory Visualizer and Health Monitor tools that are provided with DB2 provide a graphical user interface. The Health Monitor can be configured using the command line or by GUI, and can help you in your system monitoring activities. Everything works together, so let's see how it's done.

Configuring and using system monitoring

With DB2 V9.7, there is an alternative to the traditional system monitor. You can use table functions for systems, activities, or objects. Data for these elements are collected and stored in memory.

- ▶ System monitoring: The server operations as a whole can be monitored through request monitor elements, grouped in the following hierarchical fashion:
  - ❑ Service class: You can group workloads into a service class; for example, *marketing*
  - ❑ Workload: We can define a workload named *reporting*, which will belong to the service class—*marketing*
  - ❑ Unit of work: Users connected to the application *accounts* will be assigned to the *reporting* workload

- ▶ Activity monitoring: Any DML or a DDL statement triggers activities on the data server, as well as calls and the load utility. An activity can have different states, such as EXECUTING, IDLE, or QUEUED.

- ▶ Data objects monitoring: We can monitor a database object for performance indicators such as a buffer pool, table space, a table, or an index.

Getting ready

You will need to purchase a license in order to use all the features of workload management. You can change the default setting if necessary by using the *METRICS database configuration parameter.

How to do it...

1. Get the actual configuration with the following command:

```
[db2inst1@nodedb21 ~]$  db2 get db cfg | grep -e "METRICS"
 Request metrics                      (MON_REQ_METRICS) = BASE
 Activity metrics                     (MON_ACT_METRICS) = BASE
 Object metrics                       (MON_OBJ_METRICS) = BASE
```

2. Change the setting if necessary.

   If the parameter is set to NONE or 0, you can change it right away. This parameter is dynamic so the change takes effect immediately.

```
[db2inst1@nodedb21 ~]$ db2 "UPDATE DB CFG USING
>       MON_REQ_METRICS BASE
```

```
>        MON_ACT_METRICS BASE

>        MON_OBJ_METRICS BASE"

DB20000I  The UPDATE DATABASE CONFIGURATION command completed
    successfully.
```

3. You can enable workload statistics collection at a chosen interval.

    Get the current configuration with the following:

    ```
    [db2instp@ nodedb21 ~]$ db2 get db cfg | grep WLM_COLLECT_INT
     WLM Collection Interval (minutes)        (WLM_COLLECT_INT) = 0
    ```

    Set up statistics collection. We will also set up the workload management to collect system data every five minutes.

    ```
    [db2instp@ nodedb21 ~]$ db2 "UPDATE DATABASE CONFIGURATION USING
        WLM_COLLECT_INT 5 IMMEDIATE"

    DB20000I  The UPDATE DATABASE CONFIGURATION command completed
        successfully.
    ```

4. The next step involve workload management, which requires a license. This requires Workload Management Administrator (WLMADM) authority.

    Create the service class with the following command:

    ```
    db2 "CREATE SERVICE CLASS MARKETING"
    ```

5. Users connecting through the accounts application will be assigned to the REPORTING workload. You can add other workloads to this service class later.

    Create a workload with the following command:

    ```
    db2 "CREATE WORKLOAD REPORTING APPLNAME('ACCOUNTS') SERVICE CLASS
        MARKETING"
    ```

How it works...

The system monitor is enabled on new databases by default. Data is collected into memory and can be queried through table functions, much as with the dynamic V$ tables in Oracle.

There's more...

Let's have a look at the table functions that we can use for monitoring. We'll cover some examples here.

Querying system information using table functions

Data server operations are available through table functions; you can query those tables by service, workload, or by connection:

- ▶ MON_GET_SERVICE_SUBCLASS
- ▶ MON_GET_SERVICE_SUBCLASS_DETAILS
- ▶ MON_GET_WORKLOAD
- ▶ MON_GET_WORKLOAD_DETAILS
- ▶ MON_GET_CONNECTION
- ▶ MON_GET_CONNECTION_DETAILS
- ▶ MON_GET_UNIT_OF_WORK
- ▶ MON_GET_UNIT_OF_WORK_DETAILS

Ex 1: Which connections are most impacted by lock waits?

```
[db2inst1@ nodedb21 ~]$ db2 'select substr(application_name,1,30)
"APPLICATION",
           total_rqst_time "RQST TIME",
           total_wait_time "TOTAL WAIT",
           lock_wait_time "LOCK WAIT",
    (case when (total_rqst_time > 0)
       then (lock_wait_time * 100) /
            total_rqst_time
       else 0 end) as PCT_LOCK_WAIT
from table (mon_get_connection(null,-2)) as t
order by PCT_LOCK_WAIT desc fetch first 5 rows only'


APPLICATION                            RQST TIME            TOTAL WAIT
LOCK WAIT                 PCT_LOCK_WAIT
-------------------------------- -------------------- --------------------
-------------------- --------------------
db2bp                                          2914                  500
0                        0


  1 record(s) selected.
```

Ex 2: How much time has the database spent on lock waits?

```
[db2inst1@ nodedb21 ~]$ db2 "select sum(total_rqst_time) as rqst_time,
      sum(lock_wait_time) as lock_wait_time,
    (case when sum(total_rqst_time) > 0
    then (sum(lock_wait_time) * 100) / sum(total_rqst_time)
    else 0 end) as lwt_pct
from table(mon_get_connection(null,-2)) as t        "


RQST_TIME              LOCK_WAIT_TIME        LWT_PCT
-------------------   -------------------   -------------------
            2915                        0                     0


  1 record(s) selected.
```

Querying activity information using table functions

Obtaining this information is easy once you get the application handle. You can then query activity information using the application handle, and unit of work ID.

▶ MON_GET_ACTIVITY_DETAILS

▶ MON_GET_PKG_CACHE_STMT

In this example, we can query the wait time for an activity:

```
SELECT actmetrics.application_handle "appl handle",
      actmetrics.activity_id        "act id",
      actmetrics.uow_id             "uow_id",
      substr(actmetrics.stmt_text, 1, 50) "stmt text",
      actmetrics.total_act_time     "tot act time",
      actmetrics.total_act_wait_time "tot act wait",
      CASE WHEN actmetrics.total_act_time > 0
        THEN DEC
          ((FLOAT(actmetrics.total_act_wait_time)/FLOAT(actmetrics.total_
act_time)) * 100, 5, 2)
        ELSE NULL
      END    "pct wait"
FROM TABLE(MON_GET_ACTIVITY_DETAILS(for each row of
          (select application_handle,  uow_id, activity_id
```

```
                from    table(wlm_get_workload_occurrence_activities_
v97(NULL, -1))
                where   activity_id > 0), -1)) AS ACTDETAILS,
XMLTABLE (XMLNAMESPACES(
  DEFAULT 'http://www.ibm.com/xmlns/prod/db2/mon'),
  '$actmetrics/db2_activity_details'
  PASSING XMLPARSE(DOCUMENT ACTDETAILS.DETAILS) as "actmetrics"
  COLUMNS
    "APPLICATION_HANDLE"  INTEGER PATH 'application_handle',
    "ACTIVITY_ID"         INTEGER PATH 'activity_id',
    "UOW_ID"              INTEGER PATH 'uow_id',
    "STMT_TEXT"           VARCHAR(1024) PATH 'stmt_text',
    "TOTAL_ACT_TIME"      INTEGER PATH 'activity_metrics/total_act_time',
    "TOTAL_ACT_WAIT_TIME" INTEGER PATH 'activity_metrics/total_act_wait_
time'
  ) AS ACTMETRICS;


appl handle act id      uow_id      stmt text
tot act time tot act wait pct wait
----------- ----------- ----------- ------------------------------------
------------- ------------ ------------ --------
      3940           1          20 SELECT actmetrics.application_handle
"appl handle"          0           0        -


  1 record(s) selected.
```

Querying data objects information using table functions

Data server operations are available through table functions; you can query those tables by service, workload, or by connection:

- ▸ MON_GET_BUFFERPOOL
- ▸ MON_GET_TABLESPACE
- ▸ MON_GET_CONTAINER
- ▸ MON_GET_TABLE
- ▸ MON_GET_INDEX

Let's see the table space that has the maximum physical reads here:

```
SELECT substr(tbsp_name,1,20)        "tbsp name",
                member               "member",
                tbsp_type            "tbspc type",
                pool_data_p_reads    "phys reads"
FROM TABLE(MON_GET_TABLESPACE('',-2)) AS t
ORDER BY pool_data_p_reads DESC;
```

tbsp name	member	tbspc type	phys reads
SYSCATSPACE	0	DMS	223
USERSPACE1	0	DMS	34
POS_TBLS	0	DMS	18
POS_INDX	0	DMS	18
SYSTOOLSPACE	0	DMS	7
TEMPSPACE1	0	DMS	2
SYSTOOLSTMPSPACE	0	DMS	2

```
  7 record(s) selected.
```

Workload management (WLM)

Using all the functionalities of workload management requires a license; however, you can use limited functionalities of WLM without licensing, such as the following:

- Default workloads
- Default service classes
- Workload manager tables/stored procedures
- Create/activate/drop and workload management event monitors

  ```
  [db2inst1@ nodedb21 ~]$ db2 "SELECT application_handle,
    activity_id, uow_id, local_start_time
      FROM TABLE( WLM_GET_WORKLOAD_OCCURRENCE_ACTIVITIES_V97( NULL,
        -1)) AS T"


  APPLICATION_HANDLE    ACTIVITY_ID UOW_ID       LOCAL_START_TIME
  -------------------- ----------- ----------- ---------------------
  -----
                2606            1          26 2011-12-01-
  11.46.01.527879

    1 record(s) selected.
  ```

With the full license, you can create workloads and manage system resources according to the workload priorities.

See also

We cannot cover all the table functions here and all the possible query combinations you can use to monitor performance on a system-wide basis. We suggest you refer to the documentation for more details here: `ftp://ftp.software.ibm.com/ps/products/db2/info/vr97/pdf/en_US/DB2Monitoring-db2f0e972.pdf`.

Configuring and using snapshot monitoring

The snapshot monitor can be used to take a picture of the database usage statistics and connected applications at a specific point-in-time. Being used regularly, you can identify trends and act proactively on potential problems.

Getting ready

The information you can collect depends on the monitor switches. If you are not logged in as instance owner, you must have proper authority to capture a database snapshot.

How to do it...

1. Get current settings for monitor switches with the following command:

    ```
    [db2inst1@nodedb21 ~]$ db2 get monitor switches
    ```

    ```
                    Monitor Recording Switches

        Switch list for db partition number 0
        Buffer Pool Activity Information  (BUFFERPOOL) = OFF
        Lock Information                       (LOCK) = OFF
        Sorting Information                    (SORT) = OFF
        SQL Statement Information         (STATEMENT) = OFF
        Table Activity Information            (TABLE) = OFF
        Take Timestamp Information         (TIMESTAMP) = ON  09/17/2011
        05:44:48.194786
        Unit of Work Information                (UOW) = OFF
    ```

2. Set monitoring ON to enable snapshot data collection.

   We will turn all switches ON, so we can capture all levels:

   ```
   [db2inst1@nodedb21 ~]$ db2 "update monitor switches
      using bufferpool on lock on sort on statement on
      table on uow on"
   DB20000I  The UPDATE MONITOR SWITCHES command completed
      successfully.
   ```

3. Get new settings for monitor switches with the following command:

   ```
   [db2inst1@nodedb21 ~]$ db2 get monitor switches
   ```

   ```
                    Monitor Recording Switches

   Switch list for db partition number 0
   Buffer Pool Activity Information  (BUFFERPOOL) = ON  09/24/2011
   17:38:08.216907
   Lock Information                        (LOCK) = ON  09/24/2011
   17:38:08.216907
   Sorting Information                     (SORT) = ON  09/24/2011
   17:38:08.216907
   SQL Statement Information          (STATEMENT) = ON  09/24/2011
   17:38:08.216907
   Table Activity Information             (TABLE) = ON  09/24/2011
   17:38:08.216907
   Take Timestamp Information          (TIMESTAMP) = ON  09/17/2011
   05:44:48.194786
   Unit of Work Information                (UOW) = ON  09/24/2011
   17:38:08.216907
   ```

4. Execute a snapshot on the database.

   This is an excerpt of the output. You will be able to analyze performance metrics on the database. In this example, we are focusing on DML statements. There are many more indicators and snapshots available.

   ```
   [db2instp@nodedb21 ~]$ db2 "get snapshot for database
      on posp" | more
   ```

   ```
                    Database Snapshot

   Database name                          = POSP...
   Commit statements attempted            = 3094
   Rollback statements attempted          = 898
   ```

```
Dynamic statements attempted              = 18654

Static statements attempted               = 9360

Failed statement operations               = 4

Select SQL statements executed            = 9895

Xquery statements executed                = 0

Update/Insert/Delete statements executed  = 2933

DDL statements executed                   = 32

Inactive stmt history memory usage (bytes) = 0
```

Execute a snapshot on buffer pools. For the specified database, we are focusing on buffer pools. This shows performance statistics for each buffer pool in the database. We only show a few metrics which can be used to compute hit ratios, for example:

```
[db2instp@nodedb21 ~]$ db2 get snapshot for buffer pools on posp |
more
                Bufferpool Snapshot

...

Bufferpool name                     = BP_POSP_DSS32K

Database name                       = POSP

Database path                       = /data/db2/db2instp/
NODE0000/SQL00001/

Input database alias                = POSP

Snapshot timestamp                  = 01/16/2012
19:22:21.888446


Buffer pool data logical reads      = 20

Buffer pool data physical reads     = 18

...

Buffer pool index logical reads     = 0

Buffer pool index physical reads    = 0

...

Total buffer pool read time (milliseconds) = 50

Total buffer pool write time (milliseconds)= 0
```

5. Execute a snapshot on table spaces.

   Now we examine information for table spaces. For each table space, you will see its definition, the containers, and buffer pool performance statistics related to this table space. The following example is a condensed format:

```
[db2instp@nodedb21 ~]$ db2 get snapshot for tablespaces on posp |
more


                    Tablespace Snapshot


Snapshot timestamp                          = 01/16/2012
19:26:51.391520

Database name                               = POSP

Tablespace name                             = POSP_DSS_TB32K

  Tablespace ID                             = 6

  Tablespace Type                           = DMS

  Tablespace Page size (bytes)              = 32768

  File system caching                       = No


Tablespace information for node number      = 0

  Tablespace State                          = 0x'00000000'

  Tablespace Prefetch size (pages)          = 16

  Total number of pages                     = 1600

  High water mark (pages)                   = 48

  Container Name                            = /data/db2/db2instp/
NODE0000/posp/posp_dss_tb32k.dbf

      Container ID                          = 0

  Table space map:


   Range  Stripe Stripe  Max         Max  Start  End    Adj.
Containers
   Number Set    Offset  Extent      Page Stripe Stripe
   [   0] [   0]    0      98        1583     0    98    0    1 (0)


  Buffer pool data logical reads            = 20
  Buffer pool data physical reads           = 18
```

6. Execute a snapshot on locks.

For the sake of clarity, we will provoke a lock. This is optional, and you should do this in a test environment.

We will open two separate windows, Application 1 and Application 2. This is necessary for the deadlock to occur. The +c option turns auto-commit OFF for the given CLP command. So, in Application 1:

```
[db2instp@nodedb21 ~]$ db2 +c "UPDATE POSP.PRODUCTS SET
  GLACC=40050 WHERE SKU='771665871150'"

DB20000I  The SQL command completed successfully.
```

Application 1 now has an exclusive lock on a row of the PRODUCTS table. Now, we open Application 2's window and type the following command:

```
[db2inst1@nodedb21 ~]$ db2 +c "UPDATE POSP.PRODUCTS SET
  GLACC=40040 WHERE SKU='59800000215'"

DB20000I  The SQL command completed successfully.
```

Application 2 has an exclusive lock on a row of the PRODUCTS table.

Let's see what the applications are and let's follow them:

```
[db2instp@nodedb21 ~]$ db2 list applications show detail


CONNECT Auth Id
Application Name      Appl.       Application Id
Seq#  Number of  Coordinating DB  Coordinator      Status
Status Change Time          DB Name  DB Path

...
   Handle
Agents      partition number pid/thread

...
db2bp                 6333        *N0.db2instp.120117014813
00001 1        0                 236            UOW Waiting
01/16/2012 20:49:16.479471 POSP   /data/db2/db2instp/NODE0000/
SQL00001/

DB2INSTP
db2bp                 6332        *N0.db2instp.120117014803
00001 1        0                 235            UOW Waiting
01/16/2012 20:49:34.857005 POSP   /data/db2/db2instp/NODE0000/
SQL00001/

DB2INSTP
```

We can now look at the locks; here is a simplified view:

```
[db2instp@nodedb21 ~]$ db2 get snapshot for locks on posp


                 Database Lock Snapshot


Database name                              = POSP
...
Application handle                         = 6333
Application status                         = UOW Waiting
Locks held                                 = 1
List Of Locks
  Database partition         = 0
  Object Type                = Internal Plan Lock
  Mode                       = S
...
Application handle                         = 6332
Application status                         = UOW Waiting
Locks held                                 = 1
List Of Locks
  Database partition         = 0
  Object Type                = Internal Plan Lock
  Mode                       = S
```

7. Execute a snapshot on an application.

   We identified two applications, 6332 and 6333, having locks. We can now get a snapshot for application handle (agentid) 6332:

```
[db2instp@nodedb21 ~]$ db2 get snapshot for application agentid
6332


                 Application Snapshot

Application handle                         = 6332
Application status                         = UOW Waiting
Authorization level granted                =
   (authorization information ...)
Coordinator agent process or thread ID     = 235
```

```
Locks held by application              = 1
   (lock information ...)
Total sorts                            = 0
   (sort information ...)
Buffer pool data logical reads         = 0
   (buffer pool information ...)
Number of SQL requests since last commit  = 1
   (SQL statements information ...)


UOW log space used (Bytes)             = 0
   (UOW information ...)
Package cache lookups                  = 2
   (cache information ...)


Workspace Information
Memory usage for application:
Agent process/thread ID                = 235
    Database partition number          = 0
  Agent Lock timeout (seconds)         = -1
  Memory usage for agent:
    Memory Pool Type                   = Other Memory
       Current size (bytes)            = 196608
       High water mark (bytes)         = 524288
       Configured size (bytes)         = 2099658752
```

8. Execute a snapshot on dynamic SQLs.

   Now let's see which commands are executed, using the following command:

   ```
   [db2instp@ nodedb21 ~]$ db2 get snapshot for dynamic sql on posp |
   more
   ```

   ```
        Dynamic SQL Snapshot Result

    Database name                    = POSP


    Database path                    = /data/db2/db2instp/NODE0000/
   SQL00001/
    ...
   ```

```
Number of executions              = 1

Number of compilations            = 1

...

Buffer pool data logical reads    = 0

Buffer pool data physical reads   = 0

...

Statement text                    = UPDATE   POSP.PRODUCTS SET
   GLACC=40050 WHERE SKU='771665871150'
```

You can now go back to your two applications and do a `rollback` operation, so that the data stays safe.

We suggest you use the administrative views to have an automated framework. We'll discuss some scripts you can use for that later.

How it works...

The database manager collects information about its performance and other operating parameters, as well as applications using it, so that there is some overhead in the processing. To minimize this impact, we can configure the elements that we want to collect using the monitor switches. There is a lot of information available with the `get snapshot` command. You can also access this same information through administrative views that can help you maintain and analyze trends.

There's more...

You can create collection tables and produce history reports. Certain software tools such as `RRDtool` allow you to create graphic representations, which can then be displayed on a web page.

Table functions and administrative views

On instance start, metrics are collected at the following levels if the monitor switches are ON. You can query with the corresponding table functions or administrative views from SYSIBMADM.

Level	Table function	Administrative view
Database Manager	SNAPSHOT_DBM()	SYSIBMADM.SNAPDBM
Database	SNAPSHOT_DATABASE()	SYSIBMADM.SNAPDB
Application	SNAPSHOT_APPL()	SYSIBMADM.SNAPAPPL
Table	SNAPSHOT_TABLE()	SYSIBMADM.SNAPTAB
Lock	SNAPSHOT_LOCK()	SYSIBMADM.SNAPLOCK
Table space	SNAPSHOT_TBS()	SYSIBMADM.SNAPTBSP

Level	Table function	Administrative view
Container	SNAPSHOT_CONTAINER()	SYSIBMADM.SNAPCONTAINER
Buffer pool	SNAPSHOT_BP()	SYSIBMADM.SNAPBP
Statements	SNAPSHOT_STATEMENT()	SYSIBMADM.SNAPSTMT

These are the 11 scripts to help you monitor a database. Feel free to experiment with those scripts, so you can get a good indication of your database's performance.

 The (query_field + 1) construction is used to avoid division by zero errors, and does not affect the accuracy of the result.

Database load

This query helps you determine the actual load on the database. The number of selects, inserts, updates, and deletes tells us what the workload is, so we can concentrate on our tuning efforts when the workload is heavier.

```
SELECT DBPARTITIONNUM, COMMIT_SQL_STMTS, SELECT_SQL_STMTS, UID_SQL_STMTS
FROM    SYSIBMADM.SNAPDB;
```

Buffer pool hit ratios

For OLTP databases, you want to maintain 85 percent hit ratio for data and 95 percent hit ratio for indexes. For DSS databases, it is normal to have a lower hit ratio, since we're not using the same strategies for performance.

```
SELECT DBPARTITIONNUM,
      (POOL_DATA_L_READS - POOL_DATA_P_READS) * 100 /
  (POOL_DATA_L_READS + 1)
FROM SYSIBMADM.SNAPDB;
SELECT DBPARTITIONNUM,
      (POOL_INDEX_L_READS - POOL_INDEX_P_READS) * 100 /
  (POOL_INDEX_L_READS + 1)
FROM SYSIBMADM.SNAPDB;
```

You can zero-in on a specific buffer pool with this variation by using the buffer pool snapshot table (SYSIBMADM.SNAPBP):

```
SELECT DBPARTITIONNUM, BP_NAME,
      (POOL_DATA_L_READS - POOL_DATA_P_READS) * 100 /
  (POOL_DATA_L_READS + 1)
FROM    SYSIBMADM.SNAPBP;
```

Buffer pool physical reads and writes per transaction

This query tells us the average physical I/O activity per committed transaction; the commits help us have a normalized view of the activity, regardless of the actual load on the database:

```
SELECT DBPARTITIONNUM,
       (POOL_DATA_P_READS        + POOL_INDEX_P_READS +
        POOL_TEMP_DATA_P_READS + POOL_TEMP_INDEX_P_READS) /
       (COMMIT_SQL_STMTS + 1)
FROM   SYSIBMADM.SNAPDB;
```

Average sorting time

This query tells us the average time spent on each sort; you will want to keep this at a minimum:

```
SELECT DBPARTITIONNUM, TOTAL_SORT_TIME / (TOTAL_SORTS + 1)
FROM   SYSIBMADM.SNAPDB;
```

Sorting time per transaction

This query tells us how much time an average transaction spends on sorting:

```
SELECT DBPARTITIONNUM, TOTAL_SORT_TIME /
       (COMMIT_SQL_STMTS + 1)
FROM   SYSIBMADM.SNAPDB;
```

Lock wait time

This query tells us how much time each transaction waits for locks:

```
SELECT DBPARTITIONNUM, LOCK_WAIT_TIME/
       (COMMIT_SQL_STMTS + 1)
FROM   SYSIBMADM.SNAPDB;
```

Deadlocks and lock timeouts

This query tells us what the average number of deadlock and lock timeouts per transaction are:

```
SELECT DBPARTITIONNUM,
       (DEADLOCKS + LOCK_TIMEOUTS)/(COMMIT_SQL_STMTS + 1)
FROM   SYSIBMADM.SNAPDB;
```

Rows read/rows selected

Is indexing efficient? How many rows are read in order to find the ones that qualify? A large number may indicate full-table scans or Cartesian joins.

```
SELECT DBPARTITIONNUM, ROWS_READ /(ROWS_SELECTED+1)
FROM    SYSIBMADM.SNAPDB;
```

Dirty steal BP clean/transaction

Are there a lot of dirty writes per transaction? This may increase the I/O activity, so you may want to look at the buffer pool configuration.

```
SELECT DBPARTITIONNUM, POOL_DRTY_PG_STEAL_CLNS /(COMMIT_SQL_STMTS+1)
FROM    SYSIBMADM.SNAPDB;
```

Package cache inserts/transaction

Is the system reusing its SQLs? A high ratio may indicate that SQL are not being reused. This can happen with dynamic SQL not using parameter markers.

```
SELECT DBPARTITIONNUM, PKG_CACHE_INSERTS /(COMMIT_SQL_STMTS+1)
FROM    SYSIBMADM.SNAPDB;
```

Average log writes/transaction

This query tells us how much log activity is generated for an averaged transaction:

```
SELECT DBPARTITIONNUM, LOG_WRITES /(COMMIT_SQL_STMTS+1)
FROM    SYSIBMADM.SNAPDB;
```

See also

Chapter 13, DB2 Tuning and Optimization

Configuring and using event monitoring

Event monitoring lets you collect information triggered by state changes depending on event types such as databases, connections, tables, statements, transactions, deadlocks, and table spaces. It's been in DB2 for quite a while but new functionalities have been added in version 9.7. You have the choice to collect information into a file or a table.

Use caution while configuring event monitors as you may induce performance degradation if it's not configured correctly. Writing event data to files has the least impact on the database. Writing to NFS file systems is not as efficient as using a local file.

Writing event data to tables has more impact on the database, but provides easier interrogation through SQL queries. What's new in version 9.7 is the unformatted event table. It eases the burden on the database and gives you the same flexibility.

We will discuss lock monitoring as it changed in version 9.7, so we'll show you how to set it up, and start monitoring. You can then explore further on your own or investigate other aspects of monitoring, since you will have a framework to build upon.

Getting ready

We will provoke a deadlock in this exercise to demonstrate event logging, so you should prepare this exercise in a sandbox environment.

How to do it...

1. Identify the target where you want the event data to be stored. In our case, we chose to collect information into a table.

2. Event monitoring requires lots of storage, ideally separated from data in order to minimize contention for disk I/O activity. In the same frame of thought, we create its own buffer pool, so its cache won't interfere with actual data's cache.

   Create a table space with the following command:

   ```
   [db2inst1@nodedb21 tmp]$ db2 "CREATE BUFFERPOOL POS_MONBP32K
   IMMEDIATE SIZE AUTOMATIC PAGESIZE 32K"

   DB20000I  The SQL command completed successfully.
   ```

   Create the table space and assign its own buffer pool:

   ```
   [db2inst1@nodedb21 tmp]$ db2 "CREATE  LARGE  TABLESPACE POS_MON
   PAGESIZE 32 K

   >       MANAGED BY DATABASE

   >       USING ( FILE '/data1/db2/db2inst1/NODE0000/pos/pos_
   monitor.dbf' 6400 )

   >       AUTORESIZE YES MAXSIZE 500 M

   >       BUFFERPOOL  POS_MONBP32K"

   DB20000I  The SQL command completed successfully.
   ```

Create a system temporary table space with the same 32 KB page size. This will be used later by DB2 to format results:

```
[db2inst1@nodedb21 ~]$ db2 "CREATE SYSTEM TEMPORARY TABLESPACE
>        POS_TEMP32K  PAGESIZE 32K
>        MANAGED BY DATABASE
>        USING ( FILE '/data/db2/db2inst1/NODE0000/pos/pos_temp32k.
dbf' 100 M )
>        AUTORESIZE YES MAXSIZE 500 M
>        BUFFERPOOL  POS_MONBP32K"
DB20000I  The SQL command completed successfully.
```

3. DB2 creates and enables the DB2DETAILDEADLOCK event monitor on database creation by default. Since this feature is deprecated and will be removed in later versions, we will drop this event monitor and set up our own. There should be only one locking event monitor per database. First, we disable the current DB2DETAILDEADLOCK event monitor.

   Drop the deadlock monitor by using the following command:

```
[db2inst1@nodedb21 tmp]$ db2 "SET EVENT MONITOR DB2DETAILDEADLOCK
STATE 0"
DB20000I  The SQL command completed successfully.
```

   Now, we can drop it.

```
[db2inst1@nodedb21 tmp]$ db2 "DROP EVENT MONITOR
  DB2DETAILDEADLOCK"
DB20000I  The SQL command completed successfully.
```

4. We can now create the event monitor to monitor lock waits, lock timeouts, and deadlocks.

   Create the event monitor by using the following command:

```
[db2inst1@nodedb21 tmp]$ db2 "CREATE EVENT MONITOR POS_EV_LOCK
>        FOR LOCKING
>        WRITE TO UNFORMATTED EVENT TABLE (
>         TABLE EVMON.POS_EV_LOCK IN POS_MON )"
DB20000I  The SQL command completed successfully.
```

5. Activating an event monitor sets its counters to zero.

Enable the event monitor by using the following command:

```
[db2inst1@nodedb21 tmp]$ db2 "SET EVENT MONITOR POS_EV_LOCK
   STATE 1"

DB20000I  The SQL command completed successfully.
```

6. We will open two separate windows, Application 1 and Application 2. This is necessary for the deadlock to occur. The +c option turns auto commit OFF for the given CLP command. So, in Application 1, Provoke deadlock situation (optional) by using the following command:

```
[db2inst1@nodedb21 ~]$ db2 +c "UPDATE  POS.PRODUITS SET
  GLACC=40050 WHERE SKU='771665871150'"

DB20000I  The SQL command completed successfully.
```

Application 1 now has an exclusive lock on a row of the FACTURES table.

Now we open Application 2's window and type the following command:

```
[db2inst1@nodedb21 ~]$ db2 +c "UPDATE  POS.PRODUITS SET
GLACC=40040 WHERE SKU='59800000215'"

DB20000I  The SQL command completed successfully.
```

Application 2 has an exclusive lock on a row of the PRODUCTS table.

Now return to Application 1's window and do the following:

```
[db2inst1@nodedb21 ~]$ db2 +c "UPDATE  POS.PRODUITS SET
  PXCOUT=0.86 WHERE SKU='59800000215'"
```

You will notice it's taking longer; it is waiting for Application 2 to complete its update.

Now, go to Application 2 and enter the following command:

```
[db2inst1@nodedb21 ~]$ db2 +c "UPDATE  POS.PRODUITS SET DEPT=02
WHERE SKU='771665871150'"

DB21034E  The command was processed as an SQL statement because it
was not a

valid Command Line Processor command.  During SQL processing it
returned:

SQL0911N  The current transaction has been rolled back because of
a deadlock

or timeout.  Reason code "2".  SQLSTATE=40001
```

DB2 takes a few moments and realizes that we are in a deadlock so it rolls back the transaction from Application 2.

7. We start by extracting information to tables in our EVMON schema. DB2 will store these tables into our POS_MON table space.

Obtain information from the table by using the following command:

```
[db2inst1@nodedb21 ~]$ db2 "CALL EVMON_FORMAT_UE_TO_TABLES(
>          'LOCKING', NULL, NULL, NULL, 'EVMON', 'POS_MON',
'RECREATE_ONERROR', -1,
>          'SELECT * FROM EVMON.POS_EV_LOCK ORDER BY EVENT_
TIMESTAMP')"


  Return Status = 0
```

Now let's see the information we collected from the event log:

```
[db2inst1@nodedb21 ~]$ db2 "SELECT EVENT_ID, SUBSTR(EVENT_
TYPE,1,30) EVENT_TYPE, EVENT_TIMESTAMP,
>          MEMBER, DL_CONNS, ROLLED_BACK_PARTICIPANT_NO RB_
PARTIC_NO
>      FROM    EVMON.LOCK_EVENT
>      ORDER  BY EVENT_TIMESTAMP"


EVENT_ID             EVENT_TYPE                     EVENT_
TIMESTAMP            MEMBER DL_CONNS    RB_PARTIC_NO
-------------------- ------------------------------ ---------------
----------- ------ ----------- ------------
                   1 DEADLOCK                       2011-10-05-
23.58.35.785580        0          2              2


  1 record(s) selected.
```

How it works...

Event monitors can generate lots of volume, especially when there's a lot of activity, so you should allow a separate table space for this.

This data collection does have an impact on resources available, so you would usually use event monitors to zero-in on performance or troubleshooting. If you want to leave it active, we suggest you turn it off during night, batch, or backup operations, unless you need to monitor something closely.

Data is collected in binary format, so it has to be extracted into tables, which we put in EVMON schema for our case, and arrange to store those tables in our POS_MON table space we created for this use.

You can prune event monitor logs when they get full. We suggest you prepare automatic scripts to prune the tables regularly. We'll explain this further.

There's more...

There are some new features to consider for V9.7 and some tidbits of information you need to know.

Unformatted event table

What's new in DB2 9.7 is that you can have the information collected into an unformatted event table. The performance impact is minimal since data is written in binary format.

Using the db2evmonfmt tool for reporting

This tool extracts the information from this unformatted event table to be used for reports. Let's see how it's done below:

1. Compile the db2evmonfmt.java source (if not done already) with the following command:

   ```
   [db2inst1@nodedb21 ~]$ cd

   [db2inst1@nodedb21 ~]$ mkdir java; cd java

   [db2inst1@nodedb21 java]$ cp ~/sqllib/samples/java/jdbc/
   db2evmonfmt.java .

   [db2inst1@nodedb21 java]$ cp ~/sqllib/samples/java/jdbc/*xsl .

   [db2inst1@nodedb21 java]$ ~/sqllib/java/jdk64/bin/javac
      db2evmonfmt.java
   ```

2. Extract information from the event monitor table into a text report.

   This report is quite extensive so I included the parts which are most useful.

   ```
   [db2inst1@nodedb21 java]$ java db2evmonfmt -d pos -ue
      EVMON.POS_EV_LOCK -ftext

   SELECT evmon.xmlreport FROM TABLE ( EVMON_FORMAT_UE_TO_XML( 'LOG_
   TO_FILE',FOR EACH ROW OF ( SELECT * FROM EVMON.POS_EV_LOCK  ORDER
   BY EVENT_ID, EVENT_TIMESTAMP, EVENT_TYPE, MEMBER ))) AS evmon

   Event ID            : 1
   Event Type          : DEADLOCK
   Event Timestamp     : 2011-10-05-23.58.35.785580
   ```

```
Partition of detection : 0

Deadlock Graph

...

Participant No 2 requesting lock
----------------------------------
Lock Name           : 0x05000600520001000000000052
Lock wait start time : 2011-10-05-23.58.28.721919
Lock wait end time   : 2011-10-05-23.58.35.785580


...
Tablespace Name     : POS_TBLS

Table Schema        : POS
Table Name          : PRODUITS

Participant No 1 requesting lock
----------------------------------
Lock Name           : 0x05000600530001000000000052
Lock wait start time : 2011-10-05-23.58.23.547895
Lock wait end time   : 2011-10-05-23.58.35.785580
...
Tablespace Name     : POS_TBLS

Table Schema        : POS
Table Name          : PRODUITS
```

Attributes	Requester	Requester
Participant No	2	1
Application Handle	01028	01011
Application ID	*LOCAL.db2inst1.111006035454	*LOCAL.
db2inst1.111006034904		
Application Name	db2bp	db2bp
Authentication ID	DB2INST1	DB2INST1
Requesting AgentID	322	324

```
Coordinating AgentID   322                                    324
...


Current Activities of Participant No 2
----------------------------------------
...
Stmt type             : Dynamic
Stmt operation        : DML, Insert/Update/Delete
Stmt text             : UPDATE   POS.PRODUITS SET DEPT=02 WHERE
SKU='771665871150'


...


Current Activities of Participant No 1
----------------------------------------
...
Stmt type             : Dynamic
Stmt operation        : DML, Insert/Update/Delete
Stmt text             : UPDATE   POS.PRODUITS SET PXCOUT=0.86 WHERE
SKU='59800000215'
```

Table space use

When the unformatted event table is in a DMS table space, the event monitor automatically deactivates when the table space is full. If you are creating many event monitors you may specify the PCTDEACTIVATE option, so this can allow the remaining space for other event monitor tables.

If possible, use the largest page size (32K) for better performance. You should create a temporary system table space with the same page size.

Pruning event monitor tables

Event monitor target tables have to be pruned manually; you can use this command for example:

```
[db2inst1@nodedb21 ~]$ db2 "DELETE FROM EVMON.POS_EV_LOCK
>      WHERE  EVENT_TIMESTAMP < CURRENT_DATE - 1 MONTH"
SQL0100W  No row was found for FETCH, UPDATE or DELETE; or the result of
a query is an empty table.  SQLSTATE=02000
```

Resetting a monitor's counters

You just need to set the event monitor to OFF and ON again. Deactivating an event monitor does not reset counters.

```
[db2inst1@nodedb21 ~]$ db2 "SET EVENT MONITOR POS_EV_LOCK STATE 0"
DB20000I  The SQL command completed successfully.
[db2inst1@nodedb21 ~]$ db2 "SET EVENT MONITOR POS_EV_LOCK STATE 1"
DB20000I  The SQL command completed successfully.
```

Workload management (WLM)

Event monitor can be used in conjunction with workloads to provide a specific area to monitor. Using all the functionalities of workload management requires a license; however, you can use limited functionalities of WLM without licensing, such as the following:

- ▸ Default workloads
- ▸ Default service classes
- ▸ Workload manager tables/stored procs
- ▸ Create/activate/drop and workload management event monitors

See also

- ▸ *Chapter 4, Storage—Using DB2 Table Spaces*
- ▸ *Chapter 5, DB2 Buffer Pools*

Using Memory Visualizer

This GUI utility helps you visualize memory use and track it through time, by displaying a graphic plot. This tool is deprecated, though, and we recommend you use IBM's Optim™ tool.

Getting ready

On AIX systems, if you don't have an X server and the GUI utilities installed, you will need to set up a client workstation.

In our example, since we did not have any application accessing the database, we started the **Control Center** to provoke activity on the database. This ensures that the database allocates and uses memory. You won't need to do this on an active database.

How to do it...

1. Call the utility.

   Invoke the Memory Visualizer from the command line, and a pop up will appear so you can connect to an instance; click on **OK**:

   ```
   [db2instp@nodedb21 ~]$ db2memvis
   ```

   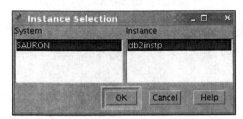

2. Configure refresh rate.

   You will see the main screen, and on the right, there is a box with **No Automatic refresh**. Click on it and select **5** seconds; the display will be refreshed regularly:

   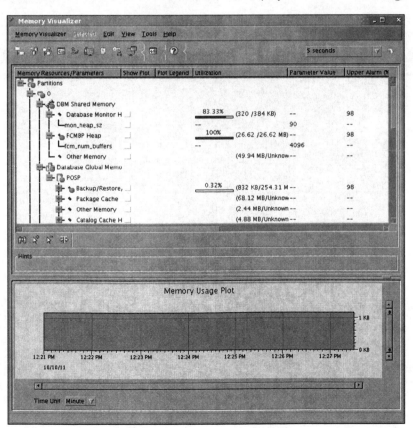

3. Make sure you have enough monitoring space.

   As monitoring is a major aspect of your database work, let's ensure that we always have optimal characteristics.

   For each instance, make sure your monitoring space usage keeps under safe thresholds. Expand **DBM Shared Memory** and **Database Monitor Heap** and click **Show Plot**. In our case, we can see 83 percent usage on partition **0**. The memory usage plot will help you visualize over a period of time:

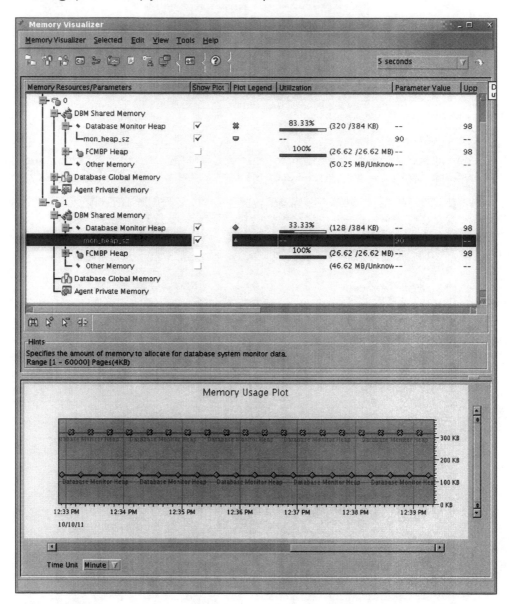

Notice the **Hints** window. You can have a brief description of a memory parameter when you click in the main pane. You can choose to hide it by unchecking the menu/View/Show hints.

4. Check for database global memory.

    You can select the partition you want to monitor, usually **0** on a single partition instance. You can see the space used, organized by components, such as **Utility Heap**, **Package Cache**, **Buffer Pools**, and so on.

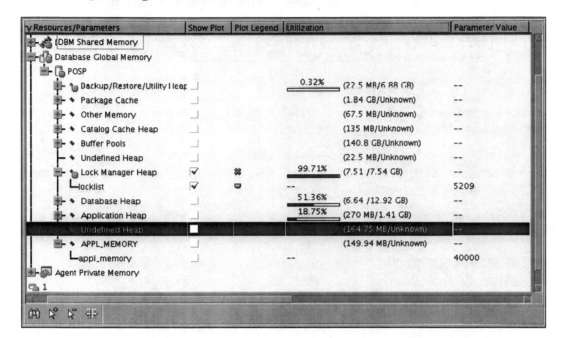

You can scroll to the right and view the warning and alarm thresholds for each item. See the Health Monitor to configure the threshold values.

There's more...

Here's a brief note on self-tuning memory for single-partitioned databases.

Self tuning memory management

DB2 does a very good job at managing memory. Self-tuning memory is activated on database creation. Unless you are using a partitioned database, we recommend that you leave the settings to automatic. In fact, an automatically-tuned database will perform as well as a manually-tuned database, when this is done well.

See also

The *Tuning memory utilization* recipe in *Chapter 13, Database Tuning and Optimization*

Using Health Monitor

The Health Monitor works on the server's side to assist the DBA in monitoring. It frees DBAs from having to constantly monitor databases' state, by performing periodic checks on predetermined warning and alarm threshold settings. You will probably have seen some in the Memory Visualizer.

Although the Health Monitor has a Health Center GUI tool, you can also use the command line to enable and configure its parameters. Since health monitoring is crucial to be aware of the databases' state at any time, the first thing we need to check is the monitoring itself.

When insufficient space is allocated for the monitor heap, monitoring operations may fail, so we can't be alerted for potential alerts.

Getting ready

Check if the health monitoring is activated on this instance. Update it if necessary.

```
[db2instp@nodedb21 ~]$ db2 get dbm cfg | grep HEALTH_MON
 Monitor health of instance and databases   (HEALTH_MON) = ON
```

How to do it...

1. Launch **Health Center** from **Control Center** by navigating to the **Tools** menu.
2. Configure the health indicator settings.

Select an instance and a database. For a new database, you have to configure the health indicator settings before use:

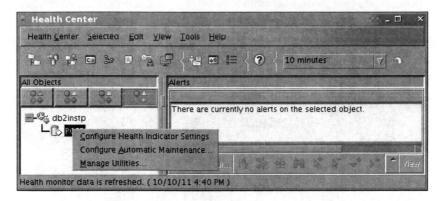

3. Configuring **Instance Settings**:

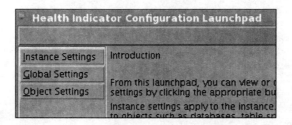

Now select **Instance settings**, and you will have three indicators to set. Normally the default value should work.

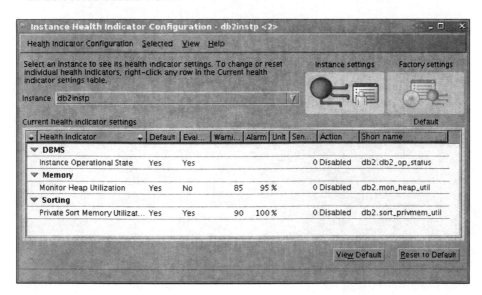

In our example, let's set up the monitor heap, which is a potential point-of-failure for monitoring. Double-click on **Monitor Heap Utilization** and check **Evaluate**, and set the thresholds to a value that suits you, or leave it at the current threshold settings:

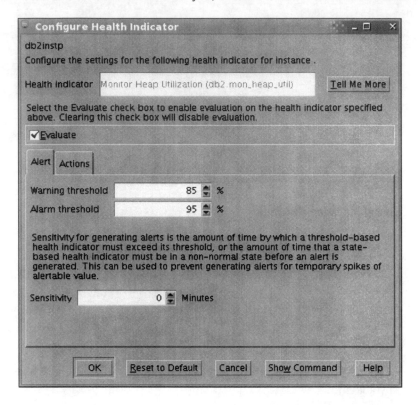

In the **Actions** tab, you can also specify actions that can be triggered. This action can be an operating system script, such as a shell script or a .bat file in Windows, or a DB2 command script.

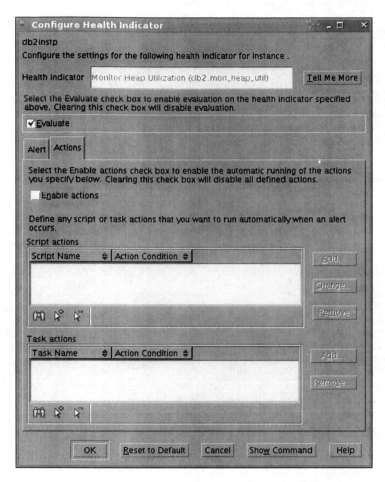

4. Configure global settings.

    You can set global settings for object types, such as databases, table spaces, and table space containers for this instance.

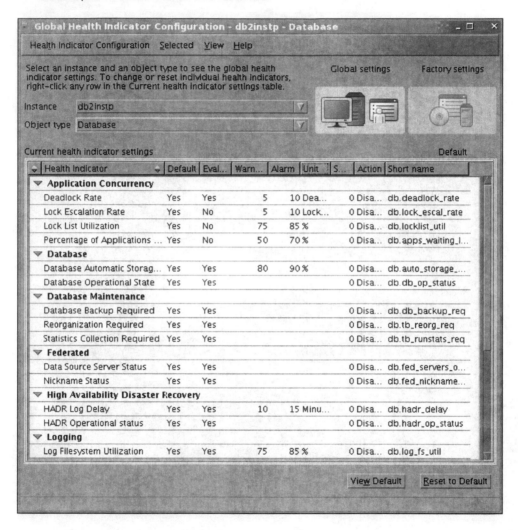

5. Configure object settings.

    You can configure settings for a specific object that will override the global settings. The procedure is the same as the previous steps.

How it works...

The Health Monitor gathers information about the health of the system without performance penalty. It does not turn ON any snapshot monitor switches to collect information. The health monitor is enabled by default when an instance is created.

The Health Monitor constantly checks health indicator settings, and acts upon an indicator setting. When notifications are enabled, the warning and alert thresholds can trigger an e-mail or a message sent to a paging device. In addition, an action can be done, depending on the health indicator's configuration, so DBAs can spend more time on actual DBA work instead of monitoring.

There's more...

DB2 can advise you on configuration changes, and issue recommendations depending on the health indicator's settings.

Getting recommendations for an alert

Once you get an alert, you can get recommendations on how to configure the database manager or database to regain normal operational settings.

```
[db2inst1@nodedb21 ~]$ db2 get recommendations for health indicator
  db2.mon_heap_util
Recommendations:


Recommendation: Investigate memory usage of monitor heap.


This parameter determines the amount of the memory, in pages, to
allocate for database system monitor data. Memory is allocated from
the monitor heap for database monitoring activities such as taking a
snapshot, turning on a monitor switch, resetting a monitor, or
activating an event monitor.
.............
```

Using the command line to check and set configuration

You can use the command line for more flexibility. You could, for example, use these commands in a script or a task:

```
[db2instp@nodedb21 ~]$ db2 get alert cfg for database manager using
  db2.mon_heap_util

                   Alert Configuration

         Indicator Name                = db2.mon_heap_util
             Default                   = No
             Type                      = Threshold-based
             Warning                   = 85
             Alarm                     = 95
             Unit                      = %
             Sensitivity               = 0
             Formula                   = ((db2.mon_heap_cur_size/
                                          db2.mon_heap_max_size)*100);
             Actions                   = Disabled
             Threshold or State checking = Enabled
```

See also

Configuring and using event monitors recipe in this chapter

13
DB2 Tuning and Optimization

In this chapter, we will cover:

- ▶ Operating system tuning
- ▶ Resolving CPU bottlenecks
- ▶ Tuning memory utilization
- ▶ Collecting object statistics with the RUNSTAT utility
- ▶ Tuning with indexes
- ▶ Tuning sorting
- ▶ Hit ratios and their role in performance improvement
- ▶ I/O tuning
- ▶ Using logging and nologging modes
- ▶ Using parallelism
- ▶ Using EXPLAIN PLAN
- ▶ Creating a benchmark testing scenario

Introduction and general tuning guidelines

You have just arrived in your organization and now have the responsibility of maintaining databases, or you have been there for a while and probably put a lot of effort into your database design. Databases still need regular attention and tuning.

We need to have a methodical approach, so a design-centred approach probably works best. You can start from the operating system as seen below, to get a global perspective. You can then move on to tuning the database, tablespaces, and specific items such as specific tables or indexes.

Start from the operating system. Examine to see if there is paging activity, and look at the network bandwidth to see if it's sufficient for the intended traffic. With SAN-based servers, storage is now transparent for DBAs. Stay informed about the physical disk layout and capabilities. Change one thing at a time, to make sure it is effective.

Here are some general guidelines to implement performance data collection:

- ▶ Collect operational data regularly and look for performance degradation trends
- ▶ Create a separate table space for this purpose
- ▶ Prepare scheduled jobs to collect data
- ▶ Do not forget to delete old data

Operating system tuning

For best results, you should examine the operating system regularly and monitor system load using `vmstat` and `iostat`. You can also collect this information in a table that you can access later.

Here are the major components of an operating system to consider:

O/S component	Things to look out for/monitor
Kernel parameters	The kernel parameters should be set before installing DB2; this requires root access.
Paging	One way to achieve this is to plan carefully for memory allocations for all the products installed on a machine. If you have databases from Oracle and IBM DB2 on the same machine, a backup server, web server, and so on, you must take into account all the memory required.
Input/Output	The next item to look for is Input/Output activity, to make sure there are enough spindles to handle the database workload. Locate potential hot spots, that is, busy disks.
CPU	Check for abnormal CPU usage, and make sure CPU load is balanced.
Network	Check for abnormal bandwidth use. Make sure transaction or diagnostic logs are not located on NFS-mounted directories.

Getting ready

Have and maintain an inventory of all software running on your server. Gather configuration settings, especially those dealing with memory. Inquire with your system administrator about how much space is needed by the operating system and for its file system cache.

Make sure database-managed table spaces have a buffer pool assigned and that they do not use file system caching, as the buffer pool is designed for that.

How to do it...

To tune the operating system, the following steps are necessary:

1. Ensure kernel parameters are set to an appropriate value. Important Linux kernel configuration parameters and their recommended values for DB2 are shown in the following table:

Kernel parameter	Description	Recommended setting
SHMMAX	Maximum size of a shared memory segment	Minimum of 1 GB
SHMALL	Maximum size of memory	90% of the available memory on the database server. SHMALL is 8 GB, by default.
kernel.sem	Specifying four kernel semaphore settings – SEMMSL, SEMMNS, SEMOPM, and SEMMNI	250 256000 32 1024
kernel.msgmni	Number of message queue identifiers	1024
kernel.msgmax	Maximum size of a message, in bytes	65536
kernel.msgmnb	Default size of a message queue, in bytes	65536

2. Get the current settings for kernel parameters with the following command:

```
[db2instp@nodedb22 ~]$ ipcs -l

------ Shared Memory Limits --------
max number of segments = 4096
max seg size (kbytes) = 2059972
max total shared memory (kbytes) = 8388608
min seg size (bytes) = 1

------ Semaphore Limits --------
max number of arrays = 1024
max semaphores per array = 250
max semaphores system wide = 256000
max ops per semop call = 32
semaphore max value = 32767

------ Messages: Limits --------
max queues system wide = 8192
max size of message (bytes) = 163840
default max size of queue (bytes) = 163840
```

3. To modify these kernel parameters, we need to edit the `/etc/sysctl.conf` file. We recycle the machine with the new settings, as shown in the following command:

```
[root@nodedb21 ~]# sysctl -p
```

4. Find out how much memory is available. For AIX, you can use `prtconf -m`. We have 2 GB, in our case. On Linux, you can use the following vmstat command:

```
[db2inst1@nodedb21 ~]$ vmstat -sM | grep 'total memory'
      2050448   total memory
```

5. Check total shared memory. Check with the shared memory segments so they do not take too much memory and allow space for the operating system:

```
[db2inst1@nodedb21 ~]$ ipcs -m
```

```
------ Shared Memory Segments --------
```

key	shmid	owner	perms	bytes	nattch	status
0xd88e8574	131072	db2instp	767	40200088	9	
0x31069b8c	65538	db2inst1	600	20500	2	
0x36069b8c	98307	db2inst1	600	20500	2	
0xd88e8668	360457	db2instp	761	50331648	1	
0x1fad7d74	393226	db2insth	767	40200088	7	
0x1fad7e68	491533	db2insth	761	50331648	1	
0x00000000	524302	db2inst1	767	40200088	1	dest
0x8f50c174	13926415	db2inst1	767	40200088	9	
0x8f50c161	13959184	db2inst1	701	50069504	6	
0x00000000	13991956	db2fenc1	701	268435456	5	
0x8f50c268	14024725	db2inst1	761	67108864	1	

We can cut and paste the results into a spreadsheet and compute the total memory allocated for shared memory segments. In this case, we have 647,118,472 bytes, that is, less than half of the total memory.

6. Check for paging or swapping. With your favorite utility, check for swap activity. Here, using `vmstat`, we need to look for large values for SI and SO. It will scan every five seconds and repeat the scan 100 times:

```
[db2instp@nodedb21 ~]$ vmstat -S M 5 100

procs -----------memory---------- ---swap-- -----io---- -system--
----cpu----
 r  b   swpd   free   buff  cache   si   so    bi    bo   in   cs
us sy id wa
```

0	0	166	425	182	483	0	0	4	7	6	3
1	0	99	0								
0	0	166	424	182	483	0	0	0	3	1123	2091
2	0	98	0								

7. Adjust the memory allocation. Here, we do not need to change anything: otherwise, we would take a look at database configuration settings, such as the following. We recommend you use the automatic settings for regular databases. We'll discuss partitioned database memory configuration, later on:

Description	Name	Recommended
Self tuning memory	SELF_TUNING_MEM	AUTOMATIC
Size of database shared memory	DATABASE_MEMORY	AUTOMATIC
Application Memory Size (4KB)		APPL_MEMORY
Database heap (4KB)	DBHEAP	AUTOMATIC

How it works...

Your system administrator has probably set up a swap area when configuring the operating system. The first thing to avoid is paging, as this introduces an immediate and perceptible loss of performance.

There's more...

Here is a recap of virtual storage and some tips on how to avoid unnecessary caching.

Virtual storage

If the total memory required by the software or applications is low, the server will use its virtual memory management facility that makes the server act as if it is has much more memory than it actually does. It does so by exchanging information from real memory and writing it to disk. This makes space for the new data stored in memory. This is great but it comes at a cost to performance, because of increased disk activity.

Disabling file system caching on table spaces

All input/output operations on table spaces are cached through the buffer pools. If the table space also has file system caching, this introduces calls to system memory, which is redundant as we already cached data in the buffer pools.

File system caching is disabled by default on Windows and Linux platforms. On AIX, HP/UX, and some other platforms, file system caching is enabled by default. On all platforms, it is enabled for SMS temporary table spaces, LOB, and large data, so we suggest you keep the default setting.

If you have assigned buffer pools to your table spaces, we recommend you disable file system caching for those table spaces. You can use the GET SNAPSHOT FOR TABLESPACES command. You won't see this with the regular LIST TABLESPACES SHOW DETAIL command:

```
[db2inst1@ nodedb21 ~]$ db2 get snapshot for tablespaces on pos | grep -E
"Tablespace name|File system caching"
Tablespace name                        = SYSCATSPACE
  File system caching                  = No
Tablespace name                        = TEMPSPACE1
  File system caching                  = No
Tablespace name                        = USERSPACE1
  File system caching                  = No
Tablespace name                        = SYSTOOLSPACE
  File system caching                  = No
Tablespace name                        = SYSTOOLSTMPSPACE
  File system caching                  = No
Tablespace name                        = POS_TBLS
  File system caching                  = No
Tablespace name                        = POS_INDX
  File system caching                  = No
Tablespace name                        = POS_MON
  File system caching                  = No
Tablespace name                        = POS_TEMP32K
  File system caching                  = No
```

Maintaining a historic record

We suggest you create some tables to capture vmstat and iostat information and keep historic data. Make sure you delete historic data so the tables stay relatively small.

See also

> ▸ *Chapter 5, DB2 Buffer Pools*

> ▸ The *Configuring and using snapshot monitoring* in *Chapter 12, Monitoring*

Resolving CPU bottlenecks

High CPU activity is normal and desirable. However, when a machine is 95 percent busy, we have to check if this is for all processors or if there is one processor that has a large load.

CPU % time is divided into 4 components:

Component	Name	Description
Us	User time	Time used by all user processes (non-kernel)
Sy	System	Time spent by operating system kernel
Id	Idle	Time spent idle
Wa	Wait	Time spent waiting for I/O

Getting ready

For this example, I compiled a C program named pos.exe. This program executes a SQL with a cartesian join to ensure that we have CPU activity for a while, so we have the time to track it down. You can open a command-line processor window and issue a SQL from there.

How to do it...

1. Get vmstat results. Issue the following command, and note the CPU columns on the right. In this example, the user CPU maintains a constant 90 percent or more activity, so immediate attention is required:

```
[db2instp@nodedb21 ~]$ vmstat 5 100
procs -----------memory---------- ---swap-- -----io---- -system-- ----cpu----
 r  b   swpd   free   buff  cache   si   so    bi    bo   in    cs us sy id wa
 3  0 522684  30876  78404 737140    0    0    10    21   13    15 90  1  9  0
 0  0 522676  30776  78420 737140    0    0     0    34 1710  2596 91  1  8  1
 0  0 522668  30652  78436 737148    0    0     0    36 1717  2578 91  1  8  1
 1  0 522664  30652  78452 737152    0    0     0    29 1685  2581 91  2  7  1
 0  0 522656  30652  78468 737160    0    0     0    34 1749  2605 91  1  8  1
 0  0 522644  30652  78484 737172    6    0     6    29 1683  2586 91  3  6  0
 0  0 522636  30652  78500 737180    0    0     0    30 1762  2611 92  1  7  1
 0  0 522632  30652  78516 737184    0    0     0    33 1667  2565 91  1  8  1
```

2. See which applications are taking the most CPU time. Let's see if any application in particular requires attention. You'll notice that pos.exe takes a lot of CPU time:

```
[db2instp@nodedb21 ~]$ db2 "
    SELECT   APPL.DBPARTITIONNUM AS DBPARTNUM,
        APPL.AGENT_ID,
        SUBSTR(APPL_NAME,1,20) AS APPL_NAME,
            AGENT_USR_CPU_TIME_S +
        AGENT_USR_CPU_TIME_MS / 1000000.0 AS USER_CPU
    FROM  SYSIBMADM.SNAPAPPL APPL,
        SYSIBMADM.SNAPAPPL_INFO APPL_INFO
    WHERE  APPL.AGENT_ID = APPL_INFO.AGENT_ID
    AND     APPL.DBPARTITIONNUM = APPL_INFO.DBPARTITIONNUM
    ORDER BY USER_CPU DESC"
```

DBPARTNUM	AGENT_ID	APPL_NAME	USER_CPU
1	67028	db2stmm	95.38
1	16376	pos.exe	46.47
0	16376	pos.exe	43.28
0	1520	db2taskd	23.46
0	1522	db2lused	21.45
0	1541	db2bp	1.29

We can use the kpd utility to track the threads and their CPU usage. Notice below EDU ID #508, which takes 6.46 seconds CPU at the time the command was issued.

```
[db2instp@nodedb21 ~]$ db2pd -edus | more


Database Partition 0 -- Active -- Up 8 days 18:24:33 -- Date
01/20/2012 18:49:30


List of all EDUs for database partition 0

db2sysc PID: 31939
db2wdog PID: 31937
db2acd  PID: 31960
```

```
EDU ID      TID                 Kernel TID      EDU Name
USR (s)           SYS (s)

================================================================
================================================================
==========

511         14007441502440025644            db2agntdp (POSP    ) 0
0.000000       0.000000

510         14007445696744025643            db2agntdp (POSP    ) 0
0.000000       0.000000

509         14007442341300824270            db2agntp 0
4.570000       0.160000

508         14007444438452823941            db2agent (POSP) 0
6.460000       0.980000

507         14007441921870422774            db2agntp (POSP) 0
3.450000       0.200000

506         14007444019022420029            db2agntdp (POSP    ) 0
0.060000       0.020000

505         14007442760731219421            db2agntdp (POSP    ) 0
3.470000       0.930000

500         14007443599592010633            db2agntdp (POSP    ) 0
0.160000       0.040000

231         14007443180161 62780            db2agent (instance) 0
0.340000       0.260000
```

3. Find the matching application handle associated with a thread. We can use EDU ID
   (# 508) to track it down to an application handle, using the following command:

   [db2instp@nodedb21 ~]$ db2pd -agents | more

   Database Partition 0 -- Active -- Up 8 days 18:22:49 -- Date
   01/20/2012 18:47:46

   Agents:

   Current agents: 113

   Idle agents: 1

   Active coord agents: 12

   Active agents total: 14

   Pooled coord agents: 97

   Pooled agents total: 98

```
Address              AppHandl [nod-index] AgentEDUID Priority
Type     State       ClientPid  Userid   ClientNm Rowsread    Ro
wswrtn   LkTmOt DBName    LastApplId
LastPooled

0x0000000200E06000 0          [000-00000] 511          0
Idle       n/a       n/a       n/a       0           0
         0     n/a       *N1.db2instp.120120234507
Fri Jan 20 18:45:05

0x0000000200756000 1307       [000-01307] 83           0
Coord    Inst-Active 18186      db2instp java      0           0
         0     n/a       n/a

...

Sun Jan 15 00:05:52

0x0000000200DF6000 6292       [000-06292] 231          0
Coord    Inst-Active 15088      db2instp db2bp     0           0
         5     n/a       *N0.db2instp.120117012511
Mon Jan 16 20:24:59

0x0000000200DC6000 16323      [000-16323] 506          0
Coord    Inst-Active 936        ROBERT   javaw.ex 445         0
         NotSet POSP     C0A80168.F30B.10D640231328
Fri Jan 20 18:13:16

0x0000000200DC0080 16376      [000-16376] 508          0
Coord    Inst-Active 3328       ROBERT   pos.exe 0           0
         NotSet POSP     C0A80168.GD0C.116980233914
Fri Jan 20 18:36:59

0x0000000200E00080 16376      [000-16376] 509          0
SubAgent Inst-Active 3328       ROBERT   pos.exe 0           0
         NotSet POSP     C0A80168.GD0C.116980233914
Fri Jan 20 18:37:04

0x0000000200D76000 16376      [000-16376] 507          0
SubAgent Inst-Active 3328       ROBERT   pos.exe 9           33
```

We found that the coordinating agent id (508) and the two subagents, 507 and 509, belong to application handle 16376.

4. Get the snapshot for the application. With the application handle, we can get a snapshot and follow its execution statistics. Note that the application handle we're using refers to the agentid keyword, instead of applid, for the following snapshot command:

```
[db2instp@nodedb21 ~]$ db2 get snapshot for application agentid
16376


                Application Snapshot
```

```
        Application handle                      = 16376
        Application status                      = UOW Waiting
        ...
        Coordinator agent process or thread ID  = 508
        Buffer pool data logical reads          = 1074
        Buffer pool data physical reads         = 0
        Buffer pool temporary data logical reads  = 17319
        Buffer pool temporary data physical reads = 2
        Buffer pool data writes                 = 324
        Buffer pool index logical reads         = 99871
        Total buffer pool read time (milliseconds) = 46
        Total buffer pool write time (milliseconds)= 2051
        ..
        Number of SQL requests since last commit  = 6941
        Dynamic SQL statements attempted          = 6941
        ...
        Rows selected                           = 14208348
        Rows read                               = 1663
        Rows written                            = 33435
        ...
        Total User CPU Time used by agent (s)   = 15.193611
        Total System CPU Time used by agent (s) = 0.000000
        ..
```

5. Obtain the active statements for this application. Look at the active statement for this application with the following command:

    ```
    [db2instp@nodedb21 ~]$ db2pd -apinfo 16376 -db posp
    ```

    ```
    Database Partition 0 -- Database POSP -- Active -- Up 5 days
    19:13:32 -- Date 01/20/2012 19:15:19

    Application :
      Address :              0x0000000200E60080
      AppHandl [nod-index] : 16376     [000-16376]
      TranHdl :             9
      Application PID :     3328
      Application Node Name : GANDALF
      IP Address:           192.168.1.104
      Connection Start Time : (1327102748)Fri Jan 20 18:39:08 2012
      Client User ID :      ROBERT
    ```

```
System Auth ID :          DB2INSTP
Coordinator EDU ID :      508
Coordinator Partition :   0
Number of Agents :        3
Locks timeout value :     NotSet
Locks Escalation :        No
Workload ID :             1
Workload Occurrence ID :  14
Trusted Context :         n/a
Connection Trust Type :   non trusted
Role Inherited :          n/a
Application Status :      UOW-Waiting
Application Name :        pos.exe
Application ID :          C0A80168.GD0C.116980233914
ClientUserID :            n/a
ClientWrkstnName :        n/a
ClientApplName :          n/a
ClientAccntng :           n/a
CollectActData:           N
CollectActPartition:      C
SectionActuals:           N

List of active statements :
  UOW-ID :          1
  Activity ID :     1
  Package Schema :   NULLID
  Package Name :     SYSSH200
  Package Version :
  Section Number :   4
  SQL Type :        Dynamic
  Isolation :       CS
  Statement Type :  DML, Select (blockable)
  Statement :        SELECT a.invid,
    to_char(a.dateinv,'YYYYMMDD') FROM POSP.invoices a, POSP.
invoices b, POSP.invoices c
```

You can choose to use EXPLAIN PLAN for this statement, and issue corrective action,
depending on your findings.

How it works...

CPU time is essential to performance, and a busy CPU is what we want, since we want it to do as much work as possible. We want to avoid runaway processes, as much as possible.

There's more...

We have seen one example of CPU bottleneck. Other sources are also possible.

Utilities

Utilities such as RUNSTATS, LOAD, or BACKUP can take a lot of resources. They can be throttled using the UTIL_IMPACT_PRIORITY keyword. Examine whether there are currently any running utilities using the following command:

```
[pse1@db01]/prod/20111016_2> db2 list utilities show detail
```

```
ID                              = 74372
Type                            = BACKUP
Database Name                   = LEDGER
Partition Number                = 0
Description                     = online db
Start Time                      = 10/18/2011 17:25:17.094883
State                           = Executing
Invocation Type                 = User
Throttling:
    Priority                    = Unthrottled
Progress Monitoring:
    Estimated Percentage Complete = 6
        Total Work              = 439687859360 bytes
        Completed Work          = 26179894432 bytes
        Start Time              = 10/18/2011 17:25:17.095180
```

Note that Unthrottled means that the backup is allowed to use 100 percent CPU.

Context switches

UNIX systems assign each process a slice of operating time. Each time the operating system handles a process, it implies a context switch. The operating system loads the last working context of a process, and then resumes processing until the next context switch.

Look for this activity using the `vmstat` command, under the `CS` column. A fair amount of activity is normal, but a rate of more than 75,000 to 100,000 context switches per second can be considered high.

See also

> ► *Chapter 9, Problem Determination*
>
> ► *Chapter 12, Monitoring*

Tuning memory utilization

Self-tuning memory is activated on database creation. Unless you are using a partitioned database, we recommend you leave the settings to automatic. You can also run the configuration advisor and do additional tweaking on parameters.

Capacity planning is crucial for performance. If you need to deactivate self-tuning, you will need some planning and preparation in order to split your server's memory into chunks for each instance. 4-8 GB per processor should be enough for most applications.

Each instance will have to go through a design process, so for each instance, we suggest you proceed from the top, at the partition level, the instance (database manager) level, and at the database level. We can consider, next, the agent's private memory:

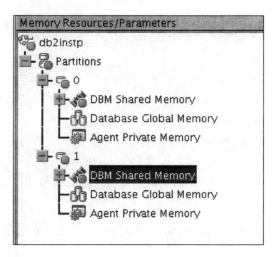

Getting ready

Monitor your system closely, and gather as much information as possible on current use. Examine `db2diag.log` for memory-related messages. Once you have your numbers ready, allow for some down time to recycle the database with new settings.

How to do it...

From here, we will consider that you want to configure memory settings manually. We'll start first at the instance level shared memory:

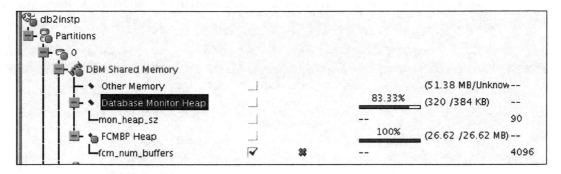

1. Configure **Fast Communication Manager** (**FCM**) on partitioned databases. You should increase `fcm_num_buffers`, if you find `SQL6040` messages in the `db2diag.log` file. If your setting is automatic, maybe some other component is using memory:

    ```
    [db2instp@nodedb21 partitioned]$ db2 "GET DBM CFG" | grep FCM

     No. of int. communication buffers(4KB)(FCM_NUM_BUFFERS) =
    AUTOMATIC(4096)

     No. of int. communication channels   (FCM_NUM_CHANNELS) =
    AUTOMATIC(2048)
    ```

2. Ensure enough memory is allowed for the monitor heap. The monitor heap (`mon_heap_sz`) has to be available to ensure that DB2 will detect and act on your monitoring requirements. Use the memory visualizer, as shown earlier, or DB2 memory tracker, as follows:

    ```
    [db2instp@nodedb21 ~]$ db2mtrk -i

    Tracking Memory on: 2011/10/26 at 00:47:06


    Memory for instance


        other       monh        fcmbp
        55.3M       320.0K       26.6M
    ```

    The `-m` flag reports the total size, and the size used without the `-km` flag. The monitor heap (`monh`) uses `320 K`.

3. Get/Set maximum databases per instance. The `numdb` parameter can impact the total memory allocated. It is recommended that you use the actual number of databases and allow aound 10 percent for growth.

```
[db2instp@nodedb21 ~]$ db2 get dbm cfg | grep NUMDB

 Max number of concurrently active databases      (NUMDB) = 8
```

You will need to restart the instance, if you change this parameter:

```
[db2instp@nodedb21 partitioned]$ db2 "update dbm cfg using numdb
5"

DB20000I  The UPDATE DATABASE MANAGER CONFIGURATION command
completed

successfully.

SQL1362W  One or more of the parameters submitted for immediate
modification

were not changed dynamically. Client changes will not be effective
until the

next time the application is started or the TERMINATE command has
been issued.

Server changes will not be effective until the next DB2START
command.
```

We have seen memory used at the instance level. Now, let's see memory used by each database at the database level. For each database, you can drill down into its components to analyze the memory distribution:

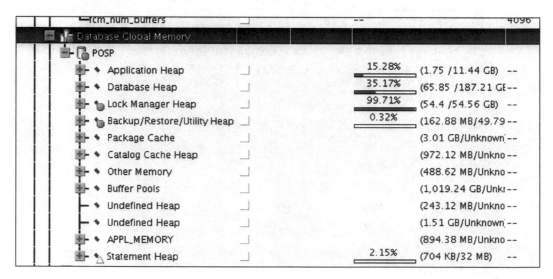

4. For each database, Get/Set global memory parameters:

 ❑ **Package cache**: This section of memory helps avoid recompiling dynamic SQL statements. Use hit ratios to tune this component, as discussed later in this chapter, in the *About hit ratios and their role in performance improvement* recipe.

 ❑ **Catalog cache**: When dynamic or static SQL references a table, information is gathered from the catalog into the cache, in an abridged format. Use hit ratios to tune this component, as discussed later in this chapter, in the *About hit ratios and their role in performance improvement* recipe.

 ❑ **Buffer pools**: The buffer pools are used to store data pages read from tables and indexes. Use hit ratios to tune this component, as discussed later in this chapter, in the *About hit ratios and their role in performance improvement* recipe.

 ❑ **Database heap**: Contains information for buffer pools, table spaces, tables, and indexes. It also contains space for the log buffer and temporary memory used by utilities. If you're not using automatic settings, here is a formula to get an approximate setting:

```
DBHEAP = 10K * NB table spaces + 4K * table + Log buffer
size
```

 ❑ **Log buffer**: This parameter allows you to specify the amount of the database heap (defined by the `dbheap` parameter) to use as a buffer for log records before writing these records to disk. Settings from 256-2000 pages are a good general configuration.

 ❑ **Lock manager heap**: Get the lock list size from the database configuration:

```
[db2instp@nodedb21 ~]$ db2 "get db cfg for posp" | grep
"LOCKLIST"

 Max storage for lock list (4KB)                (LOCKLIST) =
5209
```

5. Look at the lock entries from the db snapshot. Now convert lock list memory into pages, so 12288000/4096 = 3000 pages:

```
[db2instp@nodedb21 ~]$ db2 "get snapshot for database on posp" |
grep "Lock list memory"

Lock list memory in use (Bytes)            = 12288000
```

If the value for `Lock List memory in use` exceeds 50 percent of the defined lock list size, then increase the number of 4 KB pages in the locklist.

6. Set application global memory. This is the amount of memory needed to process a request given to an agent from an application. By default, we set this to 2500. If the db2diag.log file shows an error from an application complaining of not having enough heap storage, then increase this parameter:

```
[db2instp@nodedb21 ~]$ db2 "update db cfg for posp using
applheapsz 3000"
```

7. Look at the snapshot for the database manager. If you see that Agents stolen from another application is not equal to 0, then you may need to increase max agents to allow more agents to be available to the db manager:

```
[db2inst1@nodedb21 ~]$ db2 "get snapshot for dbm" | grep -E
"Agents stolen"

Agents stolen from another application          = 0
```

How it works...

Activity on a server is executed by **Engine Dispatchable Units** (**EDU**) that are implemented as a multi-thread architecture on all platforms. Threads require fewer resources than regular processes and can share operating system resources within the same process.

DB2 provides protection by having a separate address space for applications and the database. This provides a firewall from the application, so that application errors cannot affect database buffers, and thus preserves database integrity.

There's more...

We have seen how to manually tune memory, especially for non-uniform operations on partitioned databases. Use memory at its maximum, but make sure you do not over-allocate memory.

AUTOCONFIGURE

Use the AUTOCONFIGURE command at any time to double-check on your settings. AUTOCONFIGURE is used for initial configuration, to get a set of parameter settings that are more suited to the database than the default settings. You need to fine-tune the parameters as the database evolves.

Self-tuning memory in partitioned database environments

One of the partitions is designated as the tuning partition, and any adjustments are carried over to other partitions. When all partitions carry the same workloads, self tuning memory can be a safe choice. In a case where you have different memory requirements, hardware, or workload, you need to disable self-tuning on all partitions and adjust your memory settings on each partition.

See also

Chapter 5, DB2 Buffer Pools

Chapter 9, Problem Determination, Event Sources, and Files

Chapter 12, Monitoring

Collecting object statistics with the RUNSTAT utility

DB2's optimizer does a great job of finding the best execution path for a given SQL query. However, it relies on object statistics to achieve its purpose. We have discussed briefly, in *Chapter 2, Administration and Configuration of the DB2 Non-partitioned Database*, how to set up automatic maintenance, also called asynchronous stats collecting. We will also look briefly at synchronous stats collection.

For large tables, however, it is better to gather the statistics on just a part of the table. Since the default setting for automatic stats is to gather stats on all rows of a table, this can be time-consuming. You can override this setting for a particular table by setting a statistics profile, so DB2 can collect statistics on just a sample of the table.

How to do it...

In this case, we will run the stats on a daily sales table and set the profile. In our case, we collect samples using Bernoulli sampling, which collects a sample of 10 percent of the rows from the table. We also define priority `10`, which means the utility is throttled at 10 percent of the server's capacity:

```
[db2instp@nodedb21 ~]$ db2 "RUNSTATS ON TABLE POSP.DAILY_SALES
>       ON ALL COLUMNS AND INDEXES ALL
>       ALLOW WRITE ACCESS
>       TABLESAMPLE BERNOULLI ( 10 )
>       SET PROFILE
>       UTIL_IMPACT_PRIORITY 10"
DB20000I  The RUNSTATS command completed successfully.
```

How it works...

DB2 collects statistics, such as numbers or records, pages, and average record length. In our case, we set a profile for this table, so when the automatic runstats kicks in, it will use this profile.

There's more...

Let's see here how we can use the automatic RUNSTATS command and statistics profiles. The set priority can ease the burden of stats collection on the database; we'll see how.

Default automatic statistics collection

Auto runstats uses distribution and sampled detailed indexes all when no profile is set for a table.

Collecting statistics using a statistics profile

The SET PROFILE clause creates a statistics profile for a table, so later stats collection will use it. If you use automatic maintenance on the database, it will also use this profile for the stats collection:

```
[db2instp@nodedb21 ~]$ db2 "RUNSTATS ON TABLE POSP.DAILY_SALES
>       ON ALL COLUMNS AND INDEXES ALL
>       ALLOW WRITE ACCESS
>       TABLESAMPLE BERNOULLI ( 10 )
>       SET PROFILE
>       UTIL_IMPACT_PRIORITY 10"
```

Background stats collecting (asynchronous)

Background stats collecting (or automatic runstats) is enabled by default when creating a database. The database configuration parameter is AUTO_RUNSTATS. You can change it directly or through the control center. The characteristics for automatic runstats are as follows:

- Performed using throttled runstats, adjusts its priority automatically
- Scheduled by default to run in an online maintenance window
- Occur at two-hour intervals
- Tables remain available for update/insert/delete
- Large tables (> 4000 pages) are sampled and collected only if necessary
- Will use a statistic profile for a table, if defined

Real-time stats collecting (synchronous)

Real-time stats collecting occurs at statement compile time and provides more accurate statistics. Its source may be derived from index or metadata information.

Synchronous stats collecting is enabled by default, when creating a database. You can change this setting with the AUTO_STMT_STATS database configuration parameter. To enable this feature, AUTO_RUNSTATS must also be enabled.

Here are the main characteristics of real-time statistics collection:

- Limited to five seconds; otherwise, an asynchronous request is sent
- Occurs once per table, at the same time
- Performed for regular/MQT/global temporary tables

Setting priority

This option lets you specify the priority for CPU resources, so RUNSTATS can run at a lower priority level. A priority level of 10 will ensure not more than 10 percent of resources are used, so at least 90 percent of the resources remain available:

```
[db2instp@nodedb21 ~]$ db2 "RUNSTATS ON TABLE POSP.DAILY_SALES
>       ON ALL COLUMNS AND INDEXES ALL
>       ALLOW WRITE ACCESS
>       TABLESAMPLE BERNOULLI ( 10 )
>       SET PROFILE
>       UTIL_IMPACT_PRIORITY 10"
```

The automatic maintenance utility uses this feature automatically.

Automatic statistics profiling

Statistics profiles can be set automatically. Automatic statistics profiling is not enabled by default, so you need to enable it using the AUTO_STATS_PROF database configuration parameter. Information is collected in query feedback tables, and then statistics profiles can be generated.

- Can update statistics profiles when AUTO_PROF_UPD is enabled
- Less suited for OLTP
- Requires a supplemental set of tables in the catalog
- Not supported on partitioned databases/intra-partition parallelism

Partitioned database

If a table spans several partitions, the RUNSTAT collects information only on the database partition from which it is executed.

See also

Chapter 2, Administration and Configuration of the DB2 Non-partitioned Database.

Tuning with indexes

You will likely get requests to evaluate SQL queries and suggest indexes for best performance. Let's see together how it's done. You can use the GUI for this case, so we'll be doing it on the command line.

We will use DB2's db2advis utility. There are many ways you can use it. In our case, we have SQL commands with recommendations for indexes.

Getting ready

Now, before you can perform any EXPLAIN PLAN or performance analysis, you need to have fresh statistics on tables and indexes or reasonably recent ones; otherwise, the results may not correspond to your expectations.

How to do it...

If you're not connecting as instance owner, you will need a user with create table authority to run the EXPLAIN.DDL utility.

1. As instance owner, grant access to the database to the user who will perform SQL evaluations. That user should have profile values set and can execute DB2 from the shell or Windows command line:

    ```
    db2 connect to uatdb
    db2 grant createtab, connect on database to user rpellet
    ```

2. Create explain plan tables. You need to have tables that will permit you to do the explain plans for the queries you wish to evaluate. The script to do this is in sqllib/misc/EXPLAIN.DDL.

3. Log in and create the explain tables. The -t tells db2 to look for ; as delimiter in the SQL; -f means that the SQL is contained in EXPLAIN.DDL; -r will create an output file EXPLAIN.out with the following results:

    ```
    cd /opt/IBM/db2/V9.7/misc/
    db2 connect to uatdb
    db2 -t -f EXPLAIN.DDL -r EXPLAIN.out
    ```

4. Run queries through an explain utility. Prior to running db2advis, it may be good to do an explain plan on the query; we can use db2exfmt for the same. Look for the *Using EXPLAIN PLAN* recipe in this chapter.

5. Analyze queries through the advisor. Once explain tables are created, you're set to go. From the shell prompt, we'll change the directory where I put queries that the customer wanted me to analyze. I put the name of the SQL in a shell script variable, so I have a generic command that can be also used in a script. In this case, the SQL to be analyzed is in us_wholesale_e.sql:

```
cd 20110524_queries
input=us_wholesale_e.sql
output=us_wholesale_e.adv
db2advis -delim ';' -d uatdb -n uatdata -i $input -o $output
```

How it works...

db2advis will suggest the index, based on the tables and current indexes as well as available statistics, which is important for db2advis to make the right decisions. The following table explains the options that we used in this example:

Options	Description
-delim ;	as the end delimiter for our SQL. (;)
-d uatdb	uses uatdb database
-n uatdata	specifies uatdata as the default schema, if the SQL does not have schema identifiers for the tables
-i $input	uses $input as input file, which is defined as wholesale_e.sql
-o $output	uses $output as output file, which is defined as wholesale_e.adv

The result in the output file will suggest indexes to create, in this case, form_adjustment.sql.adv:

```
    ----
    -- LIST OF RECOMMENDED INDEXES
    -- ===========================
    --   no indexes are recommended for this workload.
```

In another case, wholesale_e.adv:

```
    --
    --
    -- LIST OF RECOMMENDED INDEXES
    -- ===========================
    -- index[1],    53.087MB
```

```
      CREATE INDEX "UATDATA    "."IDX105242216410000" ON "UATDATA
"."T4075"
      ("FTRVT" ASC, "FTNDD" ASC, "FTRFF" DESC) ALLOW REVERSE
      SCANS ;
      COMMIT WORK ;
      RUNSTATS ON TABLE "UATDATA    "."T4075" FOR INDEX "UATDATA
"."IDX105242216410000" ;
      COMMIT WORK ;
```

Take the time to examine the SQL, and edit the script to apply your naming convention for the index before running it.

```
db2 -t -f  wholesale_e.adv -r wholesale_e.log
```

There's more...

Let's take a look at the output and how to get more recommendations from the db2advis utility.

Sample output

Here is a sample from the wholesale_e.adv output file:

```
---- LIST OF RECOMMENDED INDEXES
-- ============================
-- index[1],   53.087MB
   CREATE INDEX "UATDATA    "."IDX105242216410000" ON "UATDATA    "."T4075"
   ("FTRVT" ASC, "FTNDD" ASC, "FTRFF" DESC) ALLOW REVERSE
   SCANS ;
   COMMIT WORK ;
   RUNSTATS ON TABLE "UATDATA    "."T4075" FOR INDEX "UATDATA
"."IDX105242216410000" ;
   COMMIT WORK ;
--
-- RECOMMENDED EXISTING INDEXES
-- ============================
RUNSTATS ON TABLE "UATDTA    "."T4075" FOR INDEX "UATDTA    "."T4075_9" ;
COMMIT WORK ;
--
-- UNUSED EXISTING INDEXES
-- ============================
DROP INDEX "UATDTA    "."T4075_2";
DROP INDEX "UATDTA    "."T4075_3";
DROP INDEX "UATDTA    "."T4075_4";
```

```
DROP INDEX "UATDTA  "."T4075_5";
DROP INDEX "UATDTA  "."T4075_6";
DROP INDEX "UATDTA  "."T4075_7";
DROP INDEX "UATDTA  "."T4075_8";
DROP INDEX "UATDTA  "."T4075_10";
DROP INDEX "UATDTA  "."T4075_11";
DROP INDEX "UATDTA  "."T4075_12";
DROP INDEX "UATDTA  "."T4075_13";
DROP INDEX "UATDTA  "."T4075_14";

-- =============================
```

Recommendations

For a complete set of recommendations, use option -m ICMP to get recommended MQTs, indexes, partitioning, and multidimension clustering on MQT and base tables.

See also

Chapter 6, Database Objects

Tuning sorting

Sorting occurs at two levels in the database. One is shared sort memory, located in the database global memory, and the other is at the agent level, called the private sort memory.

Getting ready

Monitor sorting activity on your database, as discussed in the previous chapter, by using snapshots, and compare sorting activity with the load on your database.

See how much sorting is done throughout a normal day's activity. In the following SQL, you can even identify the partition's sorting activity. You will see if there is enough sorting activity to make tuning worthwhile.

How to do it...

1. **Average sort time**: If average sort time per sort is long, we can start thinking about tuning.

   ```
   SELECT DBPARTITIONNUM, TOTAL_SORT_TIME / (TOTAL_SORTS + 1)
   FROM   SYSIBMADM.SNAPDB;
   ```

2. **Sort time per transaction**: If the value of `SortsPerTransaction` is greater than five, there might be too many sorts per transaction:

```
SELECT DBPARTITIONNUM, TOTAL_SORTS / ( COMMIT_SQL_STMTS +
ROLLBACK_SQL_STMTS + 1)
FROM    SYSIBMADM.SNAPDB;
```

3. **Average sort overflows**: If `PercentSortOverflow` is greater than three percent, there may be serious large sorts occurring:

```
SELECT    DBPARTITIONNUM,
       SORT_OVERFLOWS / ( TOTAL_SORTS +1 )
FROM    SYSIBMADM.SNAPDB;
```

Increasing the value of `SORTHEAP` might help, but you should consider identifying offending SQL statements and adding indexes.

How it works...

Sorts happen when no index can satisfy an order by request, a distinct or union clause is requested, or when an index is created. When the input set for the sort is small enough, DB2 executes the sort in memory; otherwise, the sort set is stored on disk.

There's more...

Let's look at sort overflows, types of sorts, and best coding practices.

Sort overflows

If the sorted data cannot fit into the sort heap, the data is stored in a temporary table that is contained in a system temporary table space owned by the database.

In any scenario, there will be a definite sort, so we can safely assume that a sort overflow of less than 10 percent should be good.

Piped sorts

A piped sort happens when the result of the sort does not require a temporary table. The sort heap is not freed until the application closes the cursor using the sort.

Coding practices

Make a point with developers to reduce sorting as much as possible. Gather best coding practices and have them enforced. Here are some tips to reduce sorting time and resources:

▶ Arrange to have `order by` clauses using indexed fields
▶ Avoid distinct clauses as much as possible
▶ Use discriminant queries to minimize result sets before sorting

See also

Tuning memory utilization recipe in this chapter.

Hit ratios and their role in performance improvement

High hit ratios indicate that the database is memory-efficient. For example, a high hit ratio for buffer cache says that, most of the time, the database will find the database records it needs in the buffer pools, instead of reading it from disk. Having fewer physical reads leads to better performance.

Getting ready

We have discussed, in *Chapter 12, Monitoring*, setting up monitor switches. Make sure monitor switches are on for buffer pools. Follow indicators regularly and tune caches in accordance. You may want to run stats on all the tables and probably check for fragmentation.

How to do it...

1. Monitor buffer pool hit ratios. Hit ratios with 90 percent or more indicate a good hit ratio:

```
[db2inst1@nodedb21 ~]$ db2 'SELECT DBPARTITIONNUM "PARTN",
>       SUBSTR(BP_NAME,1,20) "BUFFERPOOL",
>       (POOL_DATA_L_READS - POOL_DATA_P_READS) * 100 /
>       (POOL_DATA_L_READS + 1) "HIT RATIO"
>       FROM    SYSIBMADM.SNAPBP'

PARTN  BUFFERPOOL           HIT RATIO
------ -------------------- --------------------
    0  IBMDEFAULTBP                           99
    0  POS_BPT8K                              93
    0  POS_BPI8K                               0
    0  POS_MONBP32K                           50
    0  IBMSYSTEMBP4K                           0
    0  IBMSYSTEMBP8K                           0
    0  IBMSYSTEMBP16K                          0
    0  IBMSYSTEMBP32K                          0

  8 record(s) selected.
```

2. Monitor catalog cache hit ratio:

```
[db2inst1@nodedb21 ~]$ db2 'SELECT DBPARTITIONNUM "PARTN",
>        (1-(CAT_CACHE_INSERTS / CAT_CACHE_LOOKUPS))*100 "HIT RATIO"
>        FROM    SYSIBMADM.SNAPDB'


PARTN  HIT RATIO
------ --------------------
    0                    100


    1 record(s) selected.
```

3. Monitor package cache hit ratio:

```
[db2inst1@nodedb21 ~]$ db2 'SELECT (1-(PKG_CACHE_INSERTS / PKG_
CACHE_LOOKUPS))*100 "HIT RATIO"
>        FROM    SYSIBMADM.SNAPDB'


HIT RATIO
--------------------
                 100


    1 record(s) selected.
```

4. Monitor log buffer read hit ratio:

```
[db2inst1@nodedb21 ~]$ db2 "SELECT DBPARTITIONNUM,
        100-((NUM_LOG_READ_IO * 100)/(LOG_READS+1)) as LOGB_
HITRATIO
FROM    SYSIBMADM.SNAPDB"


DBPARTITIONNUM LOGB_HITRATIO
-------------- --------------------
             0                  100
             1                  100


    2 record(s) selected.
```

Dynamic SQLs can be reused only when identical code is used. Any difference forces DB2 to recompile an SQL and insert it into the package cache.

More buffer pool tips, and more on what happens in the catalog and package cache.

Buffer pools

The buffer pools are used to store data pages read from tables and indexes. When the database needs to read a page of data and finds that a page is already in the buffer pool or buffer cache, it's considered a hit.

On large databases, you can obtain better performance by having a separate buffer pool for large tables and another for smaller reference tables.

For large tables, you can gain performance by having separate buffer pools for data and for indexes.

Catalog cache

When a dynamic or static SQL references a table, information is gathered from the catalog into the cache, in an abridged format. When another SQL references a table, DB2 will look into the catalog cache, in order to minimize disk access.

Package cache

This section of memory helps avoid recompiling dynamic SQL statements, as well as reloading packages and sections for static SQLs.

 Avoid using constants in dynamic SQLs. Ensure code reuses SQLs with bind variables, to avoid having similar SQLs in the package cache.

Log buffer

The log buffer is used to store transaction data before writing it to disk. When an agent reads log data, it issues a log read request. DB2 will try to satisfy this request through the log buffer, if possible; otherwise, it will read from disk.

Chapter 5, DB2 Buffer Pools

I/O tuning

Disk Input/Output is the main bottleneck in a computer system. Since access from disk is 1000 times slower than memory, we must ensure maximum response.

The first thing we should discuss is transaction logs. Best practices in the industry recommend a separate, local, physical disk dedicated to this task, or ideally a RAID 1 configuration. Since DB2 writes to transaction logs in append mode, having a dedicated disk ensures that the write head is always ready to write without needing seek time.

The second thing to discuss is your debugging. Make sure the diagnostic logs are separated from the data. If you have event monitoring turned on, make sure it is separated from your tables and indexes. All explain plan tables (EXPLAIN.DDL) should follow the same rule.

The third thing to discuss is the number of spindles available for the database. In the case of RAID storage, or for individual drives, the rule of thumb is to configure at least 10 to 20 disks, per processor.

The next item in the list is to separate, as much as possible, tables and indexes. Tables should have their own table spaces and buffer pools, and should sit on physical spindles, separated from indexes as much as possible.

Have reorganization done regularly on tables and indexes, using automatic maintenance.

Getting ready

You may need to perform maintenance shutdown on the application or the database. For this example, we opened another window and executed a cartesian join, to make sure the database works for a while and does lots of I/O.

```
[db2inst1@nodedb21 NODE0000]$ db2 "select * from posp.invoices a, posp.
invoices b order by 1"
```

How to do it...

We'll see in the steps below how to minimize conflicting I/O's and how to find I/O hot spots:

1. Check to make sure that the log path is not the same as the database path. Get the log path:

```
[db2inst1@nodedb21 ~]$ db2 get db cfg | grep -E "[p|P]ath to log
files"
 Changed path to log files                    (NEWLOGPATH) =
 Path to log files                                        = /data/
db2/db2inst1/NODE0000/SQL00002/SQLOGDIR/
```

2. Now, compare the log path with the database path:

```
[db2inst1@nodedb21 ~]$ db2 list database directory
....
Database 4 entry:

  Database alias                        = POS
  Database name                         = POS
  Local database directory              = /data/db2
```

3. Change the log path, if necessary. The new log path must be fully qualified, that is, not a relative path:

```
[db2inst1@nodedb21 NODE0000]$ db2 "update db cfg using newlogpath
'/logs/db2/db2inst1/POS/NODE0000'"
DB20000I  The UPDATE DATABASE CONFIGURATION command completed
successfully.
SQL1363W  One or more of the parameters submitted for immediate
modification
were not changed dynamically. For these configuration parameters,
all
applications must disconnect from this database before the changes
become
effective.
```

4. Either force all applications or wait after all applications have been disconnected, then confirm change has been made effective:

```
[db2inst1@nodedb21 NODE0000]$ db2 get db cfg for pos | grep -E
"[p|P]ath to log files"
  Changed path to log files             (NEWLOGPATH) =
  Path to log files                              = /logs/
db2/db2inst1/POS/NODE0000/
```

5. Check for the amount of log activity per transaction. Transaction logging may be a system bottleneck. A high ratio indicates a high level of activity or could be a configuration issue. Check for log sizes and primary and secondary logs.

```
[db2inst1@nodedb21 NODE0000]$ db2 "SELECT DBPARTITIONNUM, LOG_
WRITES /(COMMIT_SQL_STMTS+1)
FROM    SYSIBMADM.SNAPDB"
DBPARTITIONNUM 2
-------------- --------------------
             0                 1200
             1                  560

  2 record(s) selected.
```

6. Check for I/O hot spots. Check with the system administrator for any busy device. If it is a system temporary table space, this could indicate a sorting issue or an offending query. You can confirm it is database-related by checking table space direct reads and writes.

```
[db2inst1@nodedb21 NODE0000]$ db2 update dbm cfg using DFT_MON_
BUFPOOL on DFT_MON_LOCK on DFT_MON_SORT on DFT_MON_TABLE on
[db2inst1@nodedb21 NODE0000]$ db2 "SELECT DBPARTITIONNUM,
             SUBSTR(TBSP_NAME,1,30) "TABLSPC",
             DIRECT_READS,
             DIRECT_WRITES
    FROM     SYSIBMADM.SNAPTBSP
    ORDER    BY DIRECT_WRITES DESC, DIRECT_READS DESC"
```

DBPARTITIONNUM	TABLSPC	DIRECT_READS	DIRECT_WRITES
1	TEMPSPACE1	0	528
0	TEMPSPACE1	0	528
0	SYSCATSPACE	7298	64
0	SYSTOOLSPACE	100	0
0	USERSPACE1	0	0
0	POSP_TBLS	0	0
0	POSP_DSS_TB8K	0	0
0	POSP_DSS_TB32K	0	0
0	POSP_INDX	0	0

7. Let's say, for example, we find that the /data/db2 file system is busy. We'll find corresponding table spaces with the following command:

```
[db2inst1@nodedb21 NODE0000]$ db2 "SELECT DBPARTITIONNUM "PART",
             TBSP_ID "ID",
             SUBSTR(TBSP_NAME,1,20) "TABLSPC",
             SUBSTR(CONTAINER_NAME,1,50) "CONTAINER"
    FROM     SYSIBMADM.SNAPCONTAINER
    WHERE    CONTAINER_NAME LIKE '/data/db2/%'"
```

PART	ID	TABLSPC	CONTAINER
0	0	SYSCATSPACE	/data/db2/

db2instp/NODE0000/posp/catalog.dbf

```
       0                         1 TEMPSPACE1               /data/db2/
db2instp/NODE0000/posp/temp.dbf

       0                         2 USERSPACE1               /data/db2/
db2instp/NODE0000/posp/user.dbf

       0                         3 SYSTOOLSPACE             /data/db2/
db2instp/NODE0000/SQL00001/SYSTOOLSPACE

       0                         4 POSP_TBLS                /data/db2/
db2instp/NODE0000/posp/posp_tbls.dbf

       0                         5 POSP_DSS_TB8K            /data/db2/
db2instp/NODE0000/posp/posp_dss_tb8k.dbf

       0                         6 POSP_DSS_TB32K           /data/db2/
db2instp/NODE0000/posp/posp_dss_tb32k.db

       0                        10 SYSTOOLSTMPSPACE         /data/db2/
db2instp/NODE0000/SQL00001/SYSTOOLSTMPSP

       0                        11 POSP_DSS8K_2010_Q1       /data/db2/
db2instp/node0000/posp/posp_dss8k_2010_q

       0                        12 POSP_DSS8K_2010_Q2       /data/db2/
db2instp/node0000/posp/posp_dss8k_2010_q

       0                        13 POSP_DSS8K_2010_Q3       /data/db2/
db2instp/node0000/posp/posp_dss8k_2010_q

       0                        14 POSP_DSS8K_2010_Q4       /data/db2/
db2instp/node0000/posp/posp_dss8k_2010_q

       0                        15 POSP_DS8KI_2010_Q1       /data/db2/
db2instp/node0000/posp/posp_ds8ki_2010_q

       0                        16 POSP_DS8KI_2010_Q2       /data/db2/
db2instp/node0000/posp/posp_ds8ki_2010_q

       0                        17 POSP_DS8KI_2010_Q3       /data/db2/
db2instp/node0000/posp/posp_ds8ki_2010_q

       0                        18 POSP_DS8KI_2010_Q4       /data/db2/
db2instp/node0000/posp/posp_ds8ki_2010_q

       0                        19 POSP_DSS8K_2011_Q1       /data/db2/
db2instp/node0000/posp/posp_dss8k_2011_q

       0                        20 POSP_DS8KI_2011_Q1       /data/db2/
db2instp/node0000/posp/posp_ds8ki_2011_q

       0                        21 POSP_DSS8K_2009_Q4       /data/db2/
db2instp/node0000/posp/posp_dss8k_2009_q

       0                        22 POSP_DS8KI_2009_Q4       /data/db2/
db2instp/node0000/posp/posp_ds8ki_2009_q

       1                         1 TEMPSPACE1               /data/db2/
db2instp/NODE0001/posp/temp.dbf

       1                         2 USERSPACE1               /data/db2/
db2instp/NODE0001/posp/user.dbf
```

```
        1                      4 POSP_TBLS              /data/db2/
db2instp/NODE0001/posp/posp_tbls.dbf
        1                      7 POSP_AHR_TB8K          /data/db2/
db2instp/NODE0001/posp/posp_ahr_tb8k.dbf
        1                      8 POSP_AHR_TB32K         /data/db2/
db2instp/NODE0001/posp/posp_ahr_tb32k.db
```

```
  25 record(s) selected.
```

8. Check for hot tables. While the query was running, we launched another select to pick up active tables from the SYSIBMADM.SNAPTAB administrative view:

```
[db2inst1@nodedb21 NODE0000]$ db2 "SELECT DBPARTITIONNUM,
          TBSP_ID "ID",
          SUBSTR(TABSCHEMA,1,10) "SCHEMA",
          SUBSTR(TABNAME,1,30) "TABLE",
          DATA_PARTITION_ID "PARTTBL_ID",
          ROWS_READ,
          ROWS_WRITTEN
     FROM  SYSIBMADM.SNAPTAB
     WHERE  TABSCHEMA NOT LIKE 'SYS%'"
DBPARTITIONNUM ID                        SCHEMA     TABLE
PARTTBL_ID  ROWS_READ                    ROWS_WRITTEN
------------- -------------------- ---------- ---------------
            0                         1 <424><DB2I TEMP (00001,00002)
-        2468668                         3309
            0                         4 POSP       INVOICES
-           7765                            0
            1                         1 <424><DB2I TEMP (00001,00002)
-        2534860                         3309
            1                         4 POSP       INVOICES
-           7865                            0
```

```
  4 record(s) selected.
```

Note the DB2 temporary tables and the volume of records read, which is related to our cartesian join.

How it works...

As we mentioned earlier, we recommend a separate, local, and physical disk dedicated to transaction logs, or ideally a RAID 1 configuration. Since DB2 writes to transaction logs in append mode, having a dedicated disk ensures that the write head is always ready to write without needing seek time.

There's more...

Transaction logs and disk performance for normal and partitioned databases. Another way to reduce I/O is to use the reorg command regularly. We'll see how to use reorgchk for this.

Logpath

The logpath or newlogpath database parameters determine the location of the transaction log. This location is, by default, in the database path. The transaction logs should not share the same disks as the table spaces. They should be placed on local and dedicated file systems. This applies to non-partitioned and partitioned databases as well.

Diagnostic logs on partitioned databases

Typically, the location of diagpath on all partitions is on a shared, NFS-mounted path, by default. We recommend you change diagpath to a local, non-NFS directory, for each partition. This prevents all partitions from trying to update the same file with diagnostic messages.

Reorgchk

Use automatic maintenance, or otherwise perform checks regularly. Use the following command:

```
[db2instp@nodedb21 ~]$ db2 reorgchk current statistics on table
posp.invoices


Table statistics:


F1: 100 * OVERFLOW / CARD < 5

F2: 100 * (Effective Space Utilization of Data Pages) > 70

F3: 100 * (Required Pages / Total Pages) > 80


SCHEMA.NAME                          CARD      OV     NP     FP ACTBLK
TSIZE  F1   F2   F3 REORG
-------------------------------------------------------------------
Table: POSP.INVOICES
```

```
                                        9.9e+07       0  4e+06  5e+06        -
1.24e+11   0  72  79 --*
```

Notice the F1,F2,F3 statistics. When their respective threshold are exceeded, the REORG field is marked as '*':

Index statistics:

F4: CLUSTERRATIO or normalized CLUSTERFACTOR > 80

F5: 100 * (Space used on leaf pages / Space available on non-empty leaf pages) > MIN(50, (100 - PCTFREE))

F6: (100 - PCTFREE) * (Amount of space available in an index with one less level / Amount of space required for all keys) < 100

F7: 100 * (Number of pseudo-deleted RIDs / Total number of RIDs) < 20

F8: 100 * (Number of pseudo-empty leaf pages / Total number of leaf pages) < 20


```
SCHEMA.NAME                     INDCARD   LEAF ELEAF LVLS   NDEL    KEYS
LEAF_RECSIZE NLEAF_RECSIZE LEAF_PAGE_OVERHEAD NLEAF_PAGE_OVERHEAD
F4  F5  F6  F7  F8 REORG
-----------------------------------------------------------------

Table: POSP.INVOICES

Index: POSP.INVOICES_1

                                9.9e+07 2e+05    52      3 1e+07 9.9e+07
35              35                2202                   2202  97  82
0  10   0 -----

Index: POSP.INVOICES_2

                                9.9e+07 25563   11      3 2e+07 1109537
111             111               1132                   1132  66  76
1  17   0 *----

Index: POSP.INVOICES_3

                                9.9e+07 23361   10      3 2e+07 1156602
44              44                2202                   2202  66  76
2  17   0 *----

Index: POSP.INVOICES_4

                                9.9e+07 44251   21      3 42629 2.1e+07
34              34                2274                   2274  99  91
1   0   0 -----

Index: POSP.INVOICES_5

                      9.9e+07 23103    13      3 2e+07 1095201
37              37               2428                   2428  66  76  2  17
0  *----
```

Notice the same with F4-F8 statistics. When their respective thresholds are exceeded, the REORG field is marked as *. So, even if the table does not need reorganization, one or many indexes may need a reorg.

See also

▸ *Chapter 4, Storage – Using DB2 Table Spaces*

▸ *Chapter 5, DB2 Buffer Pools*

▸ *Chapter 12, Configuring and Using Event Monitoring*

▸ *Using logging and nologging modes* recipe in this chapter

▸ *Using parallelism* recipe in this chapter

Using logging and nologging modes

Transaction logging is used for recovery. Logging, in certain cases, can introduce performance problems. When you are not concerned about recovery, you can avoid transaction logging. This may introduce additional work when recovery is needed.

The usual scenario for such operations happens when you need to perform an initialization on a table based on external data, using either LOAD, INSERT, or db2move. When the volume is especially large, the gain in performance is worthwhile.

Getting ready

You may want to perform a backup on the table space or the database, to make recovery easier.

How to do it...

Change logging characteristics on a table. This command disables logging for the current unit or work:

```
[db2inst1@nodedb21 NODE0000]$ db2 "ALTER TABLE POS.FACTDET ACTIVATE NOT
LOGGED INITIALLY"
DB20000I  The SQL command completed successfully.
```

How it works...

The alter table command disables logging until the next commit. When the current unit of work is done, the NOT LOGGED INITIALLY attribute is deactivated, and logging is resumed on the table.

If, however, the transaction fails or rolls back to a save point, the table is marked as inaccessible and has to be dropped.

There's more...

We'll see how to avoid catalog locks when using an `alter table` command, attempting recovery on a non-logged table, and considering HADR.

Catalog locks

When you activate the `NOT LOGGED INITIALLY` attribute, we recommend you use an `alter table` command just for this purpose. If you need to alter other characteristics of the same table, use a separate `alter table` command, to avoid catalog locks and contention at the catalog level.

Recovery

When attempting a roll-forward, a table cannot be recovered as it is marked as inaccessible and must be dropped.

LOAD with non-recoverable option

This has the same effect as the `NOT LOGGED INITIALLY` attribute. On failure, the unit of work is rolled back.

High Availability Disaster Recovery (HADR)

Tables with the `NOT LOGGED INITIALLY` attribute are not replicated to the standby database. Furthermore, any attempt to access these tables in an active standby database, or after a takeover, will result in an error.

See also

- ▸ *Chapter 8, DB2 High Availability*
- ▸ The *I/O Tuning* recipe, in this chapter

Using parallelism

DB2 can use more than one processor to access the database, allowing parallel execution of complex SQL requests to be divided among the processors within a single database partition.

Getting ready

Allow for downtime to restart the instance when setting DBM configuration.

How to do it...

1. Set a registry for parallel I/O.

2. For RAID 5 configuration, set this registry variable and see the discussion later on in this section:

```
[db2instp@nodedb21 ~]$ db2set DB2_PARALLEL_IO=*
```

3. Get the current configuration for intra partition parallelism. In this case, intra-partition parallelism was not set:

```
[db2inst1@nodedb21 tmp]$ db2 get dbm cfg | grep -E  "INTRA_
PARALLEL|MAX_QUERYDEGREE"
 Maximum query degree of parallelism    (MAX_QUERYDEGREE) = ANY
 Enable intra-partition parallelism     (INTRA_PARALLEL) = NO
```

4. Update the current configuration:

```
[db2inst1@nodedb21 tmp]$ db2 update dbm cfg using INTRA_PARALLEL
YES MAX_QUERYDEGREE -1
DB20000I  The UPDATE DATABASE MANAGER CONFIGURATION command
completed
successfully.
SQL1362W  One or more of the parameters submitted for immediate
modification
were not changed dynamically. Client changes will not be effective
until the
next time the application is started or the TERMINATE command has
been issued.
Server changes will not be effective until the next DB2START
command.
```

5. Restart the instance:

```
[db2inst1@nodedb21 tmp]$ db2stop force
SQL1064N  DB2STOP processing was successful.
[db2inst1@nodedb21 tmp]$ db2start
SQL1063N  DB2START processing was successful.
```

6. Connect to the database:

```
[db2inst1@nodedb21 tmp]$ db2 connect to pos

    Database Connection Information

 Database server        = DB2/LINUXX8664 9.7.4
 SQL authorization ID   = DB2INST1
 Local database alias   = POS
```

7. Prepare the next statements for parallelism:

```
[db2inst1@nodedb21 tmp]$ db2 "SET CURRENT DEGREE = 'ANY'"
DB20000I  The SQL command completed successfully.
```

Continue with the desired operation and with the operations that you need to carry out in parallel. Some SQL statements cannot use intra-partition parallelism.

How it works...

We started by setting up parallelism for disk arrays, and then at the database manager or instance level. Once the database manager settings were changed, we restarted the instance, and we are now ready to use parallelism in our queries or applications.

There's more...

Here are some considerations on parallelism related to SAN/RAID disks. We'll look at some tips to use parallelism in data loads.

RAID 5 and DB2_PARALLEL_IO

In a RAID configuration, you may see a file system as one logical disk, although there are many physical disks beneath this abstraction layer. So, only one container per table space is needed, since there is already striping at the physical level.

For this container, DB2 issues one prefetch request at a time. When a container resides on an array of disks, you can have DB2 request multiple prefetch requests simultaneously for this table space container.

To tell the DB2 system that prefetch requests can be issued to a single container in parallel, you need to change the DB2_PARALLEL_IO registry value. The simplest setting is DB2_PARALLEL_IO=*, meaning that all containers reside on multiple disks.

Allow for downtime, as you need to recycle the instance for the registry value to take effect.

Loading a table

You can improve performance on large table loads by using parallelism. In one case, we had an existing script trying to load 130 million rows into a table without using parallelism. The load was taking forever, so here is what we did to improve this load:

- Considered dropping indexes before the load
- Ensured we could use intra-partition parallelism
- Assigned memory parameters to be automatic

- ▶ Checked table space assignment
- ▶ We made sure, in this case, that we had separate table spaces for the data and index (and LOBs when present)
- ▶ Assigned buffer pools to the data, index, and temp table spaces
- ▶ Added parallelism to the load command

```
nohup db2 "load from tab415.ixf of ixf
  messages tab415.msg
  replace into DTA.FLRG_TBL
  nonrecoverable
  cpu_parallelism 8
  allow no access" &
```

See also

The *I/O Tuning* recipe, in this chapter

Using EXPLAIN PLAN

SQL tuning should be done as early as possible in the development process. Often SQLs will be developed on small development databases and will probably make it to the QA database, and even into production, with acceptable performance. When the database grows, it's not unusual to find out the same query keeps getting slower and slower. This is where you will have to check access plans.

Getting ready

Now, before you can perform any explain or performance analysis, we need fresh statistics or reasonably recent ones, on tables and indexes. Otherwise, the results may not correspond with your expectations.

How to do it...

1. User with create table privileges: If you're not connecting as instance owner, you will need a user with create table authority to run the EXPLAIN.DDL utility, as the instance owner grants database access to the user who will perform SQL evaluations. That user should have profile values set and can execute DB2 from the shell or Windows command line.

   ```
   db2 connect to uatdb
   db2 grant createtab, connect on database to user rpellet
   ```

2. Create explain plan tables: You need to have tables that will permit you to do the explain plans for the queries you wish to evaluate. The script to do this is in `sqllib/misc/EXPLAIN.DDL`. Log in with that user and create the explain tables. The `-t` tells DB2 to look for `;` as delimiter in the SQL. `-f` means the SQL is contained in `EXPLAIN.DDL`. `-r` will create an output file, `EXPLAIN.out`, with the following results:

```
cd /opt/IBM/db2/V9.7/misc/
db2 connect to uatdb
db2 -t -f EXPLAIN.DDL -r EXPLAIN.out
```

3. Run your queries through the `EXPLAIN PLAN` utility: Have your queries ready in `/home/rpellet/queries/*.db2` files, and type in the following commands:

```
cd /home/rpellet/queries
for i in *.db2
do
   db2expln -z ';' -d uatdb -stmtfile $i -o $i.out
done
```

This will change into your queries directory and will run the DB2 explain utility on all `*.db2` files, producing a report named `*.db2.out`. The database used is `UATDB`.

4. Or, you could run your queries manually. The current explain mode set to `YES` will execute the query and produce explain results:

```
db2 connect to posp
db2 set current explain mode yes
db2 "SELECT INV.DATEINV,
        INV.INVID,
        DET.ITEMID,
        INV.STOTAL,
        INV.GST,
        INV.PST,
        INV.TOTAL,
        DET.SKU,
        DET.UNPRICE,
        DET.QTY
FROM    POSP.INVOICES    INV,
        POSP.INVCDET     DET
WHERE   INV.INVID = DET.INVID" | more
```

DATEINV		INVID	ITEMID	STOTAL		GST
PST	TOTAL	S				

```
KU              UNPRICE         QTY

----------------------------- -------- ------ ----------------- -----
------- ----------- ---------------- -
-------------- ---------------- ----------------
2010-06-18-19.39.00.000000    3532.    2.                  4.56
0.23        0.41              5.20 6
80502990100              0.44              1.00
....
2011-05-31-21.01.00.000000    6512.    1.                  2.06
0.41        0.74              9.40 680502010105
2.07            4.0
```

```
4595 record(s) selected.
```

5. When the current explain mode is set to EXPLAIN, it will produce explain results without executing the query. The following message then appears:

   SQL0217W The statement was not executed as only Explain information requests

   are being processed. SQLSTATE=01604

6. The db2exfmt tool will format the plan, you specify the database and the plan table's schema (-e db2instp). It will take the latest plan (-w -1) and place the output in invoices.txt:

   [db2instp@nodedb21 tmp]$ db2exfmt -d posp -e db2instp -w -1 -n % -o invoices.txt

   DB2 Universal Database Version 9.7, 5622-044 (c) Copyright IBM Corp. 1991, 2009

   Licensed Material - Program Property of IBM

   IBM DATABASE 2 Explain Table Format Tool

   Connecting to the Database.

   Connect to Database Successful.

   Enter source schema (SOURCE_SCHEMA, Default %%) ==>

   Enter section number (0 for all, Default 0) ==>

   Output is in invoices.txt.

   Executing Connect Reset -- Connect Reset was Successful.

7. View the output. The db2exfmt tool will format the plan and place the output in invoices.txt. You can browse into this report using your favorite utility:

   [db2instp@nodedb21 tmp]$ view invoices.txt

How it works...

Based on an actual intervention for one of my clients, I had to do an explain to make sure queries were efficient. The scripts were placed as files with a `.db2` extension. We are just running it through a loop in AIX, and when statements are processed, the utility produces an output file. The statements do not get executed, so you don't have to worry about performance.

There's more...

When you have your output, you have to interpret the results. There is a lot of material to cover on this subject, and this is outside the scope of the current discussion.

Sample output

Here is an extract of the sample output. For each node, a cost is associated with the total cost of the query:

```
Access Plan:
-----------
        Total Cost:              261.295
        Query Degree:           1


                        Rows
                        RETURN
                        (    1)
                        Cost
                         I/O
                          |
                        4576
                        DTQ
                        (    2)
                        261.295
                          43
                          |
                        2288
                        ^HSJOIN
                        (    3)
                        259.859
                          43
                /-----------+----------\
        2288                            1642
```

```
        FETCH                        FETCH
        (    4)                      (    6)
       140.826                      118.858
          24                           19
      /---+----\                   /---+----\
    2288         2288           1642          1642
   IXSCAN    TABLE: POSP       IXSCAN    TABLE: POSP
   (    5)      INVCDET        (    7)      INVOICES
   64.4626        Q1          43.0079         Q2
      6                          4
      |                          |
    2288                       1642
 INDEX: POSP               INDEX: POSP
  PK_FACTDET                PK_FACTURES
     Q1                        Q2
```

Watch out for...

Make sure statistics are recent, and run complex queries through the index advisor. If a query is to be executed many times, you may consider using a **Materialized Query Table** (**MQT**).

1. **Cartesian joins**: Ensure each table accessed in the query has a matching key with the joined tables.

2. **Distinct clause**: The distinct clause makes sure no double records are returned from the query. This implies a sort operation.

> The distinct clause should be the last keyword to be coded. Test your query before adding this. You can detect a cartesian join if a query returns too many rows. The distinct clause could mask this type of result until it's in production.

3. **Full table scans**: Table scans have to be considered in the query's context. A table scan should not be considered an issue, when performed in memory or when the table's cardinality is less than a few hundred rows.

Importing production statistics

You can have a test or QA environment simulate production conditions. When you export statistics from the production database, you can import the statistics in your test or QA environment without needing to store all the production data to match the volume and the processing load.

See also

The *I/O Tuning* recipe, in this chapter

Creating a benchmark testing scenario

Creating a benchmark does involve lots of resources, including application developers and database administrators. The extra time it takes can have maximum returns in the long run. We suggest you consider this option if you are developing an application.

If your IT department is using an ERP such as JD Edwards or SAP, you can also benefit from this approach. A benchmark is useful because it helps you define a controlled environment in which you can have repeatable tests.

You can test deadlock scenarios, table space configurations, or database parameters. The same conditions and tests help you pinpoint, accurately, the best options for tuning your databases.

Getting ready

Allow for hardware and software resources, and time for an implementation team, with project lead, application developers, and system and database administrators. Make this part of your implementation project, or it could even be considered as a project on its own.

Have representative SQLs available, and a set of your top consuming SQLs available for testing. Prepare a set of statements that will simulate a typical or heavy load on the database. If you have special batch jobs, such as season end, quarterly reports, or processing, you may want to run these on your benchmark environment.

How to do it...

1. Prepare a hardware and software environment especially for this purpose. This should be a closed environment, separated from production or development servers. We want no interference to distort performance results.

2. Create a database according to logical and physical design. Have this environment match, as closely as possible, your target production environment, server model, disks, and memory configuration. This benchmark can also be used for testing migrations, software updates, and so on.

3. Populate the database with representative data, as much as possible. Try to get as much realistic data as possible, with a volume as close as possible to your production volume.

4. Make backups. A good set of backups ensures that you have repeatable conditions. Do not forget to keep a history of database and database manager configuration parameters.

5. Have representative SQLs available and maintain your database's evolution with your production environment.

6. Monitor as much as possible. Set traces and event monitors, see what works best for you, and keep a history of configurations and related results.

7. Tune the SQL/Database/Parameter. Change one thing at a time and monitor results. Act accordingly, and make backups.

8. Make the benchmark database evolve. Mirror, as much as possible, your production database, with the same database partitions/table space/database objects.

There's more...

Consider warm-up runs in testing scenarios.

Warm-up run

The first run warms up the database so to speak, by initializing buffer pools and other related resources. This always requires more time, so that in the next runs, your tests will probably run better. On three or four runs, you should not consider the first run's results and keep only the other two or three runs' results when evaluating performance.

See also

Chapter 12, Monitoring

14

IBM pureScale Technology and DB2

In this chapter, we will cover the following topics:

- Managing instances, members, and cluster facilities in DB2 pureScale
- Monitoring DB2 pureScale
- High availability in DB2 pureScale
- Backup and recovery in DB2 pureScale

Introduction

DB2 pureScale is a scalable cluster-based active-active type, shared-everything architecture. It has all the features that a clustering configuration can offer and has the main advantage that it is a real database-aware clustering solution. IBM started to include pureScale technology from version 9.8 (this version can be considered as version 9.7 with pureScale). From an architectural point of view, the DB2 pureScale inherits features from z/OS Coupling Facility technology, which was developed and has existed in z/OS for a long time. Applications that are running on normal databases can be ported without any modification to DB2 pureScale architecture. It provides transparent automated failover, automatic workload balancing, and automatic client reroute capabilities.

The software components of DB2 pureScale are as follows:

- DB2 members
- Cluster caching facilities
- DB2 cluster services instance management software, which is based on IBM Tivoli System Automation for multiple platforms.

Being a shared-everything architecture, it uses shared storage formatted with the GPFS filesystem. It has built-in storage provisioning capabilities, through special commands, for formatting, adding, or removing disks, so there is no need to administer these separately.

The databases reside on these shared disk areas and are accessible to all members and caching facilities from the schema.

Managing instances, members, and cluster facilities in DB2 pureScale

In this recipe, we will cover different operations that can be executed on instances, members, and cluster facilities. Our system configuration is composed by two members and two caching facilities. They will be presented with parameters related to pureScale and commands related to stopping, starting, and going into maintenance state.

Getting ready

In our recipes, we will use a DB2 pureScale setup, with two members and two CFs, running on IBM AIX operating system.

Being a clustered environment, the instance itself has to know about the participating member and cluster facilities, and also about the shared device path. The members are used for administrative operations; there could be up to 128 members. The CF can be considered as an instance and database extension, using two sets of parameters that control memory, locking, and diagnostic values on every member.

How to do it...

We will start the practical part of this recipe with a short introduction to pureScale instance.

Creating and managing a DB2 pureScale instance

To create a pureScale instance, you have three options: to create it during setup, to use the command line, or to use the db2isetup wizard. There is a limitation of one instance per pureScale system.

The instance has to be configured when it is being created, to be aware of the participant members, cluster facilities, and shared disk device's values on every node (node-level registry).

The instance create command format is as follows:

```
db2icrt  -d  -m <MemberHostName:Netname>  -cf <CFHostName:Netnames>
   -instance_shared_dev  <Shared_Device_Path_for_Instance>
   -tbdev <Raw_device_for_tiebreaker>
   -u <fencedID>
   <instanceID>
```

Managing DB2 pureScale members

The pureScale members constitute the processing part of pureScale architecture.

1. The command used to stop a member has the following format:

   ```
   db2stop member member-id
   ```

2. To identify the member's ID, we have multiple options. One is to query the
   DB2_MEMBERS system view, as follows:

   ```
   db2sdin1@fndb1-pre-mgt:/home/db2sdin1# db2 "select
   id,varchar(home_host,15) as member_host  from  sysibmadm.db2_
   member"


   ID       MEMBER_HOST
   ------ ---------------
    0 fndb1-pre-mgt
       1 fndb2-pre-mgt
   2 record(s) selected.
   db2sdin1@fndb1-pre-mgt:/home/db2sdin1#
   ```

3. We can also query the DB2_GET_INSTANCE_INFO table function, as follows:

   ```
   db2sdin1@fndb1-pre-mgt:/home/db2sdin1# db2 "SELECT
   ID,varchar(HOME_HOST,15) as member_host from table(DB2_GET_
   INSTANCE_INFO(null,'','','',null)) as TBL where TBL.TYPE='MEMBER'"


   ID       MEMBER_HOST
   ------ ---------------
       0  fndb1-pre-mgt
       1  fndb2-pre-mgt


    2 record(s) selected.
   ```

4. Or we can obtain information about available members by using the db2instance command as follows:

```
db2sdin1@fndb2-pre-mgt:/home/db2sdin1# db2instance -list -member
ID    TYPE     STATE        HOME_HOST              CURRENT_HOST
ALERT   PARTITION_NUMBER   LOGICAL_PORT   NETNAME

0   MEMBER              STARTED              fndb1-pre-mgt
fndb1-pre-mgt                    NO           0                   0
fndb1-pre-ib

1       MEMBER       STARTED              fndb2-pre-
mgt              fndb2-pre-mgt              NO                   0
0     fndb2-pre-ib

db2sdin1@fndb2-pre-mgt:/home/db2sdin1#
```

5. After having found the members ID, stop the member with ID 1 by issuing the following command:

```
db2sdin1@fndb1-pre-mgt:/home/db2sdin1# db2stop member 1

10/25/2011 15:25:32    1    0    SQL1064N   DB2STOP processing was
successful.

SQL1064N   DB2STOP processing was successful.

db2sdin1@fndb1-pre-mgt:/home/db2sdin1#
```

Starting pureScale members

1. The command format for starting a member is as follows:

```
db2start member member-id
```

2. Start a member with ID 1, stopped previously, by executing the following command:

```
db2sdin1@fndb1-pre-mgt:/home/db2sdin1# db2start member 1

10/25/2011 15:27:45    1    0    SQL1064N   DB2START processing was
successful.

SQL1064N   DB2START processing was successful.

db2sdin1@fndb1-pre-mgt
```

Managing the DB2 pureScale caching facilities

The caching facility is responsible for buffer pool management and global locking. The configuration of each clustering facility is controlled by a set of instances and an extended set of database parameters. The following CF server configuration parameters are updatable with the UPDATE DBM CFG command:

Parameter	Description
CF_DIAGLEVEL	Similar to database manager configuration parameter diaglevel. Valid values are: 0 – No diagnostic data captured 1 – Severe errors only 2 – All errors 3 – All errors and warnings 4 – All errors, warnings, and informational messages
CF_DIAGPATH	Similar to database manager configuration parameter diagpath.
CF_MEM_SZ	Specifies the total memory allocated to cluster facility. Memory parameter—not dynamic—possible range is AUTOMATIC [32768 - 4 294 967 295].
CF_NUM_CONNS	Initial size of CF connection pool. It is a dynamic parameter, range between 4 and 256.
CF_NUM_WORKERS	Controls the number of worker threads started by CF. It is a Dynamic parameter ranging between 1 and 31. When it has an automatic value, the number of initial worker threads is calculated as total number of CPUs-1.

CF structure configuration parameters are an extended set of database parameters. They can be configured as any other database parameters using the UPDATE DB CFG command line.

CF structure configuration parameters are updatable with the UPDATE DB CFG command:

Parameter	Description
CF_DB_MEM_SZ	This is a subset of cf_mem_sz, and controls the maximum memory allocated for databases. Every database running in the pureScale environment may have different memory requirements. Dynamic parameter possible range is AUTOMATIC [32768 - 4 294 967 295].
CF_GBP_SZ	Controls the memory allocated to group buffer pool (or GBP) for database. Dynamic parameter range between AUTOMATIC [32768 - 4 294 967 295].
CF_LOCK_SZ	Specifies the amount of memory used by CF for locking. For the global parameter, every database must have the same value. Dynamic parameter possible range is AUTOMATIC [AUTOMATIC, 4096 - 1073741824].
CF_SCA_SZ	Controls the shared communication area, control block for tables, indexes, table spaces, and catalogs. Dynamic parameter possible range is AUTOMATIC [AUTOMATIC, 2048 - 1073741824].

Every CF can have its own set of parameter values.

Stopping the caching facility

1. The command used for stopping the cluster facility has the following format:

   ```
   db2stop CF CF_id
   ```

2. Similarly with members to identify cluster facilities' ID, we have multiple sources. CF identifiers can be listed by querying the DB2_CF system view, as follows:

   ```
   db2sdin1@fndb1-pre-mgt:/home/db2sdin1#  db2 "select
   id,varchar(current_host,15) as cf_host from sysibmadm.db2_cf"


   ID     CF_HOST
   ------ ---------------
      128 fncf1-pre-mgt
      129 fncf2-pre-mgt
    2 record(s) selected.



   db2sdin1@fndb1-pre-mgt:/home/db2sdin1#
   ```

3. Use the DB2_GET_INSTANCE_INFO table function, as follows:

   ```
   db2sdin1@fndb1-pre-mgt:/home/db2sdin1# db2 "SELECT
   ID,varchar(HOME_HOST,15) as cf_host from table(DB2_GET_INSTANCE_
   INFO(null,'','','',null)) as TBL where TBL.TYPE='CF'>


   ID     CF_HOST
   ------ ---------------
      128 fncf1-pre-mgt
      129 fncf2-pre-mgt


    2 record(s) selected.



   db2sdin1@fndb1-pre-mgt:/home/db2sdin1#
   ```

   Or we can obtain information about available cluster facilities by using the db2instance command as follows:

   ```
   db2sdin1@fndb2-pre-mgt:/home/db2sdin1# db2instance -list -cf
   ID TYPE   STATE     HOME_HOST     CURRENT_HOST   ALERT    PARTITION_
   NUMBER    LOGICAL_PORT NETNAME
   -128   CF    PRIMARY                     fncf1-pre-mgt            fncf1-
   pre-mgt               NO              -                     0
   fncf1-pre-ib
   ```

```
129     CF        PEER                    fncf2-pre-
mgt               fncf2-pre-mgt                   NO                      -
0      fncf2-pre-ib

db2sdin1@fndb1-pre-mgt:/home/db2sdin1#
```

4. To stop the caching facility with ID `129`, issue the following command:

    db2sdin1@fndb1-pre-mgt:/home/db2sdin1# db2stop cf 129

    SQL1064N DB2STOP processing was successful.

5. We can verify whether our CF is really stopped, by using the following query:

    db2 "SELECT ID,varchar(HOME_HOST,15) as cf_host,state from table(DB2_GET_INSTANCE_INFO(null,'','','',null)) as TBL where TBL. TYPE='CF'"

    ```
    ID      CF_HOST          STATE

    ------- ---------------- --------------------------------

        128 fncf1-pre-mgt    PRIMARY
        129 fncf2-pre-mgt    STOPPED


      2 record(s) selected.
    ```

Starting pureScale cluster facilities

1. The command used for starting the cluster facility has the following format:

    db2start CF CF_id

2. Start the CF with ID `129`:

    db2sdin1@fndb1-pre-mgt:/home/db2sdin1# db2start cf 129

    SQL1063N DB2START processing was successful.

How it works...

Internal coordination and cluster inter-communication are implemented using **Remote Direct Memory Access** (**RDMA**) protocol instructions based upon the InfiniBand infrastructure (cards, switches, and so on). The database or databases reside on a shared storage area, and every member can access the data from it. Locks and data pages are managed by the active CF. Inside CF is a memory area named the global buffer pool, abbreviated as GPB that act as a global shared cached and coordinates page allocation cluster-wide.

The locking mechanisms implemented within locking memory area are also shared is also shared, so if a member holds a lock, the others are aware of it.

There's more...

If there is the case to replace hardware components, for example, from one LPAR, physical servers, or any maintenance operation (such as applying patches), we may put the members in maintenance mode.

Put pureScale members in maintenance mode

To enter in maintenance mode, execute the following steps:

1. Quiesce member 1 by executing the following command:

```
db2sdin1@fndb1-pre-mgt:/home/db2sdin1/sqllib/db2dump# db2stop
member 1 quiesce

10/28/2011 13:05:42     1   0   SQL1064N  DB2STOP processing was
successful.

SQL1064N  DB2STOP processing was successful.
```

2. To effectively enter maintenance mode, execute the following command:

```
db2sdin1@fndb1-pre-mgt:/home/db2sdin1/sqllib/db2dump# db2stop
instance on fndb1-pre-mgt

SQL1064N  DB2STOP processing was successful.

db2sdin1@fndb1-pre-mgt:/home/db2sdin1/sqllib/db2dump#
```

3. To exit from maintenance mode execute the following commands:

   Start the instance on member 1:

```
db2sdin1@fndb1-pre-mgt:/home/db2sdin1/sqllib/db2dump# db2start
instance on fndb2-pre-mgt
```

   Start member 1:

```
db2sdin1@fndb1-pre-mgt:/home/db2sdin1/sqllib/db2dump#db2start
member 1

db2sdin1@fndb1-pre-mgt:/home/db2sdin1/sqllib/db2dump#
```

Monitoring DB2 pureScale environments

Despite the fact that DB2 pureScale addresses high availability, we should know, at any moment, the status of the components of our system. Here we can enumerate the state of members, the current state of caching facilities, any alerts generated by cluster facilities, and performance information regarding locking mechanisms and buffer pools.

In the following recipe, we will cover the monitoring tasks and explain some monitoring elements related to DB2 pureScale components.

Getting ready

There are plenty of methods for monitoring our system, such as administrative views, table functions, clp, and shell commands.

Members and caching facilities can be in different states of functionality. Members can be in the following states:

Member state	Description
STARTED	Member is up and ready to accept connections.
STOPPED	Member has been stopped manually.
RESTARTING	Member is restarting; a member can also have this state if restarting light (When a member cannot be restarted on his original host and is restarted on other available host to perform crash recovery is called restart light.).
WAITING_FOR_FAILBACK	Processes and memory are allocated for the current member and it has been restarted in light mode. It doesn't accept any connection.
ERROR	The member could not be restarted and an alert is generated.

Caching facilities can be in the following states:

Cluster facility state	Description
STOPPED	The CF has been stopped manually.
RESTARTING	The CF is restarting automatically or manually, after issuing db2start.
BECOMING_PRIMARY	The CF attempts to be the primary CF if no other CF has this role.
CATCHUP(n%)	The CF synchronizes information with the primary CF. This is showed in percentages; after it gets 100 percent, CF goes to PEER state.
PEER	The CF is constantly synchronizing with the primary and is ready to become PRIMARY in the case of failure.
ERROR	The CF cannot be started or restarted and an alert is generated.

Table function (interfaces) used for monitoring members:

Interface	Type	Info
DB2_GET_CLUSTER_HOST_STATE	Table function	Basic
DB2_GET_INSTANCE_INFO	Table function	Detailed
DB2_CLUSTER_HOST_STATE	Administrative view	Basic
DB2_GET_INSTANCE_INFO	Administrative view	Detailed
DB2_MEMBERS	Administrative view	Detailed
DB2_INSTANCE_ALERTS	Administrative view	Detailed

Table function used for monitoring cluster facilities:

Interface	Type	Info
`DB2_GET_CLUSTER_HOST_STATE`	Table function	Basic
`DB2_GET_INSTANCE_INFO`	Table function	Detailed
`DB2_CLUSTER_HOST_STATE`	Administrative view	Basic
`DB2_GET_INSTANCE_INFO`	Administrative view	Detailed
`DB2_CF`	Administrative view	Detailed
`DB2_INSTANCE_ALERTS`	Administrative view	Detailed

Next, we will cover how to monitor members and CFs, using some of the interfaces listed in the preceding tables.

How to do it...

1. Using the `DB2_CLUSTER_HOST_STATE administrative view` to monitor the states of members and cluster facilities is done as follows:

```
db2sdin1@fndb1-pre-mgt:/home/db2sdin1# db2 "SELECT
varchar(hostname,17) as HOST_NAME, varchar(STATE,12) as
STATE,INSTANCE_STOPPED,ALERT FROM SYSIBMADM.DB2_CLUSTER_HOST_
STATE"


HOST_NAME            2                INSTANCE_STOPPED ALERT
-----------------    -------------    ---------------- --------
fncf2-pre-mgt        ACTIVE           NO               NO
fncf1-pre-mgt        ACTIVE           NO               NO
fndb2-pre-mgt        ACTIVE           NO               NO
fndb1-pre-mgt        ACTIVE           NO               NO


  4 record(s) selected.
```

2. Using the `db2instance -list` command for monitoring members and cluster facilities is done as follows:

```
db2sdin1@fndb1-pre-mgt:/home/db2sdin1#db2instance -list
ID          TYPE           STATE          HOME_HOST
CURRENT_HOST            ALERT   PARTITION_NUMBER        LOGICAL_
PORT     NETNAME

--          ----           -----          ---------
-----------            -----   ----------------        ----------
--       -------
```

```
0         MEMBER          STARTED              fndb1-pre-
mgt              fndb1-pre-mgt      NO                      0
0     fndb1-pre-ib

1         MEMBER          STARTED              fndb2-pre-
mgt              fndb2-pre-mgt      NO                      0
0     fndb2-pre-ib

128       CF                 PEER              fncf1-pre-
mgt              fncf1-pre-mgt      NO                      -
0     fncf1-pre-ib

129       CF              PRIMARY              fncf2-pre-
mgt              fncf2-pre-mgt      NO                      -
0     fncf2-pre-ib


HOSTNAME                        STATE           INSTANCE_STOPPED
ALERT

--------                        -----           ---------------
-           -----

fncf2-pre-mgt                   ACTIVE                       NO
NO

fncf1-pre-mgt                   ACTIVE                       NO
NO

fndb2-pre-mgt                   ACTIVE                       NO
NO

fndb1-pre-mgt                   ACTIVE                       NO
NO
```

3. Here's how to list alerts related to members:

    ```
    db2sdin1@fndb1-pre-mgt:/home/db2sdin1# db2cluster -cm -list -alert
    There are no alerts
    ```

Monitoring cluster facility memory structures

CF memory is divided into three areas of memory:

- ▸ GBP memory area:

  In this area, we have all the memory allocated for all the buffer pools. Buffer pool hit ratio formulae, used for non-pureScale monitoring, are also applicable here.

- ▸ Locking memory area:

  This area is used for locking across the DB2 pureScale instance. Take care to allocate enough memory, especially in high concurrency systems, to overcome lock escalations.

- ▸ Memory allocated for shared communication area:

This area contains database-wide information about tables, indexes, table spaces, and catalogs.

1. To monitor CF global buffer pool memory allocation, per host, issue the following query:

```
db2sdin1@fndb1-pre-mgt:/home/db2sdin1# db2 "SELECT varchar(HOST_
NAME,17) AS HOST,
>        ID ,
>        CURRENT_CF_GBP_SIZE as CURRENT_GLOBAL_BUFFERPOOL,
>        CONFIGURED_CF_GBP_SIZE as CONFIGURED_CF_GLOBAL_
BUFFERPOOL_SIZE,
>        TARGET_CF_GBP_SIZE as TARGET_CF_GLOBALBUFFERPOOL_SIZE,
>         current_cf_mem_size as CURRENT_CF_MEMORY_SIZE
>   FROM TABLE( MON_GET_CF(129) ) "


HOST                ID      CURRENT_GLOBAL_BUFFERPOOL CONFIGURED_CF_
GLOBAL_BUFFERPOOL_SIZE TARGET_CF_GLOBALBUFFERPOOL_SIZE CURRENT_CF_
MEMORY_SIZE
---------------- ------ ------------------------- ----------------
-------------------- ------------------------------- -------------
----------
fncf2-pre-mgt       129                            45
346624                  346880                          1751040


  1 record(s) selected.
```

2. Beside traditional OS monitoring tools such as vmstat, iostat, and so on, you may use administrative views of table functions to monitor DB2 pureScale hardware resources. Execute the following query to get detailed information about memory structures per member:

```
db2sdin1@fndb1-pre-mgt:/home/db2sdin1# db2 "
> SELECT  VARCHAR(NAME,20) AS HOST_ATTRIBUTE,
>         VARCHAR(VALUE,25) AS VALUE,
>         VARCHAR(UNIT,8) AS UNIT
> FROM SYSIBMADM.ENV_CF_SYS_RESOURCES"


HOST_ATTRIBUTE       VALUE                     UNIT
-------------------- ------------------------- --------
HOST_NAME            fncf1-pre-mgt             -
MEMORY_TOTAL         14336                     MB
```

MEMORY_FREE	9848	MB
MEMORY_SWAP_TOTAL	8192	MB
MEMORY_SWAP_FREE	8167	MB
VIRTUAL_MEM_TOTAL	22528	MB
VIRTUAL_MEM_FREE	18016	MB
CPU_USAGE_TOTAL	0	PERCENT
HOST_NAME	fncf2-pre-mgt	-
MEMORY_TOTAL	14336	MB
MEMORY_FREE	9269	MB
MEMORY_SWAP_TOTAL	8192	MB
MEMORY_SWAP_FREE	8171	MB
VIRTUAL_MEM_TOTAL	22528	MB
VIRTUAL_MEM_FREE	17441	MB
CPU_USAGE_TOTAL	0	PERCENT

```
  16 record(s) selected.


db2sdin1@fndb1-pre-mgt:/home/db2sdin1#
```

How it works...

Usually, it is recommended to set up warnings and alerts regarding the monitored elements; there could be more critical or less critical states, depending on your internal metrics and alert definition.

There's more...

You may also use a graphical tool, such as Optim Performance Manager Extended Edition, for extensive monitoring of your pureScale system.

High availability in DB2 pureScale environments

DB2 pureScale is designed to be a high-availability solution. In the case when one member is failing, for different reasons, the first step is to try to restart it; if this is not possible, then an automatic failover will be conducted on one of the available members. This is a summary description of the automatic rerouting mechanism, which is absolutely transparent for clients. The next case is related to CF failures; in this case, all the work is taken by the peer CF, which will become the new primary, after performing the synchronization steps.

Getting ready

In this recipe, we will simulate a CF failure; next, we will follow the phases of transition of the second CF until it becomes the primary CF.

How to do it...

1. Stop the primary CF gracefully, by executing the following command:

```
db2sdin1@fndb1-pre-mgt:/home/db2sdin1# db2stop cf 128
SQL1064N  DB2STOP processing was successful.
db2sdin1@fndb1-pre-mgt:/home/db2sdin1#
```

2. Query from `DB2_GET_INSTANCE_INFO`, to find the CF states. We can see, in this moment, that the former primary CF is trying to restart:

```
db2sdin1@fndb1-pre-mgt:/home/db2sdin1# db2 "SELECT
ID,varchar(HOME_HOST,15) as cf_host,state from table(DB2_GET_
INSTANCE_INFO(null,'','','',null)) as TB"


ID      CF_HOST          STATE
------  ---------------  --------------------------------
   128 fncf1-pre-mgt     RESTARTING
   129 fncf2-pre-mgt     PEER


 2 record(s) selected.


CF 128 is stopped:
```

3. If you query again in a short time, we will see that a failover to the available CF 129 is being initiated:

```
db2sdin1@fndb1-pre-mgt:/home/db2sdin1# db2 "SELECT
ID,varchar(HOME_HOST,15) as cf_host,state from table(DB2_GET_
INSTANCE_INFO(null,'','','',null)) as TB"


ID      CF_HOST          STATE
------  ---------------  --------------------------------
   128 fncf1-pre-mgt     STOPPED
   129 fncf2-pre-mgt     BECOMING_PRIMARY
 2 record(s) selected.
```

4. After a short time, the former primary CF restarts, and CF with ID `129` becomes the primary CF:

```
db2sdin1@fndb1-pre-mgt:/home/db2sdin1# db2 "SELECT
ID,varchar(HOME_HOST,15) as cf_host,state from table(DB2_GET_
INSTANCE_INFO(null,'','','',null)) as TB"


ID     CF_HOST          STATE
------ --------------- -------------------------------
   128 fncf1-pre-mgt    RESTARTING
   129 fncf2-pre-mgt    PRIMARY


  2 record(s) selected.
db2sdin1@fndb1-pre-mgt:/home/db2sdin1#
```

5. The next phase is a synchronization phase named **catchup**. All memory structures are effectively copied to the old CF, when entering into CATCHUP phase:

```
db2sdin1@fndb1-pre-mgt:/home/db2sdin1# db2 "SELECT
ID,varchar(HOME_HOST,15) as cf_host,state from table(DB2_GET_
INSTANCE_INFO(null,'','','',null)) as TB>


ID     CF_HOST          STATE
------ --------------- -------------------------------
   128 fncf1-pre-mgt    CATCHUP(2%)
   129 fncf2-pre-mgt    PRIMARY


  2 record(s) selected.
```

6. Finally, CF `128` is in PEER state:

```
db2sdin1@fndb1-pre-mgt:/home/db2sdin1# db2 "SELECT
ID,varchar(HOME_HOST,15) as cf_host,state from table(DB2_GET_
INSTANCE_INFO(null,'','','',null)) as TB"


ID     CF_HOST          STATE
------ --------------- -------------------------------
   128 fncf1-pre-mgt    PEER
   129 fncf2-pre-mgt    PRIMARY


  2 record(s) selected.
```

How it works...

All the functional mechanisms found inside are monitored continuously by the clustering services. A failover is decided after a definite series of steps. There is no data loss in database during failover. Only the uncommitted transactions running on the member that has failed are rolled back.

There's more...

If we have a configuration with one CF, in the case of failure, the instance is stopped and the system become unusable. Therefore, it is recommended to have a configuration with a minimum of two CFs, to offer real high availability.

Backup and recovery in DB2 pureScale environments

In essence, the methods used for backup and recovery are not that different from non-pureScale systems, excluding a multipartitioned database, which is a different subject. Backup and recovery in a pureScale environment can be conducted from any member. The commands used are the same as those found in non-pureScale setups.

Getting ready

In this recipe, we will perform an offline backup, followed by an online backup. Next, we will perform a restore and recovery in roll-forward mode, followed by a conventional database recovery.

How to do it...

Performing a pureScale database backup and recovery is similar to a normal database backup, with some slight differences, such as, for offline backups, all members must be consistent before performing a backup.

Performing an offline database backup

1. Prepare the database to be eligible for online backups. Configure the archive log location, number of primary logs, secondary logs, and log file size, by using the following command:

   ```
   db2sdin1@fndb1-pre-mgt:/db2sd_20110826102843/db2sdin1/NAV#  db2
   "update db for NAV using logarchmeth1 "DISK: /
   ```

```
db2sd_20110826102843610284 3/db2sdin1/NAV/archivelogs logprimary 13
logsecond 4 logfilsiz 1024 "
```

```
DB20000I   The UPDATE DATABASE CONFIGURATION command completed
successfully.
```

```
SQL1363W  Database must be deactivated and reactivated before the
changes to
```

```
one or more of the configuration parameters will be effective.
```

2. Terminate any backend connection by using the following command:

```
db2sdin1@fndb1-pre-mgt:/db2sd_20110826102843/db2sdin1/NAV# db2
terminate
```

```
DB20000I   The TERMINATE command completed successfully.
```

```
db2sdin1@fndb1-pre-mgt:/db2sd_20110826102843/db2sdin1/NAV# db2
"deactivate database NAV"
```

```
DB20000I   The DEACTIVATE DATABASE command completed successfully.
```

3. Each participant member in our configuration has its own log stream. List the path to log files on each member:

```
db2sdin1@fndb2-pre-mgt:/db2sd_20110826102843/db2sdin1# db2 "get db
cfg " | grep "Path to log files"
```

```
 Path to log files                                = /
db2sd_20110826102843/db2sdin1/NAV/DBPARTITION0000/LOGSTREAM0001/
```

```
db2sdin1@fndb2-pre-mgt:/db2sd_20110826102843/db2sdin1 # db2 "get
db cfg " | grep "Path to log files"
```

```
 Path to log files                                = /
db2sd_20110826102843/db2sdin1/NAV/DBPARTITION0000/LOGSTREAM0000/
```

4. Deactivate database NAV by using the following command:

```
db2sdin1@fndb1-pre-mgt:/home/db2sdin1# db2 "deactivate database
NAV"
```

```
DB20000I   The DEACTIVATE DATABASE command completed successfully.
```

5. Perform an offline backup for database NAV by using the following command:

```
db2sdin1@fndb1-pre-mgt:/home/db2sdin1# db2 "BACKUP DATABASE NAV TO
"/db2sd_20110826102843/db2sdin1/NAV/backup" WITHOUT PROMPTING "
```

```
Backup successful. The timestamp for this backup image is :
20111026165622
```

```
db2sdin1@fndb1-pre-mgt:/home/db2sdin1#
```

6. List current NAV database backups by using the following command:

```
db2sdin1@fndb1-pre-mgt:/home/db2sdin1# db2  " list history backup
all for NAV"


                         List History File for nav


Number of matching file entries = 1



  Op Obj Timestamp+Sequence Type Dev Backup ID
  -- --- ------------------ ---- --- --------------
   B  D  20111026165622001   F    D
  ------------------------------------------------------------------
-----------
  Contains 3 tablespace(s):

  00001 SYSCATSPACE
  00002 USERSPACE1
  00003 SYSTOOLSPACE
  ------------------------------------------------------------------
-----------
  Log Stream ID Earliest Log Current Log
  ------------- ------------ -----------
             0 S0000000.LOG S0000000.LOG
             1 S0000000.LOG S0000000.LOG
  ------------------------------------------------------------------
-----------
     Comment: DB2 BACKUP NAV OFFLINE
  Start Time: 20111026165622
    End Time: 20111026165624
      Status: A
  ------------------------------------------------------------------
-----------
   EID: 2 Location: /db2sd_20110826102843/db2sdin1/NAV/backup
```

Performing an online database backup

1. Activate database NAV by using the following command:

   ```
   db2sdin1@fndb1-pre-mgt:/home/db2sdin1# db2 "activate database NAV"
   DB20000I  The ACTIVATE DATABASE command completed successfully.
   ```

2. Perform online backup by using the following command:

   ```
   db2sdin1@fndb2-pre-mgt:/home/db2sdin1# db2 "BACKUP DATABASE NAV
   ONLINE TO "/db2sd_20110826102843/db2sdin1/NAV/backup" INCLUDE LOGS
   WITHOUT PROMPTING"


   Backup successful. The timestamp for this backup image is :
   20111026173850


   db2sdin1@fndb2-pre-mgt:/home/db2sdin1#
   ```

Performing a restore and rollforward recovery

1. Restore database NAV from a previous online backup:

   ```
   db2sdin1@fndb2-pre-mgt:/home/db2sdin1# db2 "RESTORE DATABASE
   NAV FROM /db2sd_20110826102843/db2sdin1/NAV/backup TAKEN AT
   20111026165622 TO /db2sd_20110826102843/db2sdin1/NAV"

   SQL2540W  Restore is successful, however a warning "2539" was
   encountered

   during Database Restore while processing in No Interrupt mode.
   ```

2. Use the ROLLFORWARD command on the NAV database by using the following command:

   ```
   db2sdin1@fndb2-pre-mgt:/home/db2sdin1# db2 "ROLLFORWARD DATABASE
   NAV TO END OF LOGS AND STOP"


                               Rollforward Status


    Input database alias                     = NAV
    Number of members have returned status = 2


    Member ID    Rollforward                      Next log          Log
    files processed         Last committed transaction
                 status                            to be read
    -----------  ------------------------  ------------------  ---
    ---------------------  ------------------------
   ```

```
         0   DB   working                    S0000002.LOG
   S0000000.LOG-S0000001.LOG   2011-10-26-14.42.09.000000 UTC
         1   DB   working                    S0000002.LOG
   S0000000.LOG-S0000001.LOG   2011-10-26-14.38.57.000000 UTC


   DB20000I   The ROLLFORWARD command completed successfully.
```

Performing database recovery

1. Initiate a database recovery by using the following command:

   ```
   db2sdin1@fndb1-pre-mgt:/home/db2sdin1/sqllib/db2dump# db2 "recover
   database NAV to end of logs"
   ```

   ```
                                     Rollforward Status

     Input database alias                        = NAV
     Number of members have returned status = 2


     Member ID     Rollforward                    Next log          Log
     files processed         Last committed transaction
                   status                         to be read
     -----------   -------------------------   ------------------   ---
     ----------------------   -------------------------
             0   not pending
   S0000000.LOG-S0000001.LOG   2011-10-26-17.42.09.000000 Local
             1   not pending
   S0000000.LOG-S0000001.LOG   2011-10-26-17.38.57.000000 Local


     DB20000I   The RECOVER DATABASE command completed successfully.
   ```

How it works...

The backup and recovery can be conducted from any active member.

If you want to roll forward to a timestamp, please ensure that members are synchronized; if they are not, use the maximum timestamp.

There's more...

Backups made on DB2 pureScale systems cannot be restored on non-pureScale systems. Also, backups made on a pureScale setup (number of members, CF) are not valid for restoring and recovering different pureScale configurations with different numbers of members and CFs. The main reason behind this is that there are internal configurations and dependencies between members and cluster facilities, and not last the number of log streams must be the same. Therefore, after any change in topology, such as adding or removing members, the database is placed in backup pending mode, and and a backup must be performed before connections to the database can be made before connections to the database are available.

Index

Symbols

A

Thank you for buying
IBM DB2 9.7 Advanced Administration Cookbook

About Packt Publishing

Packt, pronounced 'packed', published its first book "*Mastering phpMyAdmin for Effective MySQL Management*" in April 2004 and subsequently continued to specialize in publishing highly focused books on specific technologies and solutions.

Our books and publications share the experiences of your fellow IT professionals in adapting and customizing today's systems, applications, and frameworks. Our solution-based books give you the knowledge and power to customize the software and technologies you're using to get the job done. Packt books are more specific and less general than the IT books you have seen in the past. Our unique business model allows us to bring you more focused information, giving you more of what you need to know, and less of what you don't.

Packt is a modern, yet unique publishing company, which focuses on producing quality, cutting-edge books for communities of developers, administrators, and newbies alike. For more information, please visit our website: www.PacktPub.com.

About Packt Enterprise

In 2010, Packt launched two new brands, Packt Enterprise and Packt Open Source, in order to continue its focus on specialization. This book is part of the Packt Enterprise brand, home to books published on enterprise software – software created by major vendors, including (but not limited to) IBM, Microsoft and Oracle, often for use in other corporations. Its titles will offer information relevant to a range of users of this software, including administrators, developers, architects, and end users.

Writing for Packt

We welcome all inquiries from people who are interested in authoring. Book proposals should be sent to author@packtpub.com. If your book idea is still at an early stage and you would like to discuss it first before writing a formal book proposal, contact us; one of our commissioning editors will get in touch with you.

We're not just looking for published authors; if you have strong technical skills but no writing experience, our experienced editors can help you develop a writing career, or simply get some additional reward for your expertise.

IBM Sametime 8.5.2 Administration Guide

ISBN: 978-1-84968-304-3   Paperback: 484 pages

A comprehensive, practical book and eBook for the planning, installation, and maintenance of your Sametime 8.5.2 environment

1. Discover all the servers and components included in the new Sametime 8.5.2 architecture

2. Quickly zero in on which server components provide the features you need for your Sametime environment

3. Understand the dependencies between different servers and how to design both a pilot and production environment

IBM Rational Team Concert 2 Essentials

ISBN: 978-1-84968-160-5   Paperback: 308 pages

Improve team productivity with Integrated Processes, Planning, and Collaboration using IBM Rational Team Concert Enterprise Edition

1. Understand the core features and techniques of Rational Team Concert and Jazz platform through a real-world Book Manager Application

2. Expand your knowledge of software development challenges and find out how Rational Team Concert solves your tech, team, and collaboration worries

3. Complete overview and understanding of the Jazz Platform, Rational Team Concert, and other products built on the Jazz Platform

Please check **www.PacktPub.com** for information on our titles

IBM WebSphere Application Server v7.0 Security

ISBN: 978-1-84968-148-3   Paperback: 312 pages

Secure your IBM WebSphere applications with Java EE and JAAS security standards

1. Discover the salient and new security features offered by WebSphere Application Server version 7.0 to create secure installations

2. Explore and learn how to secure Application Servers, Java Applications, and EJB Applications along with setting up user authentication and authorization

3. With the help of extensive hands-on exercises and mini-projects, explore the various aspects needed to produce secure IBM WebSphere Application Server Network Deployment v7.0 infrastructures

IBM Cognos TM1 Cookbook

ISBN: 978-1-84968-210-7   Paperback: 490 pages

Build real world planning, budgeting, and forecasting solutions with a collection of over 60 simple but incredibly effective recipes

1. A comprehensive developer's guide for planning, building, and managing practical applications with IBM TM1

2. No prior knowledge of TM1 expected

3. Complete coverage of all the important aspects of IBM TM1 in carefully planned step-by-step practical demos

4. Part of Packt's Cookbook series: Practical recipes that illustrate the use of various TM1 features

Please check **www.PacktPub.com** for information on our titles

CPSIA information can be obtained at www.ICGtesting.com
Printed in the USA
LVOW11s1748141113

361321LV00009B/751/P